BISON
BOOKS

Johnson, Dirk.

Biting the dust.

$14.95

DATE			

WITHDRAWN

BAKER & TAYLOR

BITING THE DUST

*The Wild Ride
and Dark Romance
of the Rodeo Cowboy
and the American West*

DIRK JOHNSON

UNIVERSITY OF NEBRASKA PRESS
LINCOLN AND LONDON

First Nebraska paperback printing: 2005

Library of Congress Cataloging-in-Publication Data
Johnson, Dirk.
Biting the dust: the wild ride and dark romance of the rodeo cowboy and the
american west / Dirk Johnson.
p.   cm.
Originally published: New York: Simon & Schuster, c1994.
ISBN 0-8032-7624-9 (pbk.: alk. paper)
1. Rodeos—West (U.S.)   2. Cowboys—West (U.S.)—Social conditions.
3. West (U.S.)—Social conditions.   I. Title.
GV1834.55.W47J64   2005
791.8'4'0978—dc22   2004025466

"Wild Thing," words and music by Chip Taylor (pp. 118–19), © 1965 (Renewed 1993).
EMI Blackwood Music Inc. All rights reserved. International copyright secured. Used
by permission.

The poem on p. 160, dedicated to the memory of Deke Latham, is used with permission
of Bill Larsen, copyright © 1986 Long Loop Cow Co.

The material on pp. 236–37 from *True Unity* is used with permission of Tom Dorrance,
18425 Corral Del Cielo, Salinas, CA 93908 (price: $21.95, including shipping and han-
dling).

For Margaret

ACKNOWLEDGMENTS

I thank my mother, Karen Farley Lyons, who taught me to write, and my father, Glen Johnson, who taught me to listen.

Thanks, as well, to my sisters, Cynthia Chereskin, Rachel Strack and Jennifer Johnson, for their soft hearts and strong shoulders; to my mentor, Walter Morrison, for his example and guidance; to my friend Richard Johnson, for his generosity of spirit; and to my aunts, Sister Francelle Farley, Gertrude Farley and Eleanor Pierce, for their wit, humor and memories.

Deepest appreciation to those who helped get these pages in order, especially Heather Hach, Chuck Grant, Susan Kanode and Dory Richardson, and to those who helped keep my life in order, especially Jerome Lyons, Donna Johnson, Liz Shannon, Mary Shannon, Elizabeth Shannon, Catherine Shannon, Ben Chereskin, Ted Strack, Rich Neubauer and Tom Amenda.

A debt of gratitude is owed to my editors at the *New York Times*, especially Joseph Lelyveld, Soma Golden, David Jones, Linda Mathews, Phil Taubman, Katy Roberts and Carl Lavin; to my agent, Mary Evans; and to the editor of this book, Eric Steel, for his insight and patience.

I thank my children, Amanda, Harlan and Nora, for pounding on the study door and asking me to stop working. Most of all, I thank Margaret Shannon, my wife, whose selflessness freed me to write. Her hand is on every page.

1

THE MAN in a cowboy hat sat on a tree stump and stared at his little house, which sits on a skinny road that meanders out of Cool, Texas, population 238, a flat, dusty place without so much as a drugstore or a gas station.

On the Texas map, which it is not, Cool would be a tiny speck about three inches to the left of Fort Worth, an hour or so by pickup truck.

"It ain't exactly the Ponderosa," the man had once told his wife, as he swept his arm across the three and a half acres of scrub grass that went with the house. "But it's our little ranch."

Earlier that day, he had gotten a call from the banker, who said he wanted to have a talk. The banker didn't really want to talk, of course. He wanted some money. Who didn't? The charge cards were full. The bills were late. The checking account was overdrawn.

Joe Wimberly didn't have a nickel to his name, except for the house. And he swore he would never let that go.

Under a washboard sky that promised rain, he rose to carry a feed sack to a hungry horse, a high-strung sorrel mare. As he walked, his eyes fell on the slab near the back door, where his kids' names were etched in cement.

•   •   •

For Joe Wimberly, being a cowboy was more than a dream. It was all he knew. On his grandfather's place, Joe had learned to ride a horse by the time he was four. At seven, he was herding cattle to the sale barn with his father. At thirteen, he was climbing aboard the back of a steer.

During his school years, he had chafed in the captivity of teachers who didn't know the difference between a black Angus and a polled Hereford. He daydreamed about life on the unbroken fields and waited for the day he could follow the Wimberly men into the business of cows and calves, horses and pickups. But the day never came. Livestock prices collapsed and Joe's father and grandfather lost everything.

When Joe turned eighteen, he figured he could pack away his saddle and move to a city or town. But all the jobs seemed confined to stuffy offices, burger joints and discount stores. Nobody there gave a whit if a man could ride or rope. Joe saw the city as little more than a corral. And the people were on the wrong side of the pen.

He set out instead for a world where the Old West still lives, to the last untamed range of the true American cowboy, the rodeo. He donned buckskin chaps with silver conchas, pointed tan boots with jangly spurs and a high-crowned black hat. He stuffed a pack of chewing tobacco in his shirt pocket and climbed aboard one angry, snorting bull after another.

He saw more of America in a month than most people see in a lifetime, the wicked maw of the dizzying, razor-walled canyons of Calf Creek in Utah, the mystical plateaus of the Sangre de Cristo Mountains of New Mexico, the wordless poetry of the Painted Desert in Arizona, the rain-nourished promise of Kansas wheat fields rolling forever toward the sunset.

There were days when he walked around with $1,000 in his pocket. And there were days when he could not afford to eat. But there was never a day when he wanted to trade his chaps for a job with a boss looking over his shoulder.

"They don't write country songs about lawyers or doctors or baseball players," Joe liked to say. "But they write 'em about rodeo cowboys."

Joe wore a bushy, black mustache that matched his eyes, as dark and rich as Texas oil, set deep behind proud cheekbones. He was missing a tooth, right on the fifty-yard line. But his jaw was square and strong. And he stood much taller than his five-foot-eight-inch frame.

Whoever said cowboys don't talk much never met Joe Wimberly. He was strong, but rarely silent. To Joe's way of thinking, just about everything in life demanded some commentary, and he was happy to supply it. He talked about the rain and he talked about the drought. He talked about the past and he talked about the future. He had a story to fit every occasion. His traveling partners sometimes feigned sleep in hope that his oratory would take a rest. But then Joe might just start telling a story about sleeping rodeo cowboys. "Talking," Joe conceded, "is my best event."

•   •   •

When he got the chance, Joe would veer off the Interstate highway to call on his high school sweetheart, Paula Magee, a spirited young woman with large hazel eyes and hair the color of butterscotch. He would regale Paula with the glorious accounts of his skill and bravery. But then he had to be going. A rodeo cowboy could never sit still for long.

"My house is not a bus stop, Joe Wimberly," Paula would say with exasperation. Her grandmother looked on with narrowed eyes, hoping that "this rodeo character," as she called him, would ride off into the sunset someday soon.

Nobody could quite understand why Paula had broken it off with that other boy when Joe came along. He was nice, polite, clean-cut. And he just happened to have a wealthy grandfather. Certainly Paula's grandmother didn't understand it. Sometimes even Joe didn't understand it.

Unlike Joe, who barely squeaked through high school, Paula excelled in every subject, especially math. Every now and then, she allowed herself a fleeting thought about college. Her teachers told her she was smart enough to become an accountant. But Paula would sweep those fancy notions from her head. College was for people with money.

She took a job as a secretary, attended the Baptist church every Sunday and wondered whether she ought to forget about Joe.

She could never be sure when he might come around, or even if he would. He seemed to take his dreams more seriously than his life, and often had a hard time telling them apart. And there didn't seem to be a place for her in his rodeo world.

She vowed sometimes that she would tell him to stay away. She had spent enough Saturday nights alone by the television. For all she

cared, he could go pester some barrel racer or one of the glossy girls
in tight jeans and teased-up hairdos that linger at the beer stand after
the rodeo. That's what she would tell him.

But Paula couldn't quite get her heart to agree with her head. She
knew there was something special about Joe Wimberly.

When he walked through a room, the quick clompety-clomp of his
boots struck a certain rhythm, like he knew where he was going, or at
least where he wanted to go. Joe wasn't the type to blame the wind
for slowing him down, or curse the ground for being hard when he
landed on it.

Unlike a lot of country boys, who seemed to want to hear nothing
more from a girl than a giggle, Joe listened to what Paula had to say.
She never had to worry that an idea might seem naive or strange. In
fact, the stranger the idea, the better Joe liked it. And Paula never had
to wonder what Joe was thinking. Lord knows, he had no problem
with communication.

When Joe's truck pulled up on Valentine's Day, she decided to save
her farewell speech until his next visit. He sat on the couch and
handed her a box of candy and a big card. It was not signed "To the
woman of my dreams, Joe," or "With all of my heart, Joe," or even
plain old "Love, Joe."

It was just signed "Joe." For a man who could talk until Tuesday, he
never wasted any words with a pen.

He unwrapped a piece of her candy and popped it in his mouth.
She gave him a skeptical, sideways glance, which he returned with a
wink. He rested his head on the back of the couch, then he squirmed
a bit, like he was testing a saddle. Then he straightened up and
looked her straight in the eyes.

"Paula, I've got three days off," he said. "What do you say we get
married?"

At the courthouse wedding, Paula wore her fanciest dress. Joe
wore what he always did: a Western shirt, jeans and a cowboy hat.
Paula was eighteen. Joe was nineteen. They moved to a ramshackle
trailer thirty miles from town that came without a washing machine
or a telephone. Six months later, Paula was pregnant.

•   •   •

It scared Paula to watch Joe on a bull. She had lost her father in a
construction accident when she was a toddler. Her older brother had
died of brain cancer when she was seven. Paula's mother, a secretary,

was fired from her job for missing too much time while caring for the dying boy.

As worried as Paula got about the dangers of rodeo, she knew it was being a cowboy that put the sparkle in Joe's eyes. And she never wanted to see that fade. She had known enough death in her time to marvel at a man who reveled in life. So as he headed out the door, she would kiss him goodbye, cross her fingers and say a prayer.

Joe was a thousand miles away at a rodeo on the night that Paula gave birth to a daughter, Casey. They didn't have any insurance, and the doctor bills came to $2,500. "How we gonna pay for things, Joe?" Paula's voice cracked across the telephone wires to a pay phone in Buffalo, Minnesota, where the new father stood in the shadow of a truck stop marquee.

"I'm gonna win," Joe told her. "And I'm gonna keep on winning."

．　　　．　　　．

He was as good as his word. With the grace of a gymnast and the nerve of a bank robber, Joe dazzled the whooping, stomping crowds that filled the bleachers at little county fairs and big city stadiums throughout the West. The victory lap on horseback for the winning cowboy became as familiar a ritual for Joe as the home run trot for a major league slugger.

He would stop at home long enough to dump a stack of paychecks on the kitchen table, then drive off to conquer the next string of menacing bulls. Anybody who knew rodeo came to know the name Joe Wimberly.

In the 1980s, he qualified five times to compete in the National Finals Rodeo. In his best year, Joe won more than $40,000 in prize money, a gaudy sum for a rodeo cowboy. Out of that, he had to pay his traveling expenses and entry fees, which cut his winnings by more than a third.

Times were never easy, especially after the birth of another daughter, Sammi, but the bills got paid. They moved out of the trailer and into an apartment, and then moved again to a little rented place that had been a hunter's shack.

Joe vowed that someday they would have a house of their own, a place in the country with a yard big enough for a horse corral and plenty of trees for the kids to climb. He kept hustling on the rodeo circuit and Paula took a job in the pharmacy at Wal-Mart. They managed to save $1,500. It was enough for a down payment on a

$30,000 house on the outskirts of Cool, Texas.

The place looked like a cabin. There was no central heating, only a wood-burning stove. The wallpaper was peeling. The house needed paint. And it sat down the road from an abandoned, crumbling shack where goats rummaged inside.

But it came with three and a half acres of open space. Joe could already envision a place for a horse corral. There were trees enough for a dozen kids to climb. Before long, Paula was pregnant again.

· · ·

Even before the boxes were unpacked, Joe decided the new place needed to bear the family imprint. After all, ranch cowboys brand cattle for identification. And this little spread was now the Wimberly Ranch. So he mixed up some cement and poured a slab near the back door. He took a tree twig and carved the names of the Wimberly clan in the wet concrete: "Joe," "Paula," "Casey," "Sammi."

But this presented a problem. Soon they were going to have a new baby. "We can't leave off the name of the next Wimberly," said Joe. He and Paula had picked out names. But they didn't know whether the baby would be a boy or a girl. It was not very cowboy to have those fancy tests that determine the sex of a fetus, especially not for cowboys without medical insurance. Joe finally settled for scrawling "Baby" in the cement.

Joe had big ideas for the new place. He sawed hundreds of cedar branches and nailed them together into a fence by the road. He put together a corral and bought a horse for the kids. He built a little cabin in the backyard, complete with running water. He called it a bunkhouse, and he figured that rodeo cowboys could sleep there when they came to call. And he made plans to build a little arena on his place.

Paula had never been so happy. She could look out the kitchen window and watch deer lope through the fields. The peace of the countryside made trouble seem a world away.

Joe rescued a mangy little sheepdog from the side of the road, where it had been abandoned, and took it home. The poor mutt was terrified of people. It looked as if it had been abused. Joe named him Cowboy.

He put out milk and table scraps for the stray cats that came around. The Wimberlys were proud of the new home. And just about anybody was welcome to stay there.

Only Joe didn't get to stay there very much. He was gone to the rodeo about 200 days a year.

•   •   •

The wide open road that once symbolized freedom had lost its allure long ago. It was just a long, lonesome stretch that stood between Joe and his family. When Casey was saying her first words, her father was listening on a telephone line. And the phone wasn't any use when she took her first steps.

It was an accident of timing that Joe was around home on the morning that Paula went into labor. She gave birth to a son, McKinnon, and before sundown, Joe was on his way to a rodeo in Cleburne, Texas, where he passed out cigars behind the bucking chutes.

He seldom missed a rodeo, even when he was hurt. He had snapped his femur in three places. He had ripped ligaments in both knees. And his body was covered with scars as if it had been lashed with a whip. One of his ears had been severed and needed to be sewn back to his head.

In one rodeo, when his wrist got caught in the rope, he dangled on the side of the bull, and it kicked him in the head and knocked him unconscious. The fans shrieked in horror as Joe's limp body, still tethered to the bull, was jerked wildly.

A friend sitting next to Paula in the bleachers grabbed her head and turned it away. "Don't look," the woman cried, as Paula sat frozen in fear.

Watching from the chutes, one of Joe's fellow bull riders jumped the fence and raced into the arena. He reached in and freed Joe's hand, while a rodeo clown distracted the bull. Joe was taken away on a stretcher, his eyes glazed and his mouth hanging open. Blood ran down the right side of his face, where the bull had ripped his skin. Paula uncovered her eyes. She thought Joe was dead.

•   •   •

The narrow highway wound its way around a naked hillside and straightened out again on a flat, treeless stretch of Oklahoma. A languid sun hid behind a gauzy patch of clouds that curled like cigarette smoke in a dreary sky. Joe peered through the windshield and saw a silver water tower rising over a little town on the plains.

A hundred miles ago, Joe had pulled himself up from the dirt. He had paid $50 to enter the contest. He came away with nothing. Weeks had passed since he had taken a victory lap.

"Maybe I'm not trying hard enough," Joe thought to himself. "Maybe I'm trying too hard." He put a plug of tobacco inside his cheek and pressed a little harder on the gas pedal. The water tower disappeared in his rearview mirror.

When he got home that night, Joe had no paychecks to put on the kitchen table. The bills were all way past due. It was a wonder the electricity hadn't been cut off.

Joe and Paula couldn't even afford to fix the back window on the minivan, which had been broken by a rock hurled from a lawn mower. Paula taped a sheet of plastic over the hole in the glass.

Joe went to the bank to see if he could borrow more money. He already had one loan in arrears. He owed thousands of dollars. Where had that money gone? the banker wanted to know.

"When you're borrowing money for rodeo," Joe told him, "you're borrowing money that's already spent."

If he could just have one more loan, Joe pleaded, he was sure to make everything right. All he needed was a winning streak.

The man in the suit looked at the man in the cowboy hat. The answer was no.

"What you need," the banker said, "is a regular job."

•   •   •

With Paula and the kids visiting her relatives, Joe lay in bed past midnight and stared at the ceiling. Paula had taken a new job as a helper in the school library. She was also driving a bus. Nobody could ask her to do more. Joe wondered what he ought to ask himself to do.

The next morning, the telephone rang before the sun rose. A rancher was calling for help. His cattle had escaped through a busted fence. Joe threw on his clothes and cowboy hat and hurried over.

As they headed out to retrieve the wayward cattle, the rancher's wife came to the front porch and hollered for Joe. She said it couldn't wait.

Joe sprinted back to the house and saw a terrible look on the woman's face.

"There's been a fire at your place, Joe. You better get home right away."

He jumped in the truck and raced down a gravel road that swirled with dust from the spinning wheels. He twisted the steering wheel onto the road leading toward home, speeding past a blur of picket fences. His heart pounding, he strained to see the little house in the distance.

The place looked fine. Maybe this was all a mistake.

He killed the engine in the driveway and swung his boots out the truck door.

Now he could smell the smoke. He walked uneasily toward the house. As he stepped inside, he saw blackness everywhere. The walls were charred, the cupboards scorched, the furniture ruined.

Joe walked around in a daze. Nothing seemed real. He went to find a telephone.

"We've got a big problem," he said when Paula picked up.

"Yeah I know, the minivan, but I've been thinking, baby, and . . ."

"No, Paula," he interrupted. "We've had a fire. In the house. Some kind of short. The place is wrecked inside."

"Joe, Joe, you all right?"

"I'm fine," he said. "But the house. It's wrecked."

"I'll be right there, Joe. I'm coming home right now."

"Paula, you ain't got a home to come home to."

"I'm coming home, Joe."

●   ●   ●

The insurance man said that everything would be covered but it would take months before workers could make the place livable again.

Paula and the kids stayed in a $20 motel room for a few nights while Joe got the bunkhouse ready. It was a windowless wood hut, about twenty feet wide and fifteen feet deep, set on a concrete floor. They cooked their meals on a hot plate and slept together in a bunch.

Casey asked how long this camping trip would last. Joe told her about cowboys and cowgirls of old. They stayed in bunkhouses, too. They even went without television.

Sometimes at night, while the children were asleep, Joe would step outside and stare into the sky, as if some magical answer to their problems was hidden in the stars.

●   ●   ●

The Fourth of July was just around the corner. In the old days, they called it Cowboy's Christmas, a time when wranglers celebrated the end of a long, hard cattle drive. But for a rodeo cowboy, Independence Day was anything but a holiday. Every town and city in the West seemed to hold a contest. A hustling cowboy could hit four or five rodeos in a weekend. If he drew good livestock to ride, and stuck to their hides, a cowboy could earn enough money around the Fourth to pull out of a hole. But it could also be a disaster, since the entry fees added up to thousands of dollars.

Joe packed his bags and caught a ride with a crew of cowboys going north. "Don't worry so much about material things," Paula told Joe as she kissed him goodbye. "We've got each other. That's what matters."

The season was nearly half over, and he had won only about $5,000. He had spent that much on travel and fees. The creditors were growing impatient. And now his wife and kids were cramped in a room the size of a walk-in closet.

Joe didn't say much on the ride to Colorado. As the van pulled into the rodeo grounds in Greeley, he tried to sweep away the worries. But when his turn came, his mind was a jumble. An instant after the chute gate was pulled open, the bull sent Joe in one direction and his cowboy hat in the other. He landed with a thud. Next stop: Pecos, Texas.

On the ride south, every inch of Joe's body groaned with pain. He would be thirty on his next birthday, and it seemed that all his old injuries were flaring up. His groin was pulled. His elbow could barely bend. His knees wanted to collapse.

A doctor once asked him why he refused to have surgery on his knees. "Because it would cost five thousand dollars," Joe explained.

In the sweltering heat of the Pecos fairgrounds, Joe limped over to the contestants' area, dumped his equipment bag and shook a few familiar hands.

"How's it been goin', Joe?" asked a stout bull rider with a cheerful grin, an old friend who had known Joe since the house trailer days.

"My outside is hurtin' terrible," Joe told him. "But my inside is hurtin' worse."

•   •   •

From the platform behind the chutes, Joe looked down at the drooling bull, restless in its cage.

"You're next," the chute boss ordered.

Joe lowered himself on the back of the bull. He had ridden thousands of them. When people asked why, he always told them it was for the fun, and the money was an afterthought. But on this hot day in Pecos, the money was all Joe was thinking about.

He clenched the rope, then squirmed a bit, trying to get the right fit. Finally, he was ready. He nodded for the gate to open.

The bull saw daylight. It shot straight ahead, bucking once, twice. Joe stayed with the rhythm, his right hand secure on the rope. The clock counted down—eight seconds, seven seconds, six seconds, five seconds . . .

The bull twisted to the right. A predictable move. No threat. Easy for the cowboy to handle. Four seconds, three seconds . . .

Joe started to slip. The world was spinning out of control. The rope jerked loose. He twirled in the air. The time gun cracked. Joe slammed against the turf. "No score," called the announcer.

He knelt on the ground, not sure he wanted to get up. A rodeo clown motioned for him to get moving. He trotted over to the rails and stood among the other cowboys.

"I'm looking for a ride," he said to nobody in particular.

"We got wheels," a peach-fuzz cowboy offered. "Where you headed next? Dodge City? Prescott? Window Rock?"

Joe slung his equipment bag over his shoulder. "I'm going home," he said. "I've had enough rodeo."

2

THE AMERICAN WEST, an idea as much as a place, has always been the geography of dreams, the destination of hopes, the endless chase in search of something deep within the soul.

Suburban families in minivans spend summer vacations hoping to glimpse it. New Agers with crystals and herbs seek to commune with it. The Hollywood rich try to buy it.

As the rest of America becomes noisier, angrier, grimier, the cavernous, echoing, mystical West, real and imagined, beckons.

"Boom Time in the Rockies," blared the cover of *Time*, heralding "The New West."

In this land rush, the pioneers are galloping into town in Range Rovers and four-wheel-drive Jeeps. And they are armed with personal computers, modems, fax machines.

In the mountain West, a "ranchette" has become the coolest kind of toy. It is difficult to cast a lasso without snagging a celebrity. John Wayne is dead, but there is no shortage of movie stars in the land of piñon and juniper. "Movie Star Montana," the locals have grudgingly dubbed their state, home to Jane Fonda and Ted Turner, Whoopi Goldberg, Mel Gibson, Glenn Close.

The cowboy has become chic, or at least his clothes have. And the romance of the West has made gold mines of Santa Fe, Jackson Hole, Telluride. Rangeland, as long as it's not too far from a ski slope, brings millions.

But in the flat land of the original American cowboy, the shadowless sweep of the Great Plains, where the storied cattle drives gave the nation its most powerful myth, empty farmhouses creak in the wind. Schools are closing. Stores on Main Street are boarded up.

Movie stars aren't moving to McCook, or Colby, or Batesland, places in Nebraska and Kansas and South Dakota where cowboy hats are soiled and rumpled from days in the fields.

• • •

In so many forgotten towns on the back roads of the Great Plains, people sit on their front porches, gazing into the twilight, as if keeping watch before something else vanishes: another store, another church, another family.

These are the places the nation does not need anymore, not in today's bigger-is-better economy. A century ago, nearly half of all Americans lived on farms and ranches. Now that number has shrunk to less than one percent. Main Street has moved to the mall.

The Great Plains, home for centuries to the Sioux, were opened to the pioneers under the Homestead Act of 1862, which President Abraham Lincoln signed "so that every poor man may have a home."

And settlers came by the millions, chasing the dream of a plot of land and a new life, trudging west in covered wagons. "Nebraska or Bust!"

In the absence of timber, the settlers built houses of mud and grass and burned buffalo dung for heating fuel. In the 1890s, the Census Bureau marked an area "settled" when it had more than six people per square mile. The historian Frederick Jackson Turner declared the American Frontier to be closed.

But the population on the rural plains has been shrinking since the Dust Bowl of the 1930s. Today the populations of nearly 200 counties on the plains have dropped below the Frontier threshold.

Some say these dusty lands should never have been settled at all, that the pioneers were fools to put down roots in soil so sandy. The people who flee these towns look back on their old neighbors and wonder when they might get the sense to follow.

Mapmakers erase the names of some withered towns, as if they never existed. Grass grows up around tombstones.

But in the ceaseless, moaning wind, swirling with old ghosts and faded dreams, there is the whisper of the survivor on the Great Plains, the soul of the defiant. And when the rodeo comes to town, the whisper becomes a roar.

We're still here.

They wear cowboy hats and pointy boots, maybe a string tie or a neckerchief. They mean to look as if they belong to the plains, as if the plains belong to them. Some of the women wear bows in their hair. Some of the men wear spurs. Nobody wears Nikes.

They line the curbsides for a parade, a jaunty march through the center of town, backs arched, knees pumping high. The school band plays a fight song and banners proclaim the Ropers and Riders Association, the Sons and Daughters of the Pioneers, the 4-H Club, the Future Farmers of America.

In the grassy parking lot, near the entrance to the fairgrounds, pickups outnumber cars. There isn't a BMW in the bunch. Bumper stickers proclaim "Eat Beef" and "Ranchers Are the Real Endangered Species."

They climb the grandstands before the cowboys arrive. They sit among neighbors, and look around for a hand to shake, a back to slap, an elbow to squeeze. Their smiles are unwilted in the heat.

We're still here.

A tinny loudspeaker blares a country song, and cowboy hats bob to the rhythm. An American flag snaps in the breeze. The announcer salutes the cowboys, salutes the crowd, salutes every brave American who has fought and died.

In the flourish of the Grand Entry, the men and women of rodeo burst into the arena with the hoof-pounding thunder of a posse sweeping over the ridge, racing to the rescue. The smiling, blushing rodeo queen, wearing a sequined blouse, tight jeans and boots, waves to the crowd with a white-gloved hand. Rodeo clowns, wearing baggy trousers and coats of greasepaint, turn somersaults for the children, who giggle from their father's shoulders, as happy as life can be.

We're still here.

A cowboy comes flying out of the chutes. The crowd groans and gasps with every twist and turn, as if each one of them is taking the wild ride. The people of the plains know the danger of a sudden jolt, the fear of slipping from the edge.

The horse darts to the west, then to the east, and rears back in fury. The cowboy holds tight, summoning every ounce of strength he can muster. The crowd is right there with him.

"You can ride 'em," they cry. "Ride 'em! Ride 'em! Ride 'em!"

The cowboy hangs tough, outlasting the challenge, landing on his feet. A roar of triumph sweeps the grandstands.

We're still here.

•   •   •

Looking out from the power centers of the East, the movers and shakers of early America did not see much use in the Great Plains.

"What do we want to do with this vast, worthless area?" asked Daniel Webster in 1836.

A generation later, Horace Greeley urged, "Go west, young man, go west." But when he followed his own advice and visited the plains, he concluded grimly, "We seem to have reached the acme of barrenness and desolation."

The Great Plains start where the rainfall begins to stop, somewhere around the ninety-eighth meridian, running from Canada to the Rio Grande, through the center of Kansas, and sweeping west to the Rocky Mountains. It is where the tallgrass of the prairie gives way to the shortgrass of the plains.

The region has the hottest summers and the coldest winters, the strongest winds, the worst hail and locusts, the fiercest droughts and blizzards. Not surprisingly, it has the shortest, most fickle growing season.

Its soil is made of the clay, sand and pebbles washed from the eastern face of the Rockies by the Platte and Arkansas Rivers. Maps in some old geography books labeled it "The Great American Desert."

Francis Parkman, a historian from Boston who crossed the plains in 1846, wrote of the bleakness: "No living thing was moving throughout that vast landscape, except the lizards that darted over the sand and through the rank grass and prickly pears at our feet. Before and behind us, the level of monotony of the plains was unbroken as far as the eye could reach. Sometimes it glared in the sun, an expanse of hot, bare sand. Skulls and whitening bones of buffalo were scattered everywhere."

But a glorious future of the plains lay at the feet of the skeptics, in the grasses. The blue grama and buffalo grass survived drought in the broiling sun and remained nourishing all winter. These grasses had once supported 75 million American buffalo. In the years following the Civil War, the buffalo had been slaughtered for their hides and driven to near extinction.

These grasses grew plentiful, but went unused, except in Texas, where an obscure type of cattle, the longhorn, began to graze the rangeland in growing numbers. Descendants of the cattle brought over by the Spaniards, the longhorns roamed freely when their tenders went off to fight in the Civil War.

By the end of the war, herds in the upper Mississippi River Valley were seriously depleted. Cattle prices soared to $30 and $50 a head.

The longhorns, meanwhile, grew to perhaps 5 million, and could be had just for the effort of rounding them up.

Big money awaited the entrepreneurs who could move these cattle from Texas to lucrative markets up north. This new enterprise demanded cheap labor. The call was answered by farm boys from New England and the Midwest, soldiers mustered out of the Union and Confederate armies, cow herders from Mexico, displaced Indians, blacks newly freed from cotton plantations.

The typical cowboy worked eighteen hours a day, seven days a week. On any given day, he might be thrown from a horse or charged by a steer. He endured the baking sun of noon, the frigid gales of darkness and the eternally whining winds that literally drove some mad. He traveled 1,000 miles with nothing more comfortable for sleeping than a bedroll. Wages for a four-month drive averaged about $100, maybe enough for a new hat and a pair of fancy boots.

"We Hauled cattle out of the Mud with oxen half the day," wrote George Duffield, who drove cattle from Texas up to Iowa in 1866 and kept a diary of the trip. "Dark days are these to me. Nothing but Bread & Coffee. Hands all Growling & Swearing—every thing wet & cold . . . Sick and discouraged. Have not got the Blues but am in Hel of a fix . . . My back is Blistered badly . . . I had a sick headache bad . . . Flies worse than I ever saw them."

•   •   •

The origin of the term cowboy is uncertain. In Revolutionary War days, it was applied to Tories who rang cowbells to trick farmer patriots into the brush and ambush them. The name later referred to Texas bandits who stole cattle from Mexican herders. But after the Civil War, the name was bestowed on anyone who tended cattle on the long drives up the Great Plains.

Like the horses and the longhorns, the terms of the rangeland descended from the Spanish. *Vaquero*, or cowman, evolved to "buckaroo." The braided rope, *la reata*, became the lariat.

Every article of cowboy clothing served as a tool. The hat was used to swat away low-hanging branches, carry water from a stream, fan a campfire. The colorful bandanna kept the cowboy protected from the dust and sand, and could be used for a tourniquet in case impromptu surgery was needed for a rattlesnake bite. The boots were pointed, to make it easier to slip them in and out of the stirrups. The leather and wool chaps protected the cowboys from rope burns and horse bites. Pants were tight around the waist, since a belt buckle would have been too uncomfortable for riding.

Even the cowboy songs on the rangeland served the purpose of calming a restless cattle herd in the darkness. These Texas lullabies, as they came to be known, were often sung in a mournful tone:

> *I'm up in the mornin' afore daylight;*
> *And afore I sleep the moon shines bright.*
> *No chaps and no slicker, and it's pouring down rain,*
> *And I swear, by God, that I'll never nightherd again.*
> *Oh, it's bacon and beans most every day—*
> *I'd as soon be a-eatin' prairie hay.*
> *I went to the boss to draw my roll,*
> *He had it figured I was nine dollars in the hole.*
> *I'll sell my horse and I'll sell my saddle;*
> *You can go to hell with your longhorn cattle.*

Half of all the Texas longhorns were driven along the Chisholm Trail, named after a half-Cherokee trader named Jesse Chisholm who had carved out the path. Starting in the scrub grass near Brownsville, Texas, the trail moved up through San Antonio and Fort Worth, over the Red, Washita and Canadian Rivers in the Indian Territory that would soon become Oklahoma, toward the raucous cow towns of Kansas.

An Illinois businessman named James G. McCoy built the first cow town, Abilene, Kansas, in 1867, turning a quiet outpost of a dozen log huts into a bustling stop for cowboys that became best known for its noisy saloons and "houses of ill fame." As the railroads moved west, more cow towns came to life: Dodge City, Kansas; Ogallala, Nebraska; Cheyenne, Wyoming; Miles City, Montana.

In the course of one long drive on the plains, a trail boss bragged of a crew hand so slick he could bust a bronc while rolling and lighting a cigarette with his free hand. The boast elicited barely more than a shrug from another crew foreman. He claimed that one of his men could ride while holding a razor and mirror, tending to his grooming while breaking a recalcitrant mustang. With that kind of good-natured boast, and perhaps a wager, the game of rodeo was born.

In the early 1880s, cowboys from the brands known as Mill-Iron, Hashknife 101, and W settled their rivalries with a contest in Pecos

City, Texas, using the courthouse lawn as a corral and chasing the steers through Main Street. In the 1890s, even as the cowboy began to fade from the range, this exhibition began springing up in little towns throughout the West, a celebration of the rough-hewn ways that put them on the map, and perhaps a vow that they meant to endure and prosper. The winner might get a new suit of clothes, a medal, or just the recognition of being one tough cowboy.

The heyday of the American cowboy lasted barely a generation, from the end of the Civil War to the mid-1880s. The end of the free-wheeling days came with overgrazing, falling livestock prices, the wear and tear on cattle and men, the hazards of bushwhackers, the resistance of Indians and farmers along the trails, and the use of barbed wire to fence the rangelands.

In all, the number of cowboys on the cattle drives up the Great Plains totaled no more than 40,000. But a new emblem of America rose up from the dust, immortalized in the fanciful paintings of Frederic Remington and the exaggerated dime novels that focused more on the romance and gunfire of cowboy life than the workaday drudgery of mending fences and chasing after lost calves.

In the image of the cowboy, silhouetted against the endless Western sky, a nation of immigrants embraced a symbol that was distinctly American, apart from the cultures of older societies across the sea, a young working-class hero as strong and independent as America wished to see itself.

3

NOSTRILS FLARING, teeth flashing, eyes darting, the bronc reared back, front hooves clawing the air.

Hooves came slamming down against the turf, pulverizing dirt into dusty swirls. Writhing, twisting, shuddering, the bronc unleashed another buck, demanding to ride alone, the vow of instinct against circumstance.

High atop the horse, smacking hard against the saddle, the cowboy's 135-pound frame rose and swooped with every explosive thrust, his left hand waving freely in the air, a taunt against the odds, even as his hat bounced toward the dust.

Soaring into the air, four hooves off the ground, the ageless Western tableau of grit and chance—and then a thud, a jarring, teeth-rattling visit to earth, ever so brief, before yet another launch, a swirl of metal and leather and flesh.

Holding desperately to the reins, as the world spun around him, the cowboy started to slip, then pulled himself straight, snug in the saddle, at least for the instant, perched on the cliff's edge, struggling for balance above the hard, unforgiving earth waiting ten feet below.

Bronc and cowboy, inseparable as law and defiance, equal partners in the violent, country-and-western ballet of rodeo, streaked as one across the arena. The horse set the rhythm, the cowboy kept time.

Lusty roars echoed across the grandstands, sweeping down in great waves of admiration toward the gutsy cowboy on the raging bronc, both of them untamed, charging recklessly into the uncertain future.

Under a steel-beamed ceiling, behind tall concrete walls, smack in the middle of a congested, cemented, subdivided metropolis, the ghost of the Old West came to life.

•   •   •

The cowboys had ridden into Denver from dusty, little windswept towns with names like Mud Butte and Camp Crook, Porcupine and Hackberry, Opelousas and Okotoks. They wore Wrangler jeans, starched Western shirts and pointy boots. And under their broad-brimmed hats, every one of them harbored dreams.

They stood on the narrow platform behind the chute gates, backs arched, jaws set tight, arms folded.

The look in their eyes said, "Bring 'em on."

It was January, and the long drive along the rodeo trail was just beginning.

Chasing after glory in the dust, the cowboys would crisscross the nation, but especially the West: shadowless plains, craggy hillsides, bleached desert rock. The journey would last from the first page of the calendar to the last, or as long as bones and bank accounts held up. Somewhere along the way, the lasso would overshoot the calf, the reins would slip through the hands, the bull's horns would knife the ribs. But the season of a cowboy begins in hope. Before the taste of dirt has become as familiar as toothpaste, every cowboy still has a chance.

The gaudiest dreams were set in Las Vegas, where the top fifteen cowboys in each event would qualify for the championships. Each dollar won during the season counted for a point in the standings. The purse at the National Finals Rodeo in December, known simply as the NFR by the cowboys, would pay nearly $2 million in winnings.

In the chase for neon on the Strip, some would travel at least 100,000 miles, chasing to more than 100 rodeos around the country, a life of lonely highways, truck stop suppers and cheap motels, when they were flush, and pickup beds when they were not.

•   •   •

Unlike any other athlete, the rodeo cowboy must pay to compete. Each contest requires an entry fee, from $25 to more than $300. Travel and lodging costs cut deep into winnings, so cowboys cut corners by riding together and cramming into cheap motel rooms, often two to a bed, or sleeping outdoors.

A share of the prize money comes from ticket sales and fees on advertisers, like Royal Crown whiskey and Copenhagen chewing tobacco. But the bulk of the purse comes out of the cowboys' own pockets, the $12 million in fees paid by some 7,000 rodeo contestants, and 3 percent of that goes to the sport's corporate headquarters, the Pro Rodeo Cowboy Association in Colorado Springs.

The cowboys also pay annual dues of $260, and an insurance fee of $190 per year and $3 per rodeo. The benefits cover only injuries suffered inside the arena, or on the road between contests, and are limited to $12,500. The deductible is $500, and coverage does not extend to family members.

An ambulance always sits parked near the chute gates. Cowboys do not wonder if they will become badly hurt, but when. Rodeo promoters boast that, on average, only one cowboy a year gets killed, although some years are worse than others. The promoters do not keep figures on cowboys who become paralyzed in a crash or retire with a bad limp before age thirty.

And for all the risks, most cowboys scarcely make enough to survive. A rodeo cowboy can become a star and never earn more than $50,000 a year before expenses. Some of the sport's biggest celebrities live in house trailers.

Only one contestant in rodeo makes big money, the All-Around Cowboy, the man who wins the most points in three events or more, the rodeo equivalent of the Olympic decathlon. But even the champ's $250,000 winnings fall well short of the salary of the average benchwarmer in the NBA.

Like his predecessor on the range, the typical rodeo cowboy comes from a working-class background. Often a family ranch or farm looms somewhere in his past. It might have been sold or lost in a bank auction. Or it might be too small to support the next generation.

The newspapers in the Great Plains, most likely his home, do not run many help-wanted ads. The cowboy might have attended a community college for a while, but seldom has a university degree. He is not interested anyway in some nine-to-five job on an assembly line or behind a desk. He was born to be a cowboy. And inside the rodeo arena, if only for a handful of seconds, that's what he is.

He has memories of galloping across the open fields, of watching hawks circle over the barn at sunrise, of listening to the first bleat of a wet newborn calf in the crisp spring air. Now he lives in a town, most probably in a trailer, and breaks in a new saddle on the living room floor. But he clings to the hope that someday, if he wins enough prize money, he can buy a small herd of cattle, lease a patch of land and spend his days trotting horseback across the scrub grass, somewhere at the end of the highway.

•   •   •

Unlike basketball or football, where a lack of height or muscle can relegate the ordinary young man to the sidelines, the rodeo cowboy comes in all sizes. Some of the toughest bull riders are so short they must strain to peer over the dashboard of a car. Bronc riders are usually slender, even downright skinny. Some steer wrestlers and calf ropers could accurately be called fat, although not prudently within earshot. But whatever the event, it is not the brawn of the cowboy that counts most, but the stoutness of his heart, or what rodeo cowboys call "try."

"He ain't got much talent," the saying goes, "but he's got a whole lot of try."

Women competed in rodeos with men until the 1930s, often riding masterfully. The most famous was "Prairie Rose" Henderson, who made her debut at the Cheyenne rodeo in 1901 against howls of resistance from the judges, and outshone most of the men for a share of the prize money. But after Bonnie McCarroll's bronc, Black Cat, fell over and killed her at the Pendleton rodeo in 1929, and Marie "Ma" Gibson died in a horse wreck in 1933, the rodeo promoters and fans grew queasy about the idea of the "fairer sex" courting such danger. Despite angry protests from the cowgirls, who noted that plenty of men had died in the arenas, women were banned from competition.

Today women are allowed to compete only in the barrel-racing event of the professional rodeo circuit. The announcers often lump them together in the same breath with the rodeo queens—"All the pretty girls of rodeo." But there is no primping or preening on the back of a racing horse.

•   •   •

During the early days of rodeo, the events were drawn directly from the work of the range cowboy: roping calves and riding broncs. Steer wrestling was added years later after Bill Pickett, a black cowboy with the famous 101 Ranch, bit a surprised steer on the lips during an exhibition and wrestled it to the ground.

Rodeo promoters have since introduced the spectacles of bareback bronc riding, bull riding and barrel racing, where women on horseback speed around big drums laid out in a figure-eight pattern.

In the riding events, the cowboys and animals are judged separately, with equal weight for each, and the scores are added together for a possible total of 100 points. For the bronc, the higher the buck, the better the score. For the cowboy, points are awarded for bearing, control and spurring action. The rider is scratched if he bucks off before eight seconds elapse. Under the rules, the cowboy must use only one hand to hold the rope, and the other hand must wave freely without touching any part of the animal. In the bronc-riding events, the spurs of the cowboy must rest above the shoulders of the horse as the ride begins, or he is disqualified.

The roping, wrestling and barrel-racing events are based purely on time. The cowboy who can lasso a calf around the neck, flip it upside down and tie three of its legs together in a knot of pigging string in the shortest time is the winner. In steer wrestling, each cowboy tries to be the fastest to seize the fleeing animal, slam it to the ground and pin its horns to the turf. The winner of the barrel-racing contest is the cowgirl who can complete the pattern fastest. Knocking over a barrel brings a penalty of ten seconds, which invariably ruins any chance of placing in the money.

While each of the events claims some tie to the Old West, the real drama of rodeo, and the magnet for the crowds, is the riding of wild horses and angry bulls. The riders perform at one end of the arena, while the timed-event contestants work from the opposite end. But the two breeds of cowboy are separated by more than just 100 yards of dirt.

The biggest divide is bloodshed. Bull and bronc riders accept it as part of the bargain. Roping calves, on the other hand, might be tough on the animals but doesn't pose much of a threat to the cowboy.

The other big difference is money. The calf roper, steer wrestler and barrel racer must own a horse, as well as a trailer to haul it. The investment can run $20,000 or more. But the bull or bronc rider needs only enough cash to get to the arena and pay his entry fees, since the mounts are furnished by the rodeo. Any young man with the dream, and the guts, can climb aboard. These cowboys are known as the "roughstock" men, and their lives are a constant struggle against biting the dust.

•   •   •

The rodeo season divides into three parts: winter, summer and Las Vegas. From January through March, the cowboys compete inside stadiums in the big cities of the West. The most important are Denver, Fort Worth, Phoenix, San Antonio and Houston. From April through October, the cowboys go outdoors to state and county fairgrounds, traveling to rodeos in virtually every state in the nation, and some in Canada: "The Buffalo Bill Rodeo" in North Platte, Nebraska; "Pike's Peak or Bust" in Colorado Springs; "The Days of '47" in Salt Lake City; "Frontier Days" in Cheyenne, Wyoming, known reverently as "The Daddy of 'em All." Around the Fourth of July, when the standings have begun to take shape, they perform in more than one rodeo a day, sometimes three. By the time the leaves turn in autumn, most have abandoned the trail, too broke to continue, with only the best cowboys left to chase Las Vegas.

•   •   •

Rodeo is like a traveling ranch, a blend of sport and circus, a colorful revelry at $5 a ticket. It is sold as light-hearted entertainment, a raucous musical set in the imaginary West.

But it carries a hard edge: the shadow of debt, the hint of bloodshed, the possibility of death.

The sport has soared in popularity in recent years, now broadcast on cable television's ESPN and the Nashville Network. Millions of people attend rodeos every year. Tickets for the finals in Las Vegas are harder to get than for a championship prizefight.

But as the rodeo grandstands grow more crowded, the cowboy side of the arena fence has grown emptier. Like the ranches and windswept little towns that produce cowboys, the number of bronc and bull riders shrinks every year.

Roping clubs, a social tradition for generations in the rural West, have been folding up. High schools throughout the Great Plains are cutting rodeo as an extracurricular activity, citing a lack of participation.

And outside the Denver arena, an animal-rights activist carried a sign. It read simply: "Say No to Rodeo."

•   •   •

Sweeping out of Nebraska flat as a rug, the Great Plains run out of steam in Denver, smack against the jagged wall of the Rockies. The mile-high city is both a capital of the Old West and its antithesis.

One of America's most important cow towns in the late 1800s, Denver boomed as a railhead for beef shipped East, and for wranglers thirsting for a snort of barleycorn and a whiff of perfume on bawdy Larimer Square. But today Denver's glass and steel skyscrapers rise in salute to the New West, an economy driven by computers, not cattle.

The city skyrocketed in growth during the 1970s, when pastureland in Colorado was transformed for oil exploration, hastened by the Arab oil embargo, and Denver became a hot financial center for the energy business, as old meatpacking buildings were refurbished as plush offices for lawyers, accountants, consultants. Land and housing prices zoomed. Speculation became a parlor game, with some properties jumping 25 percent in a week, and construction exploded like chickweed along the Front Range.

These were flashy, heady times. Big-name developers and Hollywood celebrities moved to town. The International Olympic Committee chose Denver for the 1976 Winter Games, the ultimate in flattery, only to be rejected by voters already too busy to be bothered by more commotion. Lavish parties indulged in caviar and cocaine. And Denver's ethos of growth and greed inspired the television tribute to sex and power *Dynasty*.

Some of the hotshots had fled by the middle eighties, when the boom went to bust, and the holders of $200,000 mortgages gasped in the realization that their new homes were suddenly worth only half that price.

But no city so close to the magnificent peaks of the Rockies would remain in the doldrums for long. Denver is prospering again, an attractive place for up-and-coming companies and weary refugees from the East and California, enamored of Colorado's 300 days of sunshine and its slower pace. A professional baseball team, the Rockies, has arrived to lend the city a major league aura. A gleaming new airport, one of the world's biggest, promises to rival O'Hare and Dallas–Fort Worth as an engine of commerce. And a huge new Convention and Visitors Center has gone up to capitalize on America's infatuation with the West.

But Denver itself, smitten with cosmopolitan flair, fairly blushes about its old cow-town image. It hungers for recognition as a Big City. And there is, to be sure, nothing hick-town anymore about its crime statistics, from savings and loan scandals to drive-by shootings. Street gangs, virtually unknown here a decade ago, now terrorize poor neighborhoods, like Five Points, where crack dens draw more visitors than the Black Cowboy Museum.

Denver, the nation's youngest big city, barely whispers the legacy of the nation's old hero, the cowboy. Its leading image is cast in the spirit of America's current icon, the yuppie. As a metropolitan region, Denver is second only to Washington, D.C., in the percentage of college graduates. Mountain bikes on Jeep Cherokees. Nannies and ballet classes and Montessori schools. Trendy cafés without red meat on the menu. No smoking, *please.*

The fastest growing section of Denver today is Highlands Ranch, which, despite the name, is not even remotely rustic. It is a "planned community," hundreds of tidy frame and shutter houses, all in the same *Leave It to Beaver* style, an entire town drawn up on a blueprint, a section for churches here, a section for schools over there, life in the Mild West.

Rosy-cheeked Denverites spend snowy weekends at Vail and Breckenridge and Copper Mountain, but never venture to Bovina or Wild Horse or Last Chance, little Colorado towns on the plains that are no farther away than the ski slopes but might as well be on Mars.

There aren't enough ranchers on public lands in all of Colorado today to elect a city council representative in Denver. And the political clout in the gold-domed state capitol, whose fifty-fourth step marks the precise spot where the city rises exactly one mile above sea level, rests overwhelmingly with urban politicians.

Larimer Square, the old cowboy haunt, today is lined with espresso bars and pricey boutiques. And inside its tony pubs, patrons are unlikely to shout "Yahoo!" as they hoist their wine spritzers.

The older aromas of Denver, the pungent smell of horses and cattle in the streets, have long been replaced by smog, a brown cloud that hangs over the city, a by-product of progress. To civic boosters, who gaze proudly at the gleaming skyline of the new urban West, the words *cow town* have become the worst kind of insult.

•   •   •

But in the grandstands of the National Western Stock Show, a world away from computer screens and fax machines, condos and culs-de-sac, the cheers of 6,000 spectators rose in worship of America's most powerful myth.

The cowboy's name is unfamiliar. His hometown is a mystery. His face is shrouded in the shadows of his hat.

He is the lanky figure from a cigarette billboard, the silhouette on the canvas of an old painting, the character in a country-and-western ballad.

The fans have come to peer across the arena at a range without asphalt, horsepower without exhaust fumes. They take their seats with plastic cups of diet cola and boxes of salty popcorn. And they gaze out at the young man in the costume of a hero.

•   •   •

A wiry cowboy in striped Western shirt and silver-fringed chaps, boots hooked on the side rails, stared down at his draw for the afternoon performance, a frisky bay gelding snorting anxiously in its narrow cage.

As gingerly as a swimmer wading into frigid waters, the cowboy lowered his denim-covered rear, slowly and carefully, into the curved, fiberglass saddle, hard as a boulder astride the sinewy back of the 1,200-pound bronc.

Murmurs from the grandstands, rising high over the Denver arena, grew into a rumble, and then a roar, as the loudspeaker blared his name.

The horse, annoyed by the weight of the trespasser, twisted his frame, groaning angrily, and banged against the cage, rattling the rails, ready to explode.

The cowboy flinched, raised up, and reached out gently to stroke the horse's silky mane.

"It's all right, fella," the cowboy murmured. "It's all right."

In a moment, the bronc grew still, the calmness of dawn over the plains, just before the tornado. Around the horse's flanks, a sheepskin-lined strap was wrapped like a belt, which would soon be yanked a few sizes too tight, an encouragement to buck.

The cowboy clenched the reins with his gloved right hand. He slipped his boots into the stirrups, then raised his spurs over the horse's shoulders, almost grazing its neck.

And then he leaned back like a racing car driver, almost supine, arching over the cantle of the saddle.

The cowboy shifted a bit, to get just the right feel. He raised his free left arm in the air, bent at the elbow, like the hand signal for a right turn.

The knuckles on his hand squeezing the reins turned a bloodless pale. His blue eyes narrowed into defensive slits. His frame went rigid as stone.

On the other side of the gate, a rodeo worker clutched a rope tied to the chute door. He stared into the cowboy's face, waiting for the signal to pull.

The scoring judges watched from the arena turf. Pickup men on horseback straightened in their saddles. The timekeeper held a thumb over a stopwatch. The crowd fell into a hush.

•   •   •

During the last fleeting moments before the ride, the rest of the world seemed to vanish. He must do it alone. In the vernacular of rodeo, it was time to "cowboy up."

The day of a cowboy falls into two absurdly lopsided parts. Twenty-three hours, fifty-nine minutes and fifty-two seconds serve as filler, the coming and going and waiting of rodeo life.

All that really counts are those next eight seconds.

Anywhere else, eight seconds pass in a flash, an insignificant speck on the clock, a yawn in the afternoon. It is not long enough for the world's fastest man to run 100 yards, barely enough time to read a single paragraph on a page.

But on the hard back of a wild bronc or an angry bull, it is eternity—the agonizing, treacherous road from hope to fate.

In the space of eight seconds, the dreams of a rodeo cowboy can come gloriously to life, or turn to dust.

•   •   •

The cowboy nodded. The chute gate swung open. The flank strap jerked tight.

The bronc and cowboy bolted across the arena. As the fans roared, the cowboy rode high, spurring hard, clenching the reins, a racing bicyclist waiting for the rock in the road.

The horse suddenly jerked, as the cowboy lurched forward. The bronc dug his hind feet into the dirt, lifting hard, putting space between the saddle and the cowboy. The cowboy hung in the air for an instant, then slammed down against the saddle.

His face tight, the cowboy squirmed in a search for the center of gravity, bringing his free arm closer to his body. Then another thump, a jolt in the air, the saddle vanishing for a moment, and then slapping back against his jeans.

The cowboy still spurring, the horn blared, and not a moment too soon. With the contest ended, the rider leaped from the bronc, landing on his feet, wearing the smile of an answered dare.

A pickup man on horseback galloped alongside the empty-saddled bronc, reaching beneath its flanks to loose the tight strap.

The cowboy retrieved his dusty hat, flogged it against his thigh, and set it back on his head.

He listened for the score.

A score in the eighties would surely bring a good paycheck. Anything over ninety would probably win the whole shooting match. To get any kind of money, the cowboy needed to crack seventy.

"Sixty-five points," said the announcer, as dryly as if he were talking about the temperature. "A score of sixty-five."

The cowboy shook his head. He trotted toward the arena fence, pulled himself up and over the rails. A pickup man tossed his saddle over the fence.

The cowboy slung the saddle over his shoulder and disappeared down the tunnel that led from the chute gates.

A voice called out, "See you in Fort Worth."

4

ALONE IN A CORNER of the Fort Worth locker room, a dark-eyed cowboy sat on a saddle plopped on the cement floor, riding an imaginary horse.

Craig Latham clenched an invisible rein in his right hand. His legs were lifted in a V shape. Back and forth he pumped the spurs. The muscles of his face were twisted in a grimace.

Wads of white tape lay near chunks of dirt and four or five empty, unraveled cans of snuff. A hand-scrawled sign over the water fountain warned, "No Spitting."

In a few moments, Latham was going to be ready. He knew the importance of a single ride. In the last season, which ended only a month ago, he had finished seventeenth in the standings, just two spots short of qualifying for Las Vegas. He had mounted more than 100 horses during the year. A better score on just one of them might have sent him to the championships. Instead, he went home under a cloud of debt.

For Latham, rodeo only masqueraded as a game. To him, it meant survival. The Wyoming ranch where he grew up could no longer support another generation. He now lived in a house trailer in Goodwell, Oklahoma, part of the flat, dusty region known as "No Man's Land." He and his wife had a baby. The bills were mounting. If he didn't win enough money this season, which meant making it to Las Vegas, Latham could not last much longer as a cowboy.

He had paid $250 to enter and had scored well enough in the first two performances to make it to the Finals, or the "short-go," one of twelve saddle-bronc riders to qualify. Hundreds of other contestants had fallen short, had left Fort Worth without a dime. One young man, in a crash from a spinning bull, had broken his neck. The cowboy was alive. Beyond that, the doctors hadn't said much.

"Let's go buck some broncs," somebody called out.

A roster tacked on the wall listed the bulls and broncs assigned to each cowboy. Next to Latham's name, it read "Black Widow."

•   •   •

Locals boast that the East peters out in Dallas and the West begins in Fort Worth.

It was from Fort Worth, along the banks of the Trinity River, that the legendary cattle drives headed up the Great Plains. And Fort Worth is still the most Texan of Texas cities, a place where Cow Town is a proper noun and the cowboy hat is proper attire.

To be sure, there are plenty of tassled loafers and Hermes suits on the sidewalks of Fort Worth these days. But the fragrance of the old stockyards hasn't vanished just yet. On a windy day, tumbleweed still blows into town off Highway 20.

Fort Worth is the callused, plainspoken brother to Dallas, the glittery, ostentatious buckle on the Sun Belt. In almost every way, Fort Worth lives in the shadow of Big D.

Every way but one.

•   •   •

On the night of the most famous Texas rodeo of all, nearly 6,000 fans climbed the Fort Worth grandstands to glimpse cowboys who looked as cool and tough as anybody inside Billy Bob's Texas honky-tonk— and could ride to boot.

A cold, stinging drizzle fell across the city. It was the kind of wicked night once cursed by shivering cowboys on lonesome cattle drives. But under the domed roof of the Will Rogers Coliseum, only the beer was cold.

Tonight was the big dog: The Finals.

In the Grand Entry, the Six Flags of Texas were unfurled from horseback, and the spectators rose to take off their cowboy hats for the only time all evening. Galloping across the dirt came the Wise

County Sheriff's Posse, the High Ridge Riding Club, the Cowboys for Christ. And the announcer's voice rose in a patriotic quiver: "Peace—we've got it. We'll share it. And here's how you get it. Ladies and gentlemen, our 'Star-Spangled Banner.' "

To the strains of a brass band, the words of the anthem rang through the grandstands, triumphant as a battle cry.

It felt good to be American. It felt damned good to be a Texan.

In the wildly cheering crowd, a white-haired man in a bolo tie waved a cowboy hat over his head. A little boy held his thumbs up and giggled. A teenage girl jumped up and down in a T-shirt that read "Bo Don't Know Rodeo."

●   ●   ●

Latham pulled himself up onto the platform behind the bucking chutes, where the broncs had been led through a maze, one after another, standing snout to tail. Spotting Black Widow, he leaned over the rails and lowered the saddle across the mount's broad back. With a long, hooked pole, he fished for the cinch, then pulled it back across her belly, and fastened it through the O-ring to secure the saddle.

Up in the grandstands, the crowd was howling with laughter at the banter between the announcer and a clown on the arena floor.

The clown said his wife had run off with a truck driver, and ever since, the sound of a truck's horn made him sad, nervous and upset.

"Oh, I understand," the announcer said, "the sound of a horn reminds you of the truck driver, so it makes you sad about her running off."

The clown frowned through the greasepaint and wagged his head.

"Now I get it," the announcer chuckled. "The sound of the horn upsets you because you're afraid the truck driver is coming to bring her back!"

●   ●   ●

On the far side of the arena, a roper sat atop a horse, clenching pigging string between his teeth. A rope was curled around the horn of the saddle. Inside a cage, a calf peeked through a slotted gate, whimpering anxiously to get loose. The gate lifted, and the calf burst out of the chute. The horse thundered ahead, zeroing in on the target, as the frightened animal fled in a straight line, as fast as his legs could carry him, aware that trouble lurked behind.

•   •   •

The bronc riders paced. They were thinking about taming wild horses. But they were fighting butterflies.

In other sports, a case of the nerves could be shaken with a first tackle or a swing of the bat, and after a few seconds, the athlete would be relaxed and ready to play. But after a few seconds in rodeo, the cowboy is finished.

The chutes rattled. Out burst the first contestant. Latham, eighth in the order, watched, expressionless, as the cowboy rode smooth for a few seconds, but then lost control, spilling on the dirt.

Latham frowned sympathetically. These were his rivals, but also his friends. There was no trash-talking among contestants in rodeo. Cowboys stick together. The guy in the next chute might also be a travel partner later that night. And if he wins the check, he might also buy dinner.

As the chute gates opened and closed, the scores rolled in: 72, 69, 75, 72. Latham had come into the finals with an average of 74. If he could post another score in the seventies, he would be in good shape for a nice paycheck. But anything in the sixties would probably mean failure.

He pulled himself over the rails, then lowered on the saddle, waiting to hear his name. But first came the king of the cowboys: Ty Murray.

•   •   •

The announcer spoke reverently now. "Ladies and gentlemen, we needed a new leader for our sport. And the good Lord looked down and said, 'I'm gonna send you a blond-haired boy from Stephenville, Texas.' This is Ty Murray, folks, the All-Around Cowboy. And every move he makes is an eight-by-ten color photograph."

He had short-cropped hair, a baby face and a waist as skinny as a high school cheerleader's. Ty Murray measured five feet six inches in his cowboy boots and weighed all of 140 pounds, if his pockets were full of change.

But he was the All-Around Cowboy three straight years, and a sure bet to win the title again, if he didn't get hurt. While most contestants call it a day after a single event, Murray performed in three categories: bareback, saddle-bronc and bullriding. In the last season, he had won $259,000, the most ever pocketed by a rodeo cowboy, and more than ten times the sum earned by the average contestant.

He was born on October 11, 1969, the first son after two girls. Two days after he was born, he came home from the hospital in a pair of tiny cowboy boots. He started riding calves at two. As a boy, he perfected his balance by walking atop the fences around the corrals on a ranch where his father worked as a horse trainer. He started riding a unicycle at age ten and two years later his parents bought him a bucking machine. He sometimes rode the machine until one o'clock in the morning. His legs got so raw that he put a piece of cardboard inside his chaps, between his thighs and the swells of his saddle, so he could keep riding. At twenty, he won his first world title.

As the chute lifted, Murray stuck to the horse like a coat of paint, true to his gaudy billing. The judges awarded him a score of seventy-seven points, pushing him up toward the top of the standings, his familiar spot. And the crowd roared in worship.

•   •   •

Latham, now settled in his saddle, didn't watch the ride, or listen for the score. At this moment, the grandstands could have been on fire and he would not have noticed. In his mind, he ran through a checklist: keep the legs stretched high, boots pointed out, bearing straight ahead. His right hand squeezed hard on the reins. Now it was all up to him—and a mare named Black Widow.

•   •   •

Like many of the cowboys, Black Widow had come to rodeo as a castaway from ranch life.

Born eight years ago in a pasture in Oregon, the frisky horse proved too rambunctious for gentle strolls on Sunday afternoons. She showed the same fondness for a saddle that prisoners have for leg irons. And whenever somebody climbed on her back, her strong hind legs gave a hello and goodbye all in the same swift motion.

Horses are born to buck. It is nature's way of giving the horse a way to bounce predators off its back, lest they start chewing.

But an untamed horse is too dangerous for riding, and useless for any of man's other needs, which once included fighting wars and plowing fields. So the horse needs to be tamed, or broken. It is a struggle of man's will against animal instinct. In the end, if a horse remains too rebellious, it is deemed inferior.

It is not the horse that fails, of course, but the man who cannot break it. But man sets the rules. So when the horse wins, the horse loses.

After being dumped on his rear one last time, the Oregon rancher who owned the black mare called a trader, who trucked her with a slew of other horses to an auction in Fort Worth. She caught the eye of a rodeo producer who had watched her fling a man off her back like a crumpled Big Mac wrapper. He bought the horse for $850.

According to the odds, Black Widow would end up on a dinner plate somewhere in Europe, since only one horse in ten purchased by a rodeo contractor ever becomes a professional bucking horse. The rest go to the slaughterhouse, which pays about seventy cents a pound.

But Black Widow saved her life by doing what she was born to do. She threw cowboys to the dust, one after another. She became one of the contractor's finest horses, wild and quick enough to be selected for the National Finals Rodeo in 1990. Now she was still strutting proudly, five years after the rancher had tried vainly to humble her.

She rose before dawn in a pen with a dozen other horses on a feed-lot twenty miles outside of Fort Worth. She chomped down a breakfast of ten pounds of grain, and slurped water from a concrete trough. A few hours before the rodeo, the horses were hauled to the arena in an eighteen-wheeler, then shuttled to a pen near the cowboys' locker room, before finally being led to the bucking chutes.

And now she stood in the cage, snorting defiance, eager to break free once more, as Craig Latham nodded his head for the gate to swing open and the fuse to be lit.

·   ·   ·

"Here's Craig Latham," the announcer said simply. "He needs an eighty to take the lead."

Bolting out of the chute, the 1,300-pound horse raced twenty yards into the arena, as the brim of the cowboy's hat blew back in the wind. As Latham clenched tight, the horse jerked to a sudden halt, lowered her head, and started to buck, again and again, tireless as a machine, before changing directions, and bucking once more.

Straining in the saddle, Latham clenched his teeth in the same grimace he had worn on the locker room floor as the horse darted, then swooped low.

The cowboy stayed with her, spurs pumping, as their shadows danced across the dirt.

Sitting high in the saddle, Latham matched every move of the bronc, looking as if he could ride all day, or at least for the full eight seconds, an exhibition of bronc-busting mastery. If Latham had owned that Oregon ranch, Black Widow might never have been sold at all.

The horn blared. The hatless cowboy pulled his free hand to the horse, grasping its neck with both arms.

The pickup man galloped alongside. Latham lunged toward the helper, wrapping his arms around the man's chest, pulling himself from one horse to the other.

Black Widow, now riderless, raced across the turf, still bucking, as the second pickup man loosed her flank strap.

The cowboy jumped to the turf, then walked slowly along the rails, nodding politely to the cheering crowd, but feeling as anxious as a kid waiting for a report card.

"Seventy-four points for Latham," said the announcer. "He goes into second place."

Relief swept across his face. The rodeo secretary would be cutting him a check for $2,000, maybe more, depending on the last few riders.

He was still a long way from Las Vegas. But he was a couple of miles closer than he had been that morning.

He stooped to retrieve his cowboy hat. Without the hat, he looked like any ordinary young man who would be reporting to a job in the morning at a smokestack factory or a glass-and-steel office building.

Latham put the cowboy hat back on his head. And he flashed a broad smile.

5

EXCEPT FOR SOME drifting tumbleweed and the occasional beep of the radar detector, not much slowed the pickup truck as it roared north up the spine of the Great Plains.

Craig Latham and his travel partners, Billy, Danny and Robert Etbauer, each drove a stint and traded turns sleeping inside the stuffy camper slung over the bed of the pickup, which was crowded with saddles and clothes for the next week of rodeo.

The rain in Oklahoma turned to sleet in Kansas and then to snow in Nebraska. But little else changed. Every fifty miles or so, a white or silver water tower rose to mark another tiny civilization, a few dozen frame houses huddled together against the wind, and then disappeared in the embrace of wheat fields. In the long stretches between towns, weather-beaten old farmhouses, some of them empty, stared back at the road, like stranded hitchhikers too weary to wave any longer, as the highway and time swept past.

Near a curve in the road, a white cross was planted among the weeds in a gully to mark the place of a tragedy, and perhaps to serve as a warning.

The Etbauers were Craig's toughest competitors. All three brothers had made it to the championships in Las Vegas last season. Robert, the oldest at thirty, won the title in saddle-bronc riding, barely edging out Billy.

More than that, they were his closest friends. When they were rookies, Craig and Billy had never seen a city larger than 20,000. More than once, they pulled off the road to argue about who had to drive in the scary traffic of a major metropolis—like Casper, Wyoming.

Peering through the windows of the truck, they could see the sun begin to droop in the west. They were hurrying to get to Rapid City, South Dakota, where their broncs were waiting.

The day before, they had fallen behind schedule by driving 150 miles out of their way to stop at Craig's home in Oklahoma, where the cowboys sat around a kitchen table and sang "Happy Birthday" to his daughter, Chaney, who was turning one.

•   •   •

From a pay phone at a truck stop, Latham had called to learn his draw for the night. Horses are assigned to the cowboys in a random computer program at rodeo headquarters. If a cowboy draws a poor horse, he can skip the rodeo and turn out, which costs $25, as long as he notifies the headquarters twenty-four hours in advance of the contest. If he doesn't call ahead, the fine is doubled.

Even if he drew a sorry nag, Latham wouldn't be pulling out of Rapid City. It wasn't the biggest rodeo in the winter season, but it was far from the smallest. The top prize could be as much as $3,000.

The voice on the other end of the line said the bronc was Whiskey Jack, a light-footed gelding known for quick moves and a strong buck, sure to put points on the board.

It was only February, just a month into the season, too early to expect anything but more bruises. But Latham felt almost giddy. He had won paychecks in Denver, Fort Worth and El Paso. He was tied for first in Belton, Texas, when they left the rodeo. And now he had drawn a good horse for Rapid City.

He flipped through the latest copy of the *Prorodeo Sports News*. The top contenders were listed on page two, under the banner of the Crown Royal World Standings, marked by the whiskey's logo. There was Latham's name in black and white. He was in third place with earnings of $6,139.

After crossing the border into South Dakota, they veered off on Interstate 90, then rolled west past the Buffalo Gap Grasslands and the Badlands National Park. In the distance rose the Black Hills, which had been granted to the Sioux in 1868, then snatched back nine years later when gold was discovered under the earth.

Visitors from around the world now flock to the Black Hills to stare up at the faces carved on Mount Rushmore, and gamble on the slots in Deadwood Gulch, the wildest hideout in the Old West, where Wild Bill Hickok once drew eights and aces, along with a bullet in the head. A tombstone in Deadwood marks the grave of Calamity Jane, a big draw for tourists; her shoot-'em-up legend still fascinates, even though it is almost entirely fiction. The character known as Calamity, whose real name was Martha Canary, in truth led a rather bleak life. As late as 1900, she was working as a prostitute in a local brothel.

The van took the exit for Rapid City and wheeled down Main Street, where it appeared that every restaurant and tavern had a sign in the window shouting "Welcome Cowboys!"

Rapid, as it was known here, had a population of 54,000, but it seemed bigger, since it served as a hub for the country more than 100 miles around, including the Indian towns of Porcupine and Wounded Knee on the Pine Ridge Reservation, the poorest place in America.

As the truck pulled up to the Rushmore Civic Center, the parking lot was already half full, mostly with trucks. A bumper sticker on one read: "You Don't Get to SEE Much in a Small Town. But What You HEAR Makes Up for It."

The cold wind slapped the faces of the cowboys as they trudged under the weight of their gear toward the arena. Inside the locker room, a local television reporter and photographer stood waiting for the Etbauer brothers. As the camera's lights beamed on the champions, and the reporter began to ask questions, Latham slipped away to a quiet corner of the room.

•   •   •

Sitting on a narrow bench in the locker room, Latham draped the saddle across his lap and brushed the dirt from its webbing, squinting to find every last particle of dust, until it was immaculate.

A rodeo saddle looks like any other saddle, except for the absence of a horn, for obvious reasons of male preservation. It is a bronc rider's most valuable possession, just as it was for the cowboys of the Old West, who rarely owned a horse but rode whatever the cattle company provided. The phrase "He's sold his saddle" came to mean that a cowboy was finished in the trade.

Latham used to ride on an ancient saddle that had been handed down from his grandfather to his uncle to his older brother, Deke.

But not long ago, he had put the old saddle away. "I decided I couldn't ride half as good as the three guys before me," he said, "so I stopped using it."

Craig and Deke grew up on their grandfather's Red Fork Ranch in the crook of the Big Horn Mountains of Wyoming. The boys were barely out of diapers when their father, an oil field worker who led a lugubrious and nomadic life, divorced their mother, Joyce. She and her sons, who had been living in a trailer that rolled from one town to the next, moved to the ranch. During summers, they stayed in a crude mountain cabin, without running water or electricity, on a remote plateau where Joyce punched cows and tended sheep.

From the time Deke learned to talk, he was saying he would be a rodeo cowboy someday. Craig, who was two years younger than Deke, wanted to do whatever his big brother did. As they got older, the boys dreamed of becoming rodeo stars so successful they would earn enough money to save the ranch, which was always teetering on the edge of a financial cliff.

Everyone said the brothers were as different as night and day. Deke, redheaded and freckled, was a talker, a drinker, a fighter. Craig, taller and darker, always seemed as shy as a schoolboy at his first dance, reluctant to start a conversation, let alone a fight. But they were best friends. And when Deke joined the pro circuit, he often told the other cowboys: "Just wait until my brother Craig turns pro. Then we'll all be riding for second place."

Deke made the Finals in 1987, while Craig was still competing in college rodeos at Wyoming State in Torrington. Deke rode brilliantly at the championships, winning one round and finishing fifth overall. On the long drive back from Las Vegas, he stopped in Casper to spend some of his prize money on a fancy Christmas present for his mother, then hurried along the dark, snowy roads to visit her. Craig was sitting alone in his room on the campus that night, watching a videotape of his brother in a rodeo, when the telephone rang about midnight with word that Deke had been killed.

•   •   •

"Hey, stranger," a woman's voice called out.

Latham wheeled around to see his mother and grandfather. They had driven down from central Wyoming, a five-hour trip, for the chance to see Craig for just a few minutes.

The cowboy jumped up to give her a hug. And then he stretched out an arm to shake hands with his grandfather, Norris Graves, who wore a bushy white mustache, pointy boots and a black windbreaker emblazoned with the name of a tavern.

"We hear you been doin' real good," the grandfather said in a warm, raspy voice. "We're real proud."

"Oh, Granddad, just tryin' to do my best," said Craig. "You know you taught me everything I know."

"Aw," said Norris, waving a hand in the air. "Like teaching a duck to swim."

"How's that granddaughter of mine?" asked Joyce, her eyes glistening. "I sure do miss her."

"Yeah," said Craig, as his smile vanished, "so do I."

•   •   •

As the last roping calves were being slammed to the ground, Latham pulled himself over the rails and settled on the back of Whiskey Jack. The cowboy got down slowly, as he always did, careful not to graze the horse's hide with his spurs.

A false move could start the horse bucking in the chutes, leaving neither man nor horse with room to escape. The greatest number of injuries occurred not in the arena but in the chutes, where a cowboy could fall beneath the stomping hooves of the caged animal.

But except for a twitch, Whiskey Jack was calm. The bronc was nineteen years old, a codger for a rodeo horse. But some horses are still riding strong past their twenty-fifth birthday. And Jack still had plenty of kick left, to which a long line of cowboys with dirt on their britches could well attest.

Saddle-bronc riding was rodeo's classic event. It is not the wildest event, or the most dangerous, but it is the prettiest to watch, and perhaps the most difficult. Many a young tough can climb aboard a bull and ride passably the first time out. But bronc riding, a more nuanced skill, takes years of practice, which was why most contestants in the event hailed from ranches.

A scoreboard suspended from the ceiling beamed the name of each cowboy in two-foot-tall letters. When it flashed Latham's name, the announcer spoke proudly of the cowboy's roots in next-door Wyoming. The finest bronc riders tend to come from the Northern Plains, especially South Dakota and Wyoming, for reasons that have never been clear, despite endless debate over almost as much beer.

Some cowboys, especially the Texans, surmise that the northerners are all trying to follow in the footsteps of Casey Tibbs, the flamboyant, purple-kerchiefed bronc rider from South Dakota, who achieved such renown in the 1950s that he landed on the cover of *Life* magazine.

A more plausible theory held that the best bronc riders came from the Northern Plains because that's where the best broncs came from. As the last region of the nation to be settled, the remote north teemed with wild horses well into the 1950s. Some parts of Wyoming, in fact, were not fenced until astronauts started to circle the globe. To this day, thousands of mustangs still gallop the northern ranges, often fleeing the helicopters of federal land managers, who try to chase them into catch pens and then truck them to government "adopt-a-horse" sales, where a wild horse is apt to go home to a 20-by-20 backyard pen in the suburbs.

• • •

"Ready, Craig?" a chute boss called out.

Latham nodded. As the gate swung open, he kept his spurs at the neck, then swung his boots down along the horse's sides in time with the first buck. As hooves hit the ground, Latham's boots snapped back up toward the air, and then swung down again with the next buck, an arcing rhythmic motion, just the way the judges want.

The horse ran alongside a rail, near the first row of spectators. The bronc turned with a kick that sent a clod of dirt flying into the stands, smacking the forehead of a middle-aged woman. Unperturbed, she raised a finger and flicked off the dirt, never taking her gaze off the action in the arena.

Latham's lanky frame bounded as gracefully as a dancer's, moving in swoops, not jerks. It was difficult to tell where the horse left off and the cowboy began. No daylight got between his seat and the saddle. His free hand waved in the air. Even his cowboy hat stayed snug.

And when the horn blared, he simply raised a leg and jumped easily to the ground, effortless as getting off a merry-go-round.

"You're gonna have to go a long way to see a ride any better than that," the announcer marveled.

His score put him ahead of Robert, behind Danny and tied with Billy. No matter what happened in the final performance, Latham would be leaving with a paycheck for hundreds of dollars and his name would remain atop the standings in the *Prorodeo Sports News*.

In the locker room, a cup of beer was passed among the cowboys.

Latham took a swig, then changed into his street clothes. His mother and grandfather came along to say goodbye. It could be months before they saw him again.

Latham walked to a pay phone, where he called his wife and little girl, who had been kept up late waiting to hear her daddy's voice. And then he caught up with the Etbauers, who were signing autographs outside the locker room. And then the four cowboys headed to the parking lot and drove in search of a cheap motel.

6

IT WAS AN unspoken wish, one that made her feel almost disloyal, but Paula Wimberly yearned for the day when Joe would quit the rodeo.

Part of the great mystique of the rodeo cowboy was supposed to be the independence. There was no boss to answer, no time clock to punch. According to the mythology of rodeo, which sometimes got piled as high as anything the bulls left behind, the solitary cowboy had the freedom to go where he wanted, when he wanted, if he wanted.

But when the bills came due, the hard truth and romantic ideals of rodeo life went separate ways. The cowboy had the same freedom to skip a rodeo that the bricklayer had to skip the construction site: No work—no pay.

In order to survive, Joe had been hustling to every rodeo he could. He had missed plenty of family occasions, like the birth of his first child, and always vowed to make it up somehow, someday.

There was Casey's second birthday, when Joe had promised for weeks that he was going to be there. He and Paula had planned a big party. They invited friends and relatives. They bought balloons to decorate the trailer. Casey seemed almost as excited as Joe. He said there wasn't a rodeo in the world that would make him miss the party.

But on the day before the party, as Joe squeezed in one last rodeo, he was thrown from a bull and broke his leg. Joe spent his daughter's birthday in a hospital bed in Wyoming. He could not even call her to wish her a happy birthday, since the trailer didn't have a phone.

Paula never complained about the loneliness, or the unpredictability, even though there was plenty of both. She had married a cowboy, for better and for worse. And she wasn't going to try to change him into someone else. That was part of the bargain of their love.

But he had now been chasing rodeos for more than ten years. Paula wanted to have Joe at her side, not a thousand miles away, risking his life on the back of a bull. There were times when the telephone would ring late at night and Paula would be seized by some horrible image. And there were times when it did not ring, and Paula was haunted by the same fears. She needed him at home, not to fix what was broken, or carry what was heavy—Paula was capable of fending for herself—but simply to put his arms around her.

The kids were growing up. And Paula had grown impatient for the day when her cowboy would come home for good.

But now that Joe was actually uttering the words "I quit," Paula did not know exactly how she felt.

"I can't go back," Joe told her, his face drawn and his words as final as defeat. "I miss my kids, and I miss you terrible. Every time something important happens around here, I'm off in who-knows-what state. What kind of life is that for you? For the kids?

"I've watched one friend get killed. I've seen another one get paralyzed. And where has rodeo gotten me? Look at me. I'm burned out and I'm all crippled up. And we're bad, bad, bad broke."

Paula could not quite believe him. From the first day she met him, when she was fourteen years old, Joe had seen himself as a cowboy, a soul from the Old West who accidentally had been born in 1962. Rodeo was as much a part of Joe as the color of his eyes.

"What about being a cowboy?" she asked.

"Oh, Paula, there ain't much cowboying to rodeo. It's highways and truck stops and fast-food joints."

In her daydreams of Joe finally quitting the rodeo, Paula had never quite got around to thinking about what he would do for a living. That would come with tomorrow. But suddenly, tomorrow was here.

"What are you going to do?" she asked softly.

He lifted his eyes from the floor and shook his head. "I don't know."

They were $13,000 in debt.

•   •   •

Workmen had started repairs on the burned house. The contractor needed more help. He asked Joe where he could find a good worker for cheap wages.

"How cheap?" Joe asked.

"Five dollars an hour. Know anybody that'll work for that?"

"Yeah," Joe answered. "Me."

For the next few months, Joe carried boards and nails and watched the workmen bang his house back into shape. When the insurance checks arrived, Joe got paid.

After the house was finished, he answered a newspaper want ad for a cattle buyer in Fort Worth. He went to the interview in his shiny dress boots and a tie. It almost choked him. When he came home that night, he told Paula: "You're married to a businessman."

It was a commission job. And Joe was financially liable for the stock he bought. If the cattle didn't weigh the right amount, or didn't pass muster by inspectors at headquarters, Joe had to take them back to an auction. And if they sold for less on resale, he had to make up the difference. He once bought a cow that died almost as soon as he hauled it away.

The job ended up costing him more than he earned. Before long, Joe and the cattle company agreed that he should seek another career.

He took any odd job he could find. He cut firewood. He worked as a day laborer on ranches. He traded a few horses. He even tried out for a part as a cowboy extra in a beer commercial.

•   •   •

During the day, the house was noisy with the play of the kids, the ringing of the telephone, the clatter of chores. It kept Joe and Paula from concentrating on their worries.

But now the kids had been put to bed. The living room was silent.

"Paula, we got to do something," Joe said, speaking in a strained whisper so the kids wouldn't hear. "We got these bills stackin' right up to the ceiling. We're gettin' deeper and deeper in trouble every day."

He got up and paced around the room. He looked out through the window at the darkness.

"Something will come through, Joe," Paula said. "It's got to."

"Who's gonna hire me?" he shot back. "I can fool with horses and cattle, but that's about it. I ain't much use otherwise.

"Except for ridin' bulls."

For a moment, they were both silent. Paula knew what Joe was thinking.

"But Joe," she said, "your body's still hurtin'."

"Them bill collectors don't care," he answered.

Going back to the rodeo full-time was not an option. There wasn't enough money to pay for travel and entry fees.

But a rodeo just two hours away, in the Dallas suburb of Mesquite, was about to start its season. It was an indoor rodeo that ran on weekends. The top prize paid only $300. But that was a fortune ahead of Joe's current bank balance. And the entry fee was only $30.

"You sure you want to do this?" Paula asked.

"It ain't a matter of want-to," Joe said. "It's got-to."

. . .

The town of Mesquite existed before the oil boom and the LBJ Expressway and the Galleria shopping mall. But most people in Dallas wouldn't have been able to find their way there, and precious few tried.

But as oil gushed from the bowels of Texas, and Dallas burgeoned as a Sun Belt corporate center, the scrub grass around Mesquite gave way to housing developments and strip malls.

The growth pushed out the last of the old cattle ranchers in Mesquite, but elevated the profile of its theatrical descendant, the rodeo. A short businessman in a tall cowboy hat, Neal Gay, had bought some cheap, vacant land in Mesquite to run a low-budget rodeo. After the boom, he was able to sell a portion of the valuable land and build a glossy indoor rodeo stadium.

Mesquite is now the best-known rodeo in America. It is broadcast on the cable television station, the Nashville Network, where people who have never stepped in cow dung can tune in and learn about rodeo cowboys.

When Gay started the outdoor rodeo in the 1950s, the bleachers were filled mostly by rural people. Rain or shine, they sat in the stands and cheered and hooted for a few hours on an afternoon, a welcome break from their chores. Cars and pickup trucks would park in a dirt lot where spaces were marked by roofing tabs. When it rained, the lot became so muddy that Gay had to use his tractor to pull the vehicles out.

After he came into the money, some people told Gay he should never build a fancy indoor stadium. The burning sun, the driving rain, the howling wind—that was all part of the romance of the rodeo, they said.

But Gay was a businessman, not a poet. "When it comes right down to it," he said, "most people don't like that shit." And so the indoor stadium went up.

Urban people now filled most of the 5,400 seats in the Mesquite stadium. Many of them were tourists and businesspeople who had come to Dallas for a few days and wanted to see something Western before they went home. About 5 percent of the fans at the Mesquite rodeo were foreign visitors.

Air-conditioned skyboxes overlooking the arena, equipped with color televisions and wet bars, were leased for $10,000 a year. President Reagan had been here. Jerry Hall, the fashion model, was a regular. And Prince Rainier of Monaco once hired the stadium for a private rodeo for himself and thirty-five of his friends.

•   •   •

At sixty-seven years old, Neal Gay, with his ruddy complexion, narrow eyes and hands as rough as old work gloves, still looked tough enough to climb on the back of an angry bull.

Gay grew up in a hardscrabble neighborhood in South Dallas. His mother was a beautician; his father was an auto mechanic and an amateur boxer. In the 1930s, white kids in Dallas were forbidden to play with black kids. But as young blacks walked past the Gay home on the way to school, Neal's father would stop them and offer a nickel to anyone who would box with his boy.

Neal Gay learned to fight so well that, as a teenager, he wound up before a judge who told him it would be a good idea if he joined the service. "If I see you in here one more time," the judge had warned, "I'm going to send you someplace besides the military."

On his seventeenth birthday, he left Union Terminal on a train bound for the Coast Guard, where he served in the North Atlantic. But he was not cut out for the regimentation of military life, especially the yes-sir-no-sir etiquette and the subservience to commanders. He barely escaped with an honorable discharge.

When he returned to Dallas in 1945, a friend talked him into entering a few rodeos. Along the way, Gay won some, and nearly lost his life. It wasn't a stomping bull or horse that nearly killed him, but a deputy sheriff.

Gay had walked out of a rodeo in Liberty, Texas, toward the parking lot with a couple of friends, who started an argument with each other and began to fight. Gay rested against the fender of a car, sipped a beer and enjoyed the entertainment.

A cop happened on the scene, and drew back his billy club to whack one of Gay's friends. "Hey," shouted Gay, "there ain't no need for that."

Then the cop jerked out a pistol and said he had a mind to use it on Gay. After the exchange of a few more sharp words, the cop and the cowboy started wrestling around on the dirt lot, and the gun went off, blasting a hole in Gay's belly.

The cop took off, and Gay's friends stopped fighting and pulled their bleeding buddy into a car, where they raced to a hospital. In the operating room, Gay looked up at the doctor and explained that he was short on funds to pay for the mending. He had only $3 in his pocket. But he was wearing a big diamond ring. He said the hospital could hold it for collateral.

"It belongs to a gambler friend of mine," Gay warned the doctor. "He's a pretty bad guy. So make sure you don't lose it."

"Son," the doctor told him, "we're just going to try to save you, if we can."

•   •   •

A few years later, Gay married a bronc rider named Evelyn "Cookie" Foster, a tiny woman who could ride as well as almost any man. They had two sons, Pete and Donny. In February of 1954, when the oldest boy was barely two years old, Cookie was diagnosed with leukemia. She died four months later.

"I had these two little babies, and nobody to take care of them," Gay said. "So I had to quit rodeo, of course."

He opened a used-car lot and started a rodeo in Mesquite on land that he bought for next to nothing. "Even if the rodeo don't make it," he remembered saying to a friend, "this land might be worth something someday."

•   •   •

The telephone in Neal Gay's office was ringing. It was an executive with Dodge Truck calling to pitch a promotion.

If Gay would pick the meanest, wildest bull he could find, the company would put up a big prize for the cowboy who could ride it. The pot would start at $5,000, and grow by $500 every time the bull shucked a cowboy. Under the terms of the deal, the bull would be named after a new truck, Dodge Dakota. It would essentially be an advertisement, but a lot more exciting, given the possibility of blood-shed.

About thirty bull riders competed at Mesquite every weekend. But only one of the cowboys would get a crack at Dodge Dakota. The as-signment would be made randomly by computer at rodeo headquar-ters. Merely drawing the Dodge bull would take a stroke of great luck. Even so, cowboys from all around the West would enter Mesquite just for the scant chance.

Gay liked the idea. It would surely heighten the drama at Mesquite. If some cowboy could actually ride the meanest bull around, it would be a dazzling spectacle. If, on the other hand, a cow-boy fell victim under the stomping hooves of a killer beast, well, that was rodeo.

He owned 165 bucking bulls, including some of the meanest in the business. But he chose none of them. Everybody in rodeo would be following this special event. The longer the bull went unridden, the more excitement would grow, the more tickets would be sold. Gay wanted to find something exceptionally wicked.

He called a livestock trader: "If you come across something really rank, let me know."

The supplier called back with the discovery of a perfectly night-marish bull: It was black with a white face. It weighed about 1,700 pounds, as hard as rock. It had a single horn that crawled ominously down the side of its face. It had been bucked only once. And it had ex-ploded like a grenade.

"You got your Dodge Dakota," he told Gay.

•   •   •

Among traveling cowboys on the rodeo trail, Joe's name would some-times come up, especially when talk turned to hard times or bad luck.

"Whatever happened to that cowboy from Cool?" a young bull rider asked over a beer after a rodeo.

"Went broke," somebody answered in a flat voice. "He went real cold. Had some bad breaks. House burned. And you know, he's got a lot of mouths to feed."

"Stayin' home, is he?"

"Yeah. But he always enters at Mesquite. He's hoping for a chance at that Dodge Dakota."

•   •   •

For a month or so, Joe had waited nervously for the weekly call from rodeo headquarters to learn what bull he had drawn at Mesquite. He knew the chances were remote. But somebody would get Dodge Dakota. Why not him?

When he heard something in the news about South Dakota or North Dakota, when he saw a Dodge passing along the road, and especially when an overdue bill came in the mail, Joe thought about that bull.

He daydreamed about it, prayed about it, and talked and talked about it. Even the kids had come to know just about everything about this important bull that shared a name with a truck.

But the calls from rodeo headquarters never made any mention of Dodge Dakota. "Thank you now for calling," Joe would say politely, trying to keep his voice from cracking. Gradually, he stopped waiting so anxiously for the calls.

Week after week, Dodge Dakota sent the chosen cowboy hurtling through the air. The pot grew to $7,000, then $8,000, then $9,000. The fans at Mesquite started to murmur that this bull would never be ridden. It was no wonder that the Dodge company had put up such a hefty pot.

Joe was left to compete for the much smaller prize at the rodeo, along with the other twenty-nine cowboys who had lost in the lottery. Every weekend, Paula and the kids climbed into the pickup and drove to Mesquite, where they sat in the grandstand and cheered for Joe. He won his share, sometimes as much as $300. But it didn't go very far on the bills.

After the performance, they would take the kids to a Taco Bell near the stadium, the big treat for the week. When the kids asked Joe why he hadn't ordered anything for himself, he would tell them he just wasn't hungry.

•   •   •

Joe came home from the banker's office late one afternoon. He looked ashen. For a while, he didn't say a word. He just stared at the walls.

"What is it?" Paula asked uneasily, not sure she wanted to find out.

"Paula," he said finally, "we're going to have to sell the house."

For a moment, Paula was silent. It was as if her mind would not compute the terrible words she was hearing.

Through all the difficult times, the heartaches and worries and uncertainties of rodeo life, the house had been a refuge, a triumphant symbol of their struggles.

"No," Paula said softly, as breath finally returned to her. "No!"

But Joe said he didn't see any other way out. They had paid $30,000 for the house seven years ago. Maybe they could get $40,000 for it now.

"If we sell the place," he said, "we could take the difference, pay the bills, and start all over."

Paula stood in disbelief. So many memories raced through her mind. On the day they bought the place, she and Joe had giggled so happily they could barely sleep at night. There were the Thanksgiving dinners, when her grandmother came to make her special recipe for turkey and dressing, and everybody squeezed so closely in the tiny kitchen that they could barely raise their arms. There was the time when Joe was on the road and she cared for the newborn calves he raised in the yard, feeding them from baby bottles. At the time, she groused that Joe was crazy to leave her in charge of the animals. But now, it all seemed wonderful.

"This is our home, Joe. You don't just give up your home. Remember when the house burned, and people came from all around offering to paint and nail and do whatever they could? And the kids. They've never known any other home."

"Look, I've seen what bankruptcy can do to a family," Joe said. "I watched both my granddaddies go broke. I watched my father go broke. It ain't pretty to watch."

Paula's voice was growing louder. "But this is where we're meant to be. This is where God put us."

"What else can we do?" Joe asked, sounding as helpless as a lost little boy.

"Something, anything," Paula pleaded, as tears started to flood down her cheeks. "There's got to be another way we can get out of this. I'll get another job. I'll dig ditches if I have to."

"Come on, Paula. I ain't likin' this any more than you."

"But what about your plans, Joe? You were going to build an arena out back someday. What about the barn you always said you were going to build? Let's just wait a little longer, Joe. Let's see what happens."

"Paula, I put my name down on a piece of paper that said I was going to pay those debts. Right there on that paper, it says Joe Wimberly. I ain't gonna go back on that."

"I won't sign the papers, Joe. I won't do it."

Paula was angry. She glared at Joe. This wasn't the same man she had married.

"Now Paula, we got to remember. This house is just a material thing. It's boards and paint and siding. If we stay together as a family, it don't matter where we are."

He reached over and put his arms around Paula.

"I'm trying to be as smart as I can," he said, trying to manage a smile, "with what I've got to work with."

"Oh, Joe Wimberly," she whispered, as a soft laugh escaped past the tears. "I love you."

7

THE BORDER BETWEEN the Dakotas was drawn in the wrong place.

According to its hardy inhabitants, there should have been no North Dakota or South Dakota, but rather an East Dakota and West Dakota. The real divide was the Missouri River. To the east were flat, cultivated prairie in mile squares, farmers in seed caps and tidy Main Streets from a Midwestern postcard. To the west were buttes, canyons and thistly range, ranchers in cowboy hats, pickups with gun racks and the leave-me-alone politics of the rural West.

One side set the clock to Central Time. The other lay in the Mountain Zone. Dakotans identified themselves as "East River" or "West River."

Bismarck was right in the middle, set on the bank of the Missouri, chosen as the capital of North Dakota in no small part because it straddled both worlds.

The West River side had the gold, the cattle, the scenery. The East River side had the bulk of the population. But in the middle of February, all of Dakota had one thing in common: numbing cold.

At the Bismarck Stock Show and Rodeo, a button on the overcoat of an elderly woman trumpeted the silver lining of frostbite: "Minus 41 Degrees—It Keeps Out the Riffraff."

•   •   •

Behind the chutes, a twenty-five-year-old cowboy named Larry Sandvick glanced into the horse pen and appraised his dance partner for the evening, a young bay mare with white forelocks and a mane as black as midnight in Wyoming.

"Hey, look at her, Marv," he called to his traveling partner, Marvin Garrett. "She's awful cute, ain't she?"

If the horse could have talked, she would no doubt have returned the compliment. Larry Sandvick was born on a farm in North Dakota with a face that wealthy men in New York and California go to the plastic surgeon to buy: powerful jaw, sculpted cheekbones, sandy hair and deep-set eyes so blue they seemed almost purple. Women looked at Sandvick the way kids look at ice cream.

The only part of Sandvick's face that could get him into trouble was his mouth. When it wasn't wrapped around the neck of a beer bottle, it was often running in a gear two speeds ahead of his brain. Sandvick knew just about everything, except when to shut up. "If you can't brag about something," went the gospel according to Larry, "then it ain't worth doing." And he practiced what he preached.

Sandvick could be so vulgar that he sometimes embarrassed even other rodeo cowboys, a remarkable feat. He once conducted a telephone interview with the editor of *Prorodeo Sports News*, a no-nonsense woman, who became incensed when she realized that the sound of spilling water in the background was Sandvick peeing into the toilet.

One time in a bar in South Dakota, a fellow cowboy became so infuriated with Sandvick that he finally lost control and smacked him across his motoring mouth. A nervous manager beckoned the police, who arrived on the assumption that they would be carting away the smacker. But when they saw what a smart aleck Sandvick could be, they ended up jailing him instead. The fellow cowboy, feeling a bit guilty about Sandvick's predicament, decided to drive to the jail and post his bond, but not before a leisurely breakfast of pancakes and sausage.

Beneath Sandvick's swagger and swearing, though, there was a soft heart and an innocent soul. He lacked sense, but also guile. If he was the cowboy who stayed the longest and made the most noise at the beer tent, and he usually was, he was also the cowboy who stayed the longest and showed the most patience with the little cowboys and cowgirls in the special rodeos for mentally retarded children.

It was Sandvick, maybe the toughest cowboy in all of rodeo, who knelt at the head of a seriously injured bronc rider on the arena turf in Greeley, Colorado, on the Fourth of July in 1989 and cried, "Don't let him die." When the injured cowboy was hospitalized, Sandvick left the rodeo circuit and took a construction job so he could spend hours every day at the bedside of his friend, who lived for one year and sixteen days after the accident.

If a cowboy was broke, he could count on a share of whatever was jingling in Sandvick's pockets. If a cowboy needed a ride, Sandvick could always find a way to squeeze in another passenger. And if a downhearted cowboy needed a good joke or a story, Sandvick was quick to tell one on himself.

He grew up in the Badlands of North Dakota near the Little Missouri River in the town of Killdeer, population 722 and falling. As a kid, Sandvick would skip out of study hall and sneak home to the machine shed on the farm, where he taught himself to build furniture and repair saddles. The farm has been in the family since before the turn of the century, when his great-grandfather emigrated from Norway. But in today's get-big-or-get-out agriculture economy, the small operation was barely enough to support his father, and Larry read the writing on the wall.

Now he lived in a rickety trailer in Wyoming, with weeds growing up around the broken steps. Between the jerking of the horse, and the repeated landings on the hard turf, Sandvick twice needed surgery on his shoulders. In one crash against the dirt, one of his shoulders popped out of its socket, and the cowboy, still lying on the arena floor, gritted his teeth and shoved it back into place.

Sandvick drove an old, battered, heaterless Chrysler that he had bandaged with duct tape and decorated with the curled horns of a sheep for a hood ornament. He gave the car the affectionate name Goldie, and he seemed surprised, and a little hurt, when people pointed and laughed as he drove down the road.

To make ends meet, Sandvick relied on the skills he honed in the machine shed, working with furniture and leathers. Many of the rodeo cowboys used chaps made by Sandvick, including some who wore them to the National Finals in Las Vegas. But Sandvick's own pair of chaps had never made it to the championships.

•   •   •

In the drafty halls of the Bismarck stock show, a banner overhead read "Serving America's Number 1 Industry: Agriculture." There were booths on the latest in irrigation pumps, color videos of calf embryo transplants and pen after pen of shampooed show heifers and blow-dried prize lambs, including some that belonged to a local farmer named MacDonald.

Perhaps no state in America is as close to its roots as North Dakota, which joined the Union just a little over a century ago. There are men and women alive today who, as children, walked in the ruts left by the settlers' wagons.

As it always has been, North Dakota today is a land of men with callused hands, women with windburned faces, striving for nothing more, or less, than to pass on their farms and ranches to sons and daughters, as they were handed on to them.

In the cliché of rural America, it is the life of white picket fences, simple Sunday dinners, church choirs and 4-H, a world insulated from the troubles on network news. But when the rest of America was celebrating the go-go eighties, the mournful chant of the auctioneer was ringing over the farm fields, the worst agricultural depression since the Dust Bowl, and televisions in North Dakota were running suicide-prevention hot lines for desperate farmers and ranchers, as the sound of gunshots rang out from so many red barns.

Farming was just like any other business, the Washington economists explained. Go work on a computer. And Ronald Reagan cracked: "Maybe we ought to keep the grain, and export the farmers."

Little towns in North Dakota, and across the Great Plains, have been losing population so steadily that a pair of Rutgers professors, Frank and Deborah Popper, have proposed that vast parts of the region be swept clean of the last stragglers, and turned into a wildlife preserve called the Buffalo Commons.

A few years ago, the publishers of a road atlas of the United States forgot to include North Dakota. And the state endured hearty laughter in Congress over a proposed museum to honor Lawrence Welk, its most famous native son.

Young people on the Great Plains have gotten the message. They have a nickname for their forgotten land: the Outback. But its meaning is stripped of the exotic mystery of deep Australia. It is a taunt, code for hick. And when the choice of music is wrong, when the clothes are too old-fashioned, when a country kid acts too much like a country kid, peers warn sarcastically: "Don't be an Outbacker."

●   ●   ●

As the horses snorted, a fellow cowboy asked Sandvick how the winter rodeos had been going.

"Not worth a shit," he replied.

Sandvick had come to Bismarck far down in the standings. Maybe thirtieth place. Maybe fortieth. He didn't bother to check.

He pulled himself over the rails and settled on the back of the bronc, pushed down on the crown of his white cowboy hat and shoved a plug of tobacco the size of a golf ball inside his cheek.

In the bareback event, there was no saddle for balance or reins for control, only a small leather rigging, shaped like a suitcase handle, which attached to the sheepskin pad cinched around the bronc's withers.

At a nod of Sandvick's hat, the gate rose and the bronc burst from the chute, groaning as the flank strap jerked tight. The crowd roared as the bronc reared, staggering on hind hooves, while the cowboy, nearly upside down, stared up at the ceiling, blinded by the lights, deafened by the roar.

And then the horse slammed its front hooves against the turf, a 1,400-pound thunderbolt, as Sandvick's slender frame snapped forward, like a reflex to a punch in the stomach.

The unbridled bronc streaked across the arena, nearly jerking the rigging from the cowboy's clenched fist. But the cowboy's spurs kept the time, pumping in unison with every high buck.

While the seconds ticked away, Sandvick bounced like a loosely tethered saddlebag. After one sudden jolt, he looked like he might carom off at the next dart of the horse. But as the horn blared, it no longer mattered.

The cowboy dropped to the ground, knees buckling, and collapsed on the dirt. His right arm throbbed like a bad tooth. The strong horse had jerked at the cowboy's handhold like ten strong men in a tug-of-war.

Sandvick took a couple of deep breaths and rose to his feet. He dusted off his jeans with the slap of his hand, then lifted his hat to wipe the sweat from his brow.

The loudspeaker blared a score of seventy-three points. It would not be enough to win the contest, but it would place him in the money. And lately that was unfamiliar territory.

Still huffing, Sandvick climbed atop a rail to watch the rest of the cowboys. The next two contestants got dumped. And then came a couple of scores in the sixties. But when his travel partner, Garrett, came out of the chutes, everybody moved down a notch. Garrett, a two-time Las Vegas champion, posted a score of eighty to win the rodeo.

•   •   •

Sandvick clapped along with the rest of the spectators as Garrett took a victory lap on a saddle horse. And then he headed for the locker room.

He walked past a couple of paramedics who were sipping colas and trading stories from earlier rodeos. "No kidding—the bull stomped right down on the guy's balls," one of them was saying. "Man, it was bloody." His partner was not impressed. "I saw a cowboy get scalped once. I mean the top of his head actually got sliced off. I think they sewed it on later, though."

The only emergency call on this night involved a public relations woman for the city of Bismarck. She had stumbled across a step near the locker room and sprained an ankle. As the medics hurried over with a stretcher, the embarrassed woman waved them off. A cowboy standing nearby offered her a cool drink. She thanked him and raised the cup to her lips.

"Yuck!" she cried after spitting out a mouthful. "There's tobacco juice in this."

"Aw," said the cowboy, "not very much."

•   •   •

Sandvick changed into his street clothes and shouted congratulations across the locker room to Garrett.

"So that's how it's supposed to be done," Sandvick cracked with a wink.

Garrett laughed and came over to slap his partner on the back. "You had a nice ride, Lar," he said. "She darn sure was a strong devil, wasn't she?"

The cowboys would be driving all night to Minneapolis for a rodeo scheduled for the next afternoon. A steer wrestler from South Dakota had asked to come along. Since the wrestling event wouldn't start for another twenty minutes, the cowboys had some time to spare.

Sandvick walked down to the rodeo secretary's office to collect his pay. He read the check for $180, folded it, and shoved it into the pocket of his tight Wranglers. Subtracting for gas and entry fees, he would have $10 or $20 left over. But it would put some points in the standings next to his name.

Walking back through the corridors, Sandvick was stopped by a man with a little boy. The kid wanted to buy a custom-made pair of chaps.

"Be glad to," Sandvick said. "But the materials are gettin' awful expensive. With all these Hollywood types dressing up like ranchers, it's gettin' so a cowboy can't afford to look like a cowboy anymore."

The boy said he could afford it.

"What style would you like?" Sandvick asked.

"I want a pair just like Ty Murray wears."

"Oh, of course," said Sandvick, who was accustomed to such requests from the adoring fans of the champion All-Around Cowboy. "Everybody wants to look like Ty."

By the time Sandvick got back to the locker room, Garrett and the steer wrestler were ready to go. They gathered their clothes and gear and left through a back door of the Bismarck arena, as the band was playing "There's Nobody Home on the Range Anymore."

They shivered in the darkness as they climbed into Garrett's van. Sandvick got behind the steering wheel. He was supposed to appear in court in Wyoming on his last speeding violation. But a rodeo in Texas was scheduled on the same day, so naturally he couldn't make it to court. A warrant was issued for his arrest.

With eight speeding tickets in the last year, he no longer had a driver's license. But that just meant he had to be extra careful.

8

THE COWBOYS STOPPED for gasoline at U-Pump and a quick plate of dinner at Denny's, where Sandvick filled a thermos with enough caffeine to last the eight-hour trip.

By the time the van rolled onto Interstate 94, beneath a sign with an arrow that pointed toward Minnesota, it was almost midnight. The lights of Bismarck quickly faded in the rearview mirror. Only the headlights of the van pierced the blackness ahead.

"I still can't believe I forgot to enter San Angelo," moaned Sandvick, who had missed the entry deadline for the Texas rodeo.

The dashboard was covered with tapes by George Jones and Waylon Jennings, a Louis L'Amour paperback, a few cans of snuff and a copy of the *Prorodeo Sports News.* Cowboy hats swayed on hanging clips along the side windows.

"Oh, you'll probably go down there anyway," said Garrett.

"Hell yes," replied Sandvick. "You guys will be out ridin' broncs and I'll be over at the beer table, gettin' drunk and telling people: 'You know, I could have won this damned thing.' "

"Probably so, Lar," said Garrett, who had stretched out in the back seat across from the steer wrestler, Leon Etzkorn.

On this trip, Sandvick had been sober as a preacher, in deference to Garrett, who quit drinking five years ago after the birth of his first child.

"Hear anything from Mark?" Sandvick inquired about Garrett's brother, also a bareback rider, who usually traveled with them. He had broken a shoulder a month ago while trying to tame an ornery colt back home.

"Still mending," said Garrett.

Sandvick sipped coffee and punched the buttons of the radio. In eastern North Dakota, it was hard to find a station with a signal strong enough to last through a song. He gave up and switched off the dial.

Before long, the other cowboys were snoozing. Sandvick kept the speedometer up around seventy-five miles an hour, braking sharply whenever the radar detector beeped, then revving back up when the coast was clear.

•   •   •

Crossing the border into Minnesota, leaving the West, the highway swung south and east, passing white clapboard farmhouses with red wood barns and tall, corn-stocked silos. The countryside was dotted with frozen lakes: Osakis and Christina, Otter Tail and Ten Mile. And the fields, blanketed with snow, slumbered in respite before spring planting.

It was Sunday, not that it mattered much. To a rodeo cowboy, a Sunday didn't feel any different from a Tuesday. After a while, the days of the week tended to run together, like the rodeos themselves. North Dakota didn't look any different from Texas from inside the walls of an arena. Only the calendar changed, and the standings, and the view from seventy-five miles an hour.

•   •   •

About an hour west of Minneapolis, the steer wrestler suggested he take a turn behind the wheel. Sandvick pulled off the road and hopped to the passenger side, his eyes glazed, too tired to sleep. Every few miles, he popped a sunflower seed into his mouth.

The traffic became heavier and city lights began to glow in the distance, just as the sun was coming up.

They were headed for the town of Hastings, about thirty miles south of the Twin Cities. A former bull rider there had invited them to shower and rest before the rodeo.

The steer wrestler took the turnoff for Interstate 494, then veered south on Highway 35, before finally taking the exit. Hastings, with a population of 15,000, was an old farm town on the banks of the Mississippi River. But growth in the Twin Cities, sprawling deeper into the countryside every year, had nearly made a suburb out of Hastings. Many of its old Victorian houses now belonged to people wearing suits who commuted to jobs downtown. And the town's adjacent farm fields, once rich with corn and beans, now sprouted subdivisions.

"This looks like the street," said the steer wrestler, as he drove slowly through a subdivision of new homes and finally pulled into the driveway of a split-level cedar ranch. "I think so, anyway."

Instructing the other cowboys to wait, the steer wrestler loped up the steps and gave the door a few hard raps. But there was no answer. He knocked again. No answer. He crept through some bushes alongside the house and pressed his face against the windowpane.

Watching from the van, Sandvick and Garrett joked that it better be the right house. Otherwise the people inside would take one look at the prowler—a burly figure with a whiskery stubble and matted hair—and call 911.

A moment later, a woman in a pink housecoat holding a baby came to the door. She gave the steer wrestler a hug.

Sandvick and Garrett crawled out of the van, squinting in the glare of the early morning sunlight, and introduced themselves to the woman, apologizing for the inconvenience. She showed off her baby, who got a tickle from each cowboy, and then she led the sleepy men to some empty bedrooms.

•   •   •

Three hours later, Sandvick awoke to a thump at the door. In the first moment of consciousness, he didn't remember where he was. Maybe he was back in his house trailer, he surmised, and a bandit was breaking down the door. He was too sleepy to care. "Come on in and take what you want," he thought to himself. "Kill me if you have to. Just don't wake me up."

And then came another thump, harder than the last. "Gotta get going," the steer wrestler warned from the other side of the door. "The perf starts in just a couple hours."

Each of the cowboys showered, shaved and dressed. They thanked the woman again, tickled the baby once more, and headed out the door to the van. They stopped for breakfast at a Perkins restaurant in downtown Hastings. As they waited in line, Sandvick picked up a newspaper to check the sports pages.

There were pictures and articles about basketball, football, base-ball, even soccer and lacrosse. "Nothing about the rodeo," Sandvick said, shaking his head. "Damn bums."

A hostess led the bleary-eyed young men to a booth. Just about everyone in the restaurant was dressed for church. And most of them were blond.

Sandvick ordered Belgian waffles. Etzkorn ordered eggs and sausage. Garrett ordered pancakes and peanut butter.

The waitress brought over the food, including some ketchup and salsa for the eggs. "Jeez," said Garrett, "if I'da known they had salsa here, I woulda ordered something that goes with it."

The other cowboys pointed out that a man who puts peanut butter on his pancakes need not bow to dining conventions.

Garrett nodded agreeably. He picked up the salsa and began to pour it on his cakes.

•   •   •

Hustling to the arena, the cowboys noticed a car with a shattered windshield pulled over to the side of the road, next to a dead deer. The driver, a woman in her early twenties, stood outside the car looking horrified.

"Hey, Marv, a damsel in distress," said Sandvick, who noticed that she was awfully pretty. "Maybe we ought to stop and help."

"Somebody's already stopping," said Garrett, watching in the rearview mirror. "Anyway, we got to get to the arena."

The van pulled into the parking lot behind the Minneapolis Coli-seum. The sun had hidden behind the clouds and the sky was blus-tery. The cowboys held tight to the brims of their hats, against a wind that sliced through them, and trudged fifty yards to the gate marked for competitors.

At the door, a woman checked the name of each cowboy against the roster, while another stamped the hand of each contestant.

"Name?" said the woman.

"Willie Everride," said Sandvick, tipping his cowboy hat.

The woman wore a puzzled expression for a moment, then frowned.

"All right, I get it," she groaned wearily, "Ever Ride. Ha-ha."

The woman turned to her partner and wagged a finger at Sand-vick. "Stamp this one in the middle of his forehead," she said. "He's trouble."

Sandvick greeted the grimace with a wink.

Next came a man who inspected the rodeo gear, like an airport security guard, before the cowboys would be allowed into the locker room.

"That a glove?" a man asked, pointing to Sandvick's glove.

"Bingo, Dick Tracy," Sandvick replied.

The contest was billed as "The World's Toughest Rodeo." A huge color television screen was suspended from the ceiling to give instant replays of each ride. In the grandstands, there were 10,000 fans—three times the number at Bismarck. But there were not nearly as many cowboy hats.

•   •   •

Sandvick had drawn a horse named Hombre. But the bronc seemed as weary as the cowboy. It loped out of the chute, gave a few weak bucks, then galloped aimlessly. The cowboy spurred hard, like a man furiously pumping the gas pedal to start a cold engine. But Hombre had his own ideas. And when the horn blared, the stubborn horse seemed relieved to be done for the day. Sandvick jumped to the dirt and shrugged his shoulders.

The score was sixty-seven points—not worth a penny. It was time to get out of Minneapolis. The van rolled south.

•   •   •

"Who's buyin' the next round?" Sandvick snorted, as he crushed an empty beer can and set it alongside a half dozen other empties in the basement of the rodeo stadium in Phoenix.

Nobody offered.

"Cheap bastards," he cracked with a wink, as he rose and walked over to a makeshift bar for contestants.

"Old Lar's in fine form," one of the cowboys chuckled.

"Might as well get drunk," Sandvick said. "Least I'm good at that. Can't ride worth a shit."

He was trying to forget the Phoenix contest, which called itself "The Rodeo of Rodeos," although the only difference here was that spectators were sun-tanned in March. Hooting beneath cowboy hats, the fans had come to recall the Arizona of the Old West, which prided itself on the Three Big Cs, copper, cotton and cattle, never mind the New West and the influx of a fourth Big C, condominiums.

Just a few seconds into Sandvick's ride, the horse had flung him to the turf, then kicked up a cloud of dust that rose into his nostrils.

In terms of winning or losing, getting thrown was really no worse than a complete ride that got a poor score. Neither earned a paycheck. But bucking off was naked failure. Only a trained rodeo judge could discern a poor ride from a good one. But everybody in the grandstands could see that a cowboy flat on his back didn't measure up.

A band was setting up on a tiny stage near the bar. Streamers were draped across the cinderblock walls. A lighted beer sign hung from the ceiling, near some peeling plaster. And a few young women milled past the Formica tables of drinking cowboys.

A buxom woman with bleached blond hair and jeans a size too small stood alone near the bar. Her T-shirt read "Never Mind the Bull—Ride the Cowboy."

Sandvick sat gulping beer and telling stories, his voice growing hoarse as he tried to shout over the music. But soon his audience disappeared, one by one, as each of the cowboys went to look for a dance partner. He sat alone at the table and finished his drink.

When the band played "Guitars, Cadillacs and Hillbilly Music," Sandvick made his way into the crowd, and found a willing partner right away, twirling and bobbing across the dance floor, and bumping other dancers along the way. A few songs and drinks later, some cowboys decided to head downtown to a bar. Sandvick followed along, swigging a beer in the back seat of the car.

•   •   •

Denim and Diamonds was a big country-and-western discotheque. A gold lamé saddle, suspended over the dance floor, twisted in slow motion. A huge American flag was draped across a wall, near a neon Budweiser sign and a photograph of James Dean. The jukebox was blaring and strobe lights flashed.

At the bar, a petite woman with reddish hair walked up to Sandvick. She gave him an appraising glance, from his cowboy hat to his pointy boots, lingering at the parts in between, and flashed a sweet smile. She looked about thirty-five, older than almost anybody else in the bar.

She whispered in the cowboy's ear. He smiled and nodded. And the woman walked away.

Sandvick gulped down his beer. He walked over to a cowboy friend who was sharing his room at the Super 8 Motel.

"Don't come back to the room right away," he said with a smile. "Wait an hour or so."

And then he walked out of the bar and waited at the curb. A few moments later, the woman drove up in a red Peugeot. Sandvick climbed inside and the car zoomed away.

9

SWEAT TRICKLED DOWN the side of Joe Wimberly's face as he carried a fifty-pound feed sack toward the horse pen.

He heard the screen door slam and looked up to see Paula hurrying over.

"You had a phone call," she said.

Joe grimaced. He figured it was probably the banker, looking for his money, or maybe the sheriff. They take bad debts seriously in Texas.

Paula had persuaded Joe to wait just a little bit longer before putting the house up for sale. But Joe knew the banker's patience wouldn't last forever. He had been expecting the call.

"It was the rodeo, Joe," she said. "You drew Dodge Dakota for Friday night."

Joe dropped the feed sack.

"You're kiddin' me."

"No, Joe, I ain't kiddin'."

Dakota had bucked off cowboys for nine straight weeks. The pot had grown to $9,500.

He reached out to clasp Paula by the shoulders.

"This is it," he stammered, finally breaking into a smile. "This is gonna do it. This is gonna bail us out."

• • •

He started working on a game plan right away. Everywhere he went—to the horse pen, to the living room couch, to the pickup—he rode the bull in his mind. "Stay loose," he told himself. "This is just another bull."

But Joe knew it wasn't just another bull. Dakota was an outlaw, a bull so vicious it was spooky. It had sent every cowboy to the dirt, even a former world champion.

According to those who had watched and studied Dakota, the bull started every ride the same way: It would blow out of the chute, take one jump, kick over his head, step backward and then spin to the left. Joe could be sure of that much. These first moves would take about two seconds. After that, he knew, it was anybody's guess.

Some bulls will run a cowboy back off his rope. Some will jerk the rider down over its head. Some will spin violently. Dakota did it all.

Besides being strong and quick, the bull was smart. If a cowboy leaned left, Dakota went right. If a cowboy cheated to the right, the bull went left.

As a right-hander, Joe decided he would sit just to the left on the bull's back. That would give him more reach with his stronger right arm. When Dakota felt the bulk of the cowboy's weight on the left, the bull would probably try to buck him over to the right, where Joe thought he had a better chance to hang tight. It's called "setting a trap," a trick intended to force the bull's next move and stay one step ahead.

But every cowboy who had climbed aboard Dakota started with a game plan. And it had never mattered.

• • •

On Friday morning, Joe made cornflakes for the kids. Casey, his older daughter, peered over the cereal bowl at her father.

"Daddy," she asked. "You gonna ride that bull?"

"You bet I am, honey," he said, trying to summon his most confident voice.

But as the day wore on, Joe felt tight as a drum. He flipped through the pages of the *Prorodeo Sports News*. He took a walk around the house. He looked for some dishes to wash. He stared at the clock.

To try to relax, Joe and his four-year-old boy, McKinnon, sang their favorite song:

I'm a wild bull rider and I love my rodeo;
I'll ride that devil to hell and back,
For the money and the show;
My pappy was a pistol,
And I'm a son of a gun,
Yes, I'll ride that bull,
Just to have some fun.

About six o'clock, the family piled into the van and headed down the dirt road out of Cool, as sun splashed through the live oaks, making Joe squint as he drove.

The van passed through the town of Mineral Wells, founded in 1872 after the discovery of a natural spring, celebrated as a cure-all when an insane woman drank the water and regained her senses.

Joe looked out the windows at the people along Main Street going about their Friday evening routines: pulling into the grocery store, standing in line at the ice cream parlor, picking up a video, strolling lazily along the sidewalks.

They all looked so relaxed and carefree, Joe thought to himself. Farther down the road, he saw the familiar red brick of the Nation's Bank, which held the delinquent note that bore his name, and the deed to the house. His fists tightened around the steering wheel.

●   ●   ●

In the locker room of the Mesquite Arena, Joe spread his equipment out before him. There were his buckskin chaps, knee brace, elbow sleeve, old snug boots, and a colorful, striped Western shirt, the same one he wore to church on Sunday.

He changed into his riding pants, twenty-nine inches around the waist, a size bigger than his everyday jeans, and pressed a plug of tobacco under his lip.

The other cowboys, who all knew that Joe had drawn Dakota, gathered around him, chattering like bridesmaids before a wedding.

He gave them a small smile. For once, Joe didn't feel much like talking. He walked out by the chutes and hung his bull rope and cowbell over the fence. And then he returned to the locker room, where he sat silently on a narrow wood bench.

The grandstands were packed. Mesquite rodeo had always been popular among tourists to Dallas. But since the Dakota promotion began, a lot more locals had been coming, anxious to glimpse the meanest bull in Texas.

On the platform behind the chutes, Neal Gay peered across his empire: a gleaming stadium with 5,400 paying fans, pens full of prize rodeo livestock and concession stands bustling with customers.

The pickup men galloped to their stations. The chute puller crouched on the turf side of the gate. The bareback riders, who were first to compete in the performance, climbed over the rails.

The first rider bolted from the chutes. The bronc kicked high. The fans roared. And cameras zoomed in on a lanky cowboy, spurs flashing astride the wild bronc, a cable television portrait of the Old West.

•   •   •

The image flickered across a television screen in a central Nebraska farmhouse, where a fifteen-year-old boy watched in awe.

Donny Boes wanted more than anything to become a professional rodeo cowboy one day. He was only in the ninth grade at Atkinson High School. He wasn't yet old enough to drive a car.

But he had already climbed aboard plenty of wild bulls. He had been winning ribbons and trophies from the time he started in Little Britches rodeo, at the age of four, when he climbed aboard goats, and then calves and steers and shetland ponies. He graduated to bulls in the seventh grade. In his first year of high school, he joined the rodeo team and amazed the older kids with his courage and prowess.

In a rodeo in the Nebraska Sand Hills town of Valentine just a few weeks ago, he had drawn a bull that was known for its extraordinary meanness. In the weeks before, every other boy who had drawn that bull had turned out.

But Donny was too much of a cowboy to let fright keep him away, even though the other boys told him he was crazy. Even one of the rodeo clowns had tried to talk him out of riding the bull.

"You don't have to do this," one of them told him. "It doesn't mean you're not tough. This damn bull is a headhunter. Why don't you just go home?"

But Donny fastened his chaps and clenched the rope and lasted the rocky eight seconds. After the horn blared, he was still riding strong. In fact, Donny rode the snorting bull right back into the holding pen behind the chutes. When he jumped off, a clown, grateful that he didn't have to tangle with the beast, rushed over to Donny and hugged him.

The noise of adoration rang in Donny's ears. Now the sting of every failure, of every rejection, of every quiet fear that he was not strong enough, or good enough, or man enough, melted in the magnificent sun of praise and thanks and, perhaps most of all, approval.

Thunderous cheers rained down from the wooden bleachers, like confetti in a ticker-tape parade, as if this fifteen-year-old Nebraska boy had ridden for them all, dancing the rapids that lapped at the edges of every struggling farm and faded little town, cowboy fists raised in victory, laughing back at fate, triumphing in the name of every defiant soul on the Great Plains.

Crusty old ranchers tipped their cowboy hats his way. Middle-aged women in head scarves whooped like cheerleaders. Little kids gazed out from wide, awe-filled eyes.

And a pretty girl in the bleachers cheered along with the rest. She was smiling right at him.

It was all like a dream.

"We swept 'em!" his brother, Danny, who had also conquered a bull that afternoon, exulted on the ride back to Atkinson. "It's you and me on top of Nebraska."

The prize earned Donny enough points to qualify for the Nebraska state high school rodeo championship in Broken Bow in June, a remarkable feat for a freshman. The winner of the state would qualify for the national high school finals in Oklahoma, a berth that might mean a college rodeo scholarship.

Donny had already decided he wanted to attend Wyoming State in Torrington, a college known for its tough cowboys. And after that, he was going to join the pro circuit and win enough money to start a ranch. His mother and father smiled at his plans and reminded him that he needed to finish his sophomore year in high school first. But Donny didn't have a doubt in the world.

In the next rodeo at Stapleton, however, he broke his right arm in a hard fall to the turf. The doctors put it in a cast. And they didn't know whether the arm would heal in time for the championships.

●   ●   ●

The names of the cowboys at Mesquite flashed across the television screen. The announcer, a former bull riding champ himself, spoke of their strength, their grace, their courage. Between events, some of the cowboys stood before the cameras and answered the questions of an admiring interviewer.

Donny marveled at every cowboy in that faraway arena in Texas. These had once been boys like him. Now they were heroes.

In the darkness of the living room, he knew that he would someday stand before those bright camera lights.

•　　•　　•

Joe Wimberly walked slowly out of the locker room and climbed the platform behind the chutes. He had promised to pull the flank strap for a bareback rider named Robby Vacarro, a young cowboy who had been having more than his share of troubles on the trail.

After the strap was yanked, the horse took just a few steps into the arena before bucking Vacarro unceremoniously to the turf, his familiar spot.

Some of the cowboys liked to poke fun at Vacarro, who had achieved a fame, of sorts, by appearing numerous times on the rodeo videos of bad crashes and wicked falls.

"Robby don't ride too good," said one of the cowboys, shaking his head with disdain.

"Oh, he rides good," said Joe, rising to the defense of his friend. "He just don't ride too long."

During an intermission, Joe watched his son race out to the middle of the arena for the kids' calf chase. Standing in a group with about 100 others, McKinnon scanned the arena for his father, then finally spotted him and waved with a big smile. Joe smiled and waved back.

The calf was set loose in the arena, and the squealing children thundered after it, kicking up a trail of dust. A ribbon was taped to the calf's ear. The kid who grabbed it won a prize. The fans roared in amusement as the frightened calf, realizing it was trapped, finally stood frozen.

In the wild chase, some of the smaller boys and girls got knocked down and trampled by the bigger kids. A few of them burst into tears and ran back toward the grandstands.

A hefty boy in a crew cut, who elbowed his way past the others, snagged the ribbon from the calf and raised a triumphant fist in the air.

But McKinnon was nowhere in the crowd. He had found an empty patch on the turf and sat down to play in the dirt, oblivious to the commotion around the animal. Paula watched from the grandstands and thought to herself: The boy's got his priorities straight.

•　　•　　•

The cowgirls ran the barrels. The wrestlers hopped the steers. The bull riders took their turns.

Pacing along the raised platform behind the chutes, Joe drew deep breaths and exhaled the tension.

He looked up in the stands and saw his family. The three kids were jabbering away. Paula was silent.

All that was left before Joe's ride was the bullfighting exhibition. It was a relatively new rodeo event, in which a riderless bull rampaged in the arena, while a clown tried to get as close to the animal as he could, at the risk of getting hooked or stomped. The more daring the clown, the higher the score.

To the strains of a country song, the clown danced and darted under the drooling snout of the bull. At the bull's first charge, the clown reached in and slapped his face, then jumped aside. The bull wheeled in pursuit, his horns just inches from the flapping fabric of the pants of the fleeing clown, who faked left, then cut right, just an instant before it was too late.

After a few more reckless moves, the weary clown finally lifted his arms in the air, a signal to end the stunt. With sweat streaking down his greasepainted face, the clown raced to the edge of the arena, taking refuge at the top of the fence. Two other clowns emerged to chase the bull through the fence to the holding pen.

A score flashed across the lighted screen. The announcer lauded the quick moves of both man and beast. The regular performance of the Mesquite rodeo was over.

But not a single fan stood to leave.

•   •   •

The spotlight flashed on Joe Wimberly, who pulled himself over the rails and settled on the broad, humped back of the star of the show, Dodge Dakota.

The rumble in the grandstands turned to a hush. This was the moment the fans had come to see.

The bull stood still in its cage, staring straight ahead, hooves flat on the dirt, a single crooked horn crawling down the side of its black and white face.

Under a broad-brimmed hat, the cowboy's brown eyes narrowed in a determined glare. His jaw tightened. His lower lip curled over his black mustache.

One end of the rope was twisted around the belly of the beast. The other end was wrapped around the cowboy's right hand, knotted so tight it nearly stopped the blood rushing through his veins.

"Lord, I'm comin' to you like a friend," Joe pleaded silently. "You know how much I need this ride."

The bull underneath him felt as hard as the hood of a car. Joe's heart was pounding. Beads of sweat grew on his forehead. He felt short of breath.

The voice of the announcer boomed through the arena, explaining the stakes that everyone knew. "Ladies and gentlemen, the bull's name is Dodge Dakota. And he's never been ridden in nine tries. And this is Joe Wimberly of Cool, Texas.

"If he rides this bull, the cowboy wins nine thousand five hundred dollars!"

He crouched over the bull. The silver conchas of his buckskin chaps glistened in the spotlight. The rowels of his spurs dangled near the bull's hide. Six thousand rodeo fans stared down at the cowboy. The chute boss stared into his face, waiting for the signal to pull the trigger.

Joe nodded. The gate swung open. And the clock started to count down the eight most important seconds of the cowboy's life.

Dakota bolted to daylight, ten yards from the gate, then jerked to a halt. The inside of the cowboy's thighs squeezed tight against the bull. The beast bucked hard, lifting Joe into the air.

The bull slammed down hard. Joe thumped on its back. The bull bellowed and twisted to its left, as the cowboy's right hand yanked hard on the rope.

Joe's seat rose up, a flash of daylight between denim and hide. But then he thumped back, clinging tight, peering through watery eyes, the jerking rope burning his hand.

The clock showed five seconds, four seconds.

Dakota bucked, slammed, spun, then bucked again. Joe shot in the air, muscles pulled tight, his chin knocking against his chest, head snapping backward, hat flying off.

But the cowboy was surviving the wicked test. The grandstands thundered—fans on their feet, screaming, shrieking, stomping.

The clock flashed three seconds, two seconds.

Then Dakota groaned in a voice from hell, snapping its back violently, four hooves in the air. Its back snapped. And suddenly, the bull rode alone.

Crashing flat on his back, Joe looked up to see the belly of the bull and its slamming hind hooves, just ten inches away. The rope was still clenched in the cowboy's right hand.

In that terrible moment Joe's second thought was to get up and run like hell, escape the beast, save his life.

But his first thought was more powerful: The house is sold.

He scrambled away soon enough, as the clowns chased Dakota through the gate and back to its pen.

As he walked toward the chutes, Joe hung his head low, staring at the dirt. And then he raised up and gazed deep into the grandstands, searching for Paula's face.

When he saw her, he slowly mouthed the words: "I am sorry."

10

WINTER IN NEBRASKA is stark, silent, changeless. Not so much white as colorless: barren fields, frozen as death, snow-drifted country roads, impassable for days at a time, ice-shuttered windows on isolated farmhouses.

But in springtime, when the cries of newborn calves echo from the pastures, the little towns on the Great Plains celebrate survival. It is the time when rodeo cowboys, who have spent winter competing in bigger cities with indoor stadiums, come to the smaller towns like North Platte, usually just a gas stop along Interstate 80, where the rodeo unfolds under the sun and stars, and townspeople sit on wood bleachers in fresh air sweetened by cotton candy.

Behind the bucking chutes, a cowboy named Bud Longbrake wore the restless smile of a man eager to share his good news. The twenty-eight-year-old saddle-bronc rider, who had just gotten through the calving season back home in South Dakota, hollered to a friend standing at the opposite end of the walking platform behind the gates.

"We got rain last night!" he said joyfully, as if announcing the discovery of nuggets of gold, not just drops of water. "Two and forty-hundredths of an inch—it's just running!"

In places that count rainfall right down to the hundredth of an inch, a thunderstorm is reason to rejoice. For five years, the Great Plains had suffered a drought. In some places, the grass had become so scorched and withered that cattle would go hungry if it weren't for extra sacks of feed, an expense that ranchers on razor-thin margins could scarcely afford.

Ever since the Indian rain dances, people on the plains have gazed longingly at the clouds, turning at one time or another to hydrogen balloons, silver-iodide crystals, blasts of dynamite and vigils of prayer, in the hope of generating some water.

And for one brief, wet stretch, the prayers were answered. During the 1870s, uncharacteristically heavy rainfall nourished the dreams of newcomers to the Great Plains, who held to the widespread theory of the time that "rain follows the plow." The population of Kansas grew fourfold during the 1880s. The future of America seemed clearly to be headed West.

The founders of Kearney, Nebraska, in fact, argued that it made little sense for the nation's capital to be stuck way back in Washington, D.C. They started a campaign to move the capital to the Great Plains. And as good a place for it as any, they suggested, was Kearney, Nebraska.

But severe drought in the 1890s led to near starvation in Nebraska and South Dakota. Calamity hit the plains again in the 1930s, during the Dust Bowl, when winds carried dirt so high and far it clouded airplanes flying over the eastern seaboard and fouled the navigation of ships 300 miles out on the Atlantic. Swirling dirt tore the paint off houses. And some children, gasping for breath through wet rags held over their mouths, died of suffocation.

•   •   •

North Platte sits at the edge of the Nebraska Sand Hills, a million square miles of grass-covered dunes, so soft a car can sink in their grasp. Once pioneers on wagon trains had peered out on these vast empty stretches, which swept to the horizon in all directions, and felt as though they had reached the middle of a sea.

The settlers had come to the Great Plains in search of the future. When they thought they had found it, or simply became too weary to look any longer, they unhitched the horses and built little communities of sod houses, and waited for the rest of the nation to catch up to them.

A century later, some of their descendants on the Great Plains have stopped waiting. The hazards of wind and drought, the fickleness of cattle prices, the daily grind of physical labor in burning sun and freezing rain, the tedium and gossip of life in small towns, have sent many children of the plains to search for a new future of their own, closer to shopping malls than to cow pastures.

But during Nebraskaland Days, when the golden glow of the Ferris wheel rises higher than any building for 100 miles, North Platte celebrates itself.

Townspeople strap on six-shooter holsters in the annual Frontier Revue and sing "Westward Ho" and "Plow Me a Furrow." Waitresses in shot-and-a-beer taverns wear shiny black dresses with lace shoulder straps and fishnet stockings. Old women at souvenir stands sell jars of chokecherry jam and dolls made of cornstalk. The sound of gunfire rings out at a Shoot-Out at High Noon in the middle of Main Street, just a few hours after the prayer meeting at the Stockman Inn, and the local dignitaries attend both festivities.

•   •   •

The "Star-Spangled Banner" squeaked through a loudspeaker, like a song being played over a telephone, barely audible in a Nebraska wind that howled like a pack of coyotes. But in the grandstands of North Platte, where the lights cast a hazy sphere in the night sky, every word of the anthem rang as strong and clear as a hymn on Christmas morning.

Longbrake and the other cowboys stood ramrod straight, hats over hearts, eyes focused on the flag, as solemn and dignified as young men with tobacco bulging in their cheeks and belt buckles the size of salad plates could possibly look.

In the middle of the freshly raked arena, a teenage flag bearer on horseback, all smiles and rhinestones, struggled valiantly to stay in the saddle, until a strong gust finally knocked both her and Old Glory tumbling to the arena turf.

Nobody snickered, least of all the cowboys, who know the feeling of losing control. The wind was still howling as the last strains of the national anthem echoed through the crowded grandstands.

The flag bearer struggled to her feet and reached up for her saddle. All the while, she kept right on singing.

•   •   •

Longbrake bent on one knee and rested his checkbook on the other. He wrote a $60 check for the entry fee. He had drawn a good horse for the performance, a muscular bay that had been chosen for last year's championship rodeo.

"She can really buck," one cowboy told Bud, with a note of awe, and hats nodded all around.

In the brim of his white cowboy hat, Longbrake wore an eagle feather. It was the sacred gift from the elders of his tribe, who had named him Sung Wa Togla Hoksila—Wild Horse Boy.

Longbrake lived on the Cheyenne River Sioux reservation in Dupree, South Dakota, one of the poorest towns in America, where a hand-scrawled sign at the edge of Main Street proudly proclaimed: "Home of Bud Longbrake—Saddle Bronc Champion."

He was the great-grandson of Mary Sitting Eagle, who was born in 1881 during the long Sioux march back from Canada, where Chief Sitting Bull had fled with the tribe after the battle of the Little Bighorn. His Sioux grandmothers "saw the writing on the wall," his mother once told him, and married white men. Longbrake inherited the blue eyes of his Norwegian emigrant grandfather, a mark of shame in his grade school on the reservation, where the other kids called him "Custer."

The third of four children, he was born in a two-room shack without running water. The chores of his childhood included carrying pails of water from a nearby river. Bud's mother, Fay, taught school at the reservation. His father, Pete, raised cattle. On the side, he supplied bucking horses and bulls for high school and 4-H rodeos. When soaring interest rates and falling cattle prices forced many Sioux out of ranching, the Longbrakes survived on the rodeo business.

•   •   •

Longbrake reached into a wrinkled garbage bag that carried his gear—a pair of red and black chaps with silver fringe, white tube socks and slant-heel boots—and shot the breeze with the other cowboys while he got ready.

When his leggings were fastened and his boots pulled on, he stood waiting for his horse and his chance, sipping from a cup of black coffee and chewing on a toothpick. The other cowboys joked that they wouldn't recognize Longbrake without the toothpick sticking out of his smile. It was a habit he had picked up after quitting tobacco at the request of his five-year-old son, Jay.

He always kept a picture of Jay, and his two-year-old daughter,

Kayla, tucked inside his billfold. And when the rodeo trail got long and lonesome, he would sometimes take it out and just look at it for a while.

Bud and his wife, Lona, who worked as a bookkeeper for a social service agency on the reservation, had been raising their children to be proud of their Sioux identity.

But not long ago, the kids were rejected for membership in the tribe, since they were just shy of one-quarter blood, a new standard established recently by the Sioux leaders.

Lona was only one-thirty-second blood, but she had been enrolled in the tribe as a child, when the requirements were different. The rule change meant that even though Bud and Lona were both recognized as Indians, their children would not be.

The tribe's ruling had stunned Longbrake. He felt as if he had been robbed, a loss far worse than if somebody had stolen every rodeo trophy he had ever won.

He knew the reasoning behind the rule change: The tribe was short on land, short on money, short on health services. His own cousin, a councilman in the tribal government, had often lamented the problems.

Bud worried for his children's future. There were certain benefits for Indians, like college scholarships, and now his children would be ineligible.

But this went far beyond benefits. Jay and Kayla *were* Indians. They were the descendants of Mary Sitting Eagle.

Maybe being less than one-quarter blood wasn't enough to meet some new standard. But in parts of America, he knew well, it was sure as hell enough Indian to get yourself called a "buckskin" or a "gut-eater" or a "prairie nigger."

At the same time his kids were being denied their heritage, whites all over the country were suddenly claiming to have some Cherokee princess in their lineage, maybe after sitting through *Dances with Wolves*. The number of Americans claiming to be Indian on census forms has more than tripled since 1960. In New Jersey alone, the number of "Native Americans" jumped nearly 80 percent during the 1980s. And the New West was a mecca for New Agers, including plenty of "wanna-be" Indians, bred in the white suburbs, who were now running around holding vision quests and sweat lodges and ghost dances.

•   •   •

Out in the arena, a calf fled its chute as a roper chased behind, lariat in the air. But the lasso missed its mark. The calf ran free. And a cheer erupted from the grandstands.

The sport's promoters cringe at accusations of cruelty to animals. And some of the charges, to be sure, are far-fetched: the notion that sharp tacks are used to jab the horse's belly, or that flank straps squeeze the testicles of the bulls.

Rodeo is downright gentle compared to the fancy equestrian shows, where horses are rope-whipped into obedience, tails are broken for aesthetics, undersides are slammed with poles to force higher jumps and the dainty trot of Tennessee Walking Horses is helped along by training in shackles.

At least in rodeo, bulls and horses get a chance to knock a man on his ass, certainly a more dignified pursuit than pulling carriages of smooching newlyweds through Central Park.

But rodeo has a harder time defending itself on the roping of calves. Promoters like to justify it as simply mirroring an everyday chore of ranch life. But in North Platte, the heart of ranch country, plenty of people in the grandstands knew better. Jerking a sprinting calf by its neck and slamming it to the ground, the way it's done in rodeo, would get a real-life wrangler fired in a flash.

•   •   •

Longbrake had learned to ride a horse by the time he was four. As a teenager, he started entering rodeos, usually in the bull riding contest. But a piece of jewelry changed his course. It was a belt buckle crafted by Norbert Yellow Hair, an artist from Snowflake, Arizona. It was a prize for the winning saddle-bronc rider. When he saw the buckle, he thought he had never seen anything so beautiful, and decided to go after it. He entered the saddle-bronc event, won the buckle, and never went back to riding bulls.

In his early twenties, he got a loan of $200 from a local bank to try rodeo full-time. He used one of his calves for collateral. When the money ran out, he would quit. He paid the loan. And he had been riding on his winnings ever since.

But one prize still loomed beyond his grasp. The Longbrake family lived in a narrow house trailer on a dirt road in town. Someday, Bud promised, they would build a little place in the country.

•   •   •

Longbrake sat on the rails, gazing past the arena, toward the rolling plains that stretched beyond North Platte. He got up and stretched his legs. He spotted a familiar cowboy, a young man from the Sand Hills, wearing a brace from his back to his head.

"Hey, what the heck happened to your neck?" Longbrake asked.

"Oh, I broke the danged thing," the cowboy answered, as if he were talking about the handle of a coffee cup.

"Gonna quit ridin'?"

"Nah," he replied, spitting tobacco juice on the floorboards. "Doctor says I ought to. But what's he know about ranchin' and rodeo?"

•   •   •

A clapboard wall over the chute gates was emblazoned with a painting of a twinkling-eyed man in a gleaming white cowboy hat, an audacious goatee covering his chin and long, curly locks of brown hair dangling at his shoulders.

William Cody, better known as Buffalo Bill, was the most famous man ever to live in North Platte. In the 1870s, he ranched on the banks of the Dismal River, and later moved to a spread at the edge of town that he called Scout's Rest Ranch.

Cody achieved fame as the very embodiment of the nation's triumph in the West: a fourteen-year-old rider for the Pony Express, an expert shooter of buffalo for the Union Pacific Railroad, a cold-blooded fighter of Indians, a brilliant scout for the U.S. Cavalry. But more than anything else, he was a salesman. He packaged, designed, promoted and sold the image of the Old West.

In the decade after the Civil War, when the American public still thirsted for the blood-and-thunder drama of battlefield heroics, Cody took to the stages of opera houses back East to capitalize on the nation's fascination with the violent struggle for the Great Plains. The shows depicted righteous, God-fearing white settlers and brave cavalry troops on one side, and violent, barbaric red savages on the other. One theater critic of the day enthused that the show might not have been an artistic masterpiece, "but for downright fun, Injun killing, red fire and rough and tumble, it is a wonder."

But Cody believed that the theater stage was too small for the kind of wild action that could really thrill crowds. In the summer of 1882, the residents of North Platte asked Cody to help produce a Fourth of July celebration they were calling "Old Glory Blowout." He brought a stagecoach from the old Deadwood line, hired some Indians and cowboys, gathered a small buffalo herd, arranged for a sharpshooting contest and a stagecoach holdup.

The people of North Platte claim rodeo was born on that day, a contention that is disputed by at least half a dozen other towns on the plains who also claim to be the sport's birthplace.

For generations, Cody's "Wild West" shows and "Congress of the Rough Riders of the World" shaped the way Americans saw the Old West, more flash than fact, and a forerunner of the cowboy and Indians movies. But "The Noblest Whiteskin," as one book title described Cody, eventually lost it all.

The majestic figure in buffalo robes, who stood as a symbol of America's triumph on the Frontier, drank himself into bankruptcy. He died broke in 1917. His Scout's Rest Ranch, lost to foreclosure, sits near the North Platte rodeo grounds, a government-owned tourist attraction.

•   •   •

"Let 'er go," Longbrake shouted, and the chute gate swung open.

It was not by accident that this horse had been picked for the finals. She took a couple of high jumps, swooped low, then bolted ahead like gunfire. Before he knew what hit him, Bud bounced in the air and hit the swells of the saddle, just as the reins jerked loose from his hand. The horse went on jumping. Bud sat in a cloud of dust.

He shrugged his shoulders and forced a smile as he loped back to the arena fence. He pulled on his street boots and put his chaps in the plastic bag. A fellow cowboy came by to deliver a slap on the back and a word of encouragement.

"I just couldn't keep my butt down," Bud explained. "I thought I was right there, then she turned, and it slipped and . . . Aw heck, there's another rodeo tomorrow."

The cowboys laughed and shook hands. Bud started to walk toward the darkened parking lot, where the van soon would start rolling through the night. But he stopped abruptly, as if he had forgotten something. He turned and called out in a voice that caught up with his friend. "Did I tell you we got rain last night?"

11

DONNY BOES walked into the doctor's office wearing a cowboy hat, a plaster cast and a willful expression.

It was just two days before the Nebraska state high school rodeo championship in Broken Bow.

"I can't miss the rodeo," he said politely but firmly as the doctor examined the plastered arm. "If I have to, I'll cut off this cast myself."

The doctor said that wouldn't be necessary. The bones had healed sufficiently. As the cast came off, the arm looked pale and smelled awful. But it was finally free to tug on a bull rope. The doctor wished the young cowboy luck and warned: "Now be careful on those bulls."

And the fifteen-year-old walked through the clinic doors and let out a loud, joyous whoop in the June sunshine.

•   •   •

The youngest of seven children born to Allen and Lavonne Boes, two girls and five boys, Donny had been brought up to revere the rugged ways of ranching and farming. His great-grandparents had home-steaded in Nebraska a century ago. And their love for the land, along with a fierce pride in its stewards, had been passed down the genera-tions.

But not long before Donny was born, a combination of hail, drought and plunging cattle prices drove the family out of ranching.

After living in town for a while, the family bought an old, abandoned farmhouse on a nameless country road outside the little town of Atkinson in central Nebraska. They hammered and cleaned and painted. Lavonne Boes embroidered the words of the Our Father and hung it on the living room wall, near her sons' framed rodeo plaques.

Every morning, Donny's father pulled on boots and bib overalls, the chest pockets creased in the oval of a snuff can, and listened to the radio for the cattle reports. But now he was making his living as a truck driver.

"We don't ranch anymore," Donny's mother once said. "But we still have it deep inside us."

For the Boes family, the sport of rodeo was a link to their lost world. All the boys had competed as bull riders. Brent had gone to the national finals in 1981. Byron took second place in the state championships in 1984. But none of the boys took to rodeo with the natural flair of Donny.

It was against the rules for a boy so young to compete on such dangerous beasts. But Donny had begged. And his mother had finally relented and signed the paper of consent, stating her one condition: He must never compete unless she or other family members go to the rodeo with him.

She knew it wasn't completely rational, but Lavonne Boes thought that somehow her son would be safer if he stayed within her protective gaze. She also knew that Donny would find a way to compete in rodeo, no matter what anyone told him.

"You know what I like about rodeo," Donny often said. "For eight seconds, nobody in the world can tell you what to do."

•   •   •

The day before the championships, Donny and Danny Boes got into the family's camper truck, their mother behind the wheel, and headed down the country roads toward Broken Bow.

"Can you believe we really made it?" Danny giggled, as he raised a palm for a high five with his brother.

"Man," said Donny, "is this exciting, or what!"

The top thirty bull riders had qualified for the state finals. Danny had finished the regular season in sixteenth place; Donny was twenty-second. But they felt sure they would be returning home with much loftier honors.

There was a year's difference in age between the boys, but not much else. Both were dark-haired and brown-eyed, strong and handsome, popular with the girls and the football coaches. Since they were eight and nine, the boys had worked together after school and during summers as field hands for an area rancher. They stacked hay, mended fences and hauled water, ever alert for rattlesnakes and coyotes.

For their pay, they were given a heifer each year, which their boss was keeping until after they finished high school. The boys planned on becoming ranchers, and they figured this was a good way to start a herd. They now owned eight pairs of cows and calves. They had decided to name their budding cattle enterprise the Double-D Ranch, short for Danny and Donny. Just a few weeks ago, they had written to the Nebraska Department of Agriculture for the forms to register their brand, an E with a backward slash, chosen for no other reason than that it looked cool.

Donny had designed the emblem, since he was the artist in the family. His teachers had told him he had real talent for drawing, although they wished he would occasionally draw something besides bulls and ranches.

The boys belonged to the local FFA, once called the Future Farmers of America. The organization not long ago dropped the word *farmer* from its title, since so few young people could realistically expect to ever become one. Instead, the students were encouraged to go to college and aim for a corporate job in "agribusiness."

But Donny and Danny swore they would never settle for a job in some stuffy office. They were going to become dashing rodeo stars, and then use their winnings to settle down as respectable ranchers. Sometimes late into the night, they would lie awake and chart their dreams in the tiny bedroom they shared in the family's old house, which had been bought for the unpaid taxes left by its previous owner: a bankrupt rancher.

•   •   •

Just as the sun was melting into the Nebraska Sand Hills off to the west, the camper truck pulled into the dirt path on the county fairgrounds at Broken Bow, where a banner snapping in the evening breeze proclaimed the rodeo championships.

In the dusk, scores of young boys strutted around the dusty grounds, trying to look tough, or at least authentic. Some of them were nearly swallowed under big cowboy hats. Their cheeks were bulging, but inside was usually a wad of bubble gum.

Broken Bow is the seat of Custer County, where there is plenty of elbow room but not many elbows. Like 90 percent of the counties in Nebraska, it had lost population in the last decade.

Not anxious to disappear just yet, the people of Custer County had been holding "wild and crazy" brainstorming sessions to conjure up ideas for survival. There were two rules: Nobody could laugh at an idea, and nobody could say, "That won't work."

They organized a campaign to persuade people to buy locally, rather than drive forty miles to a Wal-Mart. "If everybody shops at Uncle Sam's," warned one farmwife, "we're all left out in the cold."

To recruit new residents, they mailed brochures to every graduate of Custer County schools, advertising that beautiful Victorian houses sold for less than $40,000, that the pupil-teacher ratio was only fourteen to one and that nobody could remember the last serious crime.

They convinced craftspeople in the county to pool their creations and open a store, the Devil's Den, which now employed a sales clerk. And they tried to invent ways to draw tourists to the middle of Nebraska.

"But what have we got to offer people except for the wind?" one woman had groaned.

"That's it," said another. "We'll have a kite-flying festival."

But the biggest promotion of all was the high school rodeo championship. It drew a few thousand people to town. And for once the stores of Broken Bow were almost crowded with customers.

"Boys," called Lavonne Boes, who stepped outside the camper truck and stood under a sky that had turned pitch black. "Quit flapping your jaws and come inside. You've got a big day tomorrow."

·　　·　　·

In the first round, Donny rode his horned challenger for the full eight seconds, one of only three cowboys to "cover."

The finals would come the next afternoon. If Donny could match his first performance, he might win the state and a trip to the high school championship in Oklahoma City. It would be an incredible feat for a freshman. The grandstands were buzzing with talk about this sensational young cowboy.

As they walked away from the chutes, his brother wrapped an arm around Donny's shoulders. "You know," said Danny, who had been bucked off his bull instantly, "a fella could be a little jealous of his younger brother."

But Danny had cheered as loudly as anybody. And he hoped to be rooting for his brother all the way to Oklahoma. "I'm gonna be right there with you," he said, "pulling for you all the way."

Under the stars that night, a disc jockey played country-and-western songs and the young cowboys and cowgirls twisted to the wailing music on the county fairgrounds. The Boes brothers, who had got all slicked-up for the occasion, spotted a group of pretty girls looking their way.

One of them was pointing toward Donny and smiling coyly. "That's one of the boys who won today," she said, loud enough for the brothers to hear.

Donny turned to his brother and arched an eyebrow. "Ain't it great to be a cowboy?" he whispered.

·   ·   ·

Early the next morning, as sunshine glinted through the plastic windows of the camper, Lavonne Boes hovered over a portable gas stove, frying a breakfast of bacon and eggs for her cowboys.

Donny gobbled his food and hurried down to the chutes to check the postings on the finals.

He returned to the camper with a tense expression.

"I drew Sadaam," he told Danny.

"Oooh!" his brother gasped, as if he had been stung. "That's one rank bull."

Sadaam was the most fearsome bull in the string at Broken Bow. The day before, it had shucked a young cowboy and then trampled him under its flailing hooves. The boy would recover. But he had broken a leg and cracked his skull.

Donny had ridden mean bulls before. People were still talking about his ride on that wicked beast up at Valentine. But there was something about Sadaam that seemed especially ghoulish.

Maybe it was watching that other young cowboy get hurt on the bull. Or maybe it was just the nervousness of the finals. Donny tried to shrug it off.

By the time the rodeo started, black storm clouds burst over Broken Bow with great claps of thunder that startled the livestock and the little kids. In the grandstands, fans huddled under slickers and cowboy hats dripped like gutters.

Rain was always welcome in this parched land. But its timing was awful. The field had become muddy, downright soupy in spots, a particular hazard for the rough-stock events.

On the platform behind the chute gates, Donny got drenched as he waited his turn. He stood alongside his brother, who coached him for the ride.

"Remember to keep your feet," said Danny. "Stick with him. Ride up."

A chute boss motioned for Donny to climb aboard the bull. The fans were cheering. This was the moment that he had dreamed about on all those long days of mending fence and chasing cows in the field. This was the place he had pictured himself as he sat bored in algebra class and stared out the windows.

He gripped the chute rail with both hands, then turned to his brother.

"Hey, Danny," he said. "This is for you."

He pulled himself over the rails and settled on the back of the bull. The 1,700-pound black beast jostled in the cage, its heavy hooves digging into the mud.

Raindrops pelted Donny's black cowboy hat and his leather chaps, which were stitched with four-leaf clovers. The rope was twisted tight around his right hand, the handle on Sadaam.

The loudspeaker boomed Donny's name across the fairgrounds. His mother sat in the bleachers, clutching a camera. His father, who had a long-distance truck run that week, had told Donny he would be concentrating on the bull ride all the way to Fort Worth, where he was delivering a load.

If Donny could win the state, his name would be printed in newspapers all over Nebraska. College rodeo coaches would be mailing him letters. Life would be almost too wonderful for a fifteen-year-old boy to imagine, if only he could make these next eight seconds.

The gate swung open. Sadaam charged into the arena, as Donny covered him like a shadow, absorbing the first buck, then whirled as the bull spun, still clinging tight.

His brother stood behind the chutes, fists raised in the air, hollering to the heavens. His mother watched through the camera's lens, counting the seconds, holding her breath.

Then the cowboy started to slip. His legs swung up. Spurs sliced the air. He was losing control.

The bull bucked once more, flinging the 140-pound cowboy to the turf, flat on his back, glory vanished.

But Sadaam wasn't finished. He snorted vengeance, eyes flashing, hovering over the cowboy, who writhed in the mud, trying to escape.

The bull raised its front hooves high, as the cowboy stared up in terror. The fans shrieked in disbelief.

"No!" came a cry from behind the chutes.

But the hooves came thundering down, powerful as a sledgehammer, slamming the boy's chest.

Somehow the young cowboy struggled to his feet, eyes glazed, not sure of his directions.

The clowns hurried through the mud to chase the bull away. Donny started to take a step toward the gates. He stopped suddenly, bent over, leaned his hands on his knees, pulled an arm across his chest. Then he raised up, tried to walk again. But he wobbled on rubbery legs. He tried to take another step, then collapsed.

A group of cowboys rushed to his side. They lifted him up and carried him through the rain to an ambulance. Donny's mother, who had raced down the bleachers, climbed in alongside her son. She held his hand. She told him she loved him.

"Mom," Donny mumbled weakly.

Siren blaring and lights flashing, the ambulance roared through the streets of Broken Bow, squealing into the entranceway of the hospital. Donny was carried into the emergency room.

His mother was told to stay in the waiting room, where she began to pray silently. A moment later, Donny's brother ran through the hospital doors, along with a rancher from the rodeo. A nurse came out to speak to the family.

"We're getting him stabilized," she said. "But he needs special equipment. They're going to rush him by ambulance to a hospital in Kearney."

The town of Kearney was three hours away.

The rancher told Mrs. Boes and Danny he would give them a ride. The pickup raced down Highway 21, a narrow strip that cut through the wheat fields toward Lexington, where they turned onto Interstate 80, heading east.

Tears streamed down his mother's face. Danny held her in his arms. "He's going to be all right, Mom. He's going to be all right."

The rancher held tight to the steering wheel and pushed the gas pedal to the floor. The pickup zoomed past the other trucks and cars on the highway, passing Overton, then Elm Creek, then Odessa, until finally a sign read: Kearney.

The windshield wipers clacked in the rain. Lavonne Boes held her hands together and began, in a shaking voice, to pray aloud:

"Our Father who art in Heaven . . ."

"Hallowed be thy name . . . ," joined the rancher and Donny's brother. "Give us this day . . ."

The truck swung into the parking lot. They walked through the rain and through the hospital entrance. A nurse came out from behind a desk. She had been waiting for them.

She told Mrs. Boes to wait in a closed room. The doctor would be there in a moment.

A moment later, she saw the knob twist. The door opened slowly. The doctor walked toward her. He reached for her hand.

And the mother began to cry.

"I'm sorry," he said. "Donny didn't make it."

12

"**COUNTRY AND WESTERN** is in!" trumpeted the Santa Fe rodeo parade, and on the pink cobbled sidewalks along the art galleries, people watched the passing cowboy spectacle with a kind of campy amusement.

A man in wire-rimmed glasses, who cradled a Chihuahua in his arms, let out a "Yee-haw!" A fortyish woman bedecked with turquoise jewelry set down a bulging shopping bag to do an impromptu do-si-do. On the greensward of the plaza, a callow young man with a knapsack looked up from the pages of Castaneda, and bobbed his head half-mockingly to the music of fiddlers.

But for the most part, Santa Fe's brooding, slouching mien, cool as the high desert breeze, seemed untouched by the passing burst of gaiety under the noonday sun.

In the rodeo parade, little girls sat cross-legged on hay bales in the bed of a pickup truck and clapped and sang Western campfire songs. Mustachioed men in the garb of a sheriff's posse waved pistols in the air and belted gales of lusty laughter. Palominos with silver breastplates trotted past New Age boutiques, alternative bookstores, vegetarian restaurants and self-healing salons, leaving behind a long trail of manure, which could be excused by the Santa Feans since it was, after all, organic.

•   •   •

When Santa Fe was just a town, and not yet a style, there was a Sears store here, and a Penney's. But the tourists flocking here wanted to buy art, not underwear, so both stores were leveled. Big Joe's lumber-yard, meanwhile, became the Eldorado Hotel. And nobody expects the Woolworth store to last for long.

Tourists come to marvel at the old Spanish adobe buildings, un-aware that they are actually looking at stucco, a facade that hides Vic-torian red brick underneath, the result of a campaign by the Chamber of Commerce in 1913 to make the town look more "au-thentic." It was now against Santa Fe law, literally, to build anything downtown that did not have the look of adobe, which was why the Woolworth store appeared to have been designed by the conquis-tadors.

Wealthy Anglos, infatuated with the Spanish culture of Santa Fe, started moving here in droves during the 1980s, which diluted the very heritage they came to soak up. In the last census count, Anglos became a majority for the first time in the town's history.

Founded in 1610 by Spanish explorers, Santa Fe still looked upon other Western towns as mere upstarts. By the time Pilgrims landed at Plymouth Rock, locals like to boast, the Palace of Governors in Santa Fe had already sprung a leak in its roof.

And Santa Fe claims that rodeo, too, started here long before other Western outposts even had a saloon. The evidence is a letter written from Santa Fe in 1847 by Captain Mayne Reid to a friend in his na-tive Ireland:

> The town from which I write is quaint; of the Spanish style of building and reposes in a great land kissed by the Southern sun. You have cows in Old Ireland, but you never saw cows. Yes, mil-lions of them here, I am sure, browsing on the sweet long grass of the ranges that roll from horizon to horizon. At this time of year, the cowmen have what is called the round-up, when the calves are branded and the fat beasts selected to be driven to a fair hundreds of miles away. This round-up is a great time for the cowhand, a Donny-brook fair it is indeed. They contest with each other for the best roping and throwing, and there are horse races and whiskey and wines. At night in clear moonlight, there is dancing on the streets.

•   •   •

A cool breeze swept over the grandstands at the Rodeo de Santa Fe, pronounced ro-DAY-o here, except by the cowboys.

In the bleachers, which looked out on sun-splashed hillsides sprouting expensive new homes, fans wore custom-stitched Western shirts, lizard skin boots and sparkling white cowboy hats, unsoiled by mud or blood. The parking lot swelled with Grand Wagoneers, Volvos, BMWs.

A glossy rodeo program carried ads for Tony Lama boots, a Japanese health spa, a hotel with a Jacuzzi in every room. In one ad, a man in a cowboy hat was posed on the back of a white horse, one hand on the reins and the other clutching a cellular telephone.

Down on the arena grounds, swirls of dust rose from the turf, where a forty-seven-year-old laborer named Ortiz and his son pushed and pulled rakes, working furiously to smooth the dirt, as sweat ran down their faces and drenched their white T-shirts. The father yelled instructions in Spanish to his son, who glanced back with a look that seemed to say he was hustling as fast as he could.

Joe Ortiz had tended the rodeo grounds for the past sixteen years, in exchange for permission to keep his family's mobile home on a patch outside the arena. But this property was becoming too valuable just for rodeo and the Ortiz family. Lately the Santa Fe rodeo committee, headed by a banker in a cowboy hat, had been considering lofty offers from shopping mall developers and builders of luxury homes.

•   •   •

Over the loudspeaker, the rich timbre of the rodeo announcer welcomed the crowd to "this cultural legacy of the Old West," and noted that the sport's biggest star, Ty Murray, was slated to perform.

A color photograph of Murray, his arms folded and a bull rope slung over his shoulder, graced nearly a full page inside the rodeo program, under a headline: "Cowboy and Superman Rolled into One."

The sun, moody all day, hid behind the mountains, and the wind kicked up. Some of the fans got cozy beneath shawls, awaiting the action as they sipped beer and munched on blue corn tortillas.

On the other side of the arena, Craig Latham peered through a cyclone fence, clenching a Burger King straw between his teeth.

•   •   •

The bronc rider carried his saddle under an arm, the leather straps dragging in the dirt. Perched on the other arm, his one-year-old daughter, Chaney, nestled her face against his chest. His wife, Laurie, stood at his shoulder. The cowboy had been apart from his wife and daughter for nearly a month.

From their home in Oklahoma, Laurie had borrowed a car and driven to the airport in Amarillo, Texas, to meet Craig, who had flown in from a rodeo in Calgary, Canada. They watched him ride a horse for eight seconds in Amarillo, then drove five hours to the rodeo in Santa Fe.

Since they had last been together, Chaney had grown quite a bit. "She can say 'daddy' and 'horse' real good now," Craig bragged to another cowboy.

Laurie, a tall, quiet woman with blond hair, had once been a barrel racer, but quit to stay home with her daughter. She sold her old racing horse, Snickers, for a down payment on their mobile home.

Craig gave Chaney a kiss and set her down on the ground. He took off his black corduroy jacket, stamped "Contestant," and handed it over to Laurie, whose arms had become covered with goose bumps.

Craig said he had better start toward the bucking chutes. As he began to walk away, Chaney ran to her father and threw her arms around his legs, squeezing tightly as she cried. Laurie bent down to soothe her daughter. "Oh, daddy's not going to be away for long," she said. "He'll come right back after he rides."

•   •   •

Laurie struggled to carry Chaney to the bleachers, where the mother and daughter sat next to a thirty-something couple, who seemed to frown at the new arrivals.

Whenever a cowboy burst out of the chutes, Chaney rose up and shouted, "Daddy, Daddy!" But when Craig's turn finally came, the little girl had fallen asleep on her mother's lap.

Laurie strained to see Craig in the white wooden chutes. He leaned back on the horse, his boots raised up around the animal's shoulders, his right hand squeezing the reins.

The crowd cheered as the horse bucked, then dipped and bucked again. Craig was staying in control, riding the waves, his free hand raised in the air, making it all look easy. Laurie held her breath, silently counting down the eight seconds.

The gun cracked, as Craig leaped off the horse, landing on his feet.

The scoreboard flashed seventy-five points. A smile broke out across his face. He pulled himself over the gate, then trotted toward Laurie, whose smile was even brighter.

"That's the way to do it," she said.

Still a bit winded, Craig sat down beside Laurie and squeezed her hand. "I just hope it's enough to win something," he said.

Chaney had awakened, a bit crankily, and so they decided not to stay around for the bull riding. As they rose to leave, Craig glanced around the crowd.

He noticed the fancy Western clothes, which looked like they must have cost a fortune, and joked that cattle prices must have been awfully good lately for these Santa Fe ranchers.

•   •   •

"It's Never Too Late to Be a Cowboy," read the sign in the Santa Fe clothing store.

The wrangler duds included Western yoked shirts made with Belgian silk and boots crafted with ostrich skin. "It's the perfect outfit for someone who wants to dress like a genuine cowboy," the store clerk explained, "without looking like he's been working in the corral all day."

In a cowboy antiques store, an accountant in sunglasses caressed an old leather saddle mounted on a bale of hay. The man said he didn't own a horse but thought the saddle would look striking on his banister at home.

An old pine bureau, decorated with a sheriff's badge, handcuffs and a bullet strap, was selling for $9,000. A nine-foot wood rocking horse went for $35,000, or about what it would take to buy 500 acres of scrub grass in South Dakota.

A store called Back at the Ranch was peddling shirts and jeans worn by "real-life ranch and rodeo cowboys." A pair of used Wranglers cost $30, a bit more if the back pocket was faded with the 0-shaped mark from a snuff can.

"The Western thing is very big right now," said the proprietor, Wendy Lane, who had moved to New Mexico from the Upper West Side of Manhattan to capitalize on the cowboy fad. "People are going crazy for anything that says 'cowboy,' especially the New Yorkers."

Dressed in ranch finery herself, the woman explained that being a cowboy or cowgirl was mostly a state of mind, like Santa Fe itself. "I've never actually been to a rodeo," she confessed cheerfully.

•   •   •

The rusty heap named Goldie, sheep horns curling up from a dented hood, chugged along Interstate 25 toward Santa Fe, groaning whenever the path turned uphill.

With one hand clutching the steering wheel, Larry Sandvick rolled down a window to let the fresh air slap him awake. He was tired and hungry and dirty. His faded Western shirt was wrinkled and his jeans were dusty.

The bareback rider had driven most of the night from a rodeo in Oklahoma, a dark, lonesome trail past closed gas stations and gone-in-a-blink little towns. But up ahead, he could see new pink adobe houses sprinkled along the hillsides, and an exit for Santa Fe.

Sandvick's rodeo winnings had been pretty meager so far this season. Between contests, he had been working hard on leather crafts in his drafty, cement-floored Wyoming shop, where a box of rat poison sat on a window ledge.

His proudest creation was a red leather couch engraved with the outline of a horse. A rodeo fan, a woman who worked as a vice president at a bank in Denver, had seen a photograph of the couch, which Larry liked to show off at the beer stand after the rodeos. She told him that people in Santa Fe were paying big bucks for cowboy furniture, and arranged to get it displayed in a gallery.

Sandvick, who had never been to downtown Santa Fe, decided he would try to find the gallery, even though he felt pretty beat. He turned down a narrow, winding street, but after a mile or so, it seemed to be taking him in the wrong direction. He pulled into a parking lot, leaned out the window and waved to a man strolling by.

"Excuse me there, partner," he said with a friendly twang.

The pedestrian looked up at Sandvick, shook his head that he was too busy to talk and quickened his pace.

"Not a very friendly cuss," the cowboy said to himself, as he pulled back on the road.

He drove in circles for about twenty minutes, trying to find the center of Santa Fe. There didn't seem to be a straight street in the whole town.

He turned another corner and finally saw crowds up ahead. He drove slowly, past gallery after gallery after gallery, more art places than he had ever imagined.

Sandvick knew that Santa Fe was supposed to be the cultural capital of the West. But it looked more like the East on vacation. Those surely weren't ranch hands in the fancy outdoor cafés, or Indians checking into the $200-a-night Inn of the Anasazi.

He parked Goldie along the curb, replenished his chew, and stepped outside to explore.

He strolled along the sidewalk, his heavy boots clunking on the cobblestones, his dusty cowboy hat cocked back on his head, his shirt pinned with a contestant's numeral, his face shaded with a day's growth of whiskers.

He nodded to everyone he passed, most of them dressed in hip Southwestern garb.

But nobody returned the greeting. They looked back instead with puzzled expressions. He was a curiosity.

A few people stopped and stared as he passed. One even chuckled.

Feeling embarrassed and out of place, Sandvick decided he didn't want to look any longer.

The cowboy climbed back into his car, and drove away.

13

"**WE'RE GONNA** have to haul tail, fellas," Bud Longbrake hollered, throwing his saddle into the back and jumping behind the steering wheel. "We ain't got much time."

It was the Fourth of July weekend, the crunch time for rodeo cowboys. Longbrake and two other cowboys had just competed in an afternoon performance in Prescott, Arizona. Now they were hurrying to make the evening contest at Window Rock, on the Navajo reservation, about 200 miles away.

They needed to make good time, better than the speed limits on Interstate 17 would legally allow. Longbrake took every curve in the road so fast the wheels squeaked.

But after a few miles, the traffic grew slow behind minivans stocked with kids and Winnebago trailers with bumper stickers bragging about spending the children's inheritance. Longbrake peered through the windshield and grimaced. The traffic slowed to the pace of the desert tortoise.

"What the heck's going on up here?" he groaned. "We ain't got time for a traffic jam."

The other cowboys would have used this travel time for a nap. But as they saw the traffic, and watched the clock move, they started to grow panicky. Missing a rodeo could mean the loss of hundreds of dollars in paychecks, maybe more.

"Just go off on the shoulder, and pass 'em all up," one of the cowboys said, "or we ain't never gonna make it to Window Rock."

"I can't," said Longbrake, as his teeth squeezed the life out of a toothpick between his lips. "I already got a bunch of tickets."

"Hell, let me do it," said one of the cowboys, a rookie, eager to prove his mettle. "I know how to drive offensively."

The rookie jumped behind the wheel. He veered the car to the shoulder, hurtling across the bumps, but moving past at least 100 cars.

"Hey, look out," Longbrake shouted. "There's a bunch of cops up ahead."

The flashing lights of squad cars grew brighter. It was a roadblock. The rookie veered back onto the pavement, cutting off a motorist who leaned on the horn and thrust a finger their way.

A state trooper motioned for the car to come to a halt. The rookie rolled down their window, and the officer in a Smokey Bear hat peered inside.

"We're looking for an escaped convict," the cop said. "We got reason to think he's right around here."

●　　　●　　　●

Danny Ray Hornung, an armed bank robber, was on the loose from the Arizona State Prison. For weeks, he had confounded a massive search team by hiding in the craggy reaches of the Grand Canyon, taking a few tourists as hostages along the way, but harming no one, and treating his captives with politeness.

The police had described him as an ultimate outdoorsman, a top marksman who had learned his survivalist skills in the army. With a remarkable mastery of the wilds, Hornung had traveled in figure eights to confuse police dogs tracking his scent. Now and then, he would make himself visible to reconnaissance helicopters whirring overhead, apparently as a taunt to the police. News stories had begun to call the slender five-foot-six-inch criminal "Rambo."

The fugitive had stolen a tourist's four-wheel-drive truck, used it for a few days, then left it behind with a note of apology:

Hey Bud,

I know this isn't going to mean a thing to you but I have to say it none the less. "Thanks for your donation and the use of your truck."

The rest of the stuff, I have use for, so you won't be getting it back. I know that pisses you off, and I do not blaim you one bit. All I can say is, at the moment, I need it more than you do.

I am a freedom fighter without support. Every time I do end up with something the cops steal it from me. I have tried to live in peace yet they keep coming after me. That causes me to have to steal from people like you. I do hope you have insurance. That way you'll get some of it back. That goes for your neighbors also.

Now about your truck.

I really ran it rough so you'll want to give it a good check. I could not find the transmission dip stick so I could not check it. Nor do I know anything about 4 X 4s, so really give it a good going over. These mountains are really rough on a truck, even when you don't have a nut at the wheel. I have always driven my vehicals rough, yet I also see to it they are kept up. I notice you take good care of yours also. Thats smart.

I think I may have did some harm to your 4 wheel drive system. I ran it on 4 X 4 at all times. I drove it 70 to 75 on the high way and knoticed a smell coming from it. I know I saw fluid leaken on your front wheel drums. "That can't be good." Also the bracket that holds your extra battery broke. I broke your antana off on your C.B. But it never worked as far as I could tell.

At any rate, Bud, I am sorry, I had to do this to you. I am sure you are a nice guy and didn't deserve anything like this. If you are a man of God, I would appreciate it if you would keep me in your prayers. I have a rough road ahead of me and could use all the help I can. Once again sorry.

Danny Ray

•   •   •

The chase for Hornung became the talk of coffee shops, taverns and Sunday school meetings throughout the rural West. The outlaw was daring and smart and polite to boot.

To the agitation of civic leaders, many people started pulling for Hornung. After all, the most vivid characters of the Old West had numbered not just cowboys and fur traders and gold prospectors, but also crooks. It was a spirit of independence, a rebellion against the old rules of a staid society, that had once carved a new world in the wilderness.

Westerners have always had a soft spot for outlaws. It didn't matter that Deadwood Dick, Billy the Kid and the James gang had robbed, murdered and brutalized bank tellers, Pinkerton men or innocent bystanders. The principal targets of these outlaws had been banks or railroads or other symbols of the Eastern power structure. Nor did it seem to matter much that Hornung, who had been convicted of robbing a bank in Winslow, also was a suspect in the dismemberment of a California man.

To rural Westerners, who prize nothing more than being left alone, yet see signs of urban life encroaching on all sides, the desperate flight of Danny Ray Hornung, a solitary figure being hunted in the wilds, echoed a defiance that still flickers in the New West.

A painted message on the rocky cliffs in the Grand Canyon proclaimed "Let Danny Go."

•   •   •

Satisfied that the fugitive was not hiding underneath a saddle in the back seat, the state trooper waved the cowboys along. They kept a respectable speed for a few miles, until the lights of the squad cars had disappeared in the rearview mirror.

Now the rookie kicked up the speed. The digital speedometer moved to 80, 85, 90, then past 100.

"I guess that's as fast as she'll go," he said, as it reached 108 miles an hour. "I'll put 'er on cruise."

The car whistled past the piñon and juniper of the Coconino National Forest toward the open, baking desert, dry as a bone, except for little streams with names like Crazy Creek and Tucker Flat Wash.

As they raced toward the reservation, a billboard near Holbrook beckoned to tourists: "Spend a Night in a Wigwam!"

•   •   •

The sandstone cliffs of Window Rock, the seat of the Navajo Nation, reveal a thousand different faces, depending upon the angle of the sun or the moonlight. The reservation stretches across 2 million acres of red desert, thistly brush and ancient rock. In the 1960s, Apollo astronauts trained on this barren landscape so they would feel at home on the terrain of the moon.

The Navajo Nation is the largest Indian tribe in America, with about 200,000 enrolled members. Most of its people long ago forsook the nomadic heritage of sheepherding. Some now worked in coal mines, raised small herds of cattle, or crafted jewelry for tourists stopping for trinkets and gasoline on the interstate highway, fifty miles from Window Rock. But for every Navajo with a job, at least two were unemployed. A handful of families still lived in caves or holes in the ground. There were only a few stores on the reservation, and mostly they advertised desperation: "Pawn Your Tractor" and "We Take Food Stamps."

Fourth of July in the land of the Navajo, whose ancestors were held in federal prison camps in the 1860s, bore little resemblance to Independence Day in other Western towns. There were no parades of high school marching bands, no papier-mâché floats, no towheaded kids waving plastic flags, no convertibles carrying the prim old ladies of the Daughters of the American Revolution.

On a grassy hilltop near booths selling fry bread, watermelon slices and mutton stew, a medicine man led a powwow, a celebration with roots that go much deeper than sparklers and firecrackers. "Fancy dancers" in brightly colored moccasins, regal headdresses of eagle feathers and jewelry of hollowed cow bones stepped rhythmically to the music of tambourines and drums, a ritual shaking of the body to give thanks to the creator for the gift of life.

"Song is praise to the Great Spirit," the medicine man called into a microphone, urging the crowd to sing louder. "Do not be selfish with your praise. Let us hear you sing."

White faces were scarce. One belonged to a man with a blond ponytail and an open leather vest, a lighted cigarette dangling from his lips, who peddled silk-screen T-shirts and plastic souvenirs.

"It's fourteen bucks, I tell you," the vendor snapped impatiently to a Navajo who did not understand English.

The Navajo emptied his pockets. He held up $11. The white man took it.

"All right, you win," the vendor muttered, handing over the T-shirt.

In wood bleachers, old women with eyes the color of chestnuts and deeply lined faces watched the dance in long print dresses and shawls, despite temperatures that had soared over 100 degrees.

An old man slapped the back of a friend, and they laughed quietly over old stories spoken in Navajo. A teenage girl with a long black braid wore an X hat, next to a man in his twenties who wore a Desert Storm cap.

His name was Edison Lee. He was a hero of the Gulf War, a member of the Twenty-fourth Infantry. He had come home to the reservation two months ago but had not been able to find work. He lived with two sons and his parents in a one-room shack with a dirt floor.

"My wife, she got tired and left a month ago," said Edison Lee.

In the parking lot, a crumpled copy of the *Navajo Times* lay under a car tire, covered with the broken shards of a schnapps bottle. On a page of the newspaper, an article recounted the role of the tribe in World War II, when Navajos worked as "code-talkers," relaying military strategy in a language Japanese interceptors could not decipher. The article noted that Indians had sacrificed a greater share of lives in American wars than any other ethnic group. On another page, the newspaper ran its weekly police blotter, and the names of thirty-five people who had been arrested for drunk driving.

•   •   •

Rodeo drapes itself in Americana, the legacy of the Old West, the triumph of God-fearing settlers. The announcer always invokes the glories of the Flag, and rarely misses a chance to mention The Good Lord, perhaps wearing a cowboy hat Himself, watching the performance from the heavens.

But the sport is revered nowhere else as it is in Indian Country. The people on these isolated lands, so far away from big cities, never get a visit from a professional basketball team or a big league baseball squad. Indian schools rarely have the money to buy athletic equipment or uniforms. But most kids on the reservations learn to ride a horse as soon as they learn to walk.

•   •   •

The rodeo grandstands were packed, filled with ten times the number of people who had attended the fancy dance.

Near the chute gates, a young woman paced nervously, checking the faces under every cowboy hat. But nobody looked familiar. The rodeo would start any minute. She was growing worried.

"I'm looking for my cousin," she explained to a bronc rider. "Do you know Bud Longbrake?"

"Yes ma'am," a cowboy answered. "He was up at Prescott. But they probably ain't gonna make it. We come from that way earlier. There was a helluva traffic jam."

Kyanne Dillabaugh pulled herself up on a fence post. She peered out toward the parking lot. But there weren't any cowboys out there, except for a roper casting a loop over a plastic skull on a bale of hay.

She hadn't seen her cousin Bud in three years, since she left the Sioux reservation in South Dakota to follow a boyfriend to Navajo country. The boyfriend didn't last, but Kyanne found a job at a radio station, so she stayed.

Kyanne, who had just turned twenty-one, missed everything about South Dakota, except for the January days when the thermometer plunged to minus-thirty degrees, and there were times she even missed that. She missed her family. She missed her friends. She even missed the cows. The Navajos don't raise nearly as many cattle as the Sioux. And Kyanne thought the countryside seemed awfully lonesome without them.

•   •   •

In the performance the night before, the Navajo fans had gotten a chance to see the sport's biggest star, the blond streak named Ty Murray.

As a promotion, the announcer had told the crowd that Murray would stay around for autographs after the rodeo. Young boys and girls, and some of their parents, bought programs so Murray could sign them.

Strutting behind the chutes, he looked rested and confident. Most cowboys strain to stay awake behind the wheel between rodeos. Murray had come to Window Rock with a driver, who escorted the champ for $50 a day and expenses, a better wage than most cowboys earn.

But after the chutes lifted, the star was brought back down to earth, with a thud, by a bull that was apparently unimpressed by his credentials.

Murray stomped back to the chutes, his mood as rumpled as his cowboy hat.

"Fuck!" he shouted, ripping the tape off his arm and throwing it in a heap. "Fuck! Fuck!"

He gathered his belongings and told the driver to get the car started. The champion wasn't going to stay around for any autographs.

•   •   •

"Hey Kyanne!" shouted a familiar voice.

And the young woman turned so quickly she almost tumbled off the fence post.

In a remarkable feat of luck and police radar evasion, Longbrake and the other cowboys had arrived in time, finishing the race with a sprint from the parking lot.

Bud jumped over the Cyclone fence, dropped his saddle in the dust and stretched out his arms.

"I was sure hopin' you'd be here," he said, lifting his cousin off her feet with a big hug.

"Bud, I almost gave up. Well, I didn't give up. I mean I was going to stay. But they were starting, and you weren't here, and . . ."

"Aw, shucks, we got plenty of time," he said, trying to catch his breath. "Looks like we got all day till saddle bronc ridin'. Well, twenty minutes anyway."

"Oh Bud! You look great. How's Pete and Fay and Lonna and Jay and Kayla and Delbert and Jake and Dakota and Rocky and—I mean, how's everybody?"

"Oh they're good, real good. Everybody's doin' just fine. How 'bout you? We sure miss you. They treating you all right down here?"

Arizona was fine, she told him, except of course that it was not South Dakota, and seemed terribly short on cows. The Navajos were a friendly people, she said, but much more quiet and reserved than the Sioux.

"They think we talk and make a lot of noise," she said. "What would they think of the Crows over in Montana?"

The cousins had a good laugh, and then Bud grabbed his saddle and started over toward the chutes. He stretched out his legs, which had grown stiff from the long car ride, and tried to concentrate on his horse.

Kyanne returned to the fence post to watch the rodeo. She poked the shoulder of a woman standing nearby. "See that cowboy over there?" she said, pointing toward Bud. "That's my cousin."

●   ●   ●

After each ride, the crowd applauded politely. There was no hooting and hollering. The Navajos watched rodeo the way jazz fans watch a concert, with quiet appreciation. No stomping of feet. No piercing screams. No bellowing yee-haws.

Bud saddled his horse, and settled into the stirrups. The rodeo announcer read the score of the preceding cowboy, then began to introduce Bud.

"Folks," he said, his deep voice rising an octave, "here's Bud Longbrake from Dupree, South Dakota—an Indian cowboy!"

In the next instant, people far from the arena might have looked up and wondered what was happening, as a deafening, cascading roar, like waves of an ocean rushing toward shore, thundered from the grandstands.

Deep in the crowd, an old man with windburned cheeks raised a clenched fist. Little kids bounced excitedly on wood bleachers. Teenage boys smiled broadly and exulted in daydreams.

The Wild Horse Boy, as the Sioux elders had named him, scrunched down his cowboy hat. He nodded. The chute gates swung open.

But the ride lasted only a few seconds. Bud landed on the turf even before the roars of the crowd had faded.

He jogged back to the chutes, where his cousin cast a warm smile.

"Now that wasn't too good to watch, I'm afraid," he said apologetically.

"You hush, Bud," she said, and gave his shoulder a squeeze.

He smiled and gave her a hug, then packed his saddle and chaps, and craned his neck to find his travel partners.

The other cowboys had already started for the parking lot. The driver was in a hurry. If he didn't move quickly, he would lose his spot on the ride to Greeley, Colorado, a night's drive away.

But as he started to walk briskly, a small voice stopped him.

"Can I have your autograph?" a boy asked, holding up a program.

"You bet you can," said Longbrake, bending on a knee to sign the program.

He rose and started to jog away. But an old man grabbed his arm.

"You're Bud Longbrake. I want to shake your hand."

"Can I shake your hand, too?"

"Me, too."

He visited patiently, and the men wished him good luck.

Longbrake needed to hustle. He picked up the pace, making long strides toward the parking lot.

And then another voice called out, "Can I get your autograph?"

Now he was growing a bit exasperated. He needed to catch his travel partners, if they hadn't left without him already.

"Here, let me sign real quick," he said. He scribbled his name in a dash, handed back the program and began walking fast.

"I was also hoping I could ask you some things," a young voice called out, but Longbrake kept walking. "You see, I'm thinking about becoming a cowboy. But you're in a hurry, and I understand, so . . ." The voice trailed off.

Longbrake stopped and turned around.

The Navajo boy looked about fifteen, skinny as a rail, peering out from behind glasses, standing alone in the darkness.

"I got some time," said Longbrake, setting down his bag. "Those fellas can wait. What do you want to know?"

"Is it a very hard thing to do?" the boy asked. "Being a rodeo cow-boy, I mean."

"Oh, it's pretty hard, all right," said Bud. "And it ain't just ridin' that's hard. You don't make much money in rodeo, you know. And you don't see much of your family. And that hurts a lot more than gettin' bucked off a horse."

They talked a while longer, then shook hands in the moonlight, wishing each other good luck.

"Come on Bud, let's go," a voice hollered from the parking lot.

"I'm coming. I'm coming."

To get to the car, he needed to jump over a fence. He pulled himself up gingerly, careful not to rip a hole in his pants.

"I can't afford to ruin these britches," he said. "We got a lot of rodeos yet to go. And I already got ice cream all over my Monday, Tuesday, Wednesday shirt."

·　　·　　·

The car rolled across the reservation, which had fallen black. Long-brake leaned back and closed his eyes.

Somebody switched on the radio to a country station. A song was interrupted by the voice of a news announcer.

"This just in," said the newsman. "Danny Ray Hornung, the es-caped convict who eluded police while hiding in the Grand Canyon, has been captured."

14

RAW AND JAGGED as broken glass, the bare-wire sound of an electric guitar knifed through the darkness of a Cheyenne dance hall.

And the place exploded.

It was The Song—their song, the anthem of the rodeo world.

> *Wild Thing!*
> *You make my heart sing.*
> *You make everything.*
> *Wild Thing.*

Almost anywhere else, a rodeo cowboy walks into a bar outnumbered, even in the rural West. For every fan who sees a hero under a cowboy hat, someone else sees only a backwoods hick in a funny costume, a sideshow geek with the traveling circus. A rodeo cowboy can never be sure whether some beefy beer drinker will want to shake his hand or punch out his lights.

But during Cheyenne Frontier Days, inside the Hitching Post Saloon, cowboy hats collided like bumper cars. The rodeo cowboys were at home, surrounded by family, intoxicated as much by the camaraderie as the beer.

And nobody here would ask the questions:

Why do you do it?
Why do you sleep in flea-bitten motels?
Why do you wear gaudy belt buckles and chew disgusting tobacco?
Why do you chase the highway for 100,000 miles a year?
Why do you risk your neck for such paltry reward?
Why? Why? Why?

•   •   •

Now their song was blaring. Cowboys climbed on chairs. Jumped on tables. Boot heels stomping. Arms waving.

> *Wild Thing—I think I love you.*
> *But I want to know for sure.*
> *Come on, hold me tight.*
> *I looovvve you.*

The song hailed as an anthem by rodeo cowboys was no country-and-western tune, no Old West ballad, no flag-waving hymn. It was an ancient rock-and-roll hit by the long-faded Troggs, a band that wasn't even American.

Rugged, driving, pulsating, sexual, like rodeo itself, the harsh beat seemed to shake the walls of the Hitching Post.

Dancing on the tabletops, cowboys lifted their wives and girl-friends atop their shoulders. And they chanted the words to the song, a thundered, raucous creed of a defiant subculture.

> *Come on, hold me tight.*
> *Wild Thing—you mooovvve me.*

15

ROBERT WOOD JR., a rookie cowboy from Texas, woke Saturday morning in a camper truck on the Cheyenne fairgrounds, his eyes as red as the Hitching Post stamp inked on his hand.

He was hung over, but as happy as he could ever remember. Since he was a boy, he had dreamed about competing at Cheyenne Frontier Days, the world's largest outdoor rodeo, the "Daddy of 'em All." Now he would stand boot-to-boot with the best.

Six months ago, Wood felt stuck in the eight-to-four factory trap. He had a good job with Bell Helicopters. It paid $13 an hour. But the lean young man with the square jaw and the cocky smile knew he was meant for bigger and flashier things. He had threatened to divorce his wife, Tammy, and then changed his mind. But one thing was certain: he wasn't going back to that job.

"I want to be free," he told Tammy. "Don't want no boss. Don't want nobody tellin' me what to do."

"Who does?" Tammy shot back. "Do you think anybody wakes up on Monday morning and feels good about going to work, Robert? People do it because they gotta survive. They do it because they have to."

"I don't have to," he answered.

Wood wasn't exactly burning up the rodeo trail. In fact, he was losing far more than he was winning. The savings he and Tammy had earmarked for a house were melting away. And the bills were piling up.

But he was having a ball. He lived for what he called "the rodeo atmosphere." The beer was plentiful. The music was loud. And the women were adoring.

In the celebration the night before, he had called home sometime around midnight. Or maybe it was an hour or two later.

Who was watching the clock?

While Wood chased his dream, Tammy stayed home in their cramped trailer on a dusty patch five miles outside of Glenrose, with their four-year-old boy, Robert Wood III.

She was pregnant with their second child, and the morning sickness had been awful this time around. But she rose every morning at five and drove the pickup to Blushes Beauty Parlor, where she worked as a "nail technician" on the hands of wealthy older ladies who lived in the big houses of Pecan Plantation. Later in the day, she drove to the Greenhouse Fitness Club, where she worked on the nails of younger women after they tired of pedaling the Exercycle.

When the bills came in the mail, she would spread them out on the kitchen table, and mark the calendar for the last possible due date for each. And at night, after cooking and cleaning, bathing her boy and putting him down, she would collapse on her bed and cry into the pillow.

There were times when she packed her clothes and told her absentee husband that she could not take it any longer. If he insisted on spending his life at the rodeo, he might find her gone when he returned home.

"Whatever you got to do," he would sigh, almost bored.

Among the traditions that rodeo takes from the old cattle drives, the loneliness of wives and children is one of the most enduring. The wife of one nineteenth-century cowboy wrote of being given three chickens by a ranch hand, presumably for a stew pot. She decided instead to make pets of them.

According to her diary: "They were something I could talk to."

•   •   •

Frontier Days, which started in 1896, claims to be the most famous rodeo in the world. It filled the double-deck grandstands every afternoon with 17,000 fans from around the country, and even some from Europe and Japan.

Each day the loudspeaker announced the winner of "The License Plate Derby," a parking lot check of which states sent the most cars. The Wyoming plates, emblazoned with the red silhouette of a bucking cowboy, usually ran neck and neck for the lead with Colorado, just across the border. But there were cars from almost every state. Cars from New York outnumbered those from North Dakota, an honest-to-goodness cowboy state, and nobody knew quite what to make of that.

The fans could stay around after the rodeo to see a country music star. Garth and Clint were here, and Wynonna and Reba. Or they could drive down to the Atlas Theater in downtown Cheyenne, near Gunslingers Square, where the local players were showing *The Cattleman's Daughter*, or *Can a Cowgirl Find Happiness with a Sheepish Suitor?* or *Kissin' Is a Woman's Work: Killin' Is a Man's Job*.

There were plenty of rodeo queens, dazzling young sequined beauties wrapped in banners that proclaimed their home states, and a horse-riding troupe of high school girls named "The Dandies."

The 2,000 volunteers working the rodeo were called "The Heels," a name taken during the Depression, when the contest couldn't afford to hire paid help and some generous fellow supposedly told his friends, "We'd all be heels if we didn't help out!"

The men of the Official Rodeo Committee—and they were only men—wore black cowboy hats, black tuxedos and black pearl buttons. The rodeo secretary was the widow of a bareback cowboy killed in the arena. She was twenty-four years old.

•   •   •

Wood smiled broadly, exulting in the cool sunshine of the High Plains and strutting across the fairgrounds in his bright red cowboy boots.

"Time to let the hair down," he snorted. "Let 'er rip, hang loose, free and easy."

His name was printed on page three of the rodeo program, right along with some of the biggest stars in the sport. He figured he would probably meet some of the big-name cowboys behind the chutes, or over beers. Maybe they would trade war stories, brothers in the dust and glory of rodeo life.

But he wasn't going out of his way to introduce himself. No sir. Not on your ass. Robert Wood wasn't just some factory worker in a jerkwater town anymore. He was now a rough-ridin', tobacco-spittin', dues-payin' member of the Pro Rodeo Cowboys Association.

At every other rodeo, Wood competed only in the bull riding. It drew the toughest, wildest cowboys. And that's where he belonged.

But at Cheyenne, he also entered the steer wrestling, or bulldogging. It would cost another two hundred bucks and change. But he figured it was worth every penny.

The steer wrestling at Frontier Days was the most thrilling anywhere. Unlike the rules at other rodeos, where the steer got a ten-foot head start, the Cheyenne rules gave the animal a thirty-foot lead. That meant it took longer for the mounted cowboy to catch up, and when he did, everything happened at full speed.

"You ain't lived," a steer wrestler once told Wood, "until you've dogged at Cheyenne."

So he forked over the extra entry fee. He figured if he ran low on money, he could just call Tammy and tell her to find some extra cash somehow and stick it in the checking account.

·   ·   ·

At Frontier Days, the chutes opened 180 times during every performance, once every sixty seconds, a blur of cowboy after cowboy.

The rodeo was a three-header. Each cowboy got a chance to compete in two perfs. And the top dozen scorers in each event qualified for the Finals on Sunday.

The steers and calves at Cheyenne had never been chased before, so they would be fresh right up to the moment they were collared and slammed to the dirt. The calves had come up from Florida, a bit older and bigger than their counterparts on the Great Plains, since calving season starts earlier in warmer climes.

The bulls at Cheyenne, almost always part Brahma, were as big and ornery as breeders could make them. And the bucking horses, hauled from a ranch in the Rattlesnake Hills of Colorado, were some of the friskiest in the business.

·   ·   ·

The livestock might have been fresh, but Bud Longbrake certainly wasn't.

He hadn't slept for more than an hour straight in three nights, hustling from town to town on a trail that stretched from Arizona to Colorado to Canada to Montana to Wyoming.

The latest stop was Wolf Point, Montana, where he won first place in the saddle-bronc event, good enough for a few hundred dollars. But he still hadn't won enough to pierce the standings of the top fifteen cowboys.

Longbrake ambled to the concession stand to get a cup of black coffee. It would be his ninth or tenth dose of caffeine already that day.

He was hoping to hear something from the tribe soon. When his kids were rejected for membership in the Sioux Nation, he and Lona had appealed the decision. They filled out a long form and sent it right away. Now they could only hope for the best. Waiting for somebody else to judge your fate, Bud thought, was a little like rodeo. Only he wasn't necessarily going to accept this score. No matter what the tribal government ruled, his kids were Indian.

As he stood in the long line, he chewed on a toothpick, as always, and clutched a rolled-up copy of the $2 rodeo program. On the cover was a sketch of an Indian, bare-legged and streaked with face paint, waving feathers in a wild dance. The Indian didn't look much like anybody Longbrake knew back home on the Sioux reservation.

•   •   •

As the chute flew open, the bronc underneath Bud stomped wildly across the arena. But he stayed snug in the saddle. The hat stayed firmly on his head. And the eagle feather stayed tucked in its brim.

His score was in the seventies. It wasn't all that he wanted, but certainly no failure. He still stood a good shot at making the finals on Sunday.

He trotted back to the rails, where a cowboy greeted him with a smile.

"Lookin' forward to Sunday?" he asked.

"I sure am," Bud replied. "Lona and the kids are gonna be here."

•   •   •

Since it lasted for more than a week, Frontier Days was one of the few rodeos in the West where a cowboy could stay in one place for a while.

Wives and children who rarely saw their cowboys in action came to Cheyenne, where they could watch them ply their trade and talk for a long stretch without spending a fortune on toll calls.

Rodeo used to work that way. Families traveled the circuit together, staying in campers on the fairgrounds. There was plenty of leisure time for cowboys to pitch horseshoes and play cards and arm-wrestle, even visit with their wives. After a contest, neighbors got to-gether for a potluck supper. And afterward some of the men even helped out with the dishes, although probably not most. ("Wyoming: Where the men are men and the women work.")

Expectant parents, unburdened by things like Lamaze classes, rolled from rodeo to rodeo, guessing at what state the birth certifi-cate would carry. Hospitals weren't always close by. And more than a few babies took their first breaths in the fresh air perfumed by rodeo livestock.

But interstate highways have changed all that. The speedier travel made it possible for rodeo promoters to schedule more contests and maximize their profits, since cowboys could get from place to place in a hurry. It might be no picnic to drive from Denver to Dallas in a night, but it can be done. Now there was a rodeo somewhere almost every day of the week.

In the old days, there were no standings or championship in Las Vegas to chase. Almost every big contest called itself The World Championship, and dared anyone to say otherwise. With a dozen or more rodeos all claiming to be the best, things sometimes got con-fusing. A cowboy wearing a belt buckle that proclaimed him to be, say, the world's champion bronc rider of 1949 was apt to bump into another fellow wearing a buckle inscribed with the same boast.

The old cowboys who came around to the rodeos never tired of telling the young whippersnappers how much more fun it used to be.

Cheyenne still had a few touches of the old days: cowboys strum-ming guitars under the stars, poker games on card tables of grass, and families lounging on blankets around picnic baskets. And the cowboy bulletin board, tacked on a brick wall, carried messages that could have been posted at a rodeo in the '40s.

"Wayne Herman—stop at the Applebees—if you have time."

"This note for TIM HANSEN. Go out this door and turn left and go 100 feet. You'll see us."

"Honey and kids. I'm behind chutes. bill."

There were hand-scrawled advertisements: "Appaloosa mare, $600, has packed deer, elk and bear—fairly gentle." And offers of in-surance: "Any accident, 24 hours a day; 7-day-week coverage. Wyoming cowboys only."

For the more religious cowboys, there was an invitation to "an evening of great music and testimonials," hosted by a former steer wrestler and his wife. It would be held at the Sunnyside Baptist Church, "Next to the Outlaw Saloon and Marv's Pawnshop."

·   ·   ·

Robert Wood read the notices on the board. But he knew he wouldn't be going to any church. That was for sure. He was going to wrestle a steer. Then he was going to drink. And who knew what else. Cheyenne would be one giant party town all week. This cowboy was ready.

He unhitched his horse, Bojinx, a nine-year-old gelding, mouse colored with a little black, and made his way toward the arena, where he took his place behind the chalked starter line.

He gazed out across the vast field, shadowed by double-decker grandstands. The rodeo program gloated that Cheyenne was "no teacup arena." There was no doubt about that. It was far bigger than anything Wood had ever seen.

The first wrestler in the competition bolted toward a steer. From 100 yards away, Wood watched the man time his jump perfectly, lunging sideways off a galloping horse just as the steer ran alongside, collapsing on the stunned animal's back like a 200-pound vault dropped from a window.

The cowboy grabbed it by the horns, twisting its neck backward, as the steer groaned in resistance, until finally the points touched the turf.

The triumphant cowboy, his ample belly jiggling over a belt buckle, rose with arms thrust to the sky, as the grandstands erupted in cheers, and the dazed steer loped away.

"That's what you come to see, folks!" the announcer crooned in admiration. "Bulldoggin' at its best. Here in Old Cheyenne."

Wood didn't hear the cowboy's time. But it sure seemed quick. It would be hard to beat.

His turn was next. He steadied himself on the horse. In an instant, the steer was released, fleeing as fast as it could. Wood fixed his narrowed eyes on the rodeo judge, who held a red flag over his head. The flag floated to the ground, and Wood kicked his spurs into Bojinx.

·   ·   ·

Tammy was at home in the hot trailer in Texas that afternoon, struggling with their four-year-old over one thing and the next, catching up with a week's worth of laundry, and poring fretfully over bills.

She knew that Robert was competing that day. And she hoped to get a call.

Besides everything else that goes on at those rodeos—"I wasn't born yesterday," she once told him—she worried about his health. She wanted to get a call to know at least he was all right, and not lying in a hospital bed somewhere, or worse.

She waited for the phone to ring. But she knew better than to expect it.

•   •   •

He was close, near enough to see the nape of the steer's neck, straining forward, lunging for freedom, right about where the cowboy would land with a wallop.

Bojinx kept gaining on the steer, as a mounted hazer raced along the other side, narrowing the path, shutting off any escape. But before Wood was ready to leap, the hazer's horse accidentally bumped into the steer, knocking it off balance.

As the steer crashed in the dirt, Wood hurried his leap, falling awkwardly against the animal, straining to seize its horns. But the steer twisted away, making its escape, leaving Wood on his knees in the dirt.

"No score, but a good try," the announcer called out. "Let's give this nice young cowboy from Texas a big hand."

The fans applauded politely, as Wood climbed atop Bojinx and trotted off the arena. He put away the horse and headed straight to the beer stand.

•   •   •

Wood hadn't won a penny so far at Cheyenne. But as a rookie, he hadn't figured on winning a big pile anyway. And whatever happened in the arena, it wasn't going to stop him from having a large time afterward.

The beer stand was crowded with cowboys and cowboy watchers, some of them in skimpy halters and tight-as-paint jeans. One skinny blonde, who looked barely old enough to drive, wore a T-shirt that read, "Wrangler Butts Drive Me Nuts."

Wood sipped a foamy beer and swaggered through the crowd, a smile on his face and a twinkle in his big, brown eyes.

He had come to Cheyenne for more than the livestock. There was, after all, so much of this "rodeo atmosphere."

16

LONA LONGBRAKE put down the phone inside the Plains Motel.

"Guess what?" she smiled at her kids. "Daddy's coming."

Ear-piercing screams filled the tiny motel room.

"Daddy's coming! Daddy's coming! Daddy's coming!"

Jay jumped up and down on the bed. Kayla jumped up and down on the floor. And then they traded places, and jumped some more.

Lona was exhausted from driving the 400 miles from the Cheyenne River Sioux reservation in South Dakota, with bathroom breaks in virtually every town with indoor plumbing along the way. But even she felt a little like jumping up and down.

They were meeting Bud in Cheyenne and traveling together to rodeos in Kansas. Bud even promised the kids that if they were good, they might get to stay in a motel with a swimming pool.

There was a rap on the motel door, and Lona pulled it open to see one tired but awfully happy cowboy. In a tangle of arms, the family bunched together, hugging and kissing. And then Bud fell to his knees, snorting like a bronc, "Neighhhh! Neighhhh!"

"It's the daddy horse," Kayla shouted, climbing on Bud's back, her arms tight around his neck. Jay climbed aboard the flanks, his free hand waving in the air, just like a bronc rider.

· · ·

For Craig Latham, who hung near the top of the standings, a big win in the Cheyenne finals would practically mean he could reserve a room on the Strip.

Rushing back from a rodeo in Canada, a contest squeezed into the Frontier Days week, the van sliced south on Interstate 25 in Wyoming, not far from the foothills of the Bighorn Mountains, where he first learned to ride. In the distance, mounted ranchers checked on cattle roaming in the summer pastures, cowboys too busy with the real thing to fool with rodeo.

He wheeled the van to a truck stop, and got out to hunt for a pay telephone, eager to call and learn his draw for the finals.

Latham had qualified for the Frontier Days championship by a horsehair, a single point. An impressive ride in his second performance, a score of seventy-four points, had done the trick.

Since his first ride of the season, back in frosty Denver, the saddle-bronc rider had been performing as if his future as a cowboy depended on it. And it did. Anything short of a berth in Las Vegas for the world championships could mean the end of his rodeo days.

Without a college degree, he wasn't quite sure what kind of job he could get. But if rodeo wasn't going to pay the bills, he would have to find something that did. And whatever the pay, he figured, at least the job wouldn't require an entry fee every time he went to work.

But Latham didn't need to check the help-wanted ads just yet. So far this season, he had been holding on to his cowboy hat, climbing to sixth in the world standings. His riding style wasn't flashy enough to win first place very often. But he was smooth and consistent, like the ranch cowboy he once hoped to be. The season was now just past the midpoint, and Latham had earned more than $40,000, a handsome sum for a rodeo cowboy, even after subtracting nearly half for expenses.

•   •   •

Latham walked back to the van, a strange look stamped across his face.

"Whad'ya draw?" Billy Etbauer, his traveling partner, asked.

"I didn't," Latham replied flatly.

"What?"

"They adjusted my score," he said. "Dropped a point from the second perf.

"I didn't make the finals."

•   •   •

Cheyenne is a friendly town, so friendly that in 1992 a woman in Salem, Illinois, who publishes a newsletter on civic manners, declared this city "The Most Polite Place in America."

During Frontier Days, the mayor issued a proclamation urging townspeople to be "extra special helpful" to visitors, and to greet them with a "howdy" whenever possible. The police were instructed not to issue parking tickets during the week's festivities. Motorists who returned to cars at overdue meters found, instead of a ticket, a kindly note on the windshield titled "Just a Reminder."

But Cheyenne didn't get carried away with good manners and rectitude, and never had. The town got its start with the westward rolling Union Pacific Railroad, whose boozing and brawling crews earned the nickname "Hell on Wheels."

When the rail workers arrived, in the summer of 1867, there was already a throng of 4,000 waiting for them: promoters, gamblers, soldiers, speculators and prostitutes. These were the forefathers and foremothers of Cheyenne.

As the town grew, it never quite lost its rough edges. One early visitor complained in a letter home that his Cheyenne hotel had twenty-seven beds but only one room. And each bed was meant for two.

"You never knew who you were going to have as a companion," he wrote, "very frequently a half-drunken wagon driver, who, before he got into bed, deposited a loaded revolver under his pillow."

A few blocks from the rodeo fairgrounds entrance, a police officer stepped out of a flashing squad car to inspect a fender bender, where two men in cowboy hats were talking loudly at each other and pointing fingers.

The cop, who held a police radio that stretched on a cord from inside the car, shook his head as he spoke to the dispatcher.

"Got another accident near the rodeo," he said. "I suspect they've been drinking."

"Why?" asked a fuzzy voice at the other end.

" 'Cause I suspect everybody here has been drinking."

The night before, all hell had broken loose on Capitol Street. Thousands of drunken revelers in cowboy hats poured into the streets, whooping and hollering and busting bottles on the pavement. Cars cruised nearby, as motorists hoisted their beers through windows in salute. At least one man in the crowd stopped a flying fist with his chin. And a woman with a horse tattoo, which reared over the top of a gauzy halter, moaned and heaved on the curb.

"Ain't this cooler than shit," slurred a high school boy in the mob, as he tilted a beer bottle in the direction of his mouth.

"Got that fuckin' right," replied his companion, who teetered from one leg to the other, and then hollered above the din, "Rodeo rules!"

•   •   •

It was high noon in Cheyenne. The finals of Frontier Days. And the cowboys were pumped.

They slapped backs, traded tips about their draws, shared pinches of snuff, took turns pinning contestant numerals on each other's backs.

Ty Murray leaned against a white metal post, giving one of his ten or so daily interviews to the press. He wore a big white cowboy hat, a big sparkling ring and a huge shiny belt buckle that identified him as the world's champion.

The reporter was wearing a cowboy hat, as all members of the news media at Cheyenne were required to do, so the photographs taken around the chutes would capture an authentic look. The newsman was asking Murray the meaning of "true cowboy."

Murray spat on the ground and delivered his answer. "It's what you got in your heart."

The reporter nodded with awe, as if the mystery had been unlocked. He finished scribbling. And then asked bashfully, "Ty, would you do me a favor? Would you sign my cowboy hat?"

The champ whipped a silver pen from his shirt pocket and scrawled his famous name across the hat.

•   •   •

In the last tense moments before the crack of the starter's gun, most of the cowboys attended to some personal ritual. Some paced. Some stretched. Some found a quiet corner and gazed into space.

On the whole, the cowboys were a superstitious bunch. Some would never lay a hat on a bed. Others refused to change a pair of socks after winning first place. Some carried a talisman, like the copper bracelet worn by Larry Sandvick, who had heard it emitted good vibes.

"I just don't believe in superstition, myself," Robert Etbauer, the champion bronc rider, once told a reporter for the *Prorodeo Sports*

News. "Of course, I've never been hurt real bad—knock on wood."

In preparation for the finals, one bareback rider was hanging upside down, his cowboy boots tied to a beam under the bleachers, as blood rushed to his bare head.

"Deb, what the hell are you doin'?" a fellow cowboy called out.

"Oh," said Deb Greenough, looking like a bat in repose, "the trainer said my back was compressed. So heck, I just figured, 'Why not uncompress it?' And by jimminy, my back's startin' to feel better already."

But after the others walked away, the cowboy muttered under his breath, "My head's startin' to pound a little, though."

•   •   •

The announcer instructed, "Will the male of the species please remove his headgear," and everybody in the grandstands rose for the Cowboy Prayer.

They remained standing, heads still bowed, in a moment of silence for a reading of cowboys and cowgirls who had died since the last Frontier Days rodeo. But the list missed a few names.

Jeff Grigsby was a twenty-eight-year-old rodeo clown, one of the men in greasepaint and baggy pants who rescue trapped or injured cowboys in the arena. In saving a cowboy during a rodeo in Nevada, he had been slammed in the head by a raging bull. A week later, complaining of a headache, but determined to shrug off the pain like any tough cowboy, Grigsby worked the Fourth of July rodeo at Greeley. He chased away a few mean bulls, clowned for the giggling kids in the stands, and then collapsed on the turf and died.

There had been one bad wreck at Cheyenne already this week. A Louisiana cowboy got hung up in the rope and then trampled by a bull. His limp, bloody body was hauled off the arena and laid into a waiting ambulance. The cowboy's son, who looked about eight years old, had run up to the stretcher, tears flooding his face, and screamed, "Daddy, Daddy, Daddy—oh, no, Daddy."

The cowboy's daughter, who looked closer to fifteen, stood back a few yards, her arms folded, with fright in her eyes and what looked like a flash of anger.

Many of the fans had been here three years before, on a rainy Cheyenne afternoon, when a former world champion named Lane Frost rode his final bull, Taking Care of Business. The cowboy dismounted on the muddy turf, and never saw the hooking horn. He died from internal bleeding. And for his effort, Frost was posthumously awarded a third place in the bull riding event.

The names of the deceased cowboys recited over the loudspeaker included only dues-paying members of the rodeo organization, not any amateurs. So the name of Donny Boes, the kid from Nebraska who had yearned to someday hear his name echo in the big rodeo arenas, was not mentioned.

Just the day before, the national high school rodeo finals had been held in Oklahoma, the championship that Donny had died trying to make. In the grandstands, there were some whispered words about his tragic fate. And then the fans munched popcorn and sipped colas and watched as another young cowboy, an eighteen-year-old from Loveland, Colorado, named T. R. Sprague, got thrown from a bull to his death.

•   •   •

In the chutes, Larry Sandvick sat atop a bronc, squeezing the leather handhold, as the announcer introduced the cowboy to the crowd:

"You want to talk about aggressive—this kid is wild."

Sandvick was hot. In the last week alone—a whirlwind of rodeo that took him to Spanish Fork, Utah; Medicine Hat, Alberta; and Helena, Montana; with perfs in between at Cheyenne—the bareback rider had won checks totaling more than $4,500.

His take might have been even bigger if he hadn't shown up too late to compete at Mitchell, South Dakota, where he complained that "those damned two-lane roads" had slowed his travel.

He had taken a chunk of the winnings and bought a plane ticket for a girlfriend in California, an English literature major he had met at a rodeo in Modesto, so she could fly to Cheyenne, if only for a day.

She wore wavy, flowing black hair, dark sunglasses and designer jeans that clung tightly to her long legs.

"What's it like dating him?" one of the cowboys' wives, familiar with Sandvick's colorful ways, had asked the fashionable young woman.

"Well," she replied, lowering her shades to reveal smiling eyes, "it's never boring."

•   •   •

The chute boss stared at the cowboy, waiting for the signal. Sandvick's left hand was rigid in the air. The toes of his boots pointed out.

His hat was scrunched down to his eyebrows. His cheeks bulged like an overblown balloon.

Finally, when everything felt just exactly right, he nodded.

Twisting sideways from the cage, the bronc burst into the arena, delivering a succession of hard thumps—once, twice, three times—so swiftly it was difficult to separate one buck from the next.

But Sandvick matched every move, his denim sticking to horsehide, his free hand waving in the air, outlasting the horse and the clock.

"Seventy-eight points!" the announcer cheered. Larry Sandvick went into the lead.

•   •   •

As the boys on bareback finished, the saddle-bronc finalists took their places behind the chutes.

Bud Longbrake's scores in the first two rounds had put him in a tie for twelfth place, the bottom spot among the qualifiers, what the cowboys call "the last hole."

Earlier that day, as the Longbrake family drove into the rodeo fairgrounds from the Plains Motel, the kids looked into the distance beyond the arena and saw a towering Ferris wheel, the swirling Octopus and dozens of other exciting rides. Their eyes lit up.

The rides weren't cheap. Maybe four or five dollars a pop.

Bud looked over at Lona and raised a hand to the side of his mouth. "If I do good," he whispered, "we'll take them to the carnival, okay?"

The Wyoming sun now blazed down on the splintery wood bleachers, where Lona and the kids watched intently as Bud, a hundred yards away, sank into his saddle.

Jay wore a striped red shirt with pearl buttons. Kayla wore pink nail polish, a white ribbon around a ponytail, a bright polka-dot shirt and purple slacks that matched her mom's.

•   •   •

Longbrake sat in chute number six, astride a swarthy gelding named Gentleman Jim.

The bronc charged fifteen yards into the arena, then found its spot on the turf. It bucked hard, as the cowboy rose in the saddle, his right hand clenching the braided reins, back straight, weathering every dive and swoop.

Gentleman Jim gave a jerk, changed direction, bucked again. Longbrake slid on the saddle, a minor slip, but one that would cost him some points.

The cowboy righted himself, matching the bronc's rhythm, his back straight, jaw tight, free arm waving. The last long second ticked away. The horn finally blared. And Longbrake landed on his feet, his face turned to the sky, waiting for judgment.

"Seventy points," the loudspeaker boomed.

Lona flinched. She knew it wasn't good enough. There would be no paycheck.

Jay hopped down the bleachers, two at a time, then raced toward the cowboy locker room, as fast as his five-year-old legs could carry him.

The locker room was a cement-floored, chicken-wired hut beneath the grandstands, posted with a sign "Cowboys Only!" But Jay slipped past a guard and sneaked over to his father's travel bag, a plastic garbage sack lying on the floor, and waited.

A few moments later, Longbrake walked in and plopped his saddle next to Jay, not saying a word. He pulled the leather straps over the saddle and fastened them tight. Then he poured his belongings into the plastic bag.

Jay sat cross-legged next to his kneeling father. The cowboy's eyes were shiny. His hands seemed to tremble.

Bud finally gave out a long breath. He looked over at his son and placed a hand on the boy's shoulder, giving it a squeeze.

"Hey Jay," he said softly, forcing a smile. "What do you say we go over to that carnival?"

•   •   •

Inside the locker room, the bull riders clomped nervously along the cement floor, fired with adrenaline.

But one of them, a wiry Montana cowboy, sat on a narrow wooden bench and slumped against the fence. He wasn't waiting for anything, except to go home.

Clint Branger had come to Cheyenne in first place in the bull riding standings. But a pair of mediocre scores in the first two rounds had failed to send him to the finals.

One disappointing rodeo, even the vaunted Frontier Days, wasn't going to hurt him much, though. With winnings of more than $60,000 so far this season, he had pretty much clinched a berth at Las Vegas.

Branger, a sliver of a cowboy with a chipped front tooth and a nose bent slightly to the west, was musing about the family's ranch back in Roscoe, Montana.

"Here I am having the year I always dreamed about," said the rodeo star, "and all I can think about is punching cows."

He glanced through the chicken wire, where horse hooves pounded past, leaving a trail of dust, and the tinny sound of the loudspeaker echoed somewhere in the distance.

"I mean, sometimes you wonder about this whole rodeo life."

He was talking about the broken bones and the busted marriages, the squandered bank accounts, the cheap motel rooms, the lonely highways and the greasy meals at fast-food joint after fast-food joint.

As he looked around at his fellow cowboys, Branger sometimes wondered where they were going, after it was all over.

He had known an aging bull rider, a man named Ronnie Rosin, who had neglected his ranch, neglected his family, neglected his health, all for the glory of rodeo. Still riding at "old-timers" rodeos into his fifties, Rosin was finally killed by a bull.

"I sat in a bar one time and he talked about his life," Branger said. "And he put his face in his hands and cried.

"I don't want to end up like that."

With a ranch to go home to, Branger knew he was luckier than most cowboys. But he sometimes worried about staying away too long, afraid what he might find when he returned.

The Branger ranch, which had been in the family for four generations, lay at the foot of the Beartooth Mountains, a 3,000-acre spread of grassy fields, echoing canyons and thick stands of quaking aspen, along the whispering banks of the East Rosebud River.

It used to be land that hardly anybody wanted: too rocky for planting crops, too rugged for easy cattle herding, too many miles from civilization to be commercially useful.

But places like Roscoe had lately been discovered. In the last few years, people with a deep appreciation for the beauty of the land, and even deeper pockets, had come to Montana with the kind of covetous look in their eyes that Indians must once have seen on the faces of white settlers.

Real estate brokers were peddling the "Western experience" to rich urbanites, mostly from California. And cow pastures near the Branger home were being sold and carved into ranchettes. Imported cars now zoomed along the country roads, making it difficult for a rancher to move his cattle without risking his herd, or his neck. The higher land values brought higher property taxes.

And more often all the time, somebody in a fancy, rented four-wheel-drive vehicle drove up the Brangers' dusty driveway, and knocked at the door to ask, "How much?"

Clint's father, Chris, had been listening to some mighty tempting offers: millions of dollars for a ranch that had never provided an easy life, and certainly not an affluent one.

If he sold out, he could retire with a bundle. And his two sons would be fixed for life.

"Don't do it," Clint told his father. "I want to ranch. I want to be a cowboy."

•　　•　　•

Branger rose from the bench, stretched his arms and yawned. "Guess I'll go out and watch the bull riding," he said.

He took off a pair of sunglasses. One of his eyes bore a nasty shiner.

"A bull do that?" somebody asked.

"Nah," Clint answered.

A week or so ago, he explained, it had been raining up at the ranch. So he decided to go drinking at a local bar, a place where all the faces used to be familiar.

The jukebox was good and loud. And he'd had a few beers too many. He decided to do a little dancing on a tabletop. But his feet were a bit wobbly. He tumbled over and landed in the lap of a customer, who was not amused.

"He was big and I'm little," Branger explained.

"He figured he could dot me and get away with it. And he was right."

17

In the musty locker room of the Mesquite Arena, a four-year-old boy asked his daddy to lift him up so he could pee into the urinal.

Joe Wimberly started to bend toward his son, then flinched.

"I'm sorry," said the cowboy, who had never felt so powerless in all his life. "I can't."

Pain was shooting through his neck like flames. Muscle spasms rippled up and down his back. And that wasn't even the worst of it.

Earlier that Saturday night, through the remarkable luck of the computer draw, Joe had been paired up once again with Dodge Dakota, the vicious bull no cowboy had yet been able to ride. It was a second chance at salvation, another shot to win the $10,000 prize and save the house.

But an instant after the chute gate was pulled open, the bull had slammed Joe and his dreams to the dirt, a crash so violent that the cowboy could barely make his way back to the rails.

The first time Joe had been flung from Dakota, he had looked up toward Paula and mouthed an apology. This time he just hung his head. He did not want to have to look her in the eye.

The little boy looked up from beneath his cowboy hat at his hurting father.

"Daddy," he said bravely, "I'll ride that Dodge Dakota for you."

•   •   •

When they couldn't put it off any longer, Joe and Paula sat the kids down in the living room to break the news. "It looks like we're gonna get to move," Joe said with a manufactured smile, trying to make the whole thing sound like fun.

"What do you mean?" said Casey, who was nine, old enough to detect sugarcoating when she heard it. "I don't want to move."

"It'll be all right," he said. "You'll see."

When the girl saw tears in her mother's eyes, she understood this wasn't what any of them really wanted.

In the morning, Joe called the newspaper and placed an ad in the house-for-sale section.

•   •   •

Joe was scrambling. He shod horses. He entered jackpot bull riding contests. And he organized a rodeo school featuring an authority on riding bulls and breaking bones: himself.

To draw students, he mailed flyers to Western-wear stores all over Texas, announcing his two-day clinic of "professional bull riding instruction" for a fee of $200 apiece, which included room, board and what he called tuition. Six young wanna-be cowboys signed up.

He hired two bullfighters to rescue tangled-up riders, bought food and drinks for everybody and rented an old shack in the countryside with a pen out back. He was able to borrow most of the bulls, since the local ranchers were always calling Joe to come look at some angry critter that had hooked a pickup truck or rammed a hole in a fence. A good bucking bull can bring four times what the slaughterhouses will pay.

On a wickedly hot Saturday morning, the six novices sat on the scrub grass near mesquite trees in rapt attention, while the real live cowboy expounded from a rocking chair on the rickety porch of the shack.

"You can always tell a bull rider by lookin' under his chin," Joe began his lecture, pointing to his own scarred, chewed-up flesh. "But there ain't nothin' on the outside that makes a bull rider. It's all on the inside. You get 'em all shapes and colors. All nationalities and religions. And some with no religion at all. If you're honest with yourself, you'll know when it's time to get on a bull. And when it ain't."

All of them had ridden bulls before, usually at somebody's ranch. But none had ever competed in a professional rodeo. And that's where they wanted to be. None were over twenty-five. The youngest had just turned sixteen. One of the men was a guard for the Texas Corrections Department, searching for work with a little more glamour. A couple were unemployed and uneducated, but were tough as nails, and so figured they had the résumé for rodeo.

"I've had both of my ears tore off ridin' bulls," Joe said matter-of-factly, as a few of the beginners seemed to squirm a little at the image. "Every one of my chewin' teeth is cracked. And there ain't a bull rider goin' down the road that don't have knee problems."

"Now you might be thinkin' it's all worth it for the glory. But let me ask you all a question. How many of you know the name Corey Snyder? Give me a show of hands."

A few of the cowboys scratched their heads. Nobody raised a hand.

"Well, he won the world in 1983. And not a one of you has ever heard of him.

"There's a few other things you ought to think about, too. There's plenty of ruined marriages and lonely kids because of rodeo. Darned near lost a wife myself. I got so I was concentratin' too much on the bulls, and not thinkin' about what's really important in life.

"Now I got two goals for my rodeo career: When I'm finished, I want to still have my teeth. And I want to still be married."

He looked out over the crew.

"Any questions. If not, then let's go buck some bulls."

•   •   •

As the bulls snorted in their pens, Joe jumped the rail and resumed his lecture to his students on the safe side of the fence.

"When you think of a West Texas cowboy, you think of a strong man who's short on words and long on action," Joe told them. "It's good to remember: Nobody ever stuck a foot in a shut mouth. And look like a cowboy. Wear a good pair of boots, some Wranglers and a Western shirt. If we're gonna play cowboy, we ought to dress the part.

"It's also important to keep a good mental attitude at all times. Now, this ain't always easy to do. Let's say, for instance, a friend comes up before the rodeo and says, 'Oh no, you drew Exorcist.'

"Well, you just smile a little and say, 'Yep.'

"And then you can just think about that rodeo last Friday night, the one where you rode real good. You can talk about that and how you figure on ridin' the same way today. Don't worry about that other fellow. He don't really care what you say anyway. He just wants to visit."

Joe reached through the rails and slapped a hand across the back of a muscular gray Brahma.

"Get used to lookin' at your bull. Size him up. And never leave your chaps on the rail. The bull's apt to come around and hook 'em. He wants a little taste of that cowboy even before things get started.

"Now when you get on the bull, keep your butt cocked to one side. If you're settin' in the middle, you might get jerked straight down over his head.

"And always be careful in the chute. He'll buck you off anytime. The only time you can relax is when the bull is in the back alley. And hold on to the pipe rail, or you might lose a tooth."

He flashed a gap-toothed smile. And everybody laughed nervously.

"Keep your spurs roughed up, but not sharp. You want it to just grab the skin and ripple up a little bit. But you don't want the rowel to slice the skin. You don't want to get off a bull and have him lookin' like he's been in a fight with a wildcat.

"Remember, you're in business with the stock contractor. And if you hurt his bull, he ain't gonna like you very much."

The cowboy hats nodded.

"Hold on to the bull rope tight. You're holdin' on to it for survival, for your life. And when the bull throws you, don't lie flat on the ground. I don't care if your bones are hurtin' and the wind's knocked clean out of your chest. Get up and get movin'. Even if you can only get up on your hands and knees, I want you diggin' and pullin' to get back to that fence. 'Cause that bull is gonna come back and squish you.

"But you got to be cool, too. If that bull's clear at the other end of the arena, on his way out the gate, I don't want to see you in a dead run for the fence. Now we got a couple of good bullfighters here. If you get hung up or trapped under a bull, they'll run in and help.

"But the bullfighters can't always be quick enough. So let's have a little prayer before we start."

Joe closed his eyes. And the young cowboys closed theirs.

"Father," he said, "we ask that you watch over the cowboys and the livestock. We ask that you put your angels all around us. And that we come out of this without incident."

Heads bowed, the cowboys all said "Amen."

On the desolate patch of Texas plains, the sun blazed unforgivingly. And a hawk circled overhead.

•   •   •

"Get up!" Joe hollered. "Get up! Get up! Get up!"

But the cowboy was trapped. He lay on the ground, between the stomping hooves of the bull, who stared down and snorted for the kill.

Two bullfighters in greasepaint and baggy pants slapped at the bull, trying to distract him. But the animal lowered his head at the cowboy, helpless between its stomping hooves.

With its snout, the bull rolled the cowboy over in the swirling dust, like a crumpled wad of paper, and finally reared back with hooves in the air, ready to pounce.

Just as the hooves came swinging down, the cowboy freed himself, jerked to his feet and dashed for the rails, where two other men pulled his shuddering body to safety.

"I was leanin' too far," the cowboy huffed. "Didn't have control, I guess."

"You all right?" Joe asked, looking into his eyes, making sure he wasn't knocked goofy.

"Oh yeah," said the cowboy, as blood gushed from his nose. "I'll get it right next time. You'll see."

The next few cowboys took their turns, getting spilled as soon as they came out of the chute, but averting disaster.

Joe went over everybody's ride. Some had a little more learning to do than others, he said, but they all got high marks for toughness.

The cowboys smiled broadly. It was time to ride some more.

"Owww!" came a high-pitched scream.

Joe looked around. He saw little McKinnon, wearing jeans and boots, but no shirt, racing around in a circle and screaming in pain.

Joe jumped the rails and raced over to get him.

"A bee got me," the boy wailed. "He stung me."

Joe lifted the boy into his arms and gave him a hug.

"Aw, I know it hurts," Joe said sympathetically, as he planted a kiss on the sore arm. "I'll get that mean old bee for you."

•   •   •

After the cowboys had taken another round of rides, Joe told everybody to stop for lunch.

"That old beatin' sun gets hard on the bulls and hard on the cowboys," he said. "And it gets hard on the teacher, too. Let's go inside and cool off for a spell."

They traipsed back to the shack and plopped down on the floor, talking excitedly about their conquests. "I wasn't exactly scared," one young man explained to another. "Just real nervous."

Paula was in the kitchen, heating a big pot of beans and some hot dogs for the hungry wranglers. A potbellied stove sat near the doorway. And the walls were covered with the trophies of hunters: the heads of a mountain goat, a wildcat and a deer with a cowboy hat on its antlers.

Eight years ago, Paula and Joe had lived in this cabin, back when they were saving to buy the house in Cool. It was rough living, but tolerable since they knew they would soon have a place of their own. On the day they moved out of this rickety place and drove down the dirt road, she thought they would always joke about the times they lived in a place so bleak.

Now she was staring into a pot of beans and worrying that they might end up right back where they started. Except that now they had three little kids, asking questions that were hard to answer.

The cowboys gulped down the chow, then hurried back to the bulls. There were several more hard falls. Darkness finally swept over the plains. And the tired crew retreated to the shack.

Somebody brought along a week-old newspaper. It carried a short article about the rodeo accident the week before in Terrell, Texas. A bull rider named Greg White got tangled in the rope, and then kicked in the head. He was rushed to the hospital, and pronounced dead on arrival. He was fifteen years old.

"It happens," said one of the cowboys.

They ate dinner and thanked Paula for her good cooking. And then everybody settled around the television to watch two videos that Joe had picked out: *My Heroes Have Always Been Cowboys* and *Desperados*.

18

AS **THE LITTLE** yellow Cessna airplane navigated its way toward Omak, Washington, the radio crackled with warnings from air traffic controllers.

On the ground below, ponderosa pines ignited and popped like matchsticks. Balls of fire leaped from tree crown to tree crown, like a mad relay race. Thick plumes of black smoke clouded the skies.

The Northwest had experienced the warmest winter on record, and then the driest spring in more than a century, leaving the timberlands so parched that even a tiny cigarette spark could start a monstrous blaze. In the last few months, nearly 30,000 fires had devoured a million acres of forest.

Scrunched in the back seat of the plane, Larry Sandvick snoozed, dreaming about rodeo.

In the dream, Sandvick was flying to a big contest, and he was late. The plane was drawing close to the arena. But it didn't descend. It just circled and circled. Soon it was too late, and the rodeo started.

Trapped inside the plane, Sandvick could only peer out the narrow window, looking down on the other bronc riders, now bolting from the chutes, one after the other, competing for first place, as he floated helplessly in the sky.

•   •   •

"Wake up, Lar," said a fellow cowboy, jiggling Sandvick's leg. "We're here."

With several big rodeos scheduled on the same August weekend, but a thousand miles apart, driving between contests was impossible. Sandvick and two South Dakota cowboys, Merle Temple, of Porcupine, and Mark Garrett, of Spearfish, were competing at the Omak Stampede on Saturday, and were scheduled to ride in Colorado on Sunday afternoon, just fifteen hours later.

So they hired a plane, at $65 an hour, which was piloted by a lanky, fifty-three-year-old former bareback rider named Johnny Morris, a Montana rancher who subsidized his struggling cattle operation by shuttling rodeo cowboys.

"Tray tables up," announced Morris, with a grin, as he set down the little yellow plane, which was about the size of an old Cadillac, and traveled just a bit faster.

•   •   •

The big draw at Omak was not the cowboys on bucking horses or the stomping bulls.

It was the "World Famous Suicide Race," a spectacular stunt drawn from the Old West, or at least from old westerns.

A herd of mounted riders, all of them Indians, would race off a cliff, tumbling and scrambling down the steep, brushy hillside, charge across the Okanogan River and then gallop into the rodeo arena to the screaming cheers of thousands of spectators.

In the Suicide Race in 1984, seven horses and one man were killed in the stampede. Experts on safety, as well as animal cruelty, have frowned on the event, which the rodeo program boasted had been featured on the television show *Ripley's Believe It or Not*.

In a nod to the concerns about safety, stringent new rules had been added to the Suicide Race: Contestants must be sober, be at least sixteen years old, and wear life jackets.

The promoters of the event conceded that it was wildly dangerous. Why else would tens of thousands of paying spectators flock to the obscurity of northern Washington? But they pointed to a higher cultural purpose. It was, according to the rodeo program, "a sort of rite of passage" for young Indians.

And there was a splendid by-product: "All of this exposure has created a tourism boom. . . . This generates dollars to the local economy."

•   •   •

As the Indian racers took their places high atop the bluff, thousands of giddy spectators watched from the grandstands, from the banks of the river, from the rooftops of distant houses, cheering wildly, like gawkers beneath a man on a ledge hollering, "Jump! Jump!"

The mounted Indians, distant silhouettes in the fading sun, answered the dare with raised fists and piercing screams that echoed through the valley: "Yeeee-haaaa!"

One spectator, a bare-chested visitor from Malibu in sandals and pink-framed sunglasses, turned to a local man in a cowboy hat and boots and asked, "Why do you suppose they do it?"

"Aw hell," the local answered. "You do this once. And for the rest of your life, you can tell everybody you're a real man."

The starter's gun cracked. The horses, after a kick in the ribs, started their fast gallop, and the riders howled in reckless fury.

Hooves pounded toward the edge, leaving a trail of dust, as the high-pitched whinny of twenty horses cried in startled recognition of their next steps, and the fans roared in delicious, vicarious fright.

The drop was sudden and steep—225 feet down the bluff to the river. The horses struggled at the last moment to rear back against gravity, legs pedaling like bicyclists' in the air, careening and sliding down the hillside, stabbing desperately for traction on the slope.

The first few horses finally hit the river, splashing across to the opposite bank. But a few yards behind, one of the horses stumbled and crashed, then recovered and dashed away, leaving its rider alone on the ground, where one horse trampled over him, and then another, and another.

"Did that man get killed?" a little girl asked her mother.

"Oh no, honey," said the woman, with a chuckle, as she pointed toward the man, rising to his feet, dazed, creeping to safety. "He's just going to be a little sore for a while."

•   •   •

Sandvick and the other cowboys trudged along a gravel path toward the arena, their bareback rigging slung over their shoulders. And a voice called out from the parking lot:

"Hey there, Lar!"

Sandvick looked around for the voice, and finally spotted its origin. "Duane!" he answered. "Whad'ya doin'?"

"Just trying to stay alive."

For Duane Hargo, just trying to stay alive was a full-time occupation. He was a rodeo clown, or what the cowboys call bullfighters.

In a rodeo crowd, Hargo always stood out, even if he wasn't wearing his red leotards, baggy pants and goofy hat with a green plume. Hargo, who went by the moniker "The Amazin' Raisin," was one of only a handful of black cowboys in rodeo.

As a teenager growing up in Los Angeles, he had never seen a rodeo, which he figured was a wild spectacle of big, brawny, beered-up white men with thick country twangs, not exactly the safest place for a young black guy.

But during a summer job for a rodeo contractor in Riverside, where he fed livestock and mended fence, he ran across a black rodeo cowboy.

"You're a what?" Hargo asked the black man in disbelief. "Cowboys are all white guys."

"No," the man told him. "There have always been black cowboys, even in the Old West. You just don't see them in the movies."

The rodeo cowboy, who was a bullfighter, said he was getting on in years and would soon be giving up the trade. He said he had always hoped, when he retired, that "some young brother" would step in and take his place.

"I've seen you working around here," the cowboy told young Hargo. "And you're hip to the stock."

•   •   •

In the contestants' dugout, Sandvick wrapped tape around Mark Garrett's hand—his thumb had been bent completely backward in a jerk on a horse a few weeks before.

In the first weeks of the season, Mark had been laid up with a broken back suffered in a fall while breaking a colt, and Sandvick had traveled with his brother, Marvin.

But now Marvin was home ailing, with torn ligaments in both knees, and Mark was back on the rodeo trail. He was hardly the picture of health himself, though, hobbling to the rodeo arena on crutches.

He had broken three bones in his right foot in the "Days of '47" rodeo at Salt Lake the previous month. But he was sitting in eighteenth place in the standings, so he couldn't afford to miss any contests. He was locked in a virtual tie with Sandvick.

"How's that feel, buddy?" Sandvick asked, as he finished the tape job on Mark's thumb.

"I think it'll work," he replied. "Thanks a lot, Lar."
Sandvick gave him a wink and a slap on the back.

•   •   •

Omak, a town of 4,100 just north of Grand Coulee Dam, had always relied on the riches of the earth: timber, mining, agriculture. And the rodeo was a tribute to the Old Ways, as much as the Old West.

But in recent years, waves of newcomers had been migrating to this land of pristine beauty. The traditional methods of survival here, which the locals called "working the land," had lately come under attack as "extractive" and "exploitative." The newcomers often belonged to the Sierra Club, never the Cattlemen's Association.

There were new restrictions on cattle grazing around Omak. Nearby forests had been shut down to loggers, in deference to the spotted owl. The rodeo itself had come under criticism. Even the art of the West seemed to be losing favor.

"Our art is dismissed by the elite, anymore," said Richard Beyer, a rangy, sixty-seven-year-old sculptor in a cowboy hat, whose aluminum-cast works were being exhibited in a show near the rodeo grounds. "Western art stands for the affirmative, for the power of life, for the struggle against the elements. It's not nihilistic, not snide. It's my grandpa driving a five-legged stud to pasture in the rain. Or a family in a trailer park, whipped by the winds, waiting for salvation. But people don't want that sort of thing anymore. Western art is just too, I don't know, too real, I guess. You can look at it and know what it is. I guess people think that's too simple nowadays."

•   •   •

The loudspeaker played both the national anthem and "O Canada," a courtesy for the many fans who had traveled to Omak from across the border in British Columbia, about sixty miles away.

In the dugout, Mark Garrett visited with his father, Jack, a former bronc rider himself, who has lived in Washington since the divorce some twenty years before.

The boys' mother later married a Wyoming rancher, and Marvin and Mark grew up working the fields, waiting for the day they would take over the land. But then came the hard times. Now the ranch belongs to somebody else.

The first bareback rider bolted from the chutes, then crashed hard, face first, a wicked spill.

"He's gonna be fine," the announcer assured the fans, who didn't seem to be terribly worried. "He's just sayin' to himself, 'I'm so happy to be here in central Texas tonight.' "

The fans roared with laughter. The bareback rider staggered back to the rails.

Merle Temple, the other cowboy on the Cessna, was next in the chutes. He was also chasing a berth in Las Vegas, sitting in the standings just a few hundred dollars apart from Larry and Mark.

"Come on, Merle," hollered Sandvick, as he clenched one hand on the rail and waved the other in the air. "Come on, Merle."

Temple came through with a splendid ride. The judges gave him a score of eighty points.

"Let's give that cowboy a hand," the announcer bubbled. "You know, these cowboys' hearts are as starvin' for praises as they are for raises."

Garrett leaned his crutches against a wall in the dugout and climbed aboard his bronc. With his right foot aching and his right hand so sore he could barely clench the handhold, he gave the nod to start the action.

He burst into the arena, as secure on the bucking bronc as if he had been nailed to its hide. The fans would never have guessed how much he hurt.

"Eighty-three points!" the announcer called.

From atop his horse, Sandvick had been cheering for Garrett. But now he had to attend to his own business. He was astride a muscular bay named Guildy Cat, an awesome, lightning-quick bronc that was guaranteed to deliver a wild ride, and a gaudy score, if only the cowboy could last the eight long seconds.

Just a few weeks earlier, the Cat had thrilled the crowd at the Calgary Stampede in Canada, where it danced a cowboy to the highest rodeo paycheck in all of North America—a cool $50,000.

There wasn't that kind of money on the line tonight. But a sensational ride would reward Sandvick with a couple of thousand bucks—and a slew of points.

Guildy Cat kicked against the metal cage, banging so loud it sounded like gunfire. Jostling on the horse's back, Sandvick pressed another wad of tobacco inside his cheek, like a squirrel hoarding nuts.

The bronc grew calm for a moment. And Sandvick settled into his comfortable position. Finally, he nodded. The flank strap jerked tight. The horse shot past the open gates in a whoosh.

Guildy Cat galloped so hard and so fast it seemed as if somebody had slipped amphetamines into the feed trough. The cowboy bounced on the horse's back, a vibrating blur, the muscles in his forearm rippling in a struggle to hang on.

The crowd went wild. It didn't take a rodeo expert to see that this was no ordinary bucking horse.

But this was no ordinary cowboy either, at least not tonight in the twilight of Omak. His spurs pumped an answer to every vicious buck. His face strained in gritty defiance. His free hand thrust triumphantly in the air. No matter what the horse did to lose him—swoop, dart, jerk—Sandvick wasn't going anywhere, except to the pay window.

"Can you believe this, ladies and gentlemen!" the announcer roared above the ruckus of the erupting grandstands. "A score of eighty-seven points! That's right! Eighty-seven points!

"We have a winner in the bareback riding. Let's hear it for the young man who wowed us tonight—Larry Sandvick."

He climbed aboard a saddle horse for the victory trot around the arena, tipping his hat to the applauding fans.

Back in the dugout, Garrett leaned his armpits on the crutches and freed his hands to clap. Standing beside him, Temple gave a loud whistle and a celebratory hoot.

A cowboy came along and offered Temple a beer. After pausing for a long moment, he finally answered, "No thanks."

He hadn't had a drink in forty days. He was trying hard to make it forty-one.

The airplane pilot stood behind the cowboys, his face lighting up like a billboard in Times Square.

"Well," he crowed, as he spat a glob of tobacco juice on the ground, "I reckon my boys did pretty good tonight."

19

T HE BIG FORD LTD jumped a curb, spun its wheels in a grassy ditch, passed a dozen stalled cars, then swerved back onto the county road, sneaking in between two cars, missing a crash by a whisker.

"Oh yeah!" Sandvick piped from the back seat. "Now this is rodeo-ing!"

Jack Garrett sat behind the wheel. He was giving the cowboys and their pilot a lift to the little Cessna at the Omak airport. The traffic leaving the rodeo was thick, and he didn't feel inclined to sit still in any traffic jam.

"Enough of this bullshit," he grumbled, as he wheeled the LTD into the left lane, speeding ahead of the traffic, as the cowboys hooted and marveled at his daring.

But a police officer, standing up ahead with a raised palm, was not quite so impressed.

"What seems to be the problem here?" he asked.

"Got some rodeo cowboys in here, officer," the driver replied. "They need to get agoing. Got a plane waitin' for 'em."

"Oh, I see," said the Omak cop, his tone friendly all of a sudden. "Darned good rodeo this year. Yes it was. How'd you fellas do?"

"This here cowboy won first in the bareback," Jack said, pointing toward Sandvick, who leaned forward with a humble, law-abiding nod.

"That right?" said the cop admiringly. "You know, I got a little plane myself, just a little puddle jumper. What kind's yours? Is it pressurized?"

"Naw," said Johnny Morris, the pilot, as he leaned over from the passenger side. "It ain't even turboed."

After more small talk, the cop wished the cowboys good luck and waved the LTD ahead, sailing past the backed-up cars on its way to the airport.

In the back seat, Sandvick turned to his friends with a skeptical expression.

"How the hell," he asked, "can a cop afford an airplane?"

•   •   •

Johnny radioed ahead. He was told to modify his route. Smoke from the forest fires was making travel in some parts treacherous.

It was about ten o'clock on Saturday night. The plane was headed toward Colorado to drop Sandvick off at the airport in Vail, for the Lake County rodeo, scheduled to start just after noon on Sunday. The others were going on to the Pike's Peak or Bust rodeo in Colorado Springs.

They would try to get about halfway tonight, stopping in Idaho Falls, Idaho, before heading back into the sky at daybreak.

In the darkness, the plane soared to the south and east, as the cowboys tried to talk over the rumble of the engine. Across the expanse below, the lights of ranches were scattered in the wilderness like jewels on a velvet carpet. Every now and then, a cluster of lights would appear, a little Western town, shining like a cruise ship in the middle of an empty sea.

As they crossed the Columbia River, the pilot motioned for his passengers to look down at Grand Coulee Dam, the huge, concrete trophy of man's mastery over the wild forces of nature, a triumph the bronc riders could appreciate.

"That sure is one neat bastard," said Sandvick, as the others gazed and nodded.

•   •   •

The plane touched down in Idaho Falls after midnight. The airport was closed.

A cab pulled up along the curb. "Comfort Inn, please," said Temple, as the cowboys hopped inside.

Sandvick squeezed into the front seat next to the driver. "Ain't this nice and cozy," he said with a wink and a bat of the eyes.

"Don't get fresh," the cab driver growled. "I've got a long night ahead of me."

At the entrance of the motel, the driver deposited the cowboys, rolled his eyes and muttered something unflattering about rodeo, then screeched away.

Loaded down with a week's worth of clothes and their rodeo tack, the cowboys marched to the registration counter.

"Reservation for Temple," said Merle.

The desk clerk looked up at the gang of cowboys, then looked back down at the computer screen.

"There must be some mistake," he said. "The reservation is for just one room."

"No mistake," said Temple. "That's us."

"But you're a bunch of grown men," the clerk said.

"Yep," said Temple, "pretty much, anyway."

The clerk reluctantly handed over the key, and the cowboys went off in search of room 227.

There were two beds in the room. The cowboys dropped their bags and started to figure out sleeping arrangements. According to rodeo custom, they flipped coins to see who took the bed and who took the floor.

"Aw shit," said Sandvick, "let's just split the sheets."

So they pulled the mattresses from the box springs, then laid the bedding from wall to wall.

"I'll call downstairs for the wake-up," said Temple, picking up the phone.

"Better make it five-thirty," said Johnny. "We got a long way to go."

"That's too damn early," said Merle. "Hell, it's one o'clock now. Let's make it for six."

"Five-thirty," said Sandvick, siding with the pilot.

"Six," said Merle.

"Five-thirty."

"Six."

"Aw, hell, boys," said Johnny. "We're wastin' our time squawking. Go ahead and make it for six, Merle. But we'd better hustle come morning."

Tired, unshaven and dirty, the men stripped to their shorts and crawled under the sheets.

•   •   •

It was still dark outside when the motel room phone screamed like a fire truck siren.

Sandvick sat up and rubbed his eyes. "You know," he said, "I don't feel too bad."

"Well sure," said Temple, "you had that extra half hour of sleep."

Sandvick groaned, then rolled off the mattress to get first in line for the shower.

Temple picked up the television clicker and switched it on.

"Hey," he shouted happily at a cartoon. "It's Fred and Barney."

"What are they doin' up so early," moaned Garrett, limping toward the sink with his shaving gear, one eye open.

Sandvick toweled himself off, then took the remote from Temple, who headed toward the bathroom.

He switched the channel to the sports station. It was a repeat of a golf championship, a game played somewhere with palm trees and sunshine.

"That's what we ought to be doing—playing golf and collecting some big checks," he said. "I'll bet those guys ain't staying in the Comfort Inn."

●   ●   ●

The ride to the airport took about six minutes. As they stepped outside, the air was dewy. The sun was creeping up in the sky, its soft rays bouncing against a silver grain elevator in the distance, perhaps the tallest structure in Idaho Falls. Johnny headed over to the plane, to get it warmed up.

They had had no supper the night before and were hungry as horses. They wandered inside the airport, looking for breakfast. At a vending machine, each bought a chocolate candy bar. Then they hurried out to the plane, where Johnny was waiting for his passengers.

●   ●   ●

The plane crossed into Wyoming, flying past Jackson Hole and the Shoshone National Forest, swept with pine trees like a soft green blanket.

"Hey, there's a herd of elk," Johnny said, as the plane floated over a clearing in the mountains.

"I can see a guy on horseback," said Sandvick.

As the plane headed south and east, the cowboys could see narrow, winding roads that seemingly dead-ended in nowhere. "Those are oil wells," Johnny explained.

"And you see that big black mound down there," he said. "That's an ant hill. I ain't fooling. Millions of 'em."

They passed over the continental divide, the mountain crest that serves as a traffic cop for the flow of all water in North America. Rain that falls on the east side of the divide eventually finds its way to the Atlantic Ocean. Rain that falls on the west side flows to the Pacific.

The Cessna crossed over Interstate 80, where a stream of Winnebagos and minivans from cities and suburbs back East rushed toward a summer vacation in the West.

Beyond the peaks, frosted even in August, fields of wheat looked like braided horse reins. Tall purple silos, stocked with grain, towered over little white clapboard farmhouses on acreage long ago fenced with barbed wire.

Grass as verdant as putting greens, in patterns like big bull's-eyes, marked land watered by the pivot arc, an irrigation system that turned arid cattle range into fertile croplands, and replaced cowboys with combines.

•   •   •

At the airport in Eagle, twenty miles from Vail, a building smaller than the Greyhound terminal in Denver, the cowboys got out to stretch, and to wish Sandvick good luck.

A worker at the airport with a shiny silver van gave Sandvick a lift to the rodeo. Eagle was close enough to Denver to attract some of the part-time cowboys, the "weekend warriors," who hold down regular jobs and compete for a lark.

One of them spotted Sandvick on the fairgrounds, trudging as wearily as if his boots were full of lead.

"Hey Sandwich," called Tom Neiley, with a wave.

Neiley, who lived in Boulder, looked less like a cowboy than a bond trader, which is what he was. But almost every weekend, he traded the glass-covered desk and computer terminal in a Denver skyscraper for a horse and a saddle in a dusty arena.

A native of Greenwich, Connecticut, and the scion of an old-money family, Neiley had moved to Scottsdale during high school. As a new kid in school, and a gawky one besides, he had struggled to break into the cliques of Scottsdale that distrusted outsiders, especially one with an Eastern accent.

But Neiley discovered a key to acceptance. He joined the school rodeo club, and soon proved that neither lack of size nor lack of twang could stand in the way of becoming a tough cowboy.

Even after finishing college and becoming a bond trader, he continued to compete in rodeos on weekends. In fact, after the stock market crash in October of 1987, he quit his job in disgust and joined the cowboy circuit full-time, with dreams of becoming the first MBA to win the saddle-bronc championship in Las Vegas.

But a year's worth of seedy motels and truck stop dinners was enough for Neiley. He returned to the world of high finance. Monday to Friday. Nine to five.

"Beautiful day for a rodeo," Neiley exulted.

"Yeah, I guess," Sandvick grumped.

•   •   •

As the little Cessna zoomed toward Colorado Springs, the view from the window soon changed. The alpine wilderness gave way to clogged highways and cookie-cutter subdivisions and the golden arches of Big Mac in every direction the cowboys looked.

The clock was nearing noon, and the time of the starter's gun. When the plane landed, the cowboys tried to hustle to the terminal, although Garrett's crutches slowed the pace.

From a pay phone, they called the rodeo secretary's office and asked for a cowboy named Bobby Logue.

"He don't think twice about calling us for a ride," Temple had whispered, a hand over the receiver, as he waited for Logue to come to the phone, "even if it's two in the morning."

Temple made the arrangements. And the cowboys rested on an airport bench, nervously watching the clock.

A half hour later, there was still no sign of Logue. They started to wonder if he was coming on horseback.

With the minutes shrinking, the cowboys realized they would not have time to get ready at the arena.

Garrett unzipped his gear bag and pulled on his riding boots, then spread his bareback rigging on the airport bench. He took a stainless steel file and smoothed the edges of his handhold, making it fit snugly to his grip. Temple did the same.

"Let's go," called a voice from the doorway. "We ain't got much time."

Logue had finally arrived.

•   •   •

The rodeo was moving a little behind schedule, as it turned out, so the cowboys had a few moments to relax.

The arena was nestled at the base of Pike's Peak, the jagged, snowcapped behemoth that a century ago inspired a visitor to sit down and jot the lines to a song that she named "America the Beautiful."

On the loudspeaker, the announcer boomed, "Are you proud to be Americans?"

A raucous cheer erupted in the grandstands.

"What a good-looking crowd!" the announcer said. "I think I see more people in cowboy clothes than ever before."

And the cheers thundered once more.

The arena was not far from the Professional Rodeo Cowboy Association corporate headquarters, so all of the brass was on hand.

The announcer introduced the commissioner of the sport, Lewis Cryer, the six-figure salaried boss of rodeo.

From under a big cowboy hat, Cryer waved to the cowboys and the crowd. Most of the contestants stood and removed their hats, out of respect.

But Garrett didn't budge. He was sitting on a wood bench, his crutches across his lap.

"How's that thumb?" someone asked Garrett.

"Well, if somebody had handed me a banana," he replied, "I couldn't have got 'er ate."

A crew from ESPN, the cable television station, was there to film the rodeo. When a PR man for the rodeo saw Garrett hobble to the arena on crutches, he rushed over to the television crew. "I've got a great shot for you," he said. "Why don't you interview a cowboy who came on crutches."

The television people liked the idea. But the PR man had to check with Garrett.

"I think it would be great," the publicist told Garrett. "A cowboy on crutches. And it's ESPN! But if you really, really don't want to do it, all you have to do is say no."

"No," the cowboy answered.

"You can think about it for a while if you want."

"No."

The disappointed PR man walked away.

"They can go ahead and interview me if they want," Garrett muttered. "But not with the crutches. I don't want nobody's pity. Heck, I'd rather be sittin' at home, mendin' up. But I'm sittin' in eighteenth place. I got no choice but to keep going."

He stood up, bit his lip, and used one of his crutches as a cane to make his way to the bucking chutes.

20

"**H**E CAME LIKE a whirlwind across the dry flat," the poem on the wall of the tavern began, "stirring up the dust and the grass, causing all the inhabitants to take notice."

Above it was a photograph of a young man with a toothy grin and a mop of bright red hair.

In the sepia tones of Kaycee, a dusty little Wyoming town, Deke Latham was a neon billboard in flashing color. From the time he was in the fourth grade, when he popped the school bully across the chops, Deke was a hero to just about everybody who knew him, especially his younger brother, Craig. He could crack a joke and hoist a beer as well as anybody on the rodeo trail. But he was a cowboy who consoled as well as he caroused. He was never content until everybody in the crew was wearing a smile as big as his.

Deke grew up with barely two nickels to rub together, but he swaggered like a man with a million and eager to share it, convinced that he would live to hit the jackpot.

And he did. In the national finals in 1986, he won $34,000 in the space of a week. On the night he won his first check, he hustled to a Western Union and sent a round-trip plane ticket for Las Vegas to a cowboy friend who hadn't made the finals. And then he took his family and friends out for T-bone steaks in a fancy place on the Strip.

Grown men in Wyoming do not betray much emotion. But after Deke died, tears spilled down the windburned faces of Kaycee. And taciturn ranchers sat down and wrote poetry. The words of one local cattleman were framed inside the Hole-in-the-Wall Saloon:

> *A friend of ours has left us.*
> *But hey now, he's okay,*
> *And you can bet your bottom dollar,*
> *That he's spurrin' broncs today.*
>
> *I'm settin' here athinkin'*
> *And tryin' to shake the sorrow,*
> *Hopin' that it won't be true,*
> *When the sun comes up tomorrow.*
>
> *But I know this really happened,*
> *And we've lost a great comrade,*
> *And our only consolation,*
> *Is the good times that we've had.*
>
> *But there has to be a reason,*
> *And to my mind, it's reassurin',*
> *God must have some broncs up there,*
> *That damn sure need a spurrin'.*

• • •

Not long after Deke's death, some cowboys approached his mother with the idea of holding a rodeo in his honor in Kaycee.

"If it's going to have Deke's name on it," she told them. "I want it to be a good one."

• • •

The signpost for Kaycee claimed the population was 256. But the sign was a bit out of date, like much of the town, so the true number was probably a little lower.

Kaycee has been dwindling, more or less, for as long as anybody can remember. There once was a house on almost every section, or square mile, of land, and enough people to keep the grange halls jumping with Saturday night dances. But the smaller ranches couldn't survive in the changing agricultural economy. And hundreds of homesteads have been knocked down, or allowed to crumble, leaving vast open stretches, as lonely as heartbreak.

For a while in the late seventies and early eighties, central Wyoming boomed with the exploration of oil and gas. Oil jacks, known around here as horse heads, bobbed in the cattle pastures, and oil field workers, known as roughnecks, moved into new trailer parks. Old cow towns, like Edgerton and Midwest, were transformed into thriving little centers of oil business, until the energy bust left them virtually deserted. Kaycee never yielded much oil. There was no boom, no bust. Just a kind of steady drip of life slipping away.

A gas station sits near Interstate 25, the solitary filling station for fifty miles in either direction, the only thing that brings outsiders to Kaycee, and then for just a few minutes.

But one weekend a year, Kaycee gets noisy and crowded, as every store in town, including some that have been empty for years, posts a sign in the window to celebrate "The Deke Latham Memorial Rodeo," and the jukebox is turned full volume at the Hole-in-the-Wall Saloon, just the way the redheaded cowboy liked it.

It's a one-head rodeo, spread over two days. It doesn't pay much, only about $300 for first prize in each event. The attendance is minuscule, compared to most pro rodeos, since Kaycee is a long way past nowhere, and then some. But it draws some of the best rodeo cowboys in America, especially those who called Deke their friend.

It is a rodeo as pure as country rain. Spectators sit on wooden bleachers, blankets spread on the ground, lawn chairs and the tailgates of pickups backed up to the arena fence. The trucks that belong to ranchers are easy to spot, with their bug-splattered windshields and the rolls of toilet paper on the dashboards, for those times when the nearest bathroom is twenty miles away.

Some old-timers, who might not see another rodeo all year, hobble with canes and walkers. Young parents push baby strollers. Teenagers strut around like young guns, drinking deeply from tall cups of lemonade.

After the Saturday afternoon contest, everybody gathers around picnic tables for a dinner of roast beef, scalloped potatoes, rolls and iced tea. Then they drop off their kids at the Kaycee school, where eighth-graders volunteer to watch the children until two a.m. ("After that," a sign warns, "children will be raffled off"), and head over to the Kaycee Community Center, a tin shack painted yellow, for the poetry ball.

•   •   •

"I sat down to write a grocery list," said one rancher as he took his turn on the stage, "and it turned into a poem."

Another cattleman, who looked like Christmas in his red beard and green shirt, recited a poem about a daughter who had left the ranch for a university, where she became enthralled with sophisticated city ways, even vegetarianism. The poem was titled "College Ain't All Good."

A young sheep rancher picked at a guitar and sang, "There was a blizzard comin' on, and oh how I was wishin' I was home." A skinny man in a bolo tie yodeled. And an eighty-year-old woman in cowboy boots gave a reading. It was titled "Be Yourself."

"When I was young," she began, "the ladies said to me, take off those spurs and comb your hair. You know, I never wore a dress until my wedding day. I tell my children, and I tell you: Stand up straight and be you. If the Lord had wanted us to be all the same, he'd have made us like sheep."

Afterward, the metal folding tables were cleared to make a dance floor. A white-haired man twirled his wife in a pirouette, then leaned over to kiss her cheek. A family of five, dressed in matching Western shirts and cowboy boots, held hands as they jumped to the beat. A handsome young man, a former bull rider, with clear blue eyes and a jaw as square as a box, bobbed to the music under a big black Stetson, clapping his hands with the rhythm, from his seat in a wheelchair.

•   •   •

Five hundred miles from Kaycee, in a van rambling down an empty Idaho highway, Craig Latham sprawled across the back seat, trying to get some sleep.

It was ten o'clock on Saturday night. He was tired and sore from a bronc ride earlier that day in Ellensburg, Washington. Craig and Billy Etbauer, who sat behind the wheel, would have liked to pull off the road and nap. But they were slated to compete the next afternoon in Kaycee. If they were going to arrive in time for the Sunday performance, they couldn't spare any time. And missing Deke's rodeo would have been unthinkable.

Just the other day, somebody had asked Craig about Deke, and about their mother. "Is she doing all right these days, since the accident, I mean?"

"Oh," said Craig, shaking his head. "I don't think any of us will ever be right again."

Craig and Billy met through their older brothers, Deke and Robert. Both sets of brothers became best friends. And the year after Deke died, Craig traveled to rodeos with the Etbauer brothers. On their trips, they shared stories and talked so much about Deke they sometimes half expected to hear his voice pipe up and say, "Aw hell, fellas, I can tell you a real story."

Robert had never forgotten how Deke had wired him the plane ticket from Las Vegas. He had vowed he would pay him back. But he never got the chance. In Deke's obituary, a lot of cowboys were quoted saying what a great cowboy he had been. Robert told the reporter simply, "I loved him."

•   •   •

Nearly a century ago, Craig's great-great-grandparents, Charlie and Grace Graves, had packed up a covered wagon in Brewster, Nebraska, where the hog cholera had nearly wiped them out, and headed toward the promise of a new start in the West. A diary charted the way.

MAY 19, 1902: "Got stuck. Horses balked. No good. Had to pull them out. Killed a rattler."

MAY 26: "Fine hard frost last night. Two new calves on deck this morning. Fine feed. Stock doing well. Went fishing. Caught a small mess, good but few. Read some and had some singing. Very fine day."

MAY 31: "Camped at a Mr. Dees, a tough outfit. Had a son killed in Wyoming cattle rustling. (Buffalo gnats were real bad, in our eyes.)"

JUNE 8: "Fine land, but 3/4 deserted of life. Thrown aside are mowers, plows, cultivators, binders, headers, thrashing machines. There are a good many flocks of sheep here. It looks sad to see so many fine farms deserted, drouthed out. Farms a few years ago worth 12 to 16 hundred dollars are sold for a song. One sign had a thousand dollar farm for $120, after debts."

On July 1, 1902, after a journey of 474 miles that took fourteen months, they came upon a stretch of rugged land near the Red Fork River, in the crook of the Bighorn Mountains, and unhitched their horses for good.

•   •   •

As boys, Craig and Deke lived with their mother in a cabin of rough lumber on a rugged plateau on the Red Fork Ranch. There was no bathroom, no television, no telephone.

But there were horses for each of them, Prunes and Whiskey, which they first saddled as toddlers, and they cried every time they had to get off. They also scoured for old shells and arrowheads, legacies from the days when this land was the Dull Knife Battlefield.

Their granddad, Norris, whose mother was born in the covered wagon coming West, lived down country on the ranch and came up to teach them about horses and about the wilderness.

The fog sometimes engulfed the plateau for days, so thick it was impossible to know if you were riding uphill or down. Norris showed the boys how to roll a handful of rocks to navigate the way—rocks that kept rolling meant the terrain was sloping downward.

"When you grow up to be ranchers," he told them, "you'll have to know these things to survive."

21

A BRISK WIND raked the High Plains, fluttering the field grasses like the mane of a horse at full gallop. In the distance, a mountain rose at the flanks and dipped in the middle, like the seat of a saddle, where a flock of sheep grazed in the windbreak. The sky was mottled with gray, streaky clouds, and the air smelled like rain.

"Damn this wind," said Craig Latham, holding tight to his cowboy hat, as he stood behind the chutes, where the cowboys had gathered around noon.

"Yeah," said another cowboy, "it blew so hard yesterday it blew us right into the Hole-in-the-Wall."

The cowboys chuckled as they took their places behind the chute gates. A few of the cowboys, not slated to ride today, sipped cans of beer, a little hair of the dog.

A voice on the loudspeaker welcomed the crowd, and noted that Kaycee, on this weekend, was the third largest city in all of Wyoming.

"Let us now remember why we're here," the announcer said, his voice growing somber. "We come here not to mourn the death of our friend, Deke Latham, but to celebrate his life."

Next to the chutes, a table was loaded with prizes: a collection of elk teeth, a hand-tooled leather checkbook cover, a pair of custom chaps designed by Sandvick, and a rifle, the kind Deke used for hunting.

Across the fairgrounds, the spectators now stood silently, the wind swirling dust in the bleachers, as the loudspeaker played a song.

His cowboy hat over his heart and his eyes staring down at his boots, Craig Latham softly sang the words with Garth Brooks.

●　　　●　　　●

Larry Sandvick climbed into the saddle, then hopped up and down, his seat making a suction sound on the leather like he'd had too many beans for breakfast. Then he packed some chew in his jaw and nodded for the show to begin.

"Here's a cowboy," said the announcer, introducing Sandvick, "who is, well . . . uninhibited."

Sandvick had been riding like a wild cowboy the last few weeks, and living just the same. After a rodeo in South Dakota, he had scratched up his arms in a drunken fall over a barbed-wire fence trying to keep up with a young woman who was leading him into an empty field in the moonlight. A few days later, he was getting drunk in a Rapid City bar when his travel partner, Merle Temple, took umbrage at one of Larry's jokes and popped him in the nose.

But as the standings showed, he wasn't having any problems inside the arena, except for that one rather embarrassing fall from a saddle horse during a victory lap, which the editor of the *Prorodeo Sports News*, perhaps still annoyed about his phone interview from the john, couldn't resist sharing with her readers.

The bronc darted, and Sandvick hung tight, using a sixth sense to anticipate the horse's every move. When the horn blared, another paycheck was drawn up, just waiting for his signature.

●　　　●　　　●

In the saddle-bronc event, there were ten contestants. Latham was the last. More than any other event at Kaycee, this was what the spectators had come to see. It was Deke's event, and now Craig's. And it was the event that inspired the most respect among ranch cowboys.

As Craig gripped the reins, the horse between his legs, a skittish filly with wide brown eyes named Miss Ellie, whinnied nervously and slammed against the chutes.

"She ever been out before?" Latham asked a chute boss, as he tried to calm the horse with a stroke of a hand.

"Sure, had 'er up to an Indian rodeo. She bucked all them guys off."

Latham rolled his eyes. The horses used in amateur rodeos, he knew, could never be trusted. They often get spooked in the chutes, where the hazards are greatest, and then flip a cowboy or ram his legs against the metal.

The horse calmed just long enough for the gate to be pulled open. She darted into the arena, but did more browsing than bucking, looking like she was not quite sure she understood how rodeo worked.

Craig spurred hard, but it was a lackluster ride, brought to a merciful finish by the sound of the horn. The referees decided to give Craig a reride on another horse.

"We'll put you on Mini-Bear," an official told Craig.

Some cowboys along the chutes laughed. Poor Craig was going from bad to worse.

"That derned Mini-Bear," one cowboy whispered to Craig, chewing on his words, "he's the shits."

The cowboy and bronc did a brief dance across the turf, a ride that wasn't likely to be featured in any videos at rodeo training schools.

When it was over, Craig didn't listen for the score. The day was passing quickly. And he hadn't come to Kaycee for the horses.

He hustled back to the chutes, where he stood at the shoulder of his grandfather, who was sitting nimbly on a rail.

"Good ride, Craig," said Norris Graves, in his dependable appraisal of his grandson's work.

A burning cigarette jutted past the old man's white mustache. A telephone number was scrawled in pen on the back of his leathery left hand. And he wore an old frayed windbreaker, emblazoned with the words "Deke Latham—Contestant."

"Everybody had a real good time here yesterday," he told the young cowboy. "Sure wish you was here."

"You and me both, granddad," said Craig, who climbed the rail to sit beside him.

An uncle came by to slap Craig's back. An aunt gave him a kiss on the cheek and handed over a baby. He spat out his chew before leaning over to smother the child with kisses.

Craig's half brother, Scott, stood nearby, his eyes wide with adoration. He was sixteen years old, the son of Joyce and her second husband, Joe Reculusa, a Basque sheep rancher whose father had immigrated to Wyoming from the French Pyrenees.

"You should see the way these cowboys go," said Scott, who had recently gone along with Craig on a rodeo trip that stretched from Wyoming to Canada to Kansas and back to Wyoming. "They'll drive a hundred miles an hour."

Craig gave him a wink that said *Shhh*, and reached out to squeeze his half brother's bicep.

"Scrawny as chicken legs," he smiled. "Better start liftin' some weights. Got to be ready for football."

Scott said he wanted to learn to rodeo, despite his mother's protests.

"Well, you know the best way to learn," said the cowboy star. "Just go talk to granddad."

Somebody called out, "Hey Craig, you leaving right away?"

"Nah," he answered over his shoulder. And then he turned back to Scott and gave him another wink. "I'm gonna sit awhile, talk to my brother, and then go drink a beer."

•   •   •

The beer stand on the fairgrounds was raised four feet off the ground.

"I've bellied up to a lot of bars," said one cowboy, "but I ain't used to puttin' my chin on one."

"Oh?" somebody asked. "You never been on your knees in a bar?"

"Well"— the cowboy smiled— "I guess you got a point there."

Larry Sandvick ordered a large beer, and one for a friend. The friend reached into his pocket for a dollar bill. But Sandvick waved him off.

"I'll do the buying," he said, throwing his shoulders back. "Shit, I won three thousand dollars last week."

Before he got too comfortable, Sandvick needed to find Temple and go give a jump to Goldie, his duct-taped heap of a car. Apparently there were no hard feelings about the tiff in Rapid City. Larry was giving Merle the car to drive back to his home in Porcupine.

Sandvick didn't need old Goldie anyway. With his winnings, he had bought a big, midnight-blue Cadillac, a boat of a car that was only five or six years old. Larry was one high-flying cowboy these days. He was even wearing a Rolex watch, a prize he won at a rodeo in Utah, which set off the big Budweiser ring he wore on his finger.

"Better head over to the Hole-in-the-Wall," Larry announced abruptly, "before they drink all the beer."

•   •   •

As the cowboys clomped through the street toward the saloon, they passed Craig and his mother talking quietly in the shadow of a parked van. Joyce's long hair, a mix of brown and gray, was pulled back into a ponytail. She wore the buckle Deke won in the seventh round of the rodeo finals.

On the night he was killed, she had been driving on the road behind him, in the yellow school bus she drove part-time. She was coming back from a Christmas play in town, when she saw his van in the ditch.

Before her sons joined the rodeo circuit, Joyce had never seen much of the world, had never, in fact, traveled east of Gillette, just forty miles from the Red Fork Ranch.

Through rodeo, she had logged thousands of miles, driving from contest to contest to see her sons. She got to see the skyscrapers of Denver, the canyons of Arizona, the glitter of Las Vegas.

But ever since the night she found her son's body in the snow, she had wished that nobody had ever left the ranch at all.

The Sunday-afternoon sunlight was vanishing in the dusk. She rested a hand on Craig's shoulder, and he bent to listen to some whispered words. And then she wrapped her arms around the cowboy, and squeezed tight for a very long time.

•   •   •

Inside the bar, the rodeo cowboys and local ranchers were swigging beers and trading stories, as the jukebox blared and the pool table cracked with colliding balls.

One craggy rancher, with droopy eyes that matched his mustache, shook his head when a rodeo cowboy asked how cattle prices had been holding up.

"Tell you the truth," he said heavily, "I don't know how much longer we can hang in."

The auctioneer had come to town again just last week, and a ranch family had watched their belongings sold to the highest bidder.

As a younger man, the rancher was saying, he could buy a pickup for the profit on a single cow. Now it took more than ten cows. The consumers weren't eating meat like they used to. The banks didn't want to lend to marginal cattle operations anymore. Grazing fees were going up. They couldn't use poison on coyotes anymore. And now there was talk of bringing back the damned wolves.

In the sheep country of Wyoming, predators coud put a ranch out of business. The poisons were outlawed twenty years ago, over fears that bald eagles were eating the stuff. Since then, coyotes had been multiplying.

"It's that damned Walt Disney's fault," said another rancher, as the cowboys chuckled. "I'm serious. He made all those animals seem so fartin' cute. That's why we got all these animal rights people so stirred up. They think coyotes and wolves are like damned house pets.

"But they ain't ever walked out in the field, and seen a little lamb whose leg or nose had been chewed off by a coyote, layin' there in pain.

"And these environmentalists, they got a damned selective idea of what animal's okay to kill or not. They poison rats in the big cities, don't they? Shit, that don't seem fair. Ain't a rat in New York got just as much right to life as a coyote in Wyoming?"

•   •   •

On the other side of the room, a circle of cowboys were laughing so hard their eyes were watering—all of the cowboys except one.

"It ain't that funny," said Paul Peterson, a bronc rider, who had been bitten in the nipple by a bronc up at a rodeo in Canada.

"Bit you on the tit, did she?" one of the cowboys giggled, slapping his thigh as Peterson stood straight-faced. "Just clamped right on? Sucklin' up to mama?"

"When it's somebody else's tit, it's funny," said Peterson. "When it's your tit, it ain't so damned humorous."

Sandvick stood at the bar, feeling dry, or as dry as a man can feel after a half-dozen drinks. The bartender was busy. So Sandvick just walked around the bar and helped himself to a bottle on the shelf.

He took a swig of Cactus Juice, licked his lips, then raised the bottle in the air. "To Wyoming," he shouted. "Where the men are men. And the sheep are fuckin' nervous!"

Startled by the outburst, a rancher looked up to see what caused all the commotion. "Oh," he muttered, "it's just Larry."

A little mutt, whom Sandvick named Dogie, was running loose in the bar. "Come on, Dogie," the cowboy called out to the pup. "Let's go outside and see if we can find you some dog in heat. You need a little lovin' like the rest of us." Sandvick and Dogie scampered out the door, as the screen slammed behind, and a shouted "Yee-haw!" echoed in the night.

•   •   •

Craig hadn't intended to stay very long in the Hole-in-the-Wall, at least that's what he told his traveling partners. The cowboys were slated to ride the next day in Albuquerque, fifteen hours away. They wanted to go at least as far as Denver that night, where some friends had offered a couch and some space on the living room floor for a short nap.

But it wasn't easy to leave. As the hours passed, Craig motioned to Billy Etbauer that he would have just one more beer. As the other cowboys danced and shot pool, he stood near a post and talked with his granddad.

He told him about a horse up in Canada that was so tricky it bucked him off. "I've had a few of those," said Norris Graves, shaking his head, and he recalled a horse that dumped him in the fields of the Red Fork Ranch so many years ago.

Norris had once dreamed about becoming a rodeo cowboy himself. But he was needed around the ranch, especially after his father died. So he stayed home.

"I always thought about going down the road, like you," he told Craig.

Craig replied that he'd always dreamed about staying on the ranch.

•   •   •

In the moonlight, Craig and his partners walked toward the van. Joyce came outside to give her son one last hug.

"Be careful," she said.

•   •   •

The van rolled out of town, passing the rodeo grounds and a wooden sign that marked the spot of the Johnson County Cattle Wars, which reached a bloody conclusion 100 years ago.

Cattle barons, many of them Englishmen, had come to Wyoming in the middle 1800s, staking out vast sections of land, and warning newcomers to stay away. These rich men formed the Wyoming Stock Growers Association, built sprawling homes on the High Plains, hired cowboys from Texas to do the dirty job of tending to cattle, and drew up bylaws that forbade any workingman from trying to start his own herd.

But a handful of cowboys rebelled against the rules. The brashest was Nathan D. Champion. He and his crew—Nicholas Ray, Ben Johnson and William Walker—lived in the KC cabin, which would become the site of Kaycee. The barons hired a posse of gunmen to put an end to the rule-breaking cowboy.

"Me and Nick was getting breakfast when the attack took place," Champion wrote in his diary on the morning of April 9, 1892.

Champion held out for hours, and then made a run for it. Barefoot and hatless, he was cut down by a hail of bullets as he fled. He died clutching his diary, "soaked by his heart's blood," a newspaper reported.

"It don't look as if there is much show of my getting away," the last words in the diary began. "Goodbye boys, if I never see you again."

22

"**OHHH,**" **CRAIG MOANED** from the back seat of the speeding van. "I think I'm gonna die."

"There's another beer up here somewhere," needled Billy, who had been drinking Coke all night at the Hole-in-the-Wall. "Maybe that'll help."

The highway jutted east at the Platte River, then looped around like a horseshoe, threading between the Medicine Bow Forest and Thunder Basin Grasslands, and finally straightened out again after Sheep Mountain and Chugwater.

Billy spotted a white-tailed buck in a field, mumbled something half-jokingly about grabbing his rifle from the back seat but kept driving. It was nearly midnight, and Denver was still a long way away, let alone Albuquerque.

The sky was a deep purple, lit with a flood of stars. Every forty miles or so, a truck stop marquee cast a weak yellow glare across the emptiness.

The van rolled past Cheyenne, the last gasp of Wyoming before giving way to Colorado, and Billy hit the gas hard, to make up some time.

But almost as soon as he did, the radar detector started buzzing. He peered into the rearview mirror to see a police car following behind.

"Aw shit," he muttered.

The squad car zoomed up behind the van, but didn't turn on its lights. In a moment, it veered into the passing lane and roared ahead.

"Whew," said Billy. "We got a break."

Billy had racked up nearly as many speeding tickets as prize belt buckles. While he was dating a girl in Norman, Oklahoma, he had gotten four tickets in the space of three months—including two on the same night.

He let the cop speed ahead, until he was out of sight, then pushed hard on the pedal once more. By the time the speedometer reached eighty-five, the radar detector started buzzing again. Up ahead, a squad car—the same squad car—was pulled off to the side of the road. And this time, the red and blue lights were flickering.

The cop stood by the car, waving for the van to pull over.

"Do you know how fast you were going?" the cop asked Billy.

"A little swift, was it?" the cowboy asked bashfully.

The cop frowned and began writing a citation.

"How'd you get me, though?" Billy asked. "You were way up ahead of me."

"New technology," the cop explained with a smile.

It was a timing device, he said, designed to catch sneaky drivers who thought they could speed after the police passed by. As the cop had passed, he set the timer, then zoomed ahead and waited for the car to catch up. The device calculated the average speed it took for the driver to travel so many miles in so many minutes.

"And bingo, we know how fast you were going."

"For crying out loud," Billy bristled. "You guys don't play fair."

The officer handed over the ticket, then said with a smirk, "Have a good evening."

•   •   •

Billy took the Colfax Street exit into Denver, then rolled to a stop at a red light.

He looked around. Not a soul in sight, except for a tattered old fellow carrying a sack. And he wasn't wearing a badge. Billy gunned the engine, and slipped past the red light.

Driving along Colfax, there was a strip club on his left, the U.S. Mint on his right, and the gold-domed capitol up ahead.

He made a turn onto Pennsylvania, slowed to look for the numbers, then spotted 960 and parked at the curb. He turned and woke the sleeping cowboys in the back, Craig and Paul Peterson, the bronc rider with the sore nipple, who was riding along to New Mexico.

A sleepy-eyed man opened the town house door, and his wife ushered the cowboys to the living room. Craig collapsed on the couch. Paul crashed on the floor. Billy pushed two chairs together for a bed.

●　　●　　●

In the darkness outside the Hole-in-the-Wall, Larry Sandvick fumbled for his keys. The bar was closing, but the cowboy was still rarin' to go.

During the course of the celebration, he and another cowboy had befriended a couple of young women. Now the four of them were going to take a little spin in Larry's fancy new Cadillac.

Sandvick staggered a bit, then slid behind the wheel. He fired the engine and lurched ahead, swerving across the yellow line every now and again.

The fellow cowboy was Sandvick's old friend. His name was Shane Call, a rugged bronc rider with a thick mustache and almost as much hell in his heart as Larry.

Shane Call once introduced himself to a woman, who mistook his name for "Chain Saw." And that became his nickname ever after.

Chain Saw was an expert with horses but had some difficulty when it came to books. In fact, he couldn't read. It didn't bother him much. He figured literacy wasn't a requirement in rodeo.

But Sandvick thought otherwise. He told his friend that reading could come in handy, even for a cowboy.

Sandvick decided to become his teacher. But he was puzzled about what to use for reading materials. He knew Shane certainly didn't have much interest in reading the classics, or learning about history or politics.

But he did have a keen interest in at least one subject besides rodeo: women. Sandvick soon settled on study guides—dirty magazines.

Larry would drive the car and Shane would sit and struggle to read the erotic literature. He was required to read out loud, so his progress could be gauged. And he was making steady progress. But there were times, especially during the most heated passages, when Shane would stammer over the words.

"Aw shit, this is the best damn part," Larry would say impatiently, then grab the magazine from Shane's hands. "I'll take over from here."

●　　●　　●

"Watch out!" one of the women shrieked, as the Cadillac missed a turn in the road and veered toward a ditch. But it was too late.

The passengers bounced in the air. Sandvick's head rammed against the dashboard. There was a squeal, a crunch. The Cadillac was a twisted wreck.

In a moment, the blackness of the Wyoming sky flickered with the flashing red lights of a squad car.

"Step out of the car," the cop told Sandvick.

Earlier that day, the cowboy had been able to glide on the back of a bucking horse like a sailboat on a wave and grip the reins as tight as a magnet on metal. But now he could not walk a straight line.

The cop took a step toward the cowboy.

"You're under arrest for driving while intoxicated," he said. "You have the right to remain silent . . ."

•   •   •

The sound of a crying baby woke Craig about five a.m. As he opened an eye, he noticed that the ceiling was leaking and drops of water were falling on the living room carpet. He pulled himself up and poked around the kitchen in search of a pot. He found one and placed it under the leak, then crawled back under the covers.

His head was thumping. And the pot pinged with every drop of water. After about forty-five minutes, he gave up trying to sleep.

By seven a.m., the cowboys were back in the van, cursing the bumper-to-bumper traffic, inching toward Interstate 25, braced for another 400 miles of driving.

At a gas station, Craig got behind the wheel. Billy picked up an alternative weekly Denver newspaper, *Westward*, and flipped through the pages until he got to the singles ads.

The listings were grouped according to preferences: Men Seeking Women. Women Seeking Men. Men Seeking Men. Women Seeking Women.

"Single White Female," read one. "Animal sex drive—looking for same."

"A good old-fashioned gal," Billy cackled. "Just the kind to bring home to mom."

"I'm glad I'm married," said Craig.

•   •   •

Under the lights of the Albuquerque arena, Craig trotted back to the rails, his eight-second shift completed.

The score was seventy-seven points—good enough for three or

four hundred bucks. As the other cowboys came by to pat his back, Craig loaded his travel bag and scanned the crowd.

In the front row of the bleachers, a blond-haired toddler sat squealing on her mother's lap, pointing to one of the cowboys and shouting, "Daddy! Daddy!"

Craig waited for Billy and Paul to gather their bags, then stepped off ahead of them in a hasty march toward the parking lot. Abilene was the next rodeo, the next night.

"Where do you want to stay?" Billy shouted up to Craig. "We'll want to get into Texas before we stop, don't you think?"

"Nope," said Craig.

"Where then?"

"Home."

"You ain't serious, Craig," Billy said. "Shit, we drive all the way to Goodwell tonight—we ain't gonna have more than a few hours before we got to turn around and come back to Texas."

"It's a few hours, ain't it?"

"Aw, jeez, Craig."

Goodwell, the little town in the Oklahoma panhandle where both cowboys lived, was 300 miles out of the way.

"You missin' the little girl or the big girl?" Billy asked.

"I'm missin' 'em both," Craig replied.

.   .   .

In the bedroom of the house trailer, Laurie Latham awoke from a dream and looked up to see Craig.

"You're crazy," she whispered with a smile and a hug.

It was just about four a.m.

.   .   .

Just a week or so after the accident, the pretty girl with strawberry-blond hair had come over to the table in a Wyoming bar, where Craig was sitting alone, staring into his beer and thinking about his brother.

"My name is Laurie Hart," she said. "I saw you at the funeral. And I just wanted to tell you how sorry I am."

Most people didn't bring up Deke's name after his death, worried that it would stir the pain. But Craig thought of little else besides Deke. He wanted to talk about him. And it made him lonely that everybody seemed to want to avoid the subject. He asked Laurie to pull up a chair.

They sat and talked for hours about Deke. They even laughed. There was the time Deke ran out of dishwasher soap, and put Tide into the machine, which bubbled out all over the kitchen floor. And the time Deke came back to his apartment, weak with hunger, and noticed a hunk of meat on the stove, which he may or may not have known was really Alpo, but he gulped it down anyway.

Craig confided to Laurie that he felt unsure about the direction of his life. He was a rodeo cowboy on the college team and could join the pro circuit next year. But truth be told, he was never sold on the idea of becoming a full-time cowboy. Deke was a natural. For Craig, who fought awkwardness growing up, it was more of a struggle.

"Just watching Deke ride," he told Laurie, "was more fun than riding myself."

Craig had planned on getting a teaching degree, maybe in agriculture. It would surely be a more dependable life than rodeo. But since Deke's death, he told her, he was having second thoughts. Maybe he should give rodeo a shot.

He wished his big brother was around to give him some advice. But he thought he knew. The letters Deke sent from college to his younger brother were always signed "Keep charging!"

After Craig joined the pro circuit, he moved to Goodwell, a more strategic location for a rodeo cowboy, and Laurie came with him.

Laurie had grown up in North Dakota, an East River girl, the daughter of farmers, not ranchers. They thought rodeo was tolerable as a hobby, but it certainly wasn't a career. And when Laurie moved in with Craig—compounding her poor choice in suitors with an act of sin—her father stopped speaking to her for months.

She moved back up north for a while to try to mend things but grew so achingly lonely for Craig that she soon returned.

Laurie wanted to go to college but couldn't afford the tuition. And then Panhandle State in Goodwell offered her a scholarship, as a barrel racer. She and Craig pretended they were husband and wife, so they could qualify for married student housing. Before long, they decided to tie the knot for real, and made plans for a wedding. Laurie's parents sent word that they would be unable to attend the ceremony.

Two years later, a baby girl was born. She was named Chaney, after a sparkling blue stream on the North Dakota farm where Laurie grew up.

•   •   •

Chaney woke at seven a.m., and Craig threw off his blankets to hurry over and lift her from the crib. "Da!" she shouted gleefully. "Da!"

The two of them sat on a rocking chair in the living room, beneath a sketch on the wall of Deke, the little girl on her daddy's lap, leaning back against his chest. He rested his chin on her blond head, his arms wrapped around her, both of them with closed eyes, rocking in the dawn's light.

They woke as the sun rose over the plains, and the low moan of a Santa Fe freight train swept past. They shared a breakfast of Froot Loops, then played a game with a rubber ball, and headed to the bathtub, where Craig tried to wash some of the breakfast off his little girl.

Laurie was getting dressed for her new job as a schoolteacher. For the last several years, as Craig chased broncs around the country, she had stayed home and stuck to the books. In May, she graduated from Panhandle State, the first member of the family ever to finish college.

She wore a robe and gown to the commencement, and her parents, who had softened after the birth of a granddaughter, came down from North Dakota. The ceremony was held on a Sunday, an afternoon when Craig had to work at a rodeo clinic in town. Laurie was disappointed, but figured nothing could be done about it.

As they called her name, Laurie walked across the stage to take her diploma, looking out at the crowd, where people watched in their Sunday suits and fanciest dresses. But out in the crowd was one young man in boots and jeans, her cowboy. Craig had dashed away early from the rodeo, and sat beaming proudly at his educated wife.

•   •   •

Laurie came out to the living room, where Craig was getting Chaney dressed. She looked a bit amused as he struggled with the toddler.

"You blew a pedal again," he said, as Chaney kicked off a shoe for the third time.

"She's getting pretty strong, isn't she?" Laurie said to Craig. "My mom says she's gonna grow up to be a barrel racer. But I think she's gonna ride broncs."

Laurie asked Craig what time he'd be leaving.

"If I find out I've got a sorry horse at Abilene," he said, "maybe I'll turn out and stay home."

She lifted a skeptical eyebrow, the way a mother does to a child feigning illness in hope of avoiding school.

"Oh, I guess around noon, then," he said glumly. "Can you come back home then?"

"Of course," she said with a wink.

She gave him a kiss on her way out the door, lifted her skirt as she jumped in the pickup, and headed off to her classroom.

As the morning slipped away, Craig bundled up Chaney and drove to the babysitter's house, where a car parked outside sported a bumper sticker that asked, "Have You Hugged Your Horse Today?"

After dropping off his daughter, Craig stopped at the bar and grill he owned, The Stables. It was an aluminum building at the edge of town, sometimes mistaken for a barn. It didn't bring in much money, but every little bit helped. Laurie's teaching job paid $1,200 a month. And Craig hadn't cleared a cent in rodeo last year, after expenses, since he hadn't made the finals.

A pair of horseshoes hung over the entranceway. Silver insulation was exposed on the walls. Metal folding chairs were lined up around old cable spools that served as tables. The floor was cement. The men's rest room was marked "Geldings and Studs"; the women's was marked "Fillys and Mares." A sign over the bar said "No Whining."

The place was almost empty in the late morning, except for a couple of men in overalls. The jukebox was playing "They say crime don't pay, but neither does farming these days."

•   •   •

It was time to hit the road. "Get those tires changed on the van?" Craig asked Billy.

"Naw, they didn't have time," he answered. "But they changed the oil."

The cowboys had a decision to make. They were slated to compete in two rodeos the next two days: Abilene that evening, and Pendleton the following afternoon. They couldn't miss Pendleton, since it paid so well. But they surely couldn't make it driving all night from Abilene.

"If we're gonna drive to Pendleton," said Billy, "maybe we ought to start now, and to heck with Abilene."

The only way they could hit both, they figured, would be to drive all night from Abilene to Wichita, then fly to Portland in the morning and drive to Pendleton. But the airfare could be a killer.

Craig thought for a minute, then made a phone call.

"It's all set," he said after hanging up. "We got a decent fare."

He had called a travel agent who knew how tough rodeo life could be. She had been married to a calf-roper. A year ago, her husband was flying with three other cowboys to a contest in Washington. Their single-engine plane crashed into Mount Rainier. All four of them were killed.

• • •

The van fled Oklahoma for Texas on a winding dirt road, spewing a cloud of dust a half mile long, as the cowboy hats bobbed on window hooks and the radio sang "Play, Ruby, play."

"Turn it up, Billy," Craig called out from the back seat, and the music went full throttle.

The Texas countryside was treeless and flat as the floor, the acreage cut in squares like huge city blocks, as pivot arc irrigating systems moved in imperceptible circles to coax the dry earth into growing some wheat. Out of nowhere, a billboard rose up to proclaim: "Hansford County Is Proud of Michelle Graham—Farm Business Queen."

The wind was blowing so hard it shook the van and pelted the windshield with gravel. Billy ducked behind a pickup for a windbreak, until the dust settled. And then he looked at the road map and frowned.

"Uh-oh," he said. "I'm about half-assed lost."

But near Spearman, he found Route 15, and breathed easier. The road wound around to Highway 83 and swung south across the Canadian River. He drove hard until Shamrock, and stopped to get gas and give Craig a turn behind the wheel.

Texas got a little more lush and hilly as they moved south. And the sun broke out from the clouds around Paducah. On the rickety porch of a farmhouse, a shirtless teenage boy lay on a bench and pumped a barbell. A graveyard of rusted old cars and trucks littered a farm field. And the radio faded in and out. Almost every station in Texas seemed to be full of the promise of salvation or the threat of brimstone, and sometimes both.

The radio preachers reminded Billy of a rodeo school he worked not long ago. "It was a kind of Holy Roller deal," he said. "And this one young bronc rider, he was leanin' over the neck of his horse and just a prayin', 'O Lord, O Lord, O Lord.'

"Finally, I says to the fella: If I was you, I'd stop prayin' and start cockin' my guns. You're the one that's gonna have to ride this horse."

23

T HE SEPTEMBER SUN was drooping as the cowboys pulled into the Abilene parking lot. Craig swung his boots out of the van and ducked behind an open door to slip off a pullover sweater and change into a striped Western rodeo shirt. And then he leaned back into the van to change his trousers, a bit bashful about undressing where people in the parking lot might see him.

"This is going to be tricky," he said, as he unbuttoned his jeans and glanced around furtively.

"Don't worry," said Billy, with a chuckle, "you ain't got anything that anybody's gonna see from that far away."

All zipped and buttoned, they trudged wearily past Wellshot Field and toward the indoor arena. The Texas air was still warm at six o'-clock, even a bit muggy. And the cowboys remarked how quickly the world changes: just two days ago, the people in Kaycee were looking for the first snowfall, and now here in Texas, it was still summertime.

But the world was always changing around the cowboy, even when he was standing still. The West Texas wranglers in the fields just a few miles from the rodeo grounds looked about the same as they always had, shadowed faces under broad-brimmed hats, boots locked in stirrups, hands as gnarled as mesquite branches, coaxing along cattle no less stubborn than the herds of a century ago. They still gazed across the horizon toward Abilene, "prettiest town I've ever seen," now chockablock with Wal-Marts and Burger Kings and Motel 6.

At the sidewalk near the arena entrance, a crowd of fans, hustling to get inside, elbowed past Billy and Craig, clueless that they had just rubbed shoulders with some of the sport's biggest stars. But the spectators had come to see the myth, not the man. And until the blare of the horn signaled the eight seconds under the lights, these were not cowboys, just country boys.

"After you," Billy muttered, although nobody was listening, as he stepped back on the grass until the herd of spectators made their way inside.

Since they were an hour early, and starving, the cowboys followed the smell of frying grease to the concession stand, where a woman with hair as high as a horse's head stood behind the counter.

"So are you guys cowboys?" the woman asked, as Craig ordered his usual: hamburger, fries and Coke.

"Yes, ma'am," he responded.

"What event?"

"Saddle bronc."

"Do you come here every year?"

"Yes, ma'am."

"So you know Abilene pretty good?"

"Oh no, ma'am, I wouldn't say that. I just know how to get to the rodeo grounds."

"Well, that's all there is to Abilene."

The cowboys took their dinner back to the dressing room, where a rack was hung with some samples of the new contestants' jackets for the National Finals Rodeo in Las Vegas. The jackets were eye-catchers, about as subtle as the Strip itself.

"Couldn't they have used a little more leather," said Billy, "and a little less purple?"

·   ·   ·

A cowboy bounced into the dressing room, a cup of coffee in one hand and a toothpick dangling from a wide grin.

"Hey fellas," said Bud Longbrake, shaking hands with Craig and then Billy. "How was Kaycee?"

"Real good," mumbled Craig, his words mixed with hamburger.

"Now there's a town, old Kaycee," Bud bubbled. "A fella could hole up there for three or four days and have a swell time. It wouldn't be a bad place to pitch up even if there wasn't a rodeo."

"How you been doin', Bud?" somebody asked.

Now the grin vanished.

"I been havin' heck," said Bud, who was still struggling to climb uphill into the top twenty in the standings, never mind the top fifteen.

Bud had left before sunrise on the drive from Lincoln, Nebraska, a 700-mile journey, to get to Abilene, where he was desperate to put some points on the board. He was also worried about his calves, which were due to go to auction in Pierre, South Dakota, next month. Cattle prices were erratic, and his small herd had been hit with a rash of stillbirths in the spring. On top of it all, the tribe hadn't ruled yet on whether his kids could legally be considered Indian.

He dropped his saddle and meandered out toward the arena, walking slowly across the dirt inside the fence, when a stripe-shirted referee came along and wrapped an arm around Bud's shoulders.

"When it rains, it pours," he whispered to the cowboy in a sympathetic drawl. "But you just hang in there, you hear?"

•   •   •

The town of Abilene was founded by Confederate veterans, roughhewn rebels with a sour attitude about anything North or East. But the rodeo arena was draped with so much red, white and blue bunting it looked like Yankee Stadium during the World Series. The announcer, a big man in a loose sport jacket, bellowed congratulations to the crowd for having been born American.

The star of the opening ceremony was a rodeo queen, Miss Personality, who flashed a frozen smile at the applauding crowd as she tightly clenched the reins of her horse. A friend of the queen crouched on one knee below the mounted royalty, focusing an Instamatic camera, to record the moment for posterity.

"Ladies and gentlemen, I give you Miss Personality," the announcer called out. "Now a queen wouldn't be worth much if she didn't have personality, would she?"

Behind the chutes, Craig and Billy were doing deep knee bends and waving their arms like helicopter blades. Craig wore number 546 on his back and a belt buckle from a rodeo in Elk City, Oklahoma. Billy wore number 547 and a buckle inscribed with the name of Deke Latham.

Billy was first out of the gates, a fraction of a second after the bronc, which bucked hard in a helter-skelter dance to the middle of the arena and then made a dash toward the grandstands. In the first row, a startled fan saw the bared teeth of the horse charging toward his seat like it had a ticket, and jumped so fast he spilled his popcorn.

The horse wasn't able to knock Billy off, but it scored what amounted to a TKO. "The horse's name was Hard Money," the cowboy said, shaking his head, after he pulled himself over the rails. "And he was every bit of that tonight. I got me an ass-paddling. I think he popped every bone in my body."

Craig's bronc was more cooperative. The cowboy took a nice, graceful ride, almost like he could have dropped the braided rein and just kept on riding. The scoreboard flashed a seventy-seven, the top ride of the evening.

In chute number six, Bud Longbrake straddled his horse, a muscular paint named Cotton Eye, which looked a lot more relaxed than the cowboy, whose face was pinched tight.

Bud wiggled to get just the right fit. Then he lifted his hand from the chute rail, and gave a fierce nod of the head.

On the first buck, the cowboy rode strong. On the second buck, he was still holding tight. On the third buck, he sailed through the air—and dropped to the dirt like a brick.

"Oh no!" the announcer hollered mournfully. "You won't see him do that very often."

•   •   •

In the darkness of the parking lot, Bud and his travel partner, a twenty-four-year-old Nebraskan named J. W. Simonson, shoved their saddles and bags into the back of the van, and then drove down a two-lane Texas highway. In the rearview mirror, the golden glow of a lighted Ferris wheel grew smaller and smaller, until finally it vanished.

A mile or so back, Billy sat behind the wheel of his van, with Craig in the back seat, hunched over a road map and squinting in the dome light, charting the route to Wichita.

It was already past ten p.m. The flight was scheduled to leave at seven a.m., and the drive to the airport would take maybe eight hours. There wasn't any time for dawdling.

A third cowboy had come along for the ride, Bob Logue, a slick-talking bareback rider who had grown up in Gumby, Texas, but now lived in Colorado with his wife, an airline flight attendant. He wore a thick black mustache and a gold chain around his neck.

"Feel like driving, Bob?" asked Billy.

"Aw come on, guys," he grumbled. "I been under the wheel all day."

Billy shot Craig a look that seemed to ask: Does he think we glided into Abilene on a carpet?

Before heading toward Kansas, the van pulled into a Pride gas station, a quick stop for fuel and dinner.

"How long's this hot dog been sittin' here?" Billy asked the sales clerk, as he considered the lone dog on the rotisserie rack.

"All day, I reckon," the clerk said with a shrug. "But it's fine."

"I think I'll pass," said Billy.

The cowboys finally settled on a big box of something called Lunchables, and bought some Cokes to wash it down. Since it was Craig's turn to pay, he pulled a wallet out of the neck of his cowboy boot and fished for a pair of twenties. On his way out the door, he passed a pay phone and dialed Laurie to say goodnight.

• • •

The van headed east on Route 180, then swung north on Route 281. A billboard declared, "God Watches Over Wichita Falls." The rest of Texas, apparently, was on its own.

The radio was tuned to a country music station, where a singer wailed, "I'm too dumb for New York City, and too ugly for L.A."

Logue took his shirt off, propped his legs up on the dashboard and sang along with the radio. But after a while, he suddenly leaned over and switched down the dial, and began to talk about the business of rodeo.

"It's exploitation, that's what it is," he growled. "They just want us to take each other's money."

What the cowboys needed, he said, was a union. Not just any union—not the kind where everybody belonged.

"I'm talking about a union for the top twenty or thirty cowboys, standing together. And we tell 'em: You do it our way, or you can have your rodeo without us."

Craig and Billy listened, not making a peep.

Rodeo was the only sport where the bulk of the wages came straight out of the competitors' pockets. And it used to be even worse. A group of cowboys rebelled in 1936 at the Boston Gardens, where a promoter named Colonel W. T. Johnson tried to stage a rodeo without adding a single nickel to the contestant fees that made up the purse. The cowboys walked out. Johnson finally relented and coughed up some money. The strike spawned the first cowboy association: the Turtles. Some say the name was chosen to reflect the slowness of the cowboys in finally getting organized. Others say it means you never get anywhere unless you stick your neck out.

• • •

About eighty-five miles south of Wichita, Craig woke up from a snooze in the back seat and climbed behind the wheel. It was three a.m. Pendleton started in nine hours.

The Kansas expressway was empty, so he switched on the brights. He steered with his right hand and used his left hand to rub his eyes open. In the back seat, Bob was snoring.

As Interstate 35 split off into 235, Craig veered toward the west side of the city, not certain he was on the right path until he saw a sign for the airport. He took the exit and started looking for a cheap motel, where the cowboys could scrub up before the flight to Oregon.

The first place he tried had no vacancies. He stopped at a second motel. It was full. And then a third. No luck.

"I never knew Wichita was such a danged popular place," he muttered, as he got back behind the wheel. He wasn't sure whether it was worthwhile to keep searching. But there wasn't much else to do in Kansas in the middle of the night. He kept driving.

He spotted a Motel 6 a few miles down the road, and wheeled into the parking lot. A few moments later, he came back with a key for a room.

"Get up, girls," he hollered at the sleeping cowboys. "We're here."

"Where we at?" Billy asked, without looking up.

"Tom Bodette's," he said.

The cowboys took their turns in the shower, then piled back into the van and headed toward the airport. Billy and Craig wore their usual: Western shirt and straight-legged jeans. Bob wore his gold chain, a pinky ring with a diamond-studded horseshoe, a pair of dressy jeans with pleats and enough cologne to dizzy a horse.

"I say we call ahead and rent a Lincoln or a Cadillac," said Bob. "You figure we get there at eleven a.m. The rodeo starts at noon, and they start the saddle-bronc around one. We've gotta drive two hundred miles to get there. We're gonna have to be smokin'. If we crash, I don't want to be in no little car."

The rodeo in Pendleton had special meaning for Bob. Ten years ago, he had broken his neck there. And every year, the Pendleton fans rewarded him with a special round of applause.

Inside the terminal, they bought their tickets and had enough time for breakfast. "That sure is a pretty buckle," Bob told Billy, between bites of bacon and eggs. "You know, they should never compromise on a buckle. Make 'em right, I say. Money you spend and it's gone. But a buckle, that lasts forever."

Craig wolfed down his breakfast so he'd have time to call Laurie.

An observer from the state education board was coming to her class-room today, and he knew she'd be a little nervous about it, so he wanted to wish her luck.

•   •   •

When the plane touched down in Portland, nearly an hour late, the cowboys figured they had a fifty-fifty chance to make the rodeo.

They sprinted through the terminal, snatched the keys at Budget and jumped inside the waiting car.

Interstate 84 snaked along the Canada border, with wicked twists and turns. Darting in and around the other cars, the cowboys sped beyond the city traffic, and Billy pressed the gas pedal "to the gover-nor," as the cowboys say, as far as an appeal can go, in this case some-where above 100 miles an hour.

The Cascade Mountains rose on the south. The Columbia River swept along the north. As the car raced, the cowboys leaned anx-iously toward the windshield, as if that brought them a little closer to their destination.

The heavily forested hills finally gave way to flatter, clearer terrain as they roared east, past the town of Chenoweth, then Rufus, then Blalock and Hermiston. A lot of highway sweeps past at 110 miles an hour, and the cowboys were making terrific time. A sign said Pendle-ton was only ten miles away.

But then the car started to sputter and fade, losing steam, cough-ing and lurching. "We're running out of gas!" Craig cried.

In a desperate move to tip a few last drops of gasoline into the tank, the cowboys rocked the car, jumping up and down on the seats, jerking backward and forward. But it was no use. The car came to a dead stop.

There was no time to call for help, no time to walk for gas. The cowboys decided to leave the car along the road and hitchhike to the rodeo. Billy grabbed a torn piece of cardboard from the back seat, found a pen and scrawled "RODEO" across it.

He jumped out on the road and held the sign high over his head. The first car seemed to slow down a bit, as the driver read the word, and then suddenly slammed the gas harder. A few more cars roared past, until finally a young woman pulled over to the side and rolled down her window.

"We're cowboys, ma'am," Billy told her breathlessly. "Can you help us?"

"Get in," she said.

24

SPRINTING AS FAST as their cowboy boots would let them, Billy and Craig raced toward the chutes.

It was past two, an hour into the rodeo. The bareback riders were finished. The calves had been roped. And the saddle-bronc event had started.

"Hurry up!" somebody shouted. "They've already bucked five horses."

The Oregon sky was a pale blue, unbroken except for a few skinny clouds, like little islands in a vast sea. And the grandstands thundered with the roar of 17,000 fans, the biggest rodeo in the Northwest.

Still gasping for air, the cowboys hastily fastened their saddles, then climbed into the white-board cages and settled on their waiting broncs.

As it turned out, Craig could have saved himself the trouble of hurrying. He spurred the horse for all it was worth, but that wasn't much. The ride earned a paltry score, not enough to make the finals.

Billy had more luck. He posted a score of seventy-seven, a good bet to qualify for the short-go on Saturday. Craig wished him luck and jumped in with a crew of cowboys going south. He hardly knew he had even been in Pendleton.

•   •   •

When the names of the qualifiers for the finals were posted on a cinderblock wall outside the bathroom, cowboys crowded around to read the lineup.

Bud Longbrake was 200 miles away, on a pay phone in a Spokane truck stop, calling to see if his name was on the list.

He still hadn't cracked the top twenty. In fact, he hadn't collected a paycheck in weeks. For a long time, from Cheyenne to Dodge City to Albuquerque, he had been telling himself, "Plenty of time left. I can do it. Plenty of time left. I can do it."

But now it was the middle of September, and the hopes for making Las Vegas were fading as quickly as his bank account. Maybe it was time to go home, he wondered, like a smart gambler on a bad run, who gets up from the table before losing what's still left in his pockets.

He knew that a spectacular finish could still send him to Las Vegas, where he could win back every cent he had lost during the season, and then some. But his luck showed no sign of changing.

In a truck stop call back to the reservation in South Dakota, the cowboy had asked his wife if he should keep on chasing.

"Is there still a chance?" Lona asked.

"Yeah," he answered. "A chance."

"Then keep trying," she told him.

On the blueprint for the miracle, the Pendleton Round-Up was big. It held the potential to win a couple thousand dollars or more, and just as many points in the standings. Bud would need to earn checks at nearly every rodeo left on the schedule, of course. But there were none bigger than the Round-Up. If he could place in the money at Pendleton, he still had a shot. If he didn't, it was as good as over.

The voice of a woman at rodeo headquarters answered the phone.

"This is Bud Longbrake calling about Pendleton," he said, "and I just wanted to find out if . . ."

"You made it," she answered.

•   •   •

Pendleton sits in the eastern half of Oregon, the region of the state still fairly untouched by espresso bars, vegetarian cafés and trendy brew pubs. But ranchettes, the mark of wealthy newcomers, were becoming more common.

The Round-Up, a tradition here since 1910, stood as a tribute to the way things had always been, and the hope that they wouldn't change too quickly. "The Round-Up is our only call in life, except for the woolen mills, of course," a rodeo volunteer explained. "But a lot of these newcomers—they just don't understand."

One fan wore a sticker on his cowboy hat: "Vote Yes on Number 9." It referred to an initiative on the Oregon ballot that would denounce homosexuality as, among other things, "perverse." And it was expected to pass widely in this part of the state.

"It's that fuckin' Portland," one fan told another. "They're some weird son of a bitches. Now a'course we got a few fags around here, too. And everybody knows who they are. Shit, a couple of 'em are ranchers. Nobody bothers 'em. But they ain't like them fags in Portland."

The man was sipping a beer inside the "Let 'er Buck" room, a mud-floored bar on the Pendleton rodeo grounds where the walls were posted with cardboard warnings: "Keep Your Clothes On."

But the warning was weak in the face of tradition. And before long, the patrons in the bar were roaring their approval for the old custom of the "Let 'er Buck" room: the bare-chested woman.

Perched atop the shoulders of a cowboy, where everybody could watch, a scrawny woman with a chipped front tooth pulled off her shirt, and then her bra, and waved it triumphantly over her head, as the crowd in the bar hooted in joyful lust and waved their cowboy hats in gratitude for tradition.

•   •   •

There was not a single cowboy hat in the Indian Village, a section of the campground reserved for tribes at the rodeo who wished to preserve their own traditions. Instead, there were hundreds of tepees, supported with lodgepole pines and filled with huckleberries and fry bread and deer meat. And the hand-painted rules at the entrance declared that all vestiges of white culture stay out:

"No cowboy hats, Levi's or pants of any kind other than leggings.

"No loose hair—all long hair must be braided.

"No coverups, such as shawls, blankets or scarfs, unless properly worn with costumes.

"No gunny sack cloth or campfire costumes.

"No chewing gum or cigarettes.

"No strollers, buggies or white-man baby boards.

"No drunks."

•   •   •

Inside the tepees, some of the old Indians told children about the history that had shaped the wariness of local tribes toward the white man: the Nez Percé War of 1877. Chief Joseph was leading his people across 1,300 miles of mountain wilderness, from their Wallowa home in northeast Oregon, across the Bitterroots that divide Idaho and Montana, down through Yellowstone Park, and then north toward Canada, with the U.S. Army in hot pursuit. The chase ended only a day's ride from freedom.

But there was a footnote to the story that reminded the Indian people of their place at the Round-Up. On that unsuccessful flight toward liberty was an eleven-year-old Nez Percé boy named Blanket of the Sun. Years later, when he returned to the reservation, he took up a career riding broncs. And in 1916, at the age of fifty, he competed in the Pendleton rodeo. He rode better than all the white cowboys, but the judges were reluctant to give the top prize to an Indian.

Instead, they told him to ride again. Once more, Blanket of the Sun bested the score of the other cowboys. But he was required to do it yet again, and again. And each time, the Indian registered the top score. Finally, the afternoon sun began to disappear, and it grew too dark for rodeo, as some fans cried wearily, "It's sundown, it's sundown." The officials finally relented. The prize for the "World Champion Bronc Rider" was awarded to the Nez Percé cowboy. And for the triumph at dusk, the tribe forever after called their cowboy Jackson Sundown.

•   •   •

Bud couldn't believe his good luck. For the championship, he had drawn a horse named Papa Smurf, one of the finest broncs in America, a powerful gelding with lightning feet and the bucking force of a cannon. There were no guarantees in rodeo, but Papa was as close as it comes. The horse's half of the score would surely be a winner. The rest was up to the cowboy.

From a rail behind the chutes, Bud gazed beyond the arena, toward the church steeples and groves of pine trees and soft hills that rose in the distance, barely noticing the other events down on the field.

The bareback contest had just finished, and dozens of young Indian women were perched on horses for the "Squaw Race." Earlier in the week, a seventeen-year-old girl from the Yakima reservation had been badly hurt when her horse stumbled in a groove made by calves and steers. She had been taken unconscious to a hospital.

"We salute the heritage of our friends back in the Indian Village," the announcer called out, making no mention of the accident or the girl's condition, but instead pointing to the "squaws" lined up for to-day's spectacle. "This is one of the wildest things you'll ever see!"

The Indians circled the track, their horses knocking together, as a few young women crashed to the dirt.

•   •   •

"We're going to Bud Longbrake now," the announcer called. "And Papa Smurf!"

The horse reared back, then twisted its way out of the cage and shot into the air. Bud spurred hard, matching the bronc's leap. Hooves came pounding against the ground, as the cowboy slapped in the saddle, and then another launch, four hooves in the air, the spurs still swirling.

The clock went to six, then four, then two. The bronc groaned, its teeth flashing, and gave a spectacular buck, lifting Bud fifteen feet in the air. But the cowboy matched every move, a free hand waving, un-til the horn blared the end.

The crowd erupted in thunder. The cowboy fell to the ground. He looked up at the sky. A big smile danced across his face.

"How do you like the style of the man from South Dakota?" the announcer blared, and the roaring fans gave their answer.

At the end of the day, Bud had finished in a three-way tie for first place in the short-go, and a two-way tie for second place in the rodeo overall. It earned him a thousand bucks, enough to keep him on the trail.

"Hey Bud," a friend hollered. "Hangin' around for a while?"

"Naw," he answered with a smile. "Got another rodeo to hit."

25

THE CHEYENNE RIVER Sioux reservation is hidden away in America as deeply as a forgotten old secret, a land where the white-lined pavement narrows to gravel and then to dirt, and then just stops. This is a place where the newspaper, by the time it arrives, is posted with a date that has already passed. Only the wind causes a ruckus. And only the moon and the stars, which seem infinitely closer than any big city, pierce the blackness of night.

In the dusk, Bud Longbrake stared across an empty field and dreamed of the home he wanted to build. "Maybe next year," he thought to himself, "if I can just make the finals."

The layout was stored in Bud's head: The house would be solid, so it wouldn't rattle in the wind. It would be spacious enough that each of the two kids could have a bedroom of their own. There would be a rambling front porch, maybe with a swing. And shutters and flower boxes and a kitchen window that looked out on the cow pasture.

But more than just money stood in the way of the dream. This land belonged to the tribe. It was reserved for Indians. If his children were officially deemed white, they could not inherit the lease to the land, whether or not the family's home had been built there. It would revert back to the tribe.

For today, and for as long as Bud and Lona were alive, it would not be an issue, since they were full-fledged members of the tribe. But the great-great-great-grandson of Mary Sitting Eagle knew that tomorrow does not always look like today.

"What if we build the house and something happens to us?" Bud had asked Lona. "What about the kids?"

•   •   •

Bud watched the calves graze in the pasture, not far from Rattlesnake Creek. They looked good. So did the field. There had been five long years of drought on the Great Plains, but the rains had finally come. Now the blue grama grass was providing a feast.

During the spring, Bud had spent the nights in a camper, in case any of the cows had trouble delivering. He had pulled some of the baby calves out by the hocks. In some cases, the mothers hadn't been able to stand up to break the placenta and lick the calves dry, so Bud sliced open the watery bag to let them breathe.

He had lost a slew of calves, and some mother cows, too. When a calf was orphaned, he would cut the hide from a dead calf, then wrap it around the orphan, so the mother of the dead calf would bond and eventually feed the orphan, a kind of calf adoption.

Calving was the most gratifying time for a rancher, bringing new life into the world. But to Bud, being a rancher any time of the year was the best kind of job: bundled up on horseback in the chilly dawn, sweating under a blazing sun by ten a.m., breaking a while later for a lunch of a sandwich and a Coke, then more hard work until it was time for supper with the family, and finally collapsing in bed, bone-tired and content. He would take that life in a second, if only he could afford it.

Bud had climbed into eighteenth place, just three short of the qualifying tier. Time was growing short. He needed a big win.

"Just one good rain," Bud thought to himself, as he marveled at the pasture, "can grow a foot of grass."

•   •   •

The next morning, Bud zipped his clothes in a bag and slung his saddle over his shoulder, then paced through the narrow trailer, taking one last look to make sure he didn't forget anything.

A bronze of an Indian, back bent on a rearing horse, rested on a table near a threadbare sofa. A family picture looked out from a wall paneled with fake walnut. A knickknack in the shape of a cowboy boot was etched with the name of every family member.

"When you coming home, Daddy?" asked seven-year-old Jay, who had just started the second grade.

"Soon as I can," he said, as he stooped to give the boy a hug.

And then he turned to Kayla, whose mouth was turned down at the corners, like it always was when her father left.

"You learn a lot in school today, okay?" he said, as he hugged the little girl, who was on her way to a federal program for poor children, Head Start, which Bud had also attended as a boy. "I'll want to hear all about it when I get back."

He waited for Lona to get off the telephone, so he could give his wife a kiss.

Finally she hung up. When she turned, she spoke in a low voice so the children wouldn't hear.

Lona worked for the YMCA in town. It wasn't a Y with a weight room and a sauna. It was a social service agency for all the Sioux children for hundreds of miles around. She was the secretary and book-keeper. But since there were only three full-time staff people, she ended up doing a lot of other things, like trying to convince poor Indian children surrounded by poverty and alcoholism that life was worth living.

"They found a kid hanging from the bridge this morning," she said.

•   •   •

As a teenager, Bud went to a rodeo and watched a bronc rider win first place and $1,000. At the time, he was working sixteen hours a day as a laborer on a ranch, packing square bales of hay and earning $650 a month. And here was a young guy who made a thousand bucks in eight seconds.

"I heard them cowboys talkin' after the rodeo. They was complainin' about the travel. And I thought, 'Man, what are you talkin' about. You get to see the whole country. It sounds like a pretty glamorous life to me.' "

Bud had turned thirty in June. The contest in Omaha would be his 110th of the year. So far this season, he had driven nearly 100,000 miles. The underside of his right wrist was callused from laying it across the top of the steering wheel.

The van pulled farther away from Indian country, where the towns had names like Iron Lightning and Thunder Butte and Red Elm, and deeper into white man country, and towns with solid Protestant names like Mitchell, Kimball and Fulton.

He flipped the radio dial, and the familiar voice of a broadcaster boomed and cackled and snorted the gospel of conservatism. "I just can't stand that Rush Limbaugh," he winced, and punched the radio button again. It landed on a country station, where Mary-Chapin Carpenter sang "I Take My Chances." He left it there.

The farm fields of South Dakota gave way to tidy brick-and-frame subdivisions around Sioux Falls, where a billboard claimed it was the best place in the universe to do business, at least according to *Money* magazine.

Bud's coffee mug was empty, and so was the thermos he brought to replenish it. It was getting past noon, so he pulled off at Hardy's, picked up a hamburger and filled the thermos, then wheeled next door to a gas station.

The total came to $28.49. He handed a credit card to the clerk. She ran it through the machine, frowned, and ran it through again. She handed the card back to him.

"They won't accept it," she said. "I tried it twice."

Bud dug into the jeans pocket for some cash, his head bowed, too embarrassed to look at the clerk.

It had been a tough year for Bud, and the bills were coming faster than the paychecks. The monthly phone bill alone was $300.

Bud knew it was an extravagance to call home so much. But he didn't want to be a stranger to his family. It was bad enough being gone more days than he was home. In fact, there were times when Bud would come home after a long stint on the trail, and see a man without his wife, and not dare to ask about her. In the space of time that Bud was gone to the rodeos, people died and were buried.

He worried most about Jay. The boy was getting to an age where he needed his dad around full-time. Just a month ago, Jay was hang-dog because Bud couldn't go to his Little Britches rodeo. On a fuzzy phone connection afterward, Jay told his father he won a first-prize buckle. Bud told him he was proud, and that he was sorry not to be there.

"I feel awful about missin' Jay's rodeo," Bud told Lona, when she picked up the phone.

"Oh, pretty soon he'll be caught up in something else and forget all about it," Lona reassured him.

But when Bud's van pulled into the driveway at home several days later, Jay had come running out of the trailer, holding his prize buckle high in the air for his dad to see.

•   •   •

Bud turned south on Interstate 29, which wound around to the Iowa side of the border, then passed a golfing resort along the Missouri River with a sign that declared, "Life Should Be This Good."

He took a big gulp of black coffee from his mug, and suddenly remembered that he had forgotten to use the bathroom at Hardy's. He waited about twenty miles, then spotted a rest stop and took the exit.

On his way out of the bathroom, he noticed a wooden sign that celebrated the expedition of Lewis and Clark. The explorers had met some Indians in this territory, the sign explained, "and advised them on how they were to conduct themselves," then pacified them with gifts. "They presented the chiefs with medals, a canister of powder and a bottle of whiskey."

He stuck a fresh toothpick in his mouth, hopped behind the wheel and revved up the engine. He had another two hours of driving before reaching the Omaha arena, where a bronc called Blue Duck, a name that was taken, presumably, from the vicious Indian character in *Lonesome Dove*, would be waiting for him.

●   ●   ●

Inside the Aksarben Arena (Nebraska spelled backward), Bud stood alongside the other cowboys, hats over hearts, as the Stars and Stripes waved from horseback. A banner stretched across the upper deck with the call letters of a local country station, WOW. The loudspeaker played a mournful, patriotic song. "God Bless America again . . . look at all the trouble she's been in."

The last stretch of the season was an expensive time for a cowboy clutching at Las Vegas. The rodeos were few and far between and didn't pay as well as the big summer contests. But Bud had been through this drill before. Two years ago, hustling down the stretch to make the finals, he spent $5,000 to win $500.

It had been worth it. He made the championship and then won the prize for the best average score. His father, who had once abandoned his own rodeo dreams to tend cows at home after an older brother was killed in a car crash, watched from the stands with tears in his eyes. When they awarded the prize buckle that night, Bud turned to his father and handed it over. "This belongs to you," he said.

There were thirty-five bronc riders entered at Omaha, a two-header contest, many with the same desperate visions of the Strip. The entry fees were $90 apiece. Winning a round would pay about $800. Winning the rodeo would bring double that sum.

"They were born free," the announcer's voice echoed, referring to the broncs, and maybe the cowboys, "and they insist on staying that way."

Bud fastened his chaps. He wore number 149 on his back, and the sacred eagle feather, as always, in the brim of his hat.

"Here's a cowboy's cowboy," the announcer said, as Bud's turn finally came. "I like his attitude. And I like his riding skills."

Bud clenched the reins tethered to Blue Duck and wiggled in the saddle. The gray horse hadn't been bucked much all summer and ought to be fresh. The cowboy gave the bronc a pat on the neck. He needed the best ride the horse could deliver.

The gate swung open. The flank strap jerked. But the horse just stood still for a moment.

"Come on," Bud's eyes seemed to plead. "Come on."

The bronc turned and made its way into the arena. It offered up a lazy buck, barely enough to make much of an impression.

The cowboy's spurs swept down hard, demanding some fire. But the horse just loped ahead, taking its time to get warmed up, as the precious seconds ticked away.

Finally the horse started kicking hard, and the cowboy kept spurring until the horn blared.

It was a score of seventy-three points—a single point out of the money.

Bud's heart sank to his boots. He jogged back to the rails and stood in silence, next to a freckled, red-haired cowboy, an old friend from Mud Butte, South Dakota, who knew what had been at stake for Bud.

"They ought to can that bastard," the freckled cowboy snapped, angry at the horse for letting down his friend. "Didn't even start bucking till halfway through the goddamned ride."

He lifted a callused palm and squeezed the back of Bud's neck.

"Son of a bitch," he said.

"Yeah," Bud said dryly. "Son of a bitch."

•   •   •

It had been a very long time since Bud had gotten drunk. He knew from experience that booze and rodeo don't mix well. And the bottle was the curse of the reservation.

But on this night, he walked straight to the beer stand and plopped his saddle on the cement, alongside his friend from Mud Butte, a bronc rider and scrub-grass philosopher named Red Lemmel, and his Nebraska travel partner, J. W. Simonson, whom Bud affectionately called "The J Dub."

"Well, boys," said Red, lifting a plastic cup, "here's to the authentic Old West."

The cowboys ordered another round of beers, and then another, and then one more, until a metal wall slammed shut on the counter, and a concessions attendant hollered, "Time to get on home!"

Being a long way from home, the cowboys headed instead to a saloon.

Bushwhacker's was a country-and-western bar, or the closest thing Omaha had to one. The cowboys wandered inside. And burly bouncers in broad-brimmed hats greeted them with glares. "I think I'd feel more at home in a biker bar," whispered J.W.

Bud rested an elbow against the counter, ordered a longneck, and listened to a Garth Brooks song blaring on the jukebox. After a few more beers, Bud sang along softly.

Out in the crowd, he noticed a pair of bouncers walking meanly toward some cowboys. One of them, Craig Devereaux, a small bronc rider with a gentle disposition, was holding his palms up, as if to say, "I'm not causing any trouble."

Bud set down his bottle and took a few steps toward the commotion, just in case he was needed. "Cowboy law," the rodeo boys called it. Whenever one got in a tight scrape, the others were obliged to help. Bud was a good man to have in one's corner. He never started anything, but he never backed down, either. And he was tough as nails. All the cowboys knew that, even the all-around champ, Ty Murray.

In Bud's rookie year, he had gotten into a touch football game with Murray and some other rodeo stars from Texas. But some of the Texans started playing a little rough, swinging elbows and jabbing fists. At first, Bud didn't know what to make of it. But as the play got rougher, he thought to himself, "All right, you want to play rough. We'll play rough."

He flattened a Texan. After that, Bud was always picked first in the choosing of sides for football.

•   •   •

Morning greeted Bud with a splitting headache. He rolled off a couch inside J.W.'s fiancée's apartment in Lincoln, where a few cowboys had slept the night, and headed to the van, bound for Arkansas.

It was the first day of autumn. The leaves on the trees had turned a crispy golden, and the wind carried a bite.

Bud found a McDonald's, where he loaded up his thermos with

coffee. J.W. and Devereaux were slunk in the back seat. The young Nebraskan's eyes were red and puffy, which he blamed on a new brand of shampoo.

They cut down through Iowa, then crossed into Missouri, and decided to try to make Kansas City before stopping to eat. Around Peculiar, Missouri, they found a truck stop advertising a lunchtime special for $3, and pulled into the lot.

There were six tables, all of them empty, but it still took ten minutes before a waitress wandered over and said, "I guess you'll have the chicken-fried steak."

"I guess," said Bud.

The meat was slopped with a white gravy and lumpy mashed potatoes, and came with white supermarket bread. They washed it down with coffee, then stretched their legs for a few minutes in the parking lot before climbing back in the van.

Bud scanned the road atlas, while J.W. flipped through the pages of a book called *The Wilderness Blackfoot Massacre*.

The van swept past farm fields planted with a half-dozen election signs, including a slogan for a would-be sheriff: "More Action—Less Talk."

Forty miles down the road, Bud watched a road sign for Route 71 toward Joplin, and mumbled to himself, "Was that what we wanted?" He slowed and wheeled the van over to a gully between the lanes of traffic, and traced a finger on the road map.

"You don't know where the hell we are, do you?" asked J.W., peering over his book.

"I know where we are," Bud replied. "I just ain't so sure how to get where we're going."

•   •   •

The big squares of cultivated Midwestern farmland gave way to the Ozarks: wild thickets of brush, dense woods on steep hillsides, tin-topped shacks and the secondhand bargains of perpetual yard sales.

On a rickety front porch high on a hill, a young woman in a flowered housedress, with a passel of little kids at her hem, sat and watched the traffic. A faded sign on a tiny white church read "Salvation." And lot after lot was strewn with the rusting hulks of cannibalized cars and pickups.

"Looks like *Deliverance* country," said Bud. "Bet they got some woodsy characters down here."

J.W. piped up: "I better be careful. With these puffy eyes of mine, some of these backwoods boys are likely to think I'm kinda cute."

"Naw," said Bud. "They'll just think your paw married kind of close."

As darkness fell, the cowboys were still 100 miles from Harrison, Arkansas. Bud announced that he would be turning up the speed.

"On these narrow roads?" J.W. snapped. "Bud, you're crazy."

"You worry too much," Bud answered, as he pressed hard on the gas pedal. The van roared down the narrow, winding roads, squealing around corners, rushing past walls of bared, jagged rock.

"We're gonna die!" J.W. bellowed.

"Sooner or later," Bud said.

The radar detector started whistling furiously.

"Well, I guess we'll be slowing down now," said J.W., relieved for once to be snagged by a cop.

"Nope," said Bud, stepping even harder on the gas pedal. "We ain't got time to stop and visit with the police."

"Jesus, Bud!" said J.W. "They'll throw us in jail."

But the van zoomed ahead, and before long, the radar detector stopped shrieking.

•   •   •

The Boone County Fair in Harrison looked like the fifties: women in aprons selling homemade apple pies, crew-cut boys and beribboned girls licking snow cones and giggling at a puppet show sponsored by the Baptist church, a teenager with slicked-back hair strutting triumphantly around his souped-up red convertible.

The rodeo arena was festooned with colored plastic flags, like a used-car lot. And the loudspeaker played a recording of John Wayne, set to the tune of "God Bless America": "You ask me why I love it," the Duke's voice echoed. "I'll give you a million reasons."

Rolling through the entranceway, Bud peered through the windshield. He came to a stop near a cluster of oak trees. The cowboys stepped out and ducked behind the trees to change their shirts, then lugged their saddles to the chutes.

There was a shortage of cowboys, and the announcer asked if any amateurs would like to try their luck. "How many of you girls came tonight just to see these cowboys in their tight Wranglers?" the announcer asked, eliciting a wave of titters from the women in the stands.

Bud drew an old gray mare named Red Rock. There were five cowboys in the saddle-bronc event. Bud placed fourth.

26

ON A SUN-BLEACHED Texas pasture, Joe Wimberly squatted behind an ornery black horse, cleaning its mud-caked hooves with a paring knife.

Joe had hired himself out as a farrier for five bucks an hour. The pay wouldn't put much of a dent in the bills, which had mounted to almost $14,000. But it would put some beans on the table, the usual meal at the Wimberly house these days.

There hadn't been even a whisper of wind that afternoon. Sweat was dripping down Joe's face. His lips were parched. His bad knee was throbbing. His head was pounding. And the horse had been fighting him all day.

In fact, if he hadn't ducked at just the right moment, a flying hoof would have left him with an even bigger gap in his smile.

Not that he was smiling much anyway. "I ought to just quit," Joe had told Paula. "I'm just embarrassin' myself."

The bill collectors were bearing down, and prospective buyers had started coming around to look at the house. Soon it would be time to pack up and move. And even that wouldn't erase all the debts.

Just a few days ago, Joe had paid another humiliating visit to the banker over in Mineral Wells, where he felt like a misbehaved school-boy being called into the principal's office.

"Just what are you going to do?" the banker had demanded.

"Can't I have just a little more time?" the cowboy pleaded.

There was a time when the bank might have carried him, when it was locally owned and didn't answer to corporate headquarters somewhere in the East laying down hard-and-fast rules for branches in seventeen states. In those days, a rancher or a shopkeeper in a pinch stood a chance of winning a reprieve, just because his face was familiar and his handshake was honest.

But like most places on the plains, Mineral Wells was a ghost of its former self. In the last twenty years, its population had dropped 50 percent, to about 14,000. And all signs were that it would keep shrinking.

The mainstay in town, Poston's Dry Goods, famous for its sturdy wares and friendly service, closed a few years ago. When a Wal-Mart rose at the edge of town, other doors on Main Street slammed for good.

"You've had time, Joe," the banker said flatly. "These notes have got to be paid."

•   •   •

Joe finished the horse's manicure, gathered his tools and stepped wearily toward his pickup, an old blue Ford with a rust-eaten bed. The door rattled as it closed. The handle for the passenger window was missing. A faded flag decal was stuck on the rear glass.

It was a Friday, and Joe was slated to ride at Mesquite that night, the second-to-last performance of the season.

With all the troubles at home, Joe hadn't been thinking much about bulls. He used to pore over every word of the *Prorodeo Sports News* as soon as it arrived in the mail. But he hadn't looked at the rodeo paper for weeks now.

He was up in the first section of bull riding that evening. After the regular contest, they would bring Dodge Dakota out to snort and stomp and throw off another cowboy. The purse had grown to $17,000. But that didn't seem to matter much. For twenty-four weeks, nobody had been able to ride the damned thing. And Joe had gotten his chance, twice.

A big slew of cowboys were entering the rodeo every week in hopes of getting a shot at the bull, then drawing out when their names didn't come up. The Mesquite producer had stopped announcing what cowboy would be paired with Dakota, since it was thinning the ranks of his contestants. Now he waited until intermission on the night of the rodeo and then drew a name from a box.

As Joe drove along the bumpy two-lane highway, he remembered that he was supposed to call a radio station in Fort Worth. They wanted to interview the cowboy about how it felt to get bucked off Dakota.

Nobody knew how much it really hurt, since Joe and Paula had kept quiet about their financial problems. Joe only talked about that with his horse, who wasn't apt to call him a fool for getting into such a mess, and who could keep it a secret when the hard-nosed cowboy shed a few angry tears.

Joe always saw the world through the prism of the Old West, always fancied himself as a tough hombre who couldn't be caught or broken or jailed. But he was hearing footsteps these days.

"All of them outlaws in the Old West had bounties on their head," Joe had mused. "And they ran around for a long time. But sooner or later, somebody collected that bounty."

He pulled off at a gas station and plunked his change into a pay telephone.

"This is one mean, nasty bull, wouldn't you say, cowboy?" the interviewer asked him. "And smart too, huh?"

"Well, yeah," said Joe, "I guess people just don't give animals enough credit."

"Now, you were able to stay with him longer than most," the interviewer continued, "but only for six seconds."

"You know," Joe told him, "settin' here talkin' on the phone, six seconds don't seem like much. But on the back of a bull, it's all day long."

"You wouldn't think a two-thousand-pound bull would even notice a cowboy on him," the radio man said.

"Aw, these bulls will use their tail to swat a fly settin' on their back. I think they're gonna notice a hundred-forty-pound man."

The interviewer rambled on about rodeo and the myth of the cowboy, and asked Joe if he wanted to add anything.

"I guess when you get on bulls for a living," Joe said, "the odds are stacked against you."

•   •   •

When Joe walked through the door, Paula was on the telephone.

"Well, then don't come and look at the house," she snapped and hung it up. "Smartass."

"What's wrong?" Joe asked her.

Paula was exasperated. It was bad enough to watch people inspect her home, like vultures hovering over carrion. They didn't have to get snide when she couldn't answer every question about the place.

"They're probably just poor people like us," he said.

Paula reminded him that these were people who were fixing to buy a place. So they probably weren't as poor.

"Oh, I know," he said. "Sometimes it feels like the whole world is just comin' apart."

The telephone rang again. It was a bill collector.

•   •   •

Paula and the kids sat in the top row of bleachers at the Mesquite Arena, and watched as Joe got unceremoniously dumped from his bull. It was another $40 down the drain.

After the ride, a mentally retarded man near the rail called out to the cowboy. "That's all right, Joe," he said. "You're just savin' it for Dodge Dakota, ain't that right."

Joe managed a weak smile, and walked out of his way to give the man's shoulder an affectionate squeeze. And then he headed into the locker room, where he sat on a narrow wooden bench against a cinderblock wall. He sat in silence for a while and sucked on a fresh plug of tobacco. A few moments later, he stepped out the door and peered up into the grandstands.

•   •   •

During intermission, the rodeo officials gathered around a big box filled with twenty poker chips, one for each of the bull riders, drawing to see who was to get a chance at Dodge Dakota.

The long arm of a ruddy-faced man reached into the box, fished around for a few seconds and finally pulled a lone chip from the pile.

In the grandstands, Paula was shushing her daughters, who were playing noisily in the aisles, and wrestling with her little boy, who was using his mom's lap for a saddle. She glanced down toward the arena and saw Joe standing quietly a few feet away from the crowd around the box.

Paula wasn't thinking about Dodge Dakota. She had stopped wishing a long time ago.

Fourteen weeks had passed since his second crash off the bull, when she watched their dreams vanish in the swirling dust on the arena floor. Since then, she had grown accustomed to coming to Mesquite every weekend and watching some other poor woman's husband get knocked silly by the invincible bull.

But now Paula could see a bunch of cowboys huddled around Joe. They were patting him on the back and talking a mile a minute.

"Hey, Joe Wimberly," one of the officials called out. "You got Dodge Dakota."

"No I didn't," Joe shot back, a little annoyed that anybody would kid about something like that.

"I'm telling you, Joe, you got him. You drew the darned bull. I ain't kiddin'."

And then Neal Gay, the owner of Mesquite, came by and squeezed Joe's elbow. "Third time's the charm," he said with a wink.

•   •   •

As Paula watched from the grandstands, she understood what was happening. Now her breath vanished and her heart began to pound.

She wasn't at all sure she wanted this.

Twice before, she had watched Joe's hopes soar as high as the stars, and then sink to the depths of hell.

She had listened to him curse himself mercilessly for blowing the big chance, had watched him walking in circles in the backyard, had lain beside him at night while he replayed the ride in his mind, over and over and over.

In the months that had passed, Joe's wounds had still not healed. But at least he had come to some kind of grudging peace. Her husband was a strong man, a survivor. But how much disappointment could he stand?

•   •   •

Joe climbed the steps that led to the bucking chutes. He felt almost faint. It occurred to him that he wasn't breathing. He drew in a few big gulps of air and exhaled slowly.

He looked up at the grandstands. Everything was shimmering, almost like a dream.

The season was almost over. Twenty-four times a cowboy had climbed aboard Dodge Dakota. And twenty-four times the bull had emerged victorious.

The pot had grown big enough to save the house, to pay the bills, even to have a little left over. In all his life, Joe Wimberly had rarely had anything left over.

The announcer's voice echoed across the arena:

"Ladies and gentlemen, do we have a treat for you tonight!"

The cowboy pulled himself over the rails, his boots hooked on either side, straddling the bull that snorted and stomped inside its cage.

And then he lowered himself slowly, inch by inch, until the denim touched the hide.

His eyes had narrowed to little slits. And the bull rope was wrapped around his right wrist, as tight as a noose.

Joe was a man who tried to live his life by a handful of pithy, down-to-earth aphorisms.

"A wishbone ain't no substitute for a backbone," he liked to say.

And "You won't never regret what you don't say."

And "Worry is like a rockin' horse, it just don't get you nowhere."

But as he sat on the back of Dodge Dakota, with the world at stake for the next eight seconds, only one of his favorite phrases came to mind:

"If you ain't got no choice, be brave."

•   •   •

The gate swung open. The cowboy held on for his life. And the huge black beast bellowed to the heavens.

A ton of muscle and bone, the bull thundered past the gates, as the cowboy's thighs squeezed tight, his right hand gripping the rope, his free hand in the air.

Dakota squatted, ready to spring, and then exploded. And the 140-pound cowboy summoned everything he had.

The single twisted horn crawled down the side of the bull's face. Snot spewed from its flaring nostrils. Its head snapped violently. Its eyes flashed fire. Dust rose from its kicking hooves.

And the clock ticked—six seconds . . . five seconds . . . four seconds.

The cowboy bounced on its hard, broad back. Then a shuddering buck shot him skyward, twisting in the air. He slapped back down, straining for balance. And then another punishing buck.

Joe dangled at the edge, fighting against gravity, losing control.

Two seconds, one second . . .

Joe crashed to the dirt as the horn sounded—a photo finish.

A hush swept over the arena. The faces of 5,000 fans stared down at the rodeo boss, who was staring at the timekeeper, who was staring at the clock. Joe peered up from the dirt floor, a hoof mark imprinted on his shirt back and desperation in his eyes, waiting for the official ruling.

And then the official raised his arms in the air, the sign of a touch-down.

Joe had made it by two hundredths of a second.

The grandstands shook. And the cowboy fell to his knees, tears running down his dirty cheeks.

"Thank you, Jesus," Joe cried. "Thank you, Jesus."

Paula fell sobbing into the arms of a spectator.

Sami and Casey sprinted down the stairs of the grandstands, rushing toward the arena.

McKinnon screamed, "Daddy did it! Daddy did it!"

Some fans in the top row lifted up the four-year-old boy and passed him down the bleachers, row by row, to the edge of the arena, up and over the rails, and he ran jumping and shouting toward his father.

Paula skipped down the stairs, chasing after her kids and her husband, giggling through her triumphant tears.

From his knees, Joe looked up and met Paula's eyes, as she galloped toward him with outstretched arms.

The roar of the crowd swept down on the arena floor, joyful as rain on the plains, where the Wimberly family squeezed together in a ten-armed hug, their tears spilling on the dust.

•   •   •

It was past two a.m. when they walked in the door. The kids finally settled down enough to go to bed. And Joe and Paula wrapped their arms around each other again and kissed like teenagers.

"S'pose we ought to go to bed," Paula said, as the clock showed half past two.

"In just a minute," Joe smiled. "First I got a phone call to make."

"At this hour?" Paula asked.

But the lateness of the hour had never seemed to matter to the bill collectors. He figured it could work two ways.

Joe cradled the phone and dialed the number. It rang three or four times before the sleepy banker picked up.

"Hello?" the voice answered groggily.

"How you doin' on this fine evening?" Joe boomed triumphantly into the phone.

"Who's this?" came a mumble.

"Why, this here is old Joe Wimberly," he said. "And I was just calling to say, 'I got a check for you.'"

•   •   •

Early the next morning, the telephone rang and Paula picked up. It was the banker.

"Strangest thing," the banker told her. "I got a call in the middle of the night, at least I think I got a call, and it was Joe. Or maybe I was just dreaming."

"Yeah," said Paula giddily. "That was sure one fine dream, wasn't it?"

27

HIGH IN THE neon galaxy of the Strip, a sparkling cowboy sat atop a lightbulb bronc, riding perfectly and endlessly across a blazing marquee, a 50,000-watt rodeo star who would never be thrown or hurt or broke.

Eleven months and 100 rodeos ago, the trail had begun in the knifing winds and squalling snows of Denver. Thousands of cowboys had chased the dream of Las Vegas. By the time the road reached the bright lights on the desert, only a handful were left standing. And now these cowboys gawked and giggled in the shower of colored lights, and clicked their heels to good fortune, country boys in the land of Oz.

"If I'm dreaming," said Larry Sandvick, the North Dakota farm boy who checked into a glitzy suite reserved for a champion at the Imperial Palace, "don't wake me up."

•   •   •

The National Finals Rodeo, like no convention in Las Vegas, transformed the town in its own image. Cowboy hats were everywhere, on Montana ranchers gone to town, on New Jersey slickers playing rustic, on Japanese businessmen in pinstripe suits, on ponytailed blondes in slit skirts.

Country-and-western music echoed from the show rooms of every big hotel in town, and the dance halls swooned to the ballads of cheatin' and drinkin' and thankin' God for being American.

And along Las Vegas Boulevard, the everyday tools of the cowboy trade danced in lighted images on every billboard and casino, a colorful flash of spurs and chaps and saddles and stirrups, like a tack shop in a Disney cartoon.

It did not matter that in another few weeks the towering billboards and blazing marquees would flash some other images, and a new theme-of-the-week would sweep over Las Vegas.

Nor did it matter that its garish lights and never-close bars and easy sex hardly squared with the morals handed down on the ranch. Or that the dizzying growth of Las Vegas, the fastest-growing urban center in America, exemplified the dominance of concrete and pavement over fields and barns in the economy of the New West. And it did not even matter that this quick-buck city was filled with urban-dwelling tourists who would sooner roll snake eyes than actually live in the remote lands of scrub grass and horseshit.

What mattered is that for these ten days in December, when Las Vegas becomes the cowboy capital of the world, the Old West still lives, if only for eight seconds at a time.

•   •   •

"Let's tear the roof off this place," the announcer roared, as 16,000 fans in the domed Thomas & Mack Arena answered in screams of frenzied anticipation.

The rodeo championship had been held for twenty years in Oklahoma City, the land of chicken-fried steak and the Cowboy Hall of Fame, but pulled up stakes in 1985, as the oil boom was going to bust and the ranch economy was biting the dust, and moved to burgeoning Las Vegas, where tourism promoters, looking to fill the December lull, had dangled a much bigger pot of prize money than Oklahoma could match.

Some of the older cowboys missed the friendly twang and wide-eyed enthusiasm of Oklahoma City, a place where the locals understood the language of livestock and greeted the rodeo finals as the biggest deal of the year. But it was carnival, and not culture, that footed the bills of rodeo. And the flashy ten-day show in Las Vegas had boosted the prize money for cowboys to $2 million, not to mention sweeter profits for the sport's promoters.

"Tonight in the city of neon and nylons," the loudspeaker blared, "let's rodeo!"

To the raucous strains of electric guitars, the riders of the Grand Entry, costumed as Buffalo Bill and Calamity Jane and Roy Rogers, burst through a glittering neon horseshoe and galloped across the arena floor, recently a stage for the Teenage Mutant Ninja Turtles, and now covered with eighteen inches of dirt that had been trucked in from the desert.

The Nashville band, Asleep at the Wheel, played the "Star-Spangled Banner," and just as the anthem reached "rockets' red glare," an arsenal of orange flares went shooting through the air, triggering a thunderous whoop from the crowd.

The livestock were penned in the concrete parking lot behind the stadium, not far from some condominiums, where a group of residents had been complaining to City Hall about unpleasant odors. Shortly before the performance, a cold, driving rain swept down on Las Vegas, which cleansed the air and presumably pleased the neighbors. But it did no favors for the drenched animals, who were unsheltered in the stinging storm.

The horses were finally led inside, toweled off and loaded into the chutes. The grandstands buzzed. Cowboy hats and denim mixed with high heels and spangled gowns. And the fans glanced around to search for celebrities. Nolan Ryan, the baseball star, was here, and so was Gregory Hines, the tap dancer.

All of the performances had been sold out for months, and scalpers were demanding $300 and up. One rodeo worker had been offered $10,000 for her lifetime pass, not including the cost of the $17 ticket itself. And the newspapers said a pair of front-row seats had been the object of an ugly battle in divorce court.

•   •   •

Down behind the chutes, each cowboy wore a numeral that indicated his place in the rodeo pecking order, according to winnings during the season. On the back of Ty Murray was the number 1.

The champ was announced in the reverent tone fit for a king. And the crowd exploded at the mention of his name.

Murray was shooting for his fourth straight title. But there was little drama in the pursuit. With earnings of $139,724 coming into Las Vegas, the twenty-three-year-old held a lead so large he could skip the week of rodeo for dancing-girl shows and still come back on the night of the finale to accept the crown.

"Here is a wonderful young man," the announcer said of Murray, as one superlative after the next tripped off his tongue. "And he has the quality in character to be the leader of our industry."

As the horn blared, Murray bolted into the arena, his free arm waving with the confident flair of an artist painting yet another masterpiece. And when the eight seconds had elapsed, he hopped to the turf, dusted off his chaps and waved casually toward the adoring crowd, which roared as if it had just witnessed the greatest ride in the history of rodeo, at least until the champ took his next turn.

The talents of the next contestant in the bareback event, who wore number 57 on his back, got no such lofty praise from the man behind the microphone. But the announcer did note the peculiar leggings that the cowboy was wearing.

Unlike the other cowboys, who wore conventional leathers, Larry Sandvick had donned a pair of wild and woolly angora chaps. He had sewn together the chaps as a tribute to the cowboys of old, who wore such a style during the winter, and as a nod to his adopted home state of Wyoming, where sheep were as important as cattle.

Some of the fans muttered that he looked ridiculous. And a few of the other cowboys rolled their eyes. That Sandvick. He just had to be different.

And he would not have argued the point. Sandvick never cared much for convention. After all, he figured, if a guy just wanted to be normal, he probably wouldn't rodeo for a living. And if the tongues were clucking now, just wait. He had one more surprise up his sleeve.

When the gate pulled open and the bucking started, big puffs of what looked like smoke rose off the chaps, billowing with every jerk and thrust of the horse. Sandvick had packed the angora with baby powder, a dramatic way to show that this hotshot cowboy was positively smoking.

And he was. He gave the judges and the fans a ride that was as wild as his chaps, earning a magnificent score that catapulted him right past Murray. At the end of the night, Sandvick had finished in a tie for first place. His check was $7,000.

"If you can't have a sense of humor in life," Sandvick said later, between swigs of beer with the other cowboys, who were still chuckling over his crazy chaps, "then what the hell's the point?"

•   •   •

As the time neared for the saddle-bronc event, Craig Latham stood behind the chutes and gazed up into the crowd, as if he was looking for somebody.

He had rolled up winnings of more than $55,000 during the year, and had come to Las Vegas in second place in the event, behind Billy Etbauer, his best friend. With a spectacular run, he might even catch Billy and win the championship. But Craig was grateful just to be here. If he could turn in a series of decent performances, he would be able to go home contented and put some money in the bank, poised to ride for another year.

His wife, Laurie, and little girl, Chaney, were here in the grandstands tonight, cheering him on. Laurie hadn't been able to get any time off from teaching her eleven kindergartners back in Goodwell, but she had flown in for the weekend and would fly back to Las Vegas again next weekend.

His granddad, Norris Graves, the patriarch of the Red Fork Ranch, was watching from the grandstands. And so were Craig's mother, Joyce, and father, Russell, although they didn't sit together. His aunt Bonnie was here from Wyoming. Even Laurie's parents, who hadn't been too thrilled about their daughter marrying a rodeo cowboy, had come down from North Dakota to watch him in the championship. Later that night, they were going to watch their granddaughter so Craig and Laurie could spend a night on the town.

In almost every way, this was a time of triumph for Craig, the reward for a grueling year spent rolling down so many dark highways, stopping in so many lonely truck stops. But December was a difficult time for Craig. And Las Vegas was a difficult place.

It was in December that Deke had been killed. And it was in this arena that Craig had last seen his brother alive.

Laurie always thought that Craig had chosen to become a rodeo cowboy as a way of staying close to Deke, almost as if, in the endless journey from one dusty little county fairground to the next, one noisy big-city arena to another, he was searching for a brother who was not gone, but only lost, and who might, somewhere along the trail, step out from behind the bucking chutes, or emerge from the crowd at the beer stand, and flash his wonderful grin once more.

·   ·   ·

Craig climbed aboard his bronc, Bobby Joe Skoal, leaned back in the saddle, pointed his spurs toward the sky and hung tight to the reins, as the announcer told the crowd:

"Ladies and gentlemen, here's Craig Latham, one of the finest cowboys you'll see. And if anybody can catch Billy Etbauer, this is the man right here."

He flew out of the chute, leaned to the right, absorbed the first buck, and then the next. The cowboy rode square in the center.

His score put him in a tie for first place. He loped back to the locker room, barely cracking a smile, and slowly made his way toward the Gold Coast Casino for the awards ceremony.

•   •   •

On a stage inside the Gold Coast, bedecked with red curtains and chandeliers and huge posters of Crown Royal whiskey, the winning cowboys lined up to accept their prize belt buckles, as the master of ceremonies, who wore a black sport coat and a droopy mustache, bellowed to the packed crowd on the ballroom floor, "Is anybody here drunk yet?"

The rodeo queen, perched on stage for decoration, was tall and blond and Californian. She wore a metallic green blouse, tight jeans and a black cowboy hat. The emcee introduced her to wolf whistles in the crowd, and then began to banter in a teasing voice.

"How old are you?" he asked.

"Twenty-three," she said.

"Got a boyfriend?"

"I can't answer that."

The emcee noted that her reign as queen would last for the next year of rodeos, and said her life was about to change. "You were a girl, but now you're a lady. And for the next three hundred and sixty-five days, we're gonna be walkin' and we're gonna be talkin' and we're gonna put some blisters on your bottom."

The queen smiled nervously. Somewhere out in the crowd, a beer bottle crashed to the floor. And somebody screamed a four-letter word, whether in frustration or celebration it was hard to tell.

Sandvick stood beaming on the stage, waiting to be feted. The emcee looked his way, and then began to make sport of the cowboy. "I can't let this guy get too close to the microphone," he said, casting a wary, sideways glance. "He's let his shotgun mouth overload his bee-bee-sized butt too many times."

As belly laughter erupted from the crowd, Larry looked a bit embarrassed.

"But he is a cowboy," the emcee added, a bit grudgingly. "He is what this is all about."

Sandvick had tied for first in the bareback event with Denny Mc-Clanahan, a short, skinny twenty-four-year-old from Canadian,

Texas. Both cowboys were entitled to a prize buckle. But there was only one on hand. A rodeo official told McClanahan he would get his later, and handed over the buckle to Sandvick.

Larry took it and walked over to McClanahan's father. He undid the man's belt and fastened on the gleaming buckle. "I reckon you deserve this," he told the man. And when Sandvick got his buckle later, he handed it over to his own father. "I've put you through a lot," he said, "so you ought to have this."

On his way back through the crowd, headed for another beer, Sandvick spotted two liquored women in low-cut blouses arguing loudly over the rightful dibs to some handsome cowboy.

"No need to fight," Larry said with a smile. "You can both have me."

"Shit, all right then," drawled one of the women, maybe bluffing, maybe not. "My pickup's right out back."

The answer startled the cowboy, who talked the role of the rascal more than he played it.

"Well, uh, well, uh," he mumbled, almost blushing, and walking away fast, "we'll be seeing you."

On the other side of the room, Craig made his way toward the stage, squirming past two big inebriated men. The bronc rider held tight to his wife's hand.

Craig's granddad stood somewhere in the back of the crowd, unable to fight the stampede to get close to the stage, as he strained to listen to the awards presentation through his hearing aid.

As the emcee introduced Craig, the cowboy moved haltingly toward the microphone, wearing a frozen expression as he stared into the crowd, looking like he'd be much more comfortable on the back of a raging bronc. He stammered a bit, and finally found the words.

"Everybody can't win a go-round 'cause there's fifteen of us and only ten rounds," he said. "I just wish they could add five rounds and give everybody a taste of what it's like to win."

•   •   •

Two thousand miles from the neon, Bud Longbrake sat on the couch in his house trailer, a little past midnight, watching the Las Vegas rodeo on television on tape delay.

It was a typical December night in South Dakota. A numbing wind was howling and snow was drifting across the fields, including the patch where Bud had planned to build the new house, a dream that would have to wait.

Bud had finished twentieth in the standings, missing the finals by $10,000. He had chased hard into October, until he failed to win a nickel at the Oklahoma City rodeo, and knew that his hopes were dashed. The next day, he turned out of the following week's rodeos, Yakima, Washington; Bonifay, Florida; and Hope, Arkansas; and made the long drive back home to the Cheyenne River Sioux reservation.

In a season of nearly 120 rodeos, Bud had won about $27,000. More than half of that had gone to gasoline and motels and entry fees. When he got back home, he had told his wife, "I'm so damned tired of horses and highways."

Bud thought a lot about last December, and the December before, when he made the finals, and the tribe had sent him off with a special dinner and a prayer, and he and Lona, who spent so much time apart, had gotten to talk for hours and hours as they drove past Belle Fourche and Gillette and Casper and Rawlins and Salt Lake, galloping toward Las Vegas, just the two of them.

Some friends had called to ask if he wanted to drive down to Las Vegas this year. But Bud wasn't interested. He was a cowboy, not a spectator.

Instead, he set to work in the fields, patching fence and feeding the cows, who were five months pregnant, not showing much yet, and playing with his kids.

Bud wasn't the type to wear a long face and sulk around the house. It was good to be home with the family, despite the reason. And he knew he had plenty of reasons to be thankful.

One recent morning, Lona had gone down to the post office to pick up the mail. Mixed in with the bills was a business envelope with the return address of the tribal government in Eagle Butte. Up in the left-hand corner, it read: Enrollment.

She opened the letter and read the typed words:

"This is to inform you that the Cheyenne River Sioux Tribal Council has approved the enrollment of your children."

As wind shook the trailer, the family huddled around the living room, near the bronze of the Indian bent over a bronc, and read the form over and over.

"Well, Jay," Bud told his son proudly. "You're an Indian now—I mean, you always were an Indian. But now it's official."

They called Bud's parents, who sighed with relief. For at least one more generation, the name Longbrake was Indian.

On the television set, the images of the cowboys in Las Vegas flick-

ered in the darkness. Lona waited up with her husband until the last
of the saddle-bronc riders had competed, and then went off to bed.

•   •   •

Dizzy with beer and glory, Sandvick fired up the engine on old
Goldie, the old car that had been called back into action since he
wrecked his new Cadillac, and zoomed down the streets of Las Vegas,
the reflection of colored lights overhead dancing on the cracked
windshield.

The jalopy looked bare without its curled sheep horns. But the dis-
tinctive hood ornaments had been confiscated in Canada by a cus-
toms inspector who suspected they might have come from an
endangered species. The cowboy had argued with the man, telling
him that he had the wrong sheep in mind. But he was running late for
a rodeo. He couldn't waste much time quibbling.

On this Saturday night, two fellow cowboys were crammed in the
back seat, his old friend "Chain Saw" and a bareback rider from
Hackberry, Louisiana, a young Cajun who hunted alligators in his
spare time.

Sandvick, driving without a license, flipped a U-turn on Paradise,
and scooted down the slick streets. He veered into the parking lot of
the Stardust Hotel, fastened his cowboy hat and headed toward the
ballroom, primed for some drinking and dancing.

"If you ain't livin' on the edge," he said, "then you ain't really
livin'."

He had been waiting to hear from his lawyer, who had entered a
plea on the drunk-driving charge. Sandvick was hoping to avoid
spending any time in jail, but the lawyer had told him not to count
on it.

In the week before the arrest, Sandvick had accumulated $4,500,
the biggest pile of money he had ever seen. He had even thought
about opening a savings account.

But a big chunk of the cash went for bail and the lawyer. And most
of the rest had gone to buy rodeo tickets for friends.

Now Larry was flush like never before. In the finals so far, he had
won more than $11,000. He gulped down beer after beer inside the
Stardust, and if anybody was a little short on pocket money for a
drink, Larry was happy to buy.

The next morning, he slept late, on a bed under a mirrored ceiling
in the Imperial Palace. And when he finally roused himself, he

spruced up in a gilded bathroom with a sunken tub, plumbing fit for a star.

•   •   •

That evening in the stadium, riding his third bronc of the week, Sandvick stormed out of the chutes in a cloud of dust. The fans, who were becoming accustomed to the helter-skelter rides of the bullet-proof cowboy, roared to the rhythm of the stomping dance.

But a few bucks into the ride, a hard jolt by the horse snapped Sandvick's head so far back it slammed against the top of his spine. His body jiggled like Jell-O. His eyes rolled back in his head.

Knocked cold, but still bouncing on the bronc, his lean frame somehow defied gravity for a few seconds longer, dangling woozily, until the horn sounded. One final buck of the horse seemed finally to shake some life back into his eyes. The cowboy fell to the ground, then staggered to the rails, where some medics were waiting.

A trainer knelt before him, flashing one finger before his eyes, then two, then three.

"I can't see a fucking thing," Sandvick said.

He was led into the training room, where a doctor looked him over and asked him a series of questions, like his name.

Sandvick started to come around after a while, although his eyes still weren't working as a team. When the examinations were complete, he sat shivering in his underwear, draped in a towel, looking as fragile as an old woman in a shawl.

"He was unconscious for a while on the horse," a trainer told a group of cowboys huddled around. "Just a brain bruise."

They sent Sandvick on his way, with a warning not to drink any alcohol. At two o'clock in the morning, a medic rang his room, to ask another series of questions, just to check on his mental condition.

He was asked to repeat his name, his age, his hometown and the name of the wild bronc he would climb aboard in the next go-round, just sixteen hours later.

•   •   •

In his five years as rodeo boss, Lewis Cryer had been doing a splendid job of boosting profits. When he took over as commissioner, after leaving a post as a college basketball executive, the association was drowning in debt. Now under his management, it had $3 million in the bank.

"We're running this like a business," he said.

There were a few squawks about his leadership from down below. But that was all part of the game.

Cryer had attended a ceremony for the cowboys, usually an agreeable bunch, when one of them shouted some angry words his way:

"When are you gonna get some money for the cowboys? We're starvin' out here!"

It was Sandvick. And the outburst brought glares from some of the other cowboys, who apparently thought it unkind to insult the man at the top.

But Sandvick had glared right back.

"What the hell are you lookin' at me for? You assholes are all thinkin' the same thing."

The commissioner let it roll off his back. If these vagabonds thought they were worth more than they were getting, they were dreaming. This wasn't the NBA. There were no media superstars in rodeo.

Not that he wasn't trying to change that. He had been working on a package with ESPN, and maybe a deal with a network, to get more exposure for rodeo. He had helped push the annual prize money to $20 million. Of course, $12 million of that was coming right out of the pockets of the 7,300 contestants through entry fees.

To Cryer, who wore a big black cowboy hat but had never climbed aboard a raging bull or a bucking bronc in his life, only a tiny percentage of these men seemed to have any real talent.

"There's a lot of pretenders," he said.

But he bubbled with enthusiasm about the growth potential for the sport, what with Hollywood and Madison Avenue so infatuated with the Wild West these days.

"This is a happening kind of thing," he said. "People pulling on boots and putting on hats, playing cowboy for a week."

Cryer knew there were problems on the horizon. Animal rights activists had been demonstrating outside Thomas & Mack, handing out leaflets that declared "Rodeo: Cruelty for a Buck."

He had hired a full-time staffer at rodeo headquarters to improve the sport's image with the humane groups. And he had worked to change the style of calf roping, promoting a rule that would forbid the animals from being jerked down and slammed to the turf.

"But you know, we get a lot more wrecked cowboys than wrecked animals."

That was the real magic of rodeo, of course, the drama that puts people in the seats, and draws not a peep of protest, the exquisite danger to the cowboys, the possibility of watching a young man meet his death.

"The spectacular nature of guys getting crushed, guys almost getting crushed. It's a hell of a show. People love to watch the wrecks. And there's nothing that does that like rodeo. That football player who got paralyzed—we could see that any night of the week here.

"It's dangerous, but come on, these guys are nuts, they're crazy, it's in their blood. They're obsessed. It's just a way of life with these people."

And when it ends their life, or forever stunts it, nobody can say that the rodeo business is not there to help. Take that kid up in Montana, he pointed out, the bull rider who got paralyzed at a rodeo.

"We bought him a specialized saddle and a truck equipped with a wheelchair lift. And you know, that's not the only time we've done that."

28

THE BARTENDERS at the Sands and the Stardust were hustling drinks as fast as they could. The shows for Randy Travis and Dolly Parton were selling out. And the gaming tables were piled high, in more than a few cases with the prize loot from cowboys, who were better with bulls and horses than cards and dice.

"These people are perfect for us," a tourism official enthused. "Except for two hours at the rodeo every night, they've got nothing to do. They're a captive audience."

On the sidewalks of the Strip, the visitors from America's back forty could tell they weren't in Kansas anymore. Slick flyers were being hawked with photographs of big breasts in every color, along with numbers of "real-live hot babes" who were waiting by the telephone for calls from sexed-up cowboys.

"Bo Knows Cowboys!" read the headline over the picture of a purring young blonde in fishnet stockings, blood-red fingernails pointing to her naked chest.

"Let's get naked," one ad invited. "For a midnight snack, call Kelly."

Some ads gave job descriptions: "Young Nurse." "Lonely College Student." "Busty, Sensuous, Older Woman."

There was an offer of "a night on the town" with a young woman who would wear a "matching set of pastel-colored nylons and lingerie." Prices for a date started at $250.

And since this was the nineties, even for rodeo fans, there were "The Back Street Boys," who were available to come up to the room twenty-four hours a day. "I'm Calvin," read the description over a trim fellow in tight black underwear. "I'm young, Italian and available."

Sex-for-sale was legal in Nye County, forty miles north of Las Vegas, and brochures on the cathouses noted that tourists could combine a roll in the hay with some sight-seeing at the nearby molybdenum mines and MX missile site. To be sure, some of the rodeo fans probably found their way to the Cherry Patch and Mabel's Whorehouse. But as the week wore on, the flesh peddlers lamented, the cowboy crowd was hardly any boon for business. They had done a lot better with the suit-and-tie guys at the computer convention.

•   •   •

A few hours before the Wednesday night performance, the sixth of the series, Craig and his grandfather were relaxing in the silence of a small room in the Horseshoe, a faded hotel on Fremont Street in the old part of the city. Sharing quarters, and the quiet, was a tradition between the grandfather and his grandsons.

Back in January, when the season was just beginning, and Craig was wondering whether the long haul would end in Las Vegas or in final disappointment, Norris had come down from the ranch in Wyoming to spend a month in the house trailer in Oklahoma, just to be handy if the young cowboy needed an old cowboy, or the other way around.

During each of Craig's four trips to the championship, Norris had stayed with him. And in 1986, when Deke was taking his final ride, the grandfather had shared a room with the older boy.

Craig and Norris spent the day watching a little television, talking about the snow up in Wyoming, going downstairs to play a few hands of blackjack.

It had been a fine week of performances so far for Craig. He wouldn't catch Billy, "no chance in heck," as the young cowboy put it. He might even slip a notch from his second-place ranking in the standings. But he had won more than $15,000, and there were more horses yet to buck.

Norris, who was moving through his seventies, walked a little slower this year than he had on his earlier trips to Las Vegas. And he was straining a little more from behind his glasses.

As they sat in the room, with the time of the rodeo approaching, the grandfather didn't say much, except how darned proud he was of the cowboy. He was content just to sit in silence, happy to be in his grandson's company.

Craig didn't say much either. But he wanted to.

"You know, granddad," he finally told his grandfather. "You're like John Wayne to me."

•   •   •

Inside the stadium, samples of Copenhagen chewing tobacco were being given away free to anybody who was eighteen, or looked it. Miss Crown Royal strutted in boots, ogled in the name of good whiskey. Calendars of bare-chested cowboys sold like hotcakes.

When everybody settled down, the loudspeaker blared the name of Wayne Herman, a North Dakota cowboy who was badly banged up the other night but had lived to fight another day.

"Thank you, God, for keeping him alive," the announcer boomed. "He's carrying eight stitches in his face and he's got a mile of Johnson and Johnson under his blue jeans."

Herman, who wore the insignia of the golden arches on his sleeves, a deal he worked out with a couple of McDonald's franchises in the Dakotas, had been pummeled by a horse so wickedly they needed a stretcher to carry him off. His wife had walked alongside her bleeding husband, stroking his hair, as the fans politely applauded for the brave cowboy. A few years ago, they had lost a child to cancer. But the cowboy kept on riding through the child's illness to pay the bills.

As the gate lifted, Herman bolted out of the chutes as if he didn't have a scratch, putting in his eight seconds for the check, trying not to grimace too much.

A few cowboys later, a big bronc lay down in the chutes, and the announcer muttered something about a candidate for the bucking horse sale.

•   •   •

The bull rider leading the standings was Cody Custer, who had won the $3,000 prize as the Coors Favorite Cowboy in a vote by the fans. Custer was a born-again Christian who viewed beer drinking as sinful, of course, but the world of rodeo does not spend time dwelling on contradictions.

As he had all week, Custer conquered the bull, then fell to the turf and raised his arms to the heavens in thanks and praise. "He gives the glory to God," the announcer cracked, "but he keeps the paycheck."

Custer carried a leather gear bag tooled with the inscription "Praise the Lord," and some of the other cowboys thought he carried this prayerful business a little too far.

"One of these days," Murray, the All-Around Cowboy, told some friends in the locker room, "Cody's gonna be down on his knees, giving it all up to God, and the damned bull's gonna come around and nail him right in the ass."

After the rodeo, some of the cowboys were encouraged to stop by a reception room and squeeze the palms of some of the sponsors, business executives who could then go home and talk about their friends, the rodeo cowboys.

Some other cowboys were asked to sit at a table and sign autographs for the fans, a way to promote goodwill for the sport.

"Who are you?" an autograph seeker asked one of the cowboys.

"I'm a nobody," said Larry Sandvick, as he scribbled his name on a piece of paper, "but I'm soon to be a somebody."

"You don't look like your picture in the program," said a woman in line, perhaps not sure she was meeting the real McCoy. "Your face looks thinner than the guy in the picture."

"When they took the picture," Larry explained, "I had a big wad of tobacco in my mouth."

Outside the stadium, some cowboys and their friends and families stood in the darkness and made small talk.

"Gonna do any gambling?" Craig asked his aunt, who had left the ranch for a week in the glamorous city.

"Nope," she said. "I figure we gamble enough on cattle prices and the weather."

•   •   •

On the Sunday afternoon of the final performance, a brass band played the theme song from *Bonanza*. The horses in the Grand Entry galloped across the dirt, with the riders hoisting a sign for each state represented by the cowboys, and for Canada, whose fans high in the grandstands unfurled a giant maple leaf flag.

As the bucking began, the announcer saved his most lavish praise, as always, for the introduction of Ty Murray, who had won his fourth straight title of All-Around Cowboy.

The blond cowboy under the black hat straddled his bareback horse. Cameras flashed all around him.

This was a cowboy, the announcer had gushed earlier, "who can make a bull look like a 4-H calf," and whose heroics were soon to be chronicled in *Sports Illustrated*. The loudspeaker informed the crowd that today was Ty's mother's birthday, and a cheer went up for her, a woman deserving gratitude for giving rodeo its most luminous star.

During the finals, Murray was the guest of the Gold Coast casino, where the awards were presented, so that the walk between his room and the victory stage each night would be a short one. The hotel staff had orders to show the superstar cowboy the utmost in gracious service, and had slipped up only once.

Murray's California girlfriend, who was staying with him, was keeping her little pet shih tzu in the room, a violation of the house rules. A maid asked her to remove the dog from the premises.

But the "misunderstanding" was soon rectified.

"The maid wasn't aware that this was Ty Murray's room," the management told the young woman with its deepest apologies. "You tell Ty that he can keep a horse in the room if he wants."

To the exultation of the crowd, Murray glided triumphantly across the arena on his overmatched bronc, brilliant as the sun on a Texas morning. And the thunder of applause vibrated to a room on the ground floor, where a group of old rodeo cowboys watched the performance on TV.

•   •   •

Once upon a time, Turk Greenough was one of the most sensational rodeo stars in America. "King of the Bronc-Busters," they called him. His picture was splashed across newspapers. His name echoed over radio broadcasts. At eighty-seven, he was the oldest living rodeo champ in the nation.

The old cowboys weren't given tickets to the finals, but they could sit and watch the televised performance in the drafty, cement-floored Gold Card Room. Turk sat behind a plate of chips and squinted up at the screen.

Alongside him was his old friend Johnny White Eyes, a former bronc rider from the Sioux reservation at Pine Ridge in South Dakota, who now sat in a wheelchair.

Greenough had settled in North Las Vegas after his rodeo days, and worked as a security guard for Caesar's Palace until he retired fifteen years ago. He still had a driver's license, but not a car. The old heap had blown up just a few months ago.

•   •   •

Out on the arena floor, Ty Murray and the lesser champions lined up to accept their prize buckles. The presenter of the trophies put an arm around the All-Around Cowboy and spoke into the microphone: "For all the people who aren't here, who don't see this on television, I feel sorry for them," he said. "They should try to be like Ty Murray."

Near some bundles of hay, a man dressed in the long white beard and red suit of Santa Claus sat in a high-backed chair as two little kids dressed in Western apparel bounded on his lap. The loudspeaker piped "Oh Come All Ye Faithful." And in the grandstands, a teenage boy in a cowboy hat stared at the page of the *Prorodeo Sports News* with the application form to become a rodeo contestant. There was a dotted line for the signature, near the small print: "I expressly waive any and all claims for personal injury."

•   •   •

In the locker rooms, cowboys hugged one another and filled up their beer cups. "All in all," joked one calf roper, "I guess it beats the hell out of sloppin' feed in the cold wind at two o'clock in the mornin'."

Larry Sandvick, who had scored seventy-eight points on a bronc named Flashing Jewel and upped his winnings to $49,000, walked in circles with stars in his eyes and a brace on his neck.

"Forty-nine fuckin' thousand dollars!" he said in disbelief. "Forty-nine fuckin' thousand dollars. Forty-fuckin'-nine thousand dollars!"

Neal Gay, the rodeo producer, came by to slap him on the back.

"You did real good, Sandvick," he said with a smile. "You played cowboy all week long."

"I ain't playing," Larry bellowed joyously. "Ahh *is* a cowboy."

Down the hall, Latham walked toward the locker room, lugging his saddle behind him. He wrapped an arm around his friend Billy, who had, in the end, won the saddle-bronc competition by a mile.

"Man oh man," said Billy. "I'm gonna put down my stuff and go drink a Crown Royal and Coke."

"How you gonna spend all that money, Billy?" somebody called out.

"I ain't sure yet," Etbauer replied, and then thought for a moment. "I'll have to check with Mom first."

While the other cowboys danced and hooted, Craig sat down on a bench in the locker room to catch his breath in relief. He had dropped to third in the standings during the finals. But he had still won $30,000. It was enough to keep him in the saddle. Now he could go home and play horsey with his little girl.

He hunched over to scrape the mud from his boots, pushed his chaps into a carrying bag, and then leaned on his knees, rubbing his eyes.

He sat up a moment later, and asked one of the cowboys in a low voice:

"Is everybody all right?"

"I mean," he added, "everybody here won some money, right?"

"I think so," another cowboy shrugged.

"How 'bout Terry and Butch?" Craig asked. "Did they win some?"

"Naw, that's right," the other cowboy remembered. "I don't think they won nothin'."

•   •   •

The cowboys gathered that night for the awards banquet at Caesar's Palace. Bartenders in white jackets mixed drinks for the rodeo contestants, some of them wearing black tuxedos with their cowboy hats. An acoustic band played old country songs, and the bruised and weary cowboys mingled with corporate sponsors in fancy Western attire on a plush carpet under crystal chandeliers.

After the cocktails, the cowboys sat around tables with candles and blue linen. Larry Sandvick was still wearing his jeans, his spurs and the number 57, which hung halfway off his purple shirt, but he had removed the neck brace.

Craig Latham, who had taken the time to shower and comb his hair, sat quietly with his wife, Laurie, who wore a black evening gown and a horse bracelet, which she bought with the help of the $10 gift coupon given to the cowboys in Las Vegas.

Giant Christmas trees in red ribbons and yellow lights towered in every corner. And two big-screen televisions replayed the highlights of the week. The restaurant staff served French wine and big juicy slabs of New York–cut steak.

"We're fortunate," said the emcee, "that the good people here at Caesar's had the sense to find an old dead cow and fix it up right."

From the rostrum, Baxter Black, a former large-animal veterinarian and now a "cowboy poet and philosopher," made a joke about the

PRCEWA—the Pro Rodeo Cowboys' Ex-Wives Association—and then read a poem about the death of the wildest cowboy ever, Casey Tibbs.

After some more drinking and dining, the names of the champions were called out. They stepped forward, one by one, to accept their trophies in the dark Las Vegas ballroom, full of dreams come true.

"This is as big as it gets," the emcee called out.

•　　•　　•

Ten miles from the glitter of the Strip, at a public housing project for the poor, Turk Greenough was trying to get some heat into his tiny apartment. The oven door was left open, and the former rodeo champion was wrapped in a winter jacket to ward off the chill.

Spread everywhere on the countertops and the lamp stands and the kitchen table were yellowing newspaper clips and glossy old black-and-white photographs from the glory days. A picture of Turk with Paulette Goddard. A picture of Turk with Virginia Mayo. A picture of Turk with Roy Rogers.

A smiling picture of a handsome young movie star, with an autograph scrawled in big black letters, "Yours truly, Ronald Reagan."

In his days as a rodeo star, Turk had won championships in Pendleton in 1928, in Boston in 1936, in Calgary in 1935 and 1945, in Cheyenne in 1935, '36, '37. He appeared as a stuntman in more than fifty movies, including *Gone With the Wind*, where he lay in the dust, a soldier in the Civil War.

"You know, Gary Cooper once told me," Turk recalled, "that if he could win Cheyenne just one time, he'd trade it for all his movies."

When Turk was at the top of his career, a rough-hewn darling of the Hollywood set and the pet friend of rich businessmen, he left his wife and married Sally Rand, the risqué fan dancer and movie star. The marriage lasted about six months.

"Worst mistake I ever made," said Turk. "Don't know what I was thinking." Later, he remarried his first wife, Helen, whom everybody called "Honey." She died in 1979.

A lady came by now and then to bring him a pot of soup. And his grandnephew, a rising rodeo star, helped him out when he could. But Turk was two months behind in his rent, $230 each for November and December. And he wasn't sure how he would scrape up the cash. He had long ago sold almost every trophy and saddle he ever won.

"I was a big star once," he said. "I can remember when kids would point at me when I walked down the street." But nobody had pointed his way earlier that day as the old rodeo star walked amid the crowd outside the Thomas & Mack Arena.

He rose unsteadily in black cowboy boots from the kitchen table, where an empty TV dinner sat in shredded foil, and moved slowly toward his bedroom.

On the top of the dresser were old photographs of Turk astride some famous horses, Midnight and Five Minutes to Midnight. Next to the pictures was a plaque, covered with so much dust it was impossible to read.

29

"**O**UGHT TO JUST kill her!" hollered the owner of the big Texas horse ranch. "Fuckin' thing's retarded. She's no goddamned good."

The filly knocked wildly in the pen, frightened and angry. She had resisted every effort to break her. And the ranch wasn't about to waste any more time on this two-year-old.

The slaughterhouse would give $600. That would save on feed and aggravation.

Joe Wimberly had heard about this bad-mannered filly. He figured maybe she could make a rodeo horse. He took some of the money left over from his winnings on Dodge Dakota and paid the owner the same price the killers would. If the horse could buck with a cowboy on her back, he could sell her and turn a profit of a couple hundred dollars.

"Good riddance," the ranch man snapped as Joe hauled her away.

On the day of the bucking horse sale, Joe borrowed a stock wagon, hooked it to his pickup, and carted the horse the seventy miles east to the Fort Worth Coliseum in the city known as Cow Town.

Dozens of horses had been hauled to the sale, bays and sorrels and palominos and Appaloosas, unaware that they were taking their turns in the audition of last resort. Hired hands in chaps and spurs stood ready to take each bronc for a test ride. And rodeo producers watched from the sidelines, taking mental notes on which animals might be worth a try.

Some snorting broncs showed real promise, stomping and bucking across the arena as if they were born for the rodeo, spilling cowboys on the dust and rearing toward the sky.

But when Joe's horse was loaded into the chutes, she became so startled she tried to crawl up the wall, screaming in a fury of fright, hooves clawing the air.

The workers in the chutes finally succeeded in slapping a saddle on her back, and one of the cowboys crawled aboard apprehensively.

Joe watched with hopeful eyes as the gate swung open. But she simply darted a few yards into the arena, then stopped, looking as if she didn't have a clue. Trying to trigger an explosion, the rider raked his spurs down the horse's hide and yanked her head hard with the reins.

But the mare simply twisted in a circle, groaning in confusion.

The pickup man on horseback galloped toward the horse, trying to surprise her into bucking. It was no use.

A couple of seconds before the horn, the cowboy jumped off, giving up on the horse. The pickup man reached in and unhooked the flank strap.

Now the horse kicked high in the air, bucking triumphantly across the turf, showing that she was as wild as the wind. But it was too late to impress any buyer. Rodeo horses aren't any use unless they start bucking when the clock starts ticking. A bronc that bucks afterward is just trouble. And the clock had run out on this troublesome mare. Not a single bid was entered.

Joe started down toward the horse pen, disappointed with the waste of a morning and a long drive for nothing.

"Say there," a stocky man stopped Joe with a wave of his hand. "I'll do you a favor and take her off your hands."

The man was a buyer for a slaughterhouse. He traveled around Texas to pick up useless horses and haul them back to the canners.

"I'll give you seven hundred dollars," he said.

That was $100 more than Joe had paid. And it would save him from the struggle of getting the horse back into the wagon for the drive back to Cool. Besides that, he wasn't sure what else he could do with the recalcitrant horse.

Joe didn't say anything for a moment. It had been a trying year for the cowboy. He had worried himself sick about losing the ranch, as he called his three-and-a-half-acre spread, before he finally caught a break.

Now he thought about the horse. She had looked so scared in the chutes. And out on the arena floor, she had looked lost. It was not so different from the look that Joe had worn for most of the year.

"No thanks," said the cowboy. "I believe I'll just take her on home."

•   •   •

As Joe pulled into the driveway, with the horse standing in the wagon behind the truck, Paula came out of the house and saw that the filly had come back with him.

"What's the deal?" she asked, puzzled.

"I brought her home," he replied.

"I can see that," she said. "Now what?"

"Well, I don't know," he said sheepishly. "I just felt sorry for her."

"Oh Joe Wimberly," she sighed in exasperation, feeling a little like cussing him, a little like hugging him. "What are we gonna do with you?"

•   •   •

After dinner a few nights later, Paula started the dishes and Joe stepped out into the darkness to check on the mare. He looked in the corral and gasped.

The horse was drenched in sweat, as wet as if she had been held under a hose. She rolled on the ground, kicking her belly and groaning in terrible pain. Joe ran back into the house to pick up the phone and call the vet.

"She's colicky," he told Paula as he dialed. "We got to keep her on her feet." If she rolled around, she could twist her intestines and die.

While Joe waited for the vet to pick up the phone, Paula ran outside to the horse. She bent down and wrapped her hands around its head and pulled.

"Come on baby, get up," she pleaded. "You got to get up."

On the telephone, Joe relayed the horse's symptoms to the vet. It sounded like colic to the doctor. But it was a Sunday night. He wasn't about to make any house calls.

"I guess you can bring 'er on in," the vet told Joe, "if you want."

Joe ran back outside and told Paula they needed to hurry. They coaxed the weak horse into the wagon, loaded the kids up in the truck, and sped down the Texas highways.

Thirty miles later, they pulled in at the vet's. He gave the horse a shot of sedatives to calm her nerves, and poured a laxative oil through a tube down her throat. She was constipated, the vet explained, probably from eating too much hay. The doctor said the oil should loosen her up.

Joe wrote a check, and the Wimberly family and the sick horse headed home.

But back at the ranch, she started acting up again. She was sweating heavily and trying to lie down again.

Joe pulled her up by a rope, and walked her in circles around the pasture. Paula got the kids into bed, and then came out to take her turn.

They walked and walked and walked. After a while, they were so tired they could barely stand up themselves. Paula went back inside to get some sleep. Joe saddled up another horse and led the mare behind it.

Finally, at about two o'clock in the morning, the mare stopped sweating. She had been able to move her bowels. Now she seemed relaxed.

Joe led her back to the pen, which he had swept clean of hay, and left her alone. He walked wearily to bed, and before he closed his eyes, the cowboy said a prayer for his horse.

•   •   •

When the horse was deathly sick, she hadn't minded for people to come close and touch her. But in a day or so, she was fit as a fiddle, baring her teeth and flaring her nostrils in challenge whenever Joe tried to come near.

She would never be a rodeo horse. That much was obvious. But she wasn't about to be tamed either.

Joe had broken a lot of horses in his day. But this one was different. She even looked unusual. She was a dark bay, almost the color of chocolate. A bay will usually have some white markings, a snip or a star or a streak on the nose, a dab of paint on the stockings. But this horse was solid bay, with a jet black mane and tail.

She had come from aristocracy. Her father was a champion cutting horse. Some of her half brothers and sisters—"her kin," as Joe called them—had sold for eight or nine thousand dollars. But young Cash-o-lina, as the ranch had named her, or misnamed her, wasn't worth any more alive than dead, about seventy cents a pound.

•   •   •

Like most cowboys, Joe had learned to break horses in the manner of his grandfather, and his grandfather's grandfather before him. Climb aboard and stay aboard until the horse finally loses its will to buck, the Old West practice that gave birth to the sport of rodeo.

But there is usually a little more to breaking a horse, although it is never showcased at rodeos. The horses are roped around the head, driven to the ground inside the corral, front feet tied to a snubbing post, and left to buck in panic, sometimes for hours on end. A mask is often pulled over the horse's head, to scare it with blindness. Blankets are thrown over its head and back to spook it. Ropes are whipped against its hide to beat it into submission.

After all that, the cowboy can usually climb aboard, the triumph of man over beast.

Joe could tell that Cash had been severely abused. There were some obvious signs, the gash on her forehead, the panic in her eyes. But it hadn't worked. She still would not allow a man to sit on her back. In fact, the beatings had made her all the more suspicious.

"And why wouldn't it?" Joe thought. If humans had mistreated him that way, he figured, he'd bare his teeth at them too.

Joe had broken plenty of horses with the rough style of a tough cowboy. But over time, he had started to question the practice. He had always liked horses—loved them, in fact. And it somehow didn't feel right to bully something you loved.

During a rodeo at the Cow Palace in San Francisco two years ago, Joe had picked up a book about cowboys and horses. It was titled *True Unity: Willing Communication Between Horse and Human*. Hardly a best-seller, it had been published in Fresno by an outfit called Give-It-a-Go Enterprises. And the author was an eighty-one-year-old man who had never written before.

Joe wasn't much of a reader. He had only flipped through the pages before putting the book on the shelf at home.

But now he wanted to bring Cash in from her world of anger and fear. He wanted the horse to be his partner, even his friend. He went back and picked up the book.

"It may seem like you will never get anything accomplished, but sometimes going slow is the quickest way to get there."

"I have helped riders who thought they had a horse problem. But I tell them the horse is having a 'people problem.' These riders don't seem to realize that the horse thinks he is supposed to do just what he is doing."

The author was a man named Tom Dorrance, who now lived in a

mobile home in California, but who grew up on a ranch in northeastern Oregon and had been riding horses since before matinee cowboys began talking in western movies.

As a small man, Dorrance realized that he could not overpower a horse with brute strength. Instead, he could talk to the animals and show them he meant no harm.

"I always felt freedom . . . the freedom to explore and experiment so I could develop my own character," he wrote, and realized one day that freedom was "as important to the animals as it had been to me."

Holding the book in his callused hands, Joe found himself nodding in agreement. Nothing had ever made more sense to him in all his life. The goal was not to break the horse, and kill its spirit, but to teach the animal.

"It's like seein' the light," he told Paula. "I'm tellin' you, we could raise the kids accordin' to this guy's methods."

•   •   •

Joe shared the old cowboy's wisdom with just about anybody who would listen: ranchers, store clerks, fellow church members. Most were skeptical.

"Sounds crazy to me."

"What kind of cowboyin' is that?"

"Old way works fine for me, thank you."

Maybe Joe had conquered the toughest bull in the land, they all thought, but he didn't have a chance at taming this ill-mannered filly.

•   •   •

Joe walked out to the corral to start working with Cash. She sprinted to the far side of the pen, not interested in getting friendly.

From his studies, Joe had learned that horses were prey animals. Their eyes are on the sides of their heads, always glancing around for trouble. Man is a predator. His eyes are in the front of his head. A horse smells like grass. A man smells like McDonald's. It was no wonder that a horse gets leery when a man comes around.

Joe walked behind Cash slowly, so she wouldn't think she was being chased. After a while, the horse got tired and stopped running away from him. Now she stared back at the cowboy. Joe walked in the other direction, just to show that he wasn't out to cause trouble.

He whispered goodbye and said he'd come back another time.

The next morning, when Joe walked back into the pen, the horse started to run, but not so fast this time. Then she slowed to a jog, and stopped near the cowboy.

Joe reached out his hand, to let Cash sniff it, a kind of handshake with the horse. And he started to talk.

"I know you been abused. I know it. Yeah, I do. But I ain't gonna hurt you, girl. It's all gonna be all right now. You just watch. It's all gonna be all right."

Joe brought over a pail of oats. And then he left her in peace.

•   •   •

"Hello, girl," Joe said with a smile, as he walked into the pen early the next morning.

He let her walk awhile, until she felt like stopping. Joe reached a hand to her back, and began to caress her hide. As his hand moved down the mare's right side, she flinched a bit.

"All right then," he said in a soft apology, taking his hand back. "When you're ready."

He gave the horse another sniff of his hand, and gently moved it back up to her hide. This time the horse stood still, cooperative for the moment, but still hard as a rock.

Joe gave it some time. And as he kept petting, she began to whinny, a gentle, easy sound, almost like a sigh. He walked slowly to the edge of the corral, picked up his saddle, opened the gate, and returned to the horse's side.

He let Cash have a good look at the leather, holding it near her nose, letting her inspect it.

"This here's just a saddle," he said. "It ain't gonna hurt you."

He slowly lifted the saddle to the horse's back. She flinched. And Joe took it back down. He let the horse gaze at the apparatus again.

"See," he whispered, "it ain't nothin' bad, like a cobra or somethin'. You ain't got to be afraid no more."

He lifted the saddle back up. And this time, she didn't move. He let it sit there for a long moment, then reached underneath to pull the cinches, hooking the front, and then the back.

"You're doin' real good, girl," he told her. "Real, real good."

And then he lifted up a boot to the stirrup, and pulled himself aboard the horse.

"Hey, Paula," he called toward the house, trying not to be so loud it would scare the horse, but anxious for her to see him in the saddle.

She hurried out the back door, letting the screen slam shut behind her. And then came the kids, as the screen slammed once more, twice, a third time, skipping past the cement slab where their names were etched in cement.

Joe was smiling as big as day under his cowboy hat, clenching the reins. The horse moved slowly through the gate, stepping cautiously out toward the open field.

The sun glinted through the live oaks, and a cool Texas breeze swept the field. The clucking roosters scattered and the goats across the way looked up. The old abandoned mutt, Cowboy, snuggled between the rails of the empty pen. The kids giggled. And Paula gazed proudly at these two frisky Texans who had beaten the odds.

"Let 'er go, girl," Joe whispered, as Cash began to trot. "Ride as hard as you want. Ride all that anger right out of you."

And the horse broke into a full gallop, hooves pounding furiously on the Texas scrub grass, chasing toward the sun, leaving a trail of dust to vanish in the wind.

WITHDRAWN

MATHEMATICS OF CHOICE
OR
HOW TO COUNT
WITHOUT COUNTING

NEW MATHEMATICAL LIBRARY

PUBLISHED BY

THE MATHEMATICAL ASSOCIATION OF AMERICA

Editorial Committee

Basil Gordon, Chairman (1975-76)   Anneli Lax, Editor
University of California, L.A.   *New York University*

Ivan Niven (1975-77)   *University of Oregon*
M. M. Schiffer (1975-77)   *Stanford University*

The New Mathematical Library (NML) was begun in 1961 by the School Mathematics Study Group to make available to high school students short expository books on various topics not usually covered in the high school syllabus. In a decade the NML matured into a steadily growing series of some twenty titles of interest not only to the originally intended audience, but to college students and teachers at all levels. Previously published by Random House and L. W. Singer, the NML became a publication series of the Mathematical Association of America (MAA) in 1975. Under the auspices of the MAA the NML will continue to grow and will remain dedicated to its original and expanded purposes.

MATHEMATICS OF CHOICE
OR
HOW TO COUNT
WITHOUT COUNTING

by

Ivan Niven
University of Oregon

15

THE MATHEMATICAL ASSOCIATION
OF AMERICA

Illustrated by George H. Buehler

Ninth Printing

Library of Congress Catalog Card Number: 65-17470

Complete Set ISBN-0-88385-600-X

Vol. 15 0-88385-615-8

Manufactured in the United States of America

Note to the Reader

This book is one of a series written by professional mathematicians in order to make some important mathematical ideas interesting and understandable to a large audience of high school students and laymen. Most of the volumes in the *New Mathematical Library* cover topics not usually included in the high school curriculum; they vary in difficulty, and, even within a single book, some parts require a greater degree of concentration than others. Thus, while the reader needs little technical knowledge to understand most of these books, he will have to make an intellectual effort.

If the reader has so far encountered mathematics only in classroom work, he should keep in mind that a book on mathematics cannot be read quickly. Nor must he expect to understand all parts of the book on first reading. He should feel free to skip complicated parts and return to them later; often an argument will be clarified by a subsequent remark. On the other hand, sections containing thoroughly familiar material may be read very quickly.

The best way to learn mathematics is to *do* mathematics, and each book includes problems, some of which may require considerable thought. The reader is urged to acquire the habit of reading with paper and pencil in hand; in this way mathematics will become increasingly meaningful to him.

The authors and editorial committee are interested in reactions to the books in this series and hope that readers will write to: Anneli Lax, Editor, New Mathematical Library, NEW YORK UNIVERSITY, THE COURANT INSTITUTE OF MATHEMATICAL SCIENCES, 251 Mercer Street, New York, N. Y. 10012.

The Editors

NEW MATHEMATICAL LIBRARY

Other titles in preparation

Contents

MATHEMATICS OF CHOICE

OR

HOW TO COUNT
WITHOUT COUNTING

Preface

The subject of this book is often called "combinatorial analysis" or "combinatorics". The questions discussed are of the sort "In how many ways is it possible to . . . ? ", or variations on that theme. Permutations and combinations form a part of combinatorial analysis, a part with which the reader may be already acquainted. If so, he may be familiar with some of the material in the first three chapters.

The book is self-contained with the rudiments of algebra the only prerequisite. Summaries including all formulas are given at the ends of the chapters. Throughout the book there are many problems for the reader. In fact the entire monograph is in large measure a problem book with enough background information furnished for attacking the questions. A list of miscellaneous problems follows the final chapter. Solutions, or at least sketches of solutions, are given in the back of the book for questions of any depth, and numerical answers are given for the simpler problems.

Helpful suggestions were given by the members of the S. M. S. G. Monograph Panel, and also by Herbert S. Zuckerman. Max Bell used some of the material with his students, and forwarded their comments to me. The witty subtitle of the book was suggested by Mark Kac. For all this help I express my appreciation.

CHAPTER ONE

Introductory Questions

The purpose of this chapter is to present a few sample problems to illustrate the theme of the whole volume. A systematic development of the subject is started in the next chapter. While some of the sample questions introduced here can be solved with no theoretical background, the solution of others must be postponed until the necessary theory is developed.

The idea of this book is to examine certain aspects of the question "how many?". Such questions may be very simple; for example, "How many pages are there from page 14 to page 59, inclusive?" In some cases, the answer may be nothing more than a matter of common knowledge, as for example the number of days in October, or the number of yards in a mile. In other cases, the answer may require technical information, such as the number of chemical elements known at the present time, or the number of cubic centimeters of displacement in the engine of a certain automobile. But our concern is with questions that involve thought. They may also require some prior knowledge, which will be supplied if it is not common information. Some mathematical formulas are helpful, and these will be developed in due course. However, many problems require nothing more than a little ingenuity. We begin with such a question.

PROBLEM 1.1† In any calendar year how many Friday the thirteenths can there be? What is the smallest number possible?

† This occurs as Problem E1541 on p. 919 of the *American Mathematical Monthly*, November, 1962.

Like many other questions in this book, this problem is solved in the *Answers and Solutions* section at the end. Of course the reader is urged to try the question himself before turning to the solution provided. Problem 1.1 *can* be done by simply consulting a calendar, or rather a set of annual calendars giving all possible arrangements of the days of the year. The challenge is to solve the problem in an even simpler way by devising a system. It might be noted for example that years having 365 days can be separated into seven different types, one beginning on a Monday, one on a Tuesday, etc. Similarly there are seven different types of leap years, and so there are in all fourteen types of years for the purposes of this problem. Next a system can be devised for studying the number of Friday the thirteenths in any one of these types of years. However, we drop the analysis here, and leave the rest to the reader.

PROBLEM 1.2   A manufacturer makes blocks for children, each block being a two inch cube whose faces are painted one of two colors, blue and red. Some blocks are all blue, some all red, and some have a mixture of blue and red faces. How many different kinds of blocks can the manufacturer make?

It is necessary to define what is meant by "different" blocks before the question has a precise meaning. We shall say that two blocks are the same if they can be put into matching positions so that corresponding faces have identical colors, that is, so that the bottom faces have the same color, the top faces the same color, the front faces the same color, etc. If two blocks are not the same in this sense, we say that they are different. For example, any two blocks with five blue faces and one red face are the same. But consider as another example two blocks with four red faces and two blue faces. Two such blocks may or may not be the same. If the two blue faces are adjacent on each block, then the blocks are the same. Or if the two blue faces are opposite on each block, they are the same. But if on one block the two blue faces are adjacent, whereas on the other block the two blue faces are opposite, then the blocks are different. See Figure 1.1.

This problem is also solved in the *Answers and Solutions* section, but again the reader is urged to solve it for himself, using the solution at the back of the book as a check against his work.

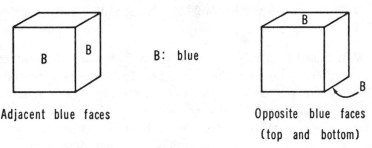

Adjacent blue faces   Opposite blue faces
                                       (top and bottom)

Figure 1.1

We turn now to three problems which are so much more difficult that the solutions are postponed until the needed theory is worked out.

PROBLEM 1.3 *A Path Problem.* A man works in a building located seven blocks east and eight blocks north of his home. (See Figure 1.2.) Thus in walking to work each day he goes fifteen blocks. All the streets in the rectangular pattern are available to him for walking. In how many different ways can he go from home to work, walking only fifteen blocks?

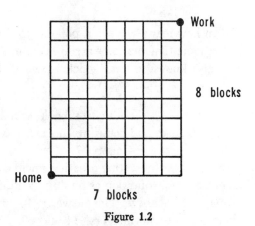

Figure 1.2

One obvious approach to this problem would be to draw diagrams of all possible paths, and then to count them. But there happen to be 6435 different paths, and so the direct approach is somewhat impractical. This problem is not very difficult if we look at it in the right way. The solution is given in Chapter 3.

We turn now to another problem whose solution must await some theoretical analysis.

PROBLEM 1.4   The governor of a state attended the centennial celebration of a famous publishing house. To express his appreciation, the publisher offered to present to the governor any selection of ten books chosen from the twenty best-sellers of the company. The governor was permitted to select ten different books from the twenty, or ten all alike (ten copies of one book), or any other combination he might prefer, provided only that the total was ten. (a) In how many ways could the governor make his selection? (b) If the governor had been requested to choose ten distinct books, in how many ways could he have made his selection?

Question (b) is easier than question (a), because (b) is a straightforward matter of choosing ten things from twenty. The number of different selections of ten things from twenty is denoted by the symbol $C(20, 10)$, and is easily evaluated as we shall see in the next chapter. The solution to part (a) of the question is given on page 59.

PROBLEM 1.5   In how many ways is it possible to change a dollar bill into coins? (Presume that the coins are in denominations 1, 5, 10, 25, and 50 cents, also known as cents, nickels, dimes, quarters and half dollars.)

This problem, like many others in this book, can be solved by simply enumerating all cases and counting them. A more systematic scheme for solving it is given in Chapter 7.

We conclude this chapter by stating a basic principle about counting. It arises in such a simple question as finding the number of pages from page 14 to page 59 inclusive. The answer is 46, one more than the difference between the two integers† 14 and 59. In general, *the number of integers from k to n inclusive is n − k + 1, where n is presumed larger than k, i.e. n > k.*

† Integers, sometimes called "whole numbers", are of three types: the positive integers or natural numbers 1, 2, 3, 4, ···, where the three dots "···" stand for "and so on"; the negative integers −1, −2, −3, −4, ···; and 0 which is neither positive nor negative. The non-negative integers are 0, 1, 2, 3, 4, ···.

Problem Set 1

1. How many integers are there from 25 to 79 inclusive?

2. What is the 53rd integer in the sequence 86, 87, 88, $\cdots$?

3. The largest of 123 consecutive integers is 307. What is the smallest?

4. The smallest of r consecutive integers is n. What is the largest?

5. The largest of r consecutive integers is k. What is the smallest?

6. How many integers are there in the sequence $n,\ n+1,\ n+2,\ \cdots,$ $n+h$?

7. How many integers x satisfy the inequalities $12 < \sqrt{x} < 15$, that is $\sqrt{x}$ exceeds 12, but $\sqrt{x}$ is less than 15?

8. How many integers are there in the sequences

   (a) 60, 70, 80, $\cdots$, 540;   (b) 15, 18, 21, $\cdots$, 144;

   (c) 17, 23, 29, 35, $\cdots$, 221?

9. How many integers between 1 and 2000   (a) are multiples of 11; (b) are multiples of 11 but not multiples of 3;   (c) are multiples of 6 but not multiples of 4?

10. What is the smallest number of coins needed to pay in exact change any charge less than one dollar? (Coins are in the denominations 1, 5, 10, 25 and 50 cents.)

11. A man has 47 cents in change coming. Assuming that the cash register contains an adequately large supply of 1, 5, 10 and 25 cent coins, with how many different combinations of coins can the clerk give the man his change?

12. A man has six pairs of cuff links scrambled in a box. No two pairs are alike. How many cuff links does he have to draw out all at once (in the dark) in order to be certain to get a pair that match?

13. A man has twelve blue socks and twelve black socks scrambled in a drawer. How many socks does he have to draw out all at once (in the dark) to be certain to get a matching pair? (Any two blue socks, or any two black socks, constitute a pair.)

14. The measure in degrees of an angle of a regular polygon is an integer. How many sides can such a polygon have?

15. A man has a large supply of wooden regular tetrahedra, all the same size. (A regular tetrahedron is a solid figure bounded by four congruent equilateral triangles; see Figure 1.3.) If he paints each tri-

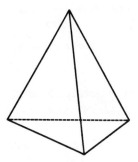

Figure 1.3

angular face in one of four colors, how many different painted tetrahedra can he make, allowing all possible combinations of colors? (Say that two blocks are different if they cannot be put into matching positions with identical colors on corresponding faces.)

16. How many paths are there from one corner of a cube to the opposite corner, each possible path being along three of the twelve edges of the cube?

17. At formal conferences of the United States Supreme Court each of the nine justices shakes hands with each of the others at the beginning of the session. How many handshakes initiate such a session?

CHAPTER TWO

Permutations and Combinations

This chapter and the next introduce some of the fundamental ideas of the subject of this book. The reader may recognize a number of these concepts from previous study. However, at several places in Chapters 2 and 3 the topics are discussed in more detail than is usually the case in elementary books on algebra. It will smooth the way for the reader in subsequent chapters if he fully understands these fundamental ideas. If he is able to answer the questions in the problem sets, he can be sure of his understanding of the subject. Much of the basic notation of combinatorics is set forth in these two chapters. Out of the variety of notation used throughout mathematical literature, we outline several of the standard forms, but subsequently stick to only one.

To introduce the subject we consider the following simple problem. A clothing store for men and boys has belts in five styles, and there are seven sizes available in each style. How many different kinds of belts does the store have?

The answer, 35, can be obtained by multiplying 5 by 7 because there are 7 belts in style number 1, 7 belts in style number 2, $\cdots$, 7 belts in style number 5, and so we have

$$7 + 7 + 7 + 7 + 7 \; = \; 5{\cdot}7 \; = \; 35.$$

This easy question illustrates a basic principle.

2.1　The Multiplication Principle

If a collection of things can be separated into m different types, and if each of these types can be separated into k different subtypes, then there are mk different types in all.

This principle can be extended beyond a classification according to two properties, such as styles and sizes of belts, to classifications according to three properties, four properties, and more. As an example consider the following question. A drugstore stocks toothpaste from seven different manufacturers. Each manufacturer puts out three sizes, each available in fluoridated form and plain. How many different kinds of toothpaste tubes does the store have? The answer, on the basis of the multiplication principle, is $7 \cdot 3 \cdot 2$ or 42, because of 7 manufacturers, 3 sizes, and 2 types as regards fluoridation.

The multiplication principle is applicable to many problems besides that of classifying objects. As an example, consider a man who decides to go to Europe by plane and to return by ship. If there are eight different airlines available to him, and nine different shipping companies, then he can make the round trip in $8 \cdot 9$ or 72 different ways.

Here is another simple example. At a big picnic the snack lunch consists of a sandwich (choice of four kinds), a beverage (choice of coffee, tea or milk) and an ice cream cup (choice of three flavors). In how many ways can a person make his selection? By the multiplication principle we see that the answer is $4 \cdot 3 \cdot 3$ or 36 ways.

Because of the various applications of the multiplication principle it is often formulated in terms of events: *If one event can occur in m ways, and a second event can occur independently of the first in k ways, then the two events can occur in mk ways.*

The word "independently" is essential here because the principle is not necessarily valid in situations where the second event is dependent on, or restricted by, the first. For example, a girl with seven skirts and five blouses might not have 35 skirt-blouse combinations because some of the colors or patterns might clash aesthetically; a certain red skirt might not go well with a certain orange blouse. However, the following example illustrates a standard kind of dependency of events wherein the principle can still be used.

PROBLEM 2.1 In how many different orders can the four letters *A, B, C, D* be written, no letter being repeated in any one arrangement?

This question can be answered by simply writing out all possible orders of the letters: *ABCD, ACBD, ABDC*, etc. But it is simpler, and in more complicated problems necessary, to devise a system to solve the problem. Consider the first letter in any arrangement. There are four choices for the letter in this position. For any given selection of the first letter, there are three possible choices for the second letter. If, for example, the first letter is *B*, then the second letter must be chosen from *A, C* or *D*. Similarly, after the first two letters of the foursome have been selected, the third letter can be chosen in two ways. And when we get to the fourth letter it can be chosen in only one way; that is, there is only one letter that can be used in the fourth place. Thus the multiplication principle gives the answer

$$4 \cdot 3 \cdot 2 \cdot 1 = 24.$$

The reader should verify this by listing all 24 cases. Here are those that begin with the letter *A*:

ABCD, ABDC, ACBD, ACDB, ADBC, ADCB.

PROBLEM 2.2 In a certain (mythical) country the automobile license plates have letters, not numbers, as distinguishing marks. Precisely three letters are used, for example, *BQJ, CCT* and *DWD*. If the alphabet has 26 letters, how many different license plates can be made?

As the examples show, repetition of letters is allowed on a license plate. There being 26 choices for each of the three letters, the answer is

$$26 \cdot 26 \cdot 26 = 17576.$$

PROBLEM 2.3 What would be the answer to Problem 2.2 if the repetition of letters on a license plate were not allowed?

An argument similar to that used in the solution of Problem 2.1 can be made. There are 26 choices for the first letter, but only 25 for the second, and only 24 for the third. Thus the answer is

$$26 \cdot 25 \cdot 24 = 15600.$$

Problem Set 2

1. Of the arrangements in Problem 2.2, how many begin with the letter Q ?

2. Of the arrangements in Problem 2.3, how many begin with the letter Q ? How many end with the letter Q ?

3. Of the arrangements in Problem 2.2, how many end with a vowel (A, E, I, O, U)?

4. Of the arrangements in Problem 2.3, how many end with a vowel?

5. A room has six doors. In how many ways is it possible to enter by one door and leave by another?

6. A tire store carries eight different sizes of tires, each in both tube and tubeless variety, each with either nylon or rayon cord, and each with white sidewalls or plain black. How many different kinds of tires does the store have?

7. A mail order company offers 23 styles of ladies' slippers. If each style were available in twelve lengths, three widths and six colors, how many different kinds of ladies' slippers would the warehouse have to keep in stock?

8. How many of the integers (whole numbers) between 10,000 and 100,000 have no digits other than 6, 7, or 8 ? How many have no digits other than 6, 7, 8 or 0 ?

2.2 Factorials

In many situations it is useful to have a simple notation for products such as

$$4 \cdot 3 \cdot 2 \cdot 1, \qquad 6 \cdot 5 \cdot 4 \cdot 3 \cdot 2 \cdot 1, \qquad 7 \cdot 6 \cdot 5 \cdot 4 \cdot 3 \cdot 2 \cdot 1,$$

each of which is the product of a sequence of consecutive integers all the way down to one. Such products are called *factorials*. The standard mathematical notation uses what is ordinarily an exclamation point; thus

$$4! = 4 \cdot 3 \cdot 2 \cdot 1 = 24$$

$$6! = 6 \cdot 5 \cdot 4 \cdot 3 \cdot 2 \cdot 1 = 720$$

$$7! = 7 \cdot 6 \cdot 5 \cdot 4 \cdot 3 \cdot 2 \cdot 1 = 5040.$$

We read 4! as "four factorial", 6! as "six factorial", and 7! as "seven factorial". In general, for any positive integer n we define $n!$ (read this as "n factorial") as

$$n! = n(n - 1)(n - 2)(n - 3) \cdots 1.$$

This is the product of all integers from n down to 1. Note that 1! is equal to 1.

Problem Set 3

1. Formulate as a product and then evaluate† each of 3!, 5! and 8!.

2. Evaluate the following: 12!/10!; 2!; 4! + 3!; (4 + 3)!.

3. Evaluate $(n + 1)!$ in case $n = 4$.

4. Evaluate $n! + 1$ in case $n = 4$.

5. Evaluate $(n - 1)!$ in case $n = 4$.

6. Evaluate $(n - r)!$ in case $n = 10$ and $r = 8$.

7. Compute $(n - r)!$ in case $n = 12$ and $r = 6$.

8. Compute $\dfrac{n!}{(n - r)!}$ in case $n = 12$ and $r = 4$; also in the case $n = 10$ and $r = 6$.

---

† Whereas the reader is asked to evaluate or compute such numbers as 5! and 8!, he would not be expected to compute (say) 20!. If such a number were the answer to a question in this book, it would be left in precisely that form. Computational techniques are very important, but they are not stressed in this volume.

9. Compute $\dfrac{n!}{r!(n-r)!}$ in case $n = 10$ and $r = 6$.

10. Which of the following are true and which false?

   (a) $8! = 8 \cdot 7!$ (b) $10!/9! = 9$ (c) $4! + 4! = 8!$

   (d) $2! - 1! = 1!$ (e) $n! = n \cdot (n-1)!$ for $n > 1$.

   (f) $n! = (n^2 - n) \cdot (n-2)!$ for $n > 2$.

2.3 Permutations

Permutations are ordered arrangements of objects. As examples of permutations, consider again Problems 2.1 and 2.3 from Section 2.1.

PROBLEM 2.1   In how many different orders can the four letters A, B, C, D be written, no letter being repeated in any one arrangement?

This is the same as asking how many permutations there are on four letters, taken four at a time. The number of such permutations is denoted by the symbol $P(4, 4)$.

PROBLEM 2.3   How many different license plates can be made if each plate has three letters and repetition of letters on a license plate is not allowed?

This is the same as asking how many permutations there are on twenty-six letters, taken three at a time. The number of such permutations is denoted by $P(26, 3)$. We have solved these problems in Section 2.1 and may now write the answers, in our new notation, as

$$P(4, 4) = 4 \cdot 3 \cdot 2 \cdot 1 = 24 \quad \text{and} \quad P(26, 3) = 26 \cdot 25 \cdot 24 = 15600.$$

Each of these $P(26, 3) = 15600$ permutations of 26 objects taken 3 at a time is called a 3-permutation. In general, an r-permutation is an ordered arrangement of r objects, and $P(n, r)$ denotes the number of r-permutations of a set of n distinct objects. This is the same as saying that $P(n, r)$ is the number of permutations of n

things taken r at a time. Of course, it is presumed that r does not exceed n, that is $r \leqslant n$. Note that the n things or objects must be distinct, i.e. we must be able to tell them apart.

To derive a formula for $P(n, r)$ we conceive of r distinct boxes into which the n objects can be put:

| 1st box | 2nd box | 3rd box | | rth box |

Then $P(n, r)$ can be thought of as the number of ways of putting n distinct objects in the r boxes, *one object in each box.*

First consider the special case where the number of objects is the same as the number of boxes. For the first box we can select any one of the n objects. That done, there remain $n - 1$ objects from which to choose for the second box. Similarly, there remain $n - 2$ objects from which to choose for the third box. Continuing in this way we see that when we get to the last box there is only one object left, so we choose one out of one. By the multiplication principle we have

$$P(n, n) = n(n - 1)(n - 2) \cdots 1 \quad \text{or} \quad P(n, n) = n! \ .$$

For example,

$$P(7, 7) = 7 \cdot 6 \cdot 5 \cdot 4 \cdot 3 \cdot 2 \cdot 1 = 7! \ ,$$
$$P(28, 28) = 28 \cdot 27 \cdot 26 \cdot \ \cdots \ \cdot 3 \cdot 2 \cdot 1 = 28! \ .$$

The argument just used to evaluate $P(n, n)$ can be applied just as well to $P(n, r)$. For instance, we note that

$$P(28, 5) = 28 \cdot 27 \cdot 26 \cdot 25 \cdot 24.$$

We observe that in this product of 5 consecutive integers the difference between the largest and the smallest, that is, between 28 and 24, is 4. In general, $P(n, r)$ is the product of the r integers n, $n - 1$, $n - 2$, $\cdots$, $n - r + 1$:

$$P(n, r) = n(n - 1)(n - 2) \cdots (n - r + 1).$$

To see that this is the product of r consecutive integers we recall that the number of integers from k to n inclusive is $n - k + 1$ (see p. 4), so the number of integers from $n - r + 1$ to n inclusive is

$$n - (n - r + 1) + 1 = r.$$

Note that, if $r = n$, this formula for $P(n, r)$ is in harmony with the earlier formula

$$P(n, n) = n(n - 1)(n - 2) \cdots 1 .$$

We now proceed to another formula for $P(n, r)$. As an example consider

$$P(10, 4) = 10 \cdot 9 \cdot 8 \cdot 7,$$

which can be written as a fraction involving factorials thus:

$$P(10, 4) = 10 \cdot 9 \cdot 8 \cdot 7 = \frac{10 \cdot 9 \cdot 8 \cdot 7 \cdot 6 \cdot 5 \cdot 4 \cdot 3 \cdot 2 \cdot 1}{6 \cdot 5 \cdot 4 \cdot 3 \cdot 2 \cdot 1} = \frac{10!}{6!} .$$

The same procedure works in the general case $P(n, r)$:

$$P(n, r) = n(n - 1)(n - 2) \cdots (n - r + 1)$$

$$= \frac{n(n - 1)(n - 2) \cdots (n - r + 1)(n - r)(n - r - 1) \cdots 1}{(n - r)(n - r - 1) \cdots 1} ,$$

$$(2.1) \qquad\qquad P(n, r) = \frac{n!}{(n - r)!} .$$

Example. How many integers between 100 and 999 inclusive consist of distinct odd digits?

Solution. The odd digits are 1, 3, 5, 7, 9; the even digits are 0, 2, 4, 6, 8. An integer such as 723 is not to be counted because it contains the even digit 2; and an integer such as 373 is not to be counted because it does not have distinct digits. The question amounts to asking for the number of permutations of the five distinct digits 1, 3, 5, 7, 9, taken three at a time. The answer is

$$P(5, 3) = \frac{5!}{(5-3)!} = \frac{5!}{2!} = 5 \cdot 4 \cdot 3 = 60$$

Formula (2.1) for $P(n, r)$ cannot be used to solve all problems about permutations, because not all such problems admit as solutions all ordered arrangements of n distinct objects, r at a time. A problem can sometimes be solved by direct use of the multiplication principle, as the following examples illustrate.

Example. How many integers between 100 and 999 have distinct digits?

Solution. This is not simply $P(10, 3)$, the number of permutations of all ten digits taken three at a time, because 086, for example, is not a number between 100 and 999. The digit 0 can be used in the units' place (as in 860), or in the tens' place (as in 806), but not in the hundreds' place. Consider three boxes to be filled by the digits of any of the integers under consideration:

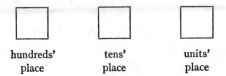

hundreds'   tens'   units'
place   place   place

There are nine choices for the digit in the hundreds' place, because 0 cannot be used. There are then nine choices for the digit in the tens' place, namely 0 together with the eight non-zero digits not used already. Similarly there are eight choices for the digit used in the units' place. Hence the answer is $9 \cdot 9 \cdot 8$ or 648.

Example. Of the 648 integers in the preceding problem, how many are odd numbers?

Solution. A number is odd if its units digit is odd, i.e. if the digit in the units' place is one of 1, 3, 5, 7, 9. So it is best to begin the argument by asking how many choices there are for the digit in the units' place; the answer is five. Next, turn to the hundreds' place; there are eight digits from which a selection can be made, namely all the non-zero digits except the one already used in the units' place. Finally there are eight choices for the digit in the tens' place, so the answer is $5 \cdot 8 \cdot 8$ or 320.

Some problems can be solved most readily by considering separate cases.

Example. How many of the first 1000 positive integers have distinct digits?

Solution. Setting aside the integer 1000, whose digits are not distinct, the others can be separated into three types:

Integers with one digit: 1, 2, 3, $\cdots$, 9;

Integers with two digits: 10, 11, 12, $\cdots$, 99;

Integers with three digits: 100, 101, 102, $\cdots$, 999.

The number of three-digit integers with distinct digits is 648, as shown in a previous example. A similar argument shows that there are 81 two-digit integers and, of course, 9 one-digit integers that meet the specification of distinct digits. Hence the answer is

$$648 + 81 + 9 = 738.$$

The idea used here is called the *addition principle:* If the things to be counted are separated into cases, the total number is the *sum* of the numbers in the various cases.

2.4 Zero Factorial

An interesting phenomenon turns up if we use formula (2.1) for $P(n, r)$ in a case such as

$$P(7, 7) = \frac{7!}{(7 - 7)!} = \frac{7!}{0!}.$$

The notation $0!$, in words, "zero factorial", has so far not been defined. In mathematics we can define the meaning of the symbols in any way we please, provided of course that there is consistency. In the present case, since we had determined earlier that $P(7, 7) = 7!$, consistency requires that

$$P(7, 7) = 7! = \frac{7!}{0!}.$$

Thus we should and do define zero factorial to be one:

$$0! = 1.$$

This may look strange but it is a useful definition. It is related to other combinatorial notation, not just to $P(n, r)$.

Problem Set 4

1. Evaluate $P(7, 3)$, $P(8, 4)$ and $P(20, 2)$.

2. Verify that $P(7, 3) = P(15, 2)$ and that $P(6, 3) = P(5, 5)$.

3. Prove that $P(n, 1) + P(m, 1) = P(n + m, 1)$ for all positive integers m and n.

4. Prove that $P(n, n) = P(n, n - 1)$ for all positive integers n.

5. How many fraternity names consisting of three different Greek letters can be formed? (There are twenty-four letters in the Greek alphabet.)

6. What would be the answer to the preceding question if repetitions of letters were allowed? What would it be if repetitions of letters were allowed and two-letter names were also included in the count?

7. How many integers between 1000 and 9999 inclusive have distinct digits? Of these how many are odd numbers?

8. From the digits 1, 2, 3, 4, 5, how many four-digit numbers with distinct digits can be constructed? How many of these are odd numbers?

9. From the digits 0, 1, 2, 3, 4, 5, 6, how many four-digit numbers with distinct digits can be constructed? How many of these are even numbers?

10. How many integers greater than 53000 have the following two properties: (a) the digits of the integer are distinct; (b) the digits 0 and 9 do not occur in the number?

11. In the preceding problem what would the answer be if condition (b) were changed to "the digits 8 and 9 do not occur in the integer"?

2.5 Combinations

Whereas a permutation is an ordered arrangement of objects, a combination is a selection made *without regard to order*. The notation $C(n, r)$ is used for the number of combinations of a certain special type, in parallel with the notation $P(n, r)$ for permutations. Thus $C(n, r)$ denotes the number of combinations, r at a time, that can be selected out of a total of n distinct objects.

Consider $C(5, 3)$ for example. Let the five objects be A, B, C, D, E. Then it can be observed that $C(5, 3) = 10$, because there are ten combinations of the objects taken three at a time:

$$
\begin{matrix}
(2.2) & A, B, C & A, B, D & A, B, E & A, C, D & A, C, E \\
 & A, D, E & B, C, D & B, C, E & B, D, E & C, D, E.
\end{matrix}
$$

Notice that each of these ten triples is simply a collection in which order does not matter. The triple C, D, E for example could have been written D, E, C or E, C, D, or in any other order; it counts as just one triple.

Given n distinct objects, $C(n, r)$ is the number of ways of choosing r objects from the total collection. Of course it is presumed that r does not exceed n, that is $r \leqslant n$. The meaning of $C(n, r)$ can also be stated in terms of a set of n elements. $C(n, r)$ is the number of subsets containing exactly r elements. For example, the listing (2.2) above gives all subsets of three elements selected from the set A, B, C, D, E.

Before deriving a general formula for $C(n, r)$, we compute the value of $C(26, 3)$ to illustrate the argument. $C(26, 3)$ can be thought of as the number of ways of choosing three letters out of a 26 letter alphabet. One such choice, for example, is the triple D, Q, X, taken without regard to order. This one combination D, Q, X corresponds to the six distinct permutations

$$
DQX \quad DXQ \quad QDX \quad QXD \quad XDQ \quad XQD.
$$

In fact, each of the $C(26, 3)$ combinations corresponds to $P(3, 3)$ or $3! = 6$ permutations. Hence there are six times as many permutations as there are combinations:

$$P(26, 3) = 6C(26, 3).$$

But we have already computed the value

$$P(26, 3) = 26 \cdot 25 \cdot 24 = 15600$$

in Problem 2.3. Hence we get

$$6C(26, 3) = 15600, \quad \text{so that} \quad C(26, 3) = 2600.$$

We now generalize this argument to get a relationship between $C(n, r)$ and $P(n, r)$ and then evaluate $C(n, r)$ by use of the formula (2.1) for $P(n, r)$. With n distinct objects, $C(n, r)$ counts the number of ways of choosing r of them without regard to order. Any one of these choices is simply a collection of r objects. Such a collection can be ordered in $r!$ different ways. Since to each combination there correspond $r!$ permutations, there are $r!$ times as many permutations as there are combinations:

$$P(n, r) = r!C(n, r) \quad \text{or} \quad C(n, r) = \frac{P(n, r)}{r!}.$$

But we know by formula (2.1) that $P(n, r)$ equals $n!/(n - r)!$, and hence we get the basic formula for $C(n, r)$,

$$(2.3) \qquad C(n, r) = \frac{n!}{r!(n - r)!}.$$

This is perhaps the most widely used formula in combinatorial analysis. The number $C(n, r)$ is often represented in other ways, for example

$$nCr, \quad {}^nCr, \quad C_r^n, \quad \text{and} \quad \binom{n}{r}.$$

The last of these is very common; it is to be read "n over r" or "the binomial coefficient n over r". Binomial coefficients occur in the expansion of a power of a sum of two terms, such as $(x + y)^8$; this is one of the topics of the next chapter.

There is one simple property of $C(n, r)$ that is almost obvious, namely

(2.4) $C(n, r) = C(n, n - r)$.

Let us take $n = 5$ and $r = 3$ as an illustration. Then the equation (2.4) becomes $C(5, 3) = C(5, 2)$ and can be verified as follows. Taking the five objects to be A, B, C, D, E, we have seen that $C(5, 3) = 10$, the ten triples having been written out in full detail in (2.2). Now when a triple, such as A, C, D, is selected, there is a pair (in this case B, E) left unselected. So corresponding to each selected triple in (2.2) we can write a corresponding unselected pair (in parentheses):

$A, B, C(D, E)$ $A, B, D(C, E)$ $A, B, E(C, D)$

$A, C, D(B, E)$ $A, C, E(B, D)$ $A, D, E(B, C)$

$B, C, D(A, E)$ $B, C, E(A, D)$ $B, D, E(A, C)$

$C, D, E(A, B)$

It follows that the number of ways of choosing three objects out of five is the same as the number of ways of choosing two objects out of five, so $C(5, 3) = C(5, 2) = 10$.

In general, corresponding to every selection of r things out of n there is a set of $n - r$ unselected things, the ones not in the selection. Hence the number of ways of choosing r things must be the same as the number of ways of choosing $n - r$ things, and so formula (2.4) is established.

If in formula (2.4) we replace r by 0 we get $C(n, 0) = C(n, n)$. Now $C(n, n)$ means the number of ways of choosing n things out of n, so $C(n, n) = 1$. But $C(n, 0)$ seems to have no meaning: "the number of ways of choosing no things out of n". It is convenient to define $C(n, 0)$ to be 1. Notice that this harmonizes with formula (2.3) which gives, for $r = 0$,

$$C(n, 0) = \frac{n!}{0!(n - 0)!} = \frac{n!}{0!n!} = 1$$

because $0! = 1$. We also define $C(0, 0) = 1$.

It is convenient to extend the definition of $C(n, r)$ to *all* integers n and r, even negative integers, for then various formulas can be written without qualification or added explanation. If n is negative, if r is negative, or if $r > n$, $C(n, r)$ is defined to be zero. For example, $C(-10, 8)$, $C(5, -8)$, and $C(10, 12)$ are zero by definition. In other words

$C(n, r) = 0$ in case one or more of n, r, $n - r$ is negative,

$$C(n, r) = \frac{n!}{r!(n - r)!} \quad \text{in all other cases.}$$

Problem Set 5

1. Evaluate $C(6, 2)$, $C(7, 4)$ and $C(9, 3)$.

2. Show that $C(6, 2) = C(6, 4)$ by pairing off the 2-subsets and the 4-subsets of the set A, B, C, D, E, F.

3. An examination consists of ten questions, of which a student is to answer eight and omit two. (a) In how many ways can a student make his selection? (b) If a student should answer two questions and omit eight, in how many ways can he make his selection?

4. A college has 720 students. In how many ways can a delegation of ten be chosen to represent the college? (Leave the answer in factorial form.)

5. Verify that $C(n, r) = C(n, n - r)$ by use of formula (2.3).

6. Twenty points lie in a plane, no three collinear, i.e. no three on a straight line. How many straight lines can be formed by joining pairs of points? How many triangles can be formed by joining triples of points?

7. In how many ways can ten persons be seated in a row so that a certain two of them are not next to each other?

8. Prove that the product of five consecutive positive integers is divisible by 5!, and more generally, that the product of r consecutive

integers is divisible by $r!$. Suggestion: Examine the formula for $C(n, r)$.

9. There are nine different books on a shelf; four are red and five are green. In how many different orders is it possible to arrange the books on the shelf if
   (a) there are no restrictions;
   (b) the red books must be together and the green books together;
   (c) the red books must be together whereas the green books may be, but need not be, together;
   (d) the colors must alternate, i.e. no two books of the same color may be adjacent?

10. A certain men's club has sixty members; thirty are business men and thirty are professors. In how many ways can a committee of eight be selected (a) if at least three must be business men and at least three professors; (b) the only condition is that at least one of the eight must be a business man? (Leave the answers in $C(n, r)$ symbols.)

11. In how many ways can a ballot be validly marked if a citizen is to choose one of three candidates for mayor, one of four for city councilman, and one of three for district attorney. A citizen is not required to vote for all three positions, but he is expected to vote for at least one.

12. If 20! were multiplied out, how many consecutive zeros would occur on the right hand end?

13. If 52! were multiplied out, how many consecutive zeros would occur on the right hand end?

14. Signals are made by running five colored flags up a mast. How many different signals can be made if there is an unlimited supply of flags of seven different colors?

15. In the preceding question what would be the answer if (a) adjacent flags in a signal must not be of the same color; (b) all five flags in a signal must be of different colors?

16. From the 26 letters of the alphabet, how many subsets of three letters are there such that no two of the three are consecutive letters of the alphabet?

17. In how many ways can all of n distinct objects be put in k distinct boxes, not more than one in each box, if there are more boxes than things?

2.6   Permutations of Things in a Circle

The permutations that we have considered so far are called *linear permutations* because they are permutations of things in a line or in a row. Permutations of things in a circle, or *circular permutations*, occur in such a problem as: In how many ways can five persons be seated at a round table?

First solution. If we label the persons A, B, C, D, E, we see that the five linear permutations

$$ABCDE, \quad BCDEA, \quad CDEAB, \quad DEABC, \quad EABCD$$

are identical when thought of as circular permutations. This is so because two arrangements of people at a round table are considered to form the same circular permutation if one can be obtained from the other by rotating everybody around the circle by the same amount and in the same direction. This is the case, for example, if everybody moves one place to his right. Hence we can get at the number of circular permutations by relating them to the linear permutations: each circular permutation corresponds to five linear permutations, so there are only $\frac{1}{5}$ as many circular permutations as there are linear permutations. But there are 5! linear permutations of five objects, and hence the answer to the question is

$$\tfrac{1}{5}(5!) \; = \; \tfrac{1}{5}(5\cdot4\cdot3\cdot2\cdot1) \; = \; 4\cdot3\cdot2\cdot1 \; = \; 4!\,.$$

Second solution. Since a circular arrangement is unchanged if every object (or every person) is moved uniformly one place to the right, or uniformly two places to the right, etc., we can fix the place of one person and arrange the others with reference to him around the table. Putting A in a fixed place, we see that any one of four persons can be immediately to A's right, then any one of three remaining persons in the next place to the right, any one of two in the next place, and the remaining person in the final place; see Figure 2.1. Using the multiplication principle we get the answer $4\cdot3\cdot2\cdot1$.

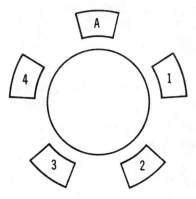

Figure 2.1

In general there are $(n - 1)!$ circular permutations of n distinct objects. To show this, we can argue as we did in the solutions just given for the special case $n = 5$. In particular, let us follow the second solution. We think of n persons, say $A, B, C, D, \cdots$, being seated at a round table. Since a uniform rotation of the persons does not alter an arrangement, we might as well put person A in one fixed place and then consider the number of ways of arranging all the others. In the chair to the right of A we can put any of the other $n - 1$ people. That done, we move to the next chair to the right into which we can place any one of the remaining $n - 2$ persons. Continuing in this counterclockwise fashion around the circle, we see that the multiplication principle gives the answer

$$(n - 1)(n - 2)(n - 3) \cdots 1 = (n - 1)!.$$

Problem Set 6

1. In how many ways is it possible to seat eight persons at a round table?

2. In the preceding question, what would be the answer if a certain two of the eight persons must not sit in adjacent seats?

3. In how many ways can four men and four ladies be seated at a round table, if no two men are to be in adjacent seats?

4. In the preceding question, suppose the persons are four married couples. What would be the answer to the question if no husband and wife, as well as no two men, are to be in adjacent seats?

5. How many different firing orders are theoretically possible in a six cylinder engine? (If the cylinders are numbered from 1 to 6, a firing order is a list, such as 1, 4, 2, 5, 3, 6, giving the rotational order in which the fuel is ignited in the cylinders.)

6. How many differently colored blocks of a fixed cubical shape can be made if six colors are available, and a block is to have a different color on each of its six faces? The definition of differently colored blocks is the same as in Problem 1.2 in Chapter 1.

7. How many different cubes with the six faces numbered from 1 to 6 can be made, if the sum of the numbers on each pair of opposite faces is 7?

2.7 Summary

The multiplication principle: If one event can occur in m ways, and a second event can occur independently of the first in k ways, then the two events can occur in mk ways.

Formula for n factorial:

$$n! = n(n-1)(n-2) \cdots 1 \quad \text{for positive integers } n,$$

$$0! = 1.$$

The number of permutations (i.e. ordered arrangements) of n distinct objects, taken r at a time, is

$$P(n, r) = \frac{n!}{(n-r)!}.$$

The number of combinations (i.e. selections, without regard to order) of n distinct objects, taken r at a time, is

$$C(n, r) = \frac{n!}{r!(n-r)!}.$$

$C(n, r)$ can also be interpreted as the number of r-subsets (subsets containing r elements) of a set of n objects. A frequently used alternative notation for $C(n, r)$ is $\binom{n}{r}$. A basic property of $C(n, r)$ is

$$C(n, r) \;=\; C(n, n - r).$$

The symbol $C(n, r)$ was given a numerical value for all pairs of integers n and r, as follows:

$C(n, r) \;=\; 0$ in case one or more of n, r, $n - r$ is negative;

$$C(n, r) \;=\; \frac{n!}{r!(n - r)!} \quad \text{in all other cases.}$$

The number of circular permutations (i.e. arrangements in a circle) of n distinct objects is $(n - 1)!$.

The formulas for $P(n, r)$ and $C(n, r)$ apply only to special situations of ordered arrangements and unordered selections where the n objects are distinct and repetitions in the r-sets are not allowed. They are not universal formulas for permutations and combinations. However, in later chapters many problems are reduced to these special cases.

CHAPTER THREE

Combinations and Binomial Coefficients

There are other ways, besides those in the preceding chapter, of looking at $C(n, r)$, the number of combinations of n different things taken r at a time. Several of these possibilities are studied in this chapter. We begin by pointing out that we can easily solve the path problem which was listed as Problem 1.3 in Chapter 1. For convenience, we repeat the statement of the question.

3.1 A Path Problem

A man works in a building located seven blocks east and eight blocks north of his home. Thus in walking to work each day he goes fifteen blocks. All the streets in the rectangular pattern are available to him for walking. In how many different paths can he go from home to work, walking only fifteen blocks?

Let us denote by E the act of walking a block east, and by N the act of walking a block north, and let us interpret a string of E's and N's such as

$$EENNNENN$$

as meaning (reading from left to right) that a man walks two blocks east, then three blocks north, then one block east, and finally two blocks north. Then any path from home to work can be identified with an appropriate pattern of seven E's and eight N's in a row. For example, the path beginning with three blocks east, then two north, then four east, and finally six north is

$$EEENNEEEENNNNNN.$$

Thus to each path there corresponds a string of seven E's and eight N's properly interspersed in a row; and conversely, to any such string of E's and N's there corresponds exactly one path. We can therefore rephrase the problem as follows: In how many ways can seven E's and eight N's be written in a row?

□ □ □ □ □ □ □ □ □ □ □ □ □ □ □

If we think of fifteen boxes to be filled with seven E's and eight N's, we see that the answer to this question is just the number of ways we can choose seven boxes out of fifteen to fill with E's, and this number is

$$C(15, 7) \; = \; \frac{15!}{7!8!} \; = \; \frac{15 \cdot 14 \cdot 13 \cdot 12 \cdot 11 \cdot 10 \cdot 9}{7 \cdot 6 \cdot 5 \cdot 4 \cdot 3 \cdot 2} \; = \; 6435.$$

It is also the same as the number of ways we can choose eight boxes out of fifteen to fill with N's, that is $C(15, 8)$. In Chapter 2 we saw that

$$C(n, r) \; = \; C(n, n - r), \text{ and so } C(15, 7) \; = \; C(15, 8) \; = \; 6435.$$

3.2 Permutations of Things Not All Alike

We have just seen that $C(15, 7)$ can be interpreted as the number of permutations of fifteen things of which seven are alike and the other eight are alike. In general $C(n, r)$ can be interpreted as the number of permutations of n things of which r are alike and the other $n - r$ are alike. This idea can also be generalized from two batches of things, like E's and N's, to more batches. We begin with an example.

PROBLEM 3.1 How many different permutations are there of the letters of the word *Mississippi*, taken all at a time? In other words, in how many different orders is it possible to write the letters of the word *Mississippi*?

SOLUTION. There are eleven letters of which four are alike (the i's), another four alike (the s's), and another two alike (the p's). Consider eleven boxes for insertion of letters to give the various permutations. Choose four of these for the i's; there are $C(11, 4)$ ways of doing this. Then choose four of the remaining seven boxes for the s's; there are $C(7, 4)$ ways of doing this. Then from the remaining three choose two boxes for the p's; there are $C(3, 2)$ ways of doing this. The letter M will fill the remaining box. By the multiplication principle we get the answer

$$C(11, 4) \cdot C(7, 4) \cdot C(3, 2) = \frac{11!}{4!7!} \frac{7!}{4!3!} \frac{3!}{2!1!} = \frac{11!}{4!4!2!1!}.$$

Of course, if we choose the letters for the boxes in some other order, the calculation looks a little different, but the final answer is the same. For example, suppose we begin by choosing one box out of the eleven for the letter M, then four boxes for the s's, then two boxes for the p's, with the remaining four boxes for the i's; then the total number of different arrangements of the letters is

$$C(11, 1) \cdot C(10, 4) \cdot C(6, 2) = \frac{11!}{1!10!} \cdot \frac{10!}{4!6!} \cdot \frac{6!}{2!4!} = \frac{11!}{4!4!2!1!},$$

the same as before.

SECOND SOLUTION. An alternative argument of quite a different kind goes like this: Let x denote the number of permutations in our answer. If we were to replace the four i's by four letters different from each other and from the remaining letters of *Mississippi*, such as $i, j, k,$ and l, we would obtain $x \cdot 4!$ permutations from the original x because each of the original permutations would give rise to $4!$. Similarly if the four s's were replaced by four distinct letters, again we would have $4!$ times as many permutations. And if the two p's were replaced by unlike letters, we would have $2!$ times as many permutations as before. But now we would have eleven letters, all *different*, and so 11! permutations. This gives the equation

$$x \cdot 4! \cdot 4! \cdot 2! = 11!, \quad \text{so that} \quad x = \frac{11!}{4!4!2!}.$$

More generally, if there are n things of which a are alike, another b are alike, another c are alike, and finally the remaining d are alike, we can find the number of permutations of the $n = a + b + c + d$ things taken all at a time by a similar argument: If x denotes the number of different permutations,

$$x \cdot a! \cdot b! \cdot c! \cdot d! = n!, \quad \text{so that} \quad x = \frac{n!}{a!b!c!d!}.$$

There need not be just four batches of like things. In general, if there are n things of which a are alike, another b are alike, another c are alike, etc., then the number of permutations of the n things taken all at a time is

$$(3.1) \qquad \frac{n!}{a!b!c! \cdots}, \quad \text{where} \quad n = a + b + c + \cdots.$$

Here the dots in the denominator stand for "and so on", that is, for as many additional factorial terms as may be necessary.

Problem Set 7

1. How many permutations are there of the letters, taken all at a time, of the words (a) assesses, (b) humuhumunukunukuapuaa (Hawaiian word for a species of fish).

2. Derive formula (3.1) in the case of four batches, $n = a + b + c + d$, by paralleling the first argument given for Problem 3.1.

3. In the path problem in Section 3.1, denote the north-south streets by $A, B, C, \cdots, H$ and the east-west streets by 1st, 2nd, $\cdots$, 9th. Presume that the man lives at the corner of 1st and A, and works at the corner of 9th and H. Given the information that all streets are available for walking with one exception, namely that E street from 5th

to 6th is not cut through, in how many different paths can the man walk from home to work, walking only fifteen blocks?

4. As a generalization of the path problem to three dimensions, consider a three-dimensional steel framework; how many different paths of length fifteen units are there from one intersection point in the framework to another that is located four units to the right, five units back, and six units up?

5. In how many different orders can the following 17 letters be written?

$$x\,x\,x\,x\,y\,y\,y\,y\,y\,z\,z\,z\,z\,z\,z\,w\,w$$

3.3 Pascal's Formula for $C(n, r)$

Consider the r-subsets, i.e. subsets consisting of r elements, of a set of n objects. The number of r-subsets is $C(n, r)$. Of the set of n objects, let us single out one and label it T. The r-subsets can be separated into two types:

  (a) those that contain the object T;

  (b) those not containing the object T.

Those that contain the object T are in number $C(n - 1, r - 1)$, because along with T in any r-subset there are $r - 1$ other objects selected from $n - 1$ objects. Those that do not contain the object T are in number $C(n - 1, r)$, because these r-subsets are selected from $n - 1$ objects, T being out. We have separated the entire collection of r-subsets into two types and then determined the number of each type, thus establishing Pascal's formula

$$(3.2) \qquad C(n, r) \;=\; C(n - 1, r) + C(n - 1, r - 1).$$

There is a simple device that extends the use of such formulas. We observe that the reasoning leading to relation (3.2) does not depend on the precise number of objects n or r. The argument would have made equally good sense if we had begun with m objects from which k were to be selected to form k-subsets, and would have led to the equally meaningful formula

$$C(m, k) \;=\; C(m - 1, k) + C(m - 1, k - 1).$$

Similarly, had we begun with $n + 1$ objects and selected r of these, we would have derived the formula

(3.3) $C(n + 1, r) = C(n, r) + C(n, r - 1).$

There is really no need to rethink the whole process to get formula (3.3); it can be obtained from (3.2) by replacing n by $n + 1$; thus

$C(n, r)$ becomes $C(n + 1, r)$;

$C(n - 1, r)$ becomes $C(n + 1 - 1, r)$ or $C(n, r)$;

$C(n - 1, r - 1)$ becomes $C(n + 1 - 1, r - 1)$ or $C(n, r - 1)$;

and formula (3.2) becomes formula (3.3).

We can replace n by $n + 1$ in formula (3.2) and wind up with a valid formula because formula (3.2) holds *for any positive integers n and r, provided only that* $n \geqslant r$. So we can replace the symbols n and r by any other symbols subject only to the conditions that (i) the new symbols denote positive integers and (ii) the symbol replacing n stands for an integer at least as large as the integer denoted by the symbol replacing r. For example, in formula (3.2) we can replace n by $n + 1$, or $n + 2$, or $n + 3$. [We cannot replace n by $(n + 1)/2$, because of (i), nor by $r - 3$, because of condition (ii).]

In one sense such replacements give no new information. For example, formula (3.2) with $n = 20$ and $r = 6$ gives the information

$$C(20, 6) = C(19, 6) + C(19, 5).$$

Exactly the same equation comes from (3.3) with $n = 19$ and $r = 6$. However, if we add equations (3.2) and (3.3) we get

$C(n, r) + C(n + 1, r)$
$\qquad = C(n, r) + C(n, r - 1) + C(n - 1, r) + C(n - 1, r - 1);$

and, by subtracting $C(n, r)$ from both sides, we obtain the new formula

(3.4) $C(n+1, r) = C(n, r-1) + C(n-1, r) + C(n-1, r-1).$

This illustrates the fact that we can get new formulas from simpler ones like (3.2) without making any arguments about the meaning of the symbols themselves, but just by the manipulation of the notation.

Problem Set 8

1. Calculate $C(6, 2)$, $C(5, 2)$ and $C(5, 1)$ and verify that the first of these is the sum of the other two.

2. Write $C(9, 4) + C(9, 3)$ as a single combination form $C(n, r)$.

3. Write $C(50, 10) - C(49, 9)$ as a single combination form $C(n, r)$.

4. What is the resulting equation if   (a) we replace n by $n - 1$ in formula (3.2);   (b) we replace n by $n - 1$ and r by $r - 1$ in (3.2)?

5. What are the resulting formulas, if, in

$$C(n, r) = \frac{n!}{r!(n - r)!},$$

(a) we replace n by $n - 1$;   (b) we replace n by $n - 1$ and r by $r - 1$?

6. Using the results of the preceding question give a proof of formula (3.2) different from the one given in the text, by an argument involving factorials.

7. The proof in the text of formula (3.2) involved consideration of a special one, T, of the n things. Consider now two special ones, say S and T. The combinations can be divided into four classes: those that contain both S and T; those that contain S but not T; those that contain T but not S; those that contain neither S nor T. What formula results if we write $C(n, r)$ as a sum of the numbers of members of these four classes? Derive the formula thus obtained in another way, by using formula (3.2).

8. Apart from one exception, Pascal's formula (3.2) holds for all pairs of integers n and r, positive, negative or zero. What is this one exception?

3.4 The Binomial Expansion

Any sum of two unlike symbols, such as $x + y$, is called a binomial. The binomial expansion, or binomial theorem, is a formula for the powers of a binomial. If we compute the first few powers of $x + y$, we obtain

$$(x + y)^1 = x + y$$

$$(x + y)^2 = x^2 + 2xy + y^2$$

$$(x + y)^3 = x^3 + 3x^2y + 3xy^2 + y^3.$$

$$(x + y)^4 = x^4 + 4x^3y + 6x^2y^2 + 4xy^3 + y^4,$$

(3.5) $$(x + y)^5 = x^5 + 5x^4y + 10x^3y^2 + 10x^2y^3 + 5xy^4 + y^5.$$

Using equation (3.5) as a basis for discussion, we note that the right member has six terms: x^5, $5x^4y$, $10x^3y^2$, $10x^2y^3$, $5xy^4$ and y^5. What we want to do is explain the coefficients of these terms, 1, 5, 10, 10, 5, 1, by means of the theory of combinations.

First let us examine the results of multiplying several binomials. For example, to multiply $(a + b)$ by $(c + d)$ we apply the distributive law and obtain

$(a + b)(c + d) = (a + b)c + (a + b)d = ac + bc + ad + bd.$

Each of the terms in this sum is a product of two symbols, one taken from the first parenthesis of our original product and the other from the second. Notice that there are precisely $2 \cdot 2 = 4$ different ways of selecting one symbol from the first binomial and one symbol from the second.

We now examine the product of three binomials

$(a + b)(c + d)(e + f)$

$$= ace + acf + ade + adf + bce + bcf + bde + bdf$$

and observe that it consists of eight terms, each a product of three symbols selected, respectively, from the three binomials. Again we observe that $8 = 2 \cdot 2 \cdot 2$ is precisely the number of different ways that three symbols can be selected, one from each binomial. Similar results hold for the expanded product of four or more binomials. Let us consider the product

$$(a + b)(c + d)(e + f)(p + q)(r + s).$$

Its expansion which we will not write out in full, is a sum of $2^5 = 32$ terms. As sample terms we cite

adeqs   and   *bceps*.

Each term is a product of five symbols, one selected from each of the five original binomials.

Now in the light of these observations let us look at $(x + y)^5$ as the product

$$(x + y)(x + y)(x + y)(x + y)(x + y).$$

There are 32 ways of selecting five symbols, one from each parenthesis, but the resulting 32 expressions are not all distinct. For example, multiplication of the particular x's and y's shown here

$$(x + y)(x + y)(x + y)(x + y)(x + y)$$

with arrows directed at them results in the product

$$xyyxx = x^3y^2.$$

But x^3y^2 also arises if we select x's from the first three parentheses and y's from the remaining two. In fact, the expression x^3y^2 arises in the expansion of $(x + y)^5$ in exactly as many ways as three x's and two y's can be written in different orders:

$$xyyxx, \quad xxxyy, \quad yxxxy, \quad \text{etc.}$$

By the theory of Section 3.2 there are

$$C(5, 2) = \frac{5!}{2!3!} = 10$$

different arrangements of these symbols. This analysis explains the coefficient 10 of x^3y^2 in equation (3.5), the expansion of $(x + y)^5$. The other coefficients can be obtained in a similar way, so we have

$$(x + y)^5 = C(5, 0)x^5 + C(5, 1)x^4y + C(5, 2)x^3y^2$$
$$+ C(5, 3)x^2y^3 + C(5, 4)xy^4 + C(5, 5)y^5.$$

This is not as concise as formula (3.5), but it suggests a general pattern. It suggests that the coefficient of x^3y^3 in the expansion of $(x + y)^6$ is $C(6, 3)$, the number of ways of writing three x's and three y's in a row; and that the coefficient of x^2y^4 in the same expansion is $C(6, 4)$, the number of ways of writing two x's and four y's in a row. (Of course $C(6, 4)$ is the same as $C(6, 2)$, but we shall make the combination symbol follow the number of y's rather than the number of x's. It could be done the other way around.)

Now let n be any positive integer. The expression $(x + y)^n$ is defined as

$$(x + y)(x + y)(x + y) \cdots (x + y) \qquad (n \text{ factors}).$$

In the expansion of this product $x^{n-j}y^j$ arises in as many ways as a batch of $n - j$ x's and a batch of j y's can be written in a row. Hence the coefficient of $x^{n-j}y^j$ is $C(n, j)$. Thus the binomial expansion can be written as

$$\begin{aligned}
(x + y)^n = \; & C(n, 0)x^n + C(n, 1)x^{n-1}y + C(n, 2)x^{n-2}y^2 \\
& + C(n, 3)x^{n-3}y^3 + \cdots + C(n, j)x^{n-j}y^j \\
& + \cdots + C(n, n)y^n.
\end{aligned}$$

As was remarked in Chapter 2, the notation $\binom{n}{j}$ is often used in place of $C(n, j)$, particularly in the binomial expansion. So in many books it looks like this:

$$\begin{aligned}
(x + y)^n = \; & \binom{n}{0} x^n + \binom{n}{1} x^{n-1}y + \binom{n}{2} x^{n-2}y^2 + \binom{n}{3} x^{n-3}y^3 \\
& + \cdots + \binom{n}{j} x^{n-j}y^j + \cdots + \binom{n}{n} y^n.
\end{aligned}$$

The first and last terms can be written more simply as x^n and y^n, and this suggests yet another form in which the binomial expansion is often given:

$$(x + y)^n = x^n + nx^{n-1}y$$

$$+ \frac{n(n-1)}{2 \cdot 1} x^{n-2}y^2 + \frac{n(n-1)(n-2)}{3 \cdot 2 \cdot 1} x^{n-3}y^3$$

$$+ \frac{n(n-1)(n-2)(n-3)}{4 \cdot 3 \cdot 2 \cdot 1} x^{n-4}y^4 + \cdots + y^n.$$

Problem Set 9

1. How many terms are there in the expansion of $(x + y)^5$? of $(x + y)^n$?

2. Write out the expansion of $(x + y)^6$ with the coefficients in the $C(n, r)$ form. Substitute 1 for x and 1 for y and so evaluate the sum

$$C(6,0) + C(6,1) + C(6,2) + C(6,3) + C(6,4) + C(6,5) + C(6,6).$$

3. Substitute 1 for x and -1 for y in the expansion of $(x + y)^6$ and so evaluate the sum

$$C(6,0) - C(6,1) + C(6,2) - C(6,3) + C(6,4) - C(6,5) + C(6,6).$$

4. What is the coefficient of u^3v^7 in $(u + v)^{10}$, expressed as a natural number?

5. Write out the full expansion of $(u + v)^7$ with the coefficients written as natural numbers.

6. Verify that the expansion of $(x + y)^8$ can be expressed in this way: the sum of all terms of the form

$$\frac{8!}{a!b!} x^a y^b,$$

where a and b range over all pairs of non-negative integers a and b such that $a + b = 8$.

7. Verify that $(x + y)^n$ is the sum of all terms of the form

$$\frac{n!}{a!b!}\, x^a y^b,$$

where a and b range over all possible pairs of non-negative integers such that $a + b = n$.

8. Without expanding the product

$$(a + b + c)(d + e + f)(p + q + r + s)(x + y + u + v + w)$$

answer the following questions: How many terms will there be? Which of the following are actual terms in the expansion? *adps*, *bdsw*, *bfpu*, *bfxw*.

3.5 The Multinomial Expansion

The idea of the preceding section carries over from binomials to sums of more than two elements. As an example consider the expression

$$(x + y + z + w)^{17};$$

this, by definition, is a product of seventeen identical factors $x + y + z + w$:

$$(x + y + z + w)(x + y + z + w) \cdots (x + y + z + w).$$

The expansion of this has a term, for example, of the form $x^4 y^5 z^6 w^2$, because the sum of the exponents is $4 + 5 + 6 + 2 = 17$. This particular term occurs in the expansion as often as x can be chosen from four of the seventeen factors, y from five of the remaining thirteen factors, z from six of the remaining eight factors, and w then taken automatically from the other two factors. Paralleling the argument made in the case of the binomial expansion, we see that this is simply

$$C(17, 4)\cdot C(13, 5)\cdot C(8, 6)\cdot 1 \;=\; \frac{17!}{13!4!}\cdot\frac{13!}{8!5!}\cdot\frac{8!}{6!2!} \;=\; \frac{17!}{4!5!6!2!}.$$

The expansion of $(x + y + z + w)^{17}$ has been shown to contain the term

$$\frac{17!}{4!5!6!2!} x^4 y^5 z^6 w^2.$$

This coefficient is very much like the numbers obtained in Section 3.2; and this is not surprising since all we are calculating here is the number of ways of ordering the following seventeen letters:

$$x\,x\,x\,x\,y\,y\,y\,y\,y\,z\,z\,z\,z\,z\,z\,w\,w.$$

More generally, we can say that the expansion of $(x + y + z + w)^{17}$ is the sum of all terms of the form

$$\frac{17!}{a!b!c!d!} x^a y^b z^c w^d,$$

where a, b, c, d range over all possible sets of non-negative integers satisfying $a + b + c + d = 17$. As a simple case we note the solution $a = 17$, $b = 0$, $c = 0$, $d = 0$, belonging to the term

$$\frac{17!}{17!0!0!0!} x^{17} y^0 z^0 w^0$$

or more simply x^{17} in the expansion. Other solutions of

$$a + b + c + d = 17$$

are, for example, $a = 4$, $b = 5$, $c = 6$, $d = 2$ and $a = 4$, $b = 5$, $c = 2$, $d = 6$ and belong to the terms

$$\frac{17!}{4!5!6!2!} x^4 y^5 z^6 w^2 \quad \text{and} \quad \frac{17!}{4!5!2!6!} x^4 y^5 z^2 w^6,$$

respectively.

Further generalization is apparent. For any positive integer n (in place of the special number 17) we see that the expansion of $(x + y + z + w)^n$ is the sum of all terms of the form

$$\frac{n!}{a!b!c!d!} x^a y^b z^c w^d,$$

where a, b, c, d range over all solutions of $a + b + c + d = n$ in non-negative integers.

There is no reason to restrict attention to a sum of four elements x, y, z, w. For any positive integer n, the multinomial expansion of

$$(x + y + z + w + \cdots)^n$$

is the sum of all terms of the form

$$\frac{n!}{a!b!c!d! \cdots} x^a y^b z^c w^d \cdots,$$

where $a, b, c, d, \cdots$ range over all solutions of

$$a + b + c + d + \cdots = n$$

in non-negative integers.

Problem Set 10

1. Write out the trinomial expansion of $(x + y + z)^4$ in full.

2. What is the coefficient of $x^2 y^2 z^2 w^2 u^2$ in the expansion of
$$(x + y + z + w + u)^{10}?$$

3. What is the coefficient of $xyzwuv$ in the expansion of
$$(x + y + z + w + u + v)^6?$$

4. What is the sum of all the coefficients in the expansion of $(x + y + z)^8$? of $(x + y + z + w)^{17}$?

5. What is the sum of all numbers of the form
$$\frac{12!}{a!b!c!},$$
where a, b, c range over all non-negative integers satisfying
$$a + b + c = 12?$$

3.6 Pascal's Triangle

The binomial coefficients in the expansion of $(x + y)^n$ form an interesting pattern if listed with increasing values of n. We begin with $(x + y)^0 = 1$ to give symmetry to the table:

1										from $(x + y)^0$
1	1									from $(x + y)^1$
1	2	1								from $(x + y)^2$
1	3	3	1							from $(x + y)^3$
1	4	6	4	1						etc.
1	5	10	10	5	1					
1	6	15	20	15	6	1				
1	7	(21)	(35)	35	21	7	1			
1	8	28	(56)	70	56	28	8	1		

This array, listed here as far as $n = 8$, is called Pascal's triangle.

The recursion relation $C(n, r) = C(n - 1, r) + C(n - 1, r - 1)$ of Section 3.3 reveals how this table can be made and extended without difficulty. For example, the three numbers 21, 35 and 56 that have been circled are the same as $C(7, 2)$, $C(7, 3)$ and $C(8, 3)$, the last of which is the sum of the first two by the recursion relation. Thus, any number $C(n, r)$ in Pascal's triangle is the sum of the number directly above, $C(n - 1, r)$, and the one to the left of that, $C(n - 1, r - 1)$. For example, if we wanted to extend the above table to the next row, namely the tenth row, we would write

$$1, \quad 1 + 8, \quad 8 + 28, \quad 28 + 56, \quad 56 + 70, \quad 70 + 56,$$
$$56 + 28, \quad 28 + 8, \quad 8 + 1, \quad 1$$

or

$$1, \ 9, \ 36, \ 84, \ 126, \ 126, \ 84, \ 36, \ 9, \ 1 \,.$$

These numbers are the coefficients in the expansion of $(x + y)^9$, and if we substitute $x = 1$ and $y = 1$ we get $(1 + 1)^9$ or 2^9.

Hence the sum of the elements in the tenth row of Pascal's triangle, $1 + 9 + 36 + 84 + \cdots$, is 2^9. In general, if we substitute $x = 1$ and $y = 1$ in $(x + y)^n$ we get 2^n, and so we can conclude that the sum of the elements in the $(n + 1)$st row of Pascal's triangle is

$$(3.6) \quad C(n, 0) + C(n, 1) + C(n, 2) + \cdots + C(n, n) = 2^n.$$

On the other hand, if we substitute $x = 1$ and $y = -1$ in $(x + y)^n$ we get 0^n or 0, and so we can conclude that

$$(3.7) \quad C(n, 0) - C(n, 1) + C(n, 2) - C(n, 3)$$
$$+ \cdots + (-1)^n C(n, n) = 0.$$

Problem Set 11

1. Extend Pascal's triangle to include $n = 9, 10, 11, 12, 13$.

2. Prove that the sum of the elements in the ninth row equals the sum of the elements of all previous rows, with 1 added.

3. Prove that in any row of Pascal's triangle the sum of the first, third, fifth, $\cdots$ elements equals the sum of the second, fourth, sixth, $\cdots$ elements.

3.7 The Number of Subsets of a Set

A man says to his son, "In cleaning up the attic I came across seven issues of an old magazine named *Colliers*. Look them over and take any you want. Whatever you don't want I will throw away." How many different selections are possible? Another way of stating this problem is: How many subsets are there of a set of seven things?

One way to solve the problem is to say that the son may select all seven, $C(7, 7)$, or six out of seven, $C(7, 6)$, or five out of seven, $C(7, 5)$, and so on. This gives the answer

$$C(7, 7) + C(7, 6) + C(7, 5) + C(7, 4) + C(7, 3)$$
$$+ C(7, 2) + C(7, 1) + C(7, 0).$$

By formula (3.6) on page 42 this is the same as 2^7.

Another way to solve the problem is to concentrate on the individual copies of the magazine rather than on sets of them. Let us denote the seven issues of the magazine by A, B, C, D, E, F, G. Then A may be taken or rejected (two possibilities); B may be taken or rejected (two possibilities); $\cdots$; G may be taken or rejected (two possibilities). Using the multiplication principle we have the answer

$$2 \cdot 2 \cdot 2 \cdot 2 \cdot 2 \cdot 2 \cdot 2 = 2^7.$$

Thus a set of seven different things has 2^7 subsets, including the whole set of all seven, and the empty set or null set with no elements. If we disregard the whole set, the others are called *proper subsets*, and so a set of seven different things has $2^7 - 1$ proper subsets. In general, a set of n different things has 2^n subsets of which $2^n - 1$ are proper subsets. Among these subsets there are exactly $C(n, r)$ having r members.

Problem Set 12

1. How many different sums of money can be made up using one or more coins selected from a cent, a nickel, a dime, a quarter, a half dollar, and a silver dollar?

2. The members of a club are to vote "yes" or "no" on each of eight issues. In marking his ballot, a member has the option of abstaining on as many as seven of the issues, but he should not abstain in all eight cases. In how many ways can a ballot be marked?

3. A travel agency has ten different kinds of free folders. The agent tells a boy to take any he wants, but not more than one of a kind. Assuming that the boy takes at least one folder, how many selections are possible?

4. A biologist is studying patterns of male (M) and female (F) children in families. A family type is designated by a code; for example, FMM denotes a family of three children of which the oldest is a female and the other two males. Note that FMM, MFM, and MMF are different types. How many family types are there among families with at least one but not more than seven children?

3.8 Sums of Powers of Natural Numbers

As a by-product of the theory of combinations we can get formulas for the sum

$$1 + 2 + 3 + 4 + \cdots + n$$

of positive integers (natural numbers) from 1 to n, for the sum of their squares,

$$1^2 + 2^2 + 3^2 + 4^2 + \cdots + n^2,$$

for the sum of their cubes, and so on. The idea is to use the recursion relation (3.2) for $C(n, r)$, which we rewrite in the form

(3.8) $C(n - 1, r - 1) \; = \; C(n, r) - C(n - 1, r).$

As an example to illustrate the method, let us write formula (3.8) in succession with $n = 9$, $n = 8$, $n = 7$, $\cdots$, $n = 3$, but with $r = 2$ in all cases:

$$C(8, 1) \; = \; C(9, 2) - C(8, 2)$$
$$C(7, 1) \; = \; C(8, 2) - C(7, 2)$$
$$C(6, 1) \; = \; C(7, 2) - C(6, 2)$$
(3.9) $$C(5, 1) \; = \; C(6, 2) - C(5, 2)$$
$$C(4, 1) \; = \; C(5, 2) - C(4, 2)$$
$$C(3, 1) \; = \; C(4, 2) - C(3, 2)$$
$$C(2, 1) \; = \; C(3, 2) - C(2, 2).$$

If we add these equations there is much cancellation on the right, with the result

$$C(2, 1) + C(3, 1) + C(4, 1) + C(5, 1)$$
$$+ \, C(6, 1) + C(7, 1) + C(8, 1) = C(9, 2) - C(2, 2),$$
$$2 + 3 + 4 + 5 + 6 + 7 + 8 = \tfrac{1}{2} 9 \cdot 8 - 1.$$

After adding 1 to both sides of this identity, we see that we have found the sum of the natural numbers from 1 to 8 by an indirect method, and this sum is $\tfrac{1}{2}(72)$ or 36.

To do this in general, replace n in formula (3.8) successively by $m + 1,\ m,\ m - 1,\ \cdots\ ,\ 4, 3$, keeping r fixed as before, $r = 2$. This gives a chain of equations

$$C(m, 1)\ =\ C(m + 1, 2) - C(m, 2)$$
$$C(m - 1, 1)\ =\ C(m, 2) - C(m - 1, 2)$$
$$(3.10)\quad C(m - 2, 1)\ =\ C(m - 1, 2) - C(m - 2, 2)$$
$$\cdots\cdots\cdots\cdots\cdots$$
$$C(3, 1)\ =\ C(4, 2) - C(3, 2)$$
$$C(2, 1)\ =\ C(3, 2) - C(2, 2).$$

Adding these equations we note that again there is considerable cancellation on the right side, and the result is

$$C(2, 1) + C(3, 1) + \cdots + C(m{-}2, 1)$$
$$+ C(m{-}1, 1) + C(m, 1) = C(m{+}1, 2) - C(2, 2),$$

or

$$2 + 3 + \cdots + (m - 2) + (m - 1) + m\ =\ \tfrac{1}{2}(m + 1)m - 1,$$

so that

$$(3.11)\quad 1 + 2 + 3 + \cdots + (m{-}2) + (m{-}1) + m = \tfrac{1}{2}m(m{+}1).$$

It should be understood that if for example $m = 2$, the left side is to be interpreted simply as $1 + 2$.

To get a formula for the sum of the squares of the natural numbers, we write the analogues of (3.10) with all values of n and r raised by 1; that is, we write equation (3.8) with $r = 3$ and n replaced successively by $m + 2,\ m + 1,\ m,\ \cdots,\ 5, 4$ to get

$$C(m + 1, 2)\ =\ C(m + 2, 3) - C(m + 1, 3)$$
$$C(m, 2)\ =\ C(m + 1, 3) - C(m, 3)$$
$$(3.12)\quad C(m - 1, 2)\ =\ C(m, 3) - C(m - 1, 3)$$
$$\cdots\cdots\cdots\cdots\cdots$$
$$C(4, 2)\ =\ C(5, 3) - C(4, 3)$$
$$C(3, 2)\ =\ C(4, 3) - C(3, 3).$$

Adding these, and then substituting the values for the combination symbols, we have

$$C(3, 2) + C(4, 2) + \cdots + C(m - 1, 2) + C(m, 2)$$
$$+ C(m + 1, 2) = C(m + 2, 3) - C(3, 3),$$

$$\tfrac{1}{3}3 \cdot 2 + \tfrac{1}{4}4 \cdot 3 + \cdots + \tfrac{1}{2}m(m - 1)$$
$$+ \tfrac{1}{2}(m + 1)m = \tfrac{1}{6}(m + 2)(m + 1)m - 1.$$

By adding 1 to both sides, then multiplying both sides by 2, we bring this into the form

$$1 \cdot 2 + 2 \cdot 3 + 3 \cdot 4 + \cdots + (m - 1)m$$
$$+ m(m + 1) = \tfrac{1}{3}m(m + 1)(m + 2).$$

The products on the left side of this equation can be rewritten as

$$1 \cdot 2 = 1(1 + 1) = 1^2 + 1,$$
$$2 \cdot 3 = 2(2 + 1) = 2^2 + 2,$$
$$3 \cdot 4 = 3(3 + 1) = 3^2 + 3,$$
$$\cdot \quad \cdot \quad \cdot \quad \cdot \quad \cdot \quad \cdot \quad \cdot \quad \cdot \quad \cdot$$
$$(m-2)(m-1) = (m-2)[(m-2) + 1] = (m-2)^2 + (m-2),$$
$$(m-1)m = (m-1)[(m-1) + 1] = (m-1)^2 + (m-1),$$
$$m(m + 1) = m^2 + m.$$

Substituting these we obtain

$$1^2 + 1 + 2^2 + 2 + 3^2 + 3 + \cdots$$
$$+ (m - 1)^2 + (m - 1) + m^2 + m = \tfrac{1}{3}m(m + 1)(m + 2)$$

or

$$[1^2 + 2^2 + \cdots + (m - 1)^2 + m^2]$$
$$+ [1 + 2 + \cdots + (m - 1) + m] = \tfrac{1}{3}m(m + 1)(m + 2).$$

We recognize the second expression in brackets as the sum of the first m natural numbers calculated in formula (3.11). Using formula (3.11) we see that

$$[1^2 + 2^2 + \cdots + (m - 1)^2 + m^2]$$
$$+ \tfrac{1}{2}m(m + 1) = \tfrac{1}{3}m(m + 1)(m + 2).$$

This can be rewritten as

$$[1^2 + 2^2 + \cdots + (m - 1)^2 + m^2]$$
$$= \tfrac{1}{3}m(m + 1)(m + 2) - \tfrac{1}{2}m(m + 1).$$

The right member of this equation reduces to $\tfrac{1}{6}m(m + 1)(2m + 1)$, as can be readily calculated by simple algebra. Hence we have derived the formula for the sum of the squares of the first m natural numbers:

$$1^2 + 2^2 + 3^2 + \cdots + m^2 = \tfrac{1}{6}m(m + 1)(2m + 1).$$

Problem Set 13

1. Find the sum of the integers from 1 to 100 inclusive.

2. Do the preceding problem again by writing the sum of the numbers both forwards and backwards:†

1	2	3	4	$\cdots$	97	98	99	100
100	99	98	97	$\cdots$	4	3	2	1

   Note that the addition of each pair of numbers in this array (i.e., $1 + 100$, $2 + 99$, $3 + 98$, $4 + 97$, etc.) always gives a total of 101. Hence the sum of the numbers from 1 to 100, taken twice, is the same as 101 added to itself 100 times. The rest is left to the reader.

3. Generalize the method outlined in the preceding problem to the integers from 1 to n inclusive, and thereby derive formula (3.11) in a different way. (Note that this device will not work on the sum of the squares of the numbers from 1 to n.)

† This method of adding the integers from 1 to 100 is said to have been used by a famous nineteenth century mathematician, C. F. Gauss, when he was a schoolboy. A teacher (so the story goes) assigned the problem to the class, hoping to keep them occupied for perhaps fifteen or twenty minutes, and was startled when the young Gauss gave the answer in a much shorter time.

4. Find the sum of the squares of the integers from 1 to 100 inclusive.

5. How many solutions in positive integers x and y are there of the equation $x + y = 100$? (In counting solutions in this and subsequent problems, treat such solutions as $x = 10$, $y = 90$ and $x = 90$, $y = 10$, as different. In other words, by a solution, we mean an ordered pair (x, y) that satisfies the equation.) How many solutions in non-negative integers?

6. How many solutions in positive integers are there of the equation $x + y = n$, where n is a fixed positive integer? How many solutions in non-negative integers?

7. How many ordered triples (x, y, z) of positive integers are solutions of $x + y + z = 100$? How many triples of non-negative integers?

8. Generalize Problem 7 to $x + y + z = n$.

9. How many terms are there in the expansion of $(x + y + z)^3$? of $(x + y + z)^4$? of $(x + y + z)^n$?

10. Extend the procedure used in equations (3.10), (3.11), (3.12) and so on, to get a formula for $1^3 + 2^3 + 3^3 + 4^3 + \cdots + m^3$.

3.9 Summary

Given n things which are alike in batches: a are alike; another b are alike; another c are alike, and so on; then the number of permutations of the n things taken all at a time is

$$\frac{n!}{a!\,b!\,c!\,\cdots}.$$

Pascal's formula for $C(n, r)$ is

$$C(n, r) = C(n - 1, r) + C(n - 1, r - 1).$$

The binomial expansion of $(x + y)^n$, for any positive integer n, is

$$(x + y)^n = C(n, 0)x^n + C(n, 1)x^{n-1}y + C(n, 2)x^{n-2}y^2$$
$$+ \cdots + C(n, j)x^{n-j}y^j + \cdots + C(n, n)y^n.$$

An alternative notation for this expansion is

$$(x + y)^n = x^n + \binom{n}{1} x^{n-1}y + \binom{n}{2} x^{n-2}y^2 + \binom{n}{3} x^{n-3}y^3$$

$$+ \cdots + \binom{n}{j} x^{n-j}y^n + \cdots + y^n.$$

The multinomial expansion of $(x + y + z + w + \cdots)^n$ is the sum of all terms of the form

$$\frac{n!}{a!b!c!d! \cdots} x^a y^b z^c w^d \cdots,$$

where $a, b, c, d, \cdots$ range over all solutions of

$$a + b + c + d + \cdots = n$$

in non-negative integers.

Pascal's triangle is given as far as $n = 8$ in Section 3.6. Also the following two relations were proved:

$$C(n, 0) + C(n, 1) + C(n, 2) + C(n, 3) + \cdots + C(n, n) = 2^n,$$
$$C(n, 0) - C(n, 1) + C(n, 2) - C(n, 3) + \cdots + (-1)^n C(n, n) = 0.$$

The number of subsets of a set of n different things is 2^n; the number of proper subsets is $2^n - 1$; the number of subsets having r elements is $C(n, r)$.

Methods for deriving the sum of kth powers of the first n natural numbers were sketched. In particular, the sum of the natural numbers from 1 to n (i.e., $k = 1$)and the sum of their squares (i.e. $k = 2$) were obtained:

$$1 + 2 + 3 + 4 + \cdots + n = \tfrac{1}{2}n(n + 1),$$
$$1^2 + 2^2 + 3^2 + 4^2 + \cdots + n^2 = \tfrac{1}{6}n(n + 1)(2n + 1).$$

CHAPTER FOUR

Some Special Distributions

Many a problem in combinatorial analysis is solved by first reformulating it. This point was illustrated on page 28 where a path problem was reduced to an equivalent question involving combinations. In this chapter we look at some other problems which, when viewed from the proper perspective, also reduce to questions involving combinations.

4.1 Fibonacci Numbers

Consider the question: In how many ways can eight plus signs and five minus signs be lined up in a row so that no two minus signs are adjacent? An example of such an arrangement is:

$$+ + - + - + + + - + - + - .$$

The problem is easy to solve if we look at it this way; write the eight plus signs as an expression (4.1) with m's between, and also m's at the start and finish:

$$(4.1) \qquad m + m + m + m + m + m + m + m + m .$$

Thus we have eight plus signs and nine m's. Now the five minus signs can be selected as any of the nine m's, and so the answer to the question is $C(9, 5)$.

In general, we can say that *the number of ways of writing k plus signs and r minus signs in a row so that no two minus signs are adjacent is $C(k + 1, r)$*. The reason for this is exactly the same as in the special case above where $k = 8$ and $r = 5$. In place of (4.1) we now have

$$(4.2) \qquad m + m + m + m + \cdots + m + m,$$

namely k plus signs separating $k + 1$ symbols m. We convert r of the m's into minus signs and let the others disappear. Thus we select r out of the $k + 1$ symbols m, turn them into minus signs, and obtain the answer $C(k + 1, r)$.

If r exceeds $k + 1$ the notation $C(k + 1, r)$ has value zero. This is as it should be because, if $k = 8$ and $r = 12$ for example, there is no way to write eight plus signs and twelve minus signs in a row so that no two minus signs are adjacent.

Next we turn to another question. Consider a series of ten x's in a row,

$$x\ x\ x\ x\ x\ x\ x\ x\ x\ x.$$

Suppose that each x may be a plus sign or a minus sign, so that there are 2^{10} or 1024 cases in all. The question is: How many of the 1024 cases do not have two minus signs in adjacent positions? By considering successively the types,

10 plus signs,

9 plus signs and 1 minus sign,

8 plus signs and 2 minus signs,

7 plus signs and 3 minus signs, etc.,

and using the result previously developed, we get the answer

$$C(11, 0) + C(10, 1) + C(9, 2) + C(8, 3) + C(7, 4) + C(6, 5).$$

There are other ·terms, $C(5, 6)$, $C(4, 7)$, and so on, but each of these is zero. The calculation is simple:

$$1 + 10 + 36 + 56 + 35 + 6 = 144.$$

More generally, let us use n in place of 10. If there were n symbols x in a row, and if each x could be a plus sign or a minus sign, there would be 2^n cases in all. Of these, the number not having two minus signs in adjacent positions is

$$(4.3) \quad C(n+1,0) + C(n,1) + C(n-1,2) + C(n-2,3) + \cdots,$$

where the sum continues until symbols of the sort $C(u, v)$ with $u < v$ are reached; such symbols denote zero by definition. Thus (4.3) denotes *the number of ways of writing n signs in a row, each being a plus sign or a minus sign, so that no two minus signs are adjacent.* This number is a function of n; we write it as $F(n)$, and then look at the question another way.

First consider those of the $F(n)$ sequences of signs that begin with a plus. They are $F(n-1)$ in number, because each of them is obtained by placing a plus sign in front of each of the $F(n-1)$ arrangements of $n-1$ signs.

Second consider those of the $F(n)$ sequences of signs that begin with a minus. The next sign in any such sequence must be plus, since adjacent minus signs are ruled out. Thus we are considering sequences of n signs beginning with $- +$. These are $F(n-2)$ in number, because each of them can be obtained by placing the pair $- +$ in front of each of the $F(n-2)$ arrangements of $n-2$ signs. Thus we conclude that

$$(4.4) \qquad F(n) = F(n-1) + F(n-2).$$

This formula is a recursion relation for the Fibonacci numbers, as the numbers $F(n)$ are called. It can be used to compute $F(n)$ whenever $F(n-1)$ and $F(n-2)$ are known. For $n = 3$, for example, it states that

$$F(3) = F(2) + F(1).$$

From the definition (4.3) of $F(n)$ we see that $F(1) = 2$ and

$F(2) = 3$, so that $F(3) = 5$. Similarly, by use of (4.4) we can compute

$$F(4) = F(3) + F(2) = 5 + 3 = 8,$$
$$F(5) = F(4) + F(3) = 8 + 5 = 13,$$
$$F(6) = F(5) + F(4) = 13 + 8 = 21,$$
$$F(7) = F(6) + F(5) = 21 + 13 = 34, \text{ etc.}$$

The Fibonacci sequence† is usually written with additional terms at the start, for example $1, 2, 3, 5, 8, 13, \cdots$, or $1, 1, 2, 3, 5, 8, 13, \cdots$, or $0, 1, 1, 2, 3, 5, 8, 13, \cdots$. We shall use the first of these three versions. To do this we define $F(0) = 1$, and then use our results $F(1) = 2$, $F(2) = 3$, etc., each term being the sum of the preceding two.

Fibonacci numbers are usually *defined* by property (4.4), $F(n) = F(n - 1) + F(n - 2)$, whereas we approached them through a problem in arrangements. This approach gave us not only formula (4.4), but also the fact that $F(n)$ is expressible in the form (4.3), which can be visualized by means of Pascal's triangle:

$F(0)$	1	1						
$F(1)$	1	2	1					
$F(2)$	1	3	3	1				
$F(3)$	1	4	6	4	1			
$F(4)$	1	5	10	10	5	1		
$F(5)$	1	6	15	20	15	6	1	
$F(6)$	1	7	21	35	35	21	7	1
$F(7)$	1	8	28	56	70	56	28	8	1

The sum of the elements along the diagonals are the values of $F(n)$. For example, consider $F(5)$. By (4.3) we see that

† For another approach to these sequences see, for example, C. D. Olds, *Continued Fractions*, Vol. 9 in this series, p. 80.

$$F(5) = C(6, 0) + C(5, 1) + C(4, 2) + C(3, 3)$$
$$= 1 + 5 + 6 + 1 = 13.$$

Problem Set 14

1. Evaluate $F(11)$ by use of (4.4). Check the answer by use of (4.3).

2. For which integers n is $F(n)$ an even number, for which odd?

3. What does formula (4.4) become if n is replaced by $n + 1$?

4. Prove that $F(n + 1) = 2F(n - 1) + F(n - 2)$.

5. In how many ways can ten A's and six B's be lined up in a row so that no two B's are adjacent?

6. In how many ways can ten A's, six B's and five C's be lined up in a row so that no two B's are adjacent?

7. How many permutations are there of the letters of the word *Mississippi*, taken all at a time, subject to the restriction that no two *i*'s are adjacent?

4.2   Linear Equations with Unit Coefficients

Consider the solutions of the equation $x + y + z + w = 12$ in positive integers x, y, z, w. (Recall that the positive integers are 1, 2, 3, 4, $\cdots$.) In counting the solutions we shall say that, for example,

$x = 9$	$x = 1$	$x = 1$	$x = 1$
$y = 1$	$y = 9$	$y = 1$	$y = 1$
$z = 1$	$z = 1$	$z = 9$	$z = 1$
$w = 1$	$w = 1$	$w = 1$	$w = 9$

are four different solutions because, as *ordered* quadruples of integers, they are distinct. In general, solutions are regarded as the same only if the values of x are equal, of y are equal, of z are equal, and of w are equal. (The situation where the four solutions just given are treated as though they were a single solution comes under the heading of "partitions of the number 12"; such questions will be considered in Chapter 6.) The number of solutions of the given equation is easily determined by viewing the problem in this way: If 12 units (denoted by 12 u's) separated by 11 spaces (denoted by 11 s's) are lined up,

$$(4.5) \qquad u\,s\,u\,s\,u\,s\,u\,s\,u\,s\,u\,s\,u\,s\,u\,s\,u\,s\,u\,s\,u\,s\,u,$$

and if we choose any 3 of the s's and let the others disappear, for example,

$$u \quad u\,s\,u \quad u \quad u \quad u\,s\,u \quad u \quad u \quad u \quad u\,s\,u,$$

then the remaining s's separate the units into four batches. The number of units in these batches can be used as the values of x, y, z, w. In the example the values are $x = 2$, $y = 4$, $z = 5$, $w = 1$. Thus any selection of three of the s's in (4.5) gives a solution of $x + y + z + w = 12$ in positive integers, and any solution corresponds to such a selection. It follows that the number of solutions of this equation in positive integers is the same as the number of ways of choosing 3 things out of 11, which is

$$C(11, 3) \;=\; \frac{11 \cdot 10 \cdot 9}{3 \cdot 2 \cdot 1} \;=\; 165 \,.$$

For a more general result let us replace 12 by m and $x + y + z + w$ by a sum of k variables, and ask for the number of solutions in positive integers of the equation

$$(4.6) \qquad x_1 + x_2 + x_3 + \cdots + x_k \;=\; m \,.$$

In the special case just studied, $m = 12$ and $k = 4$, so the equation could have been written $x_1 + x_2 + x_3 + x_4 = 12$; using x_1, x_2, x_3, x_4 in place of x, y, z, w makes no difference in the number of solutions, of course.

The number of solutions of equation (4.6) *in positive integers* $x_1, x_2, \cdots, x_k$ *is*

$$(4.7) \qquad C(m - 1, k - 1).$$

This can be seen by a direct generalization of the argument used in the special case $m = 12$, $k = 4$. We now have the symbol u repeated m times and the symbol s repeated $m - 1$ times, separating the u's:

$$u\,s\,u\,s\,u\,s\,u\,s \cdots s\,u\,s\,u.$$

We choose $k - 1$ of the symbols s (and let the others disappear) in order to separate the u's into k batches. Such a selection will give a unique solution of (4.6), namely x_1 is the number of u's in the first batch, x_2 the number in the second batch, and so on. Hence the number of solutions of (4.6) in positive integers is the same as the number of ways of selecting $k - 1$ of the symbols s out of $m - 1$, and that number is given in (4.7).

It may be noted that if k is larger than m, then equation (4.6) has no solutions in positive integers, and formula (4.7) is still valid since by our definition (see p. 21) the value of $C(m - 1, k - 1)$ is zero in this case.

Let us turn to the question of the number of solutions of an equation in non-negative integers, the difference here being that zero values for the variables are now allowed. To begin with a special case, we ask for the number of solutions of the equation

$$x + y + z + w = 12$$

in non-negative integers. Let us take 12 u's and 3 s's lined up in a row, for example:

(4.8) $u\,s\,u\,u\,u\,u\,u\,s\,u\,u\,s\,u\,u\,u\,u$

If we look upon the s's as separators of the 12 u's into four batches, we see that the illustration (4.8) gives batches of 1, 5, 2, 4 corresponding to the solution $x = 1$, $y = 5$, $z = 2$, $w = 4$ of the equation $x + y + z + w = 12$ under discussion.

We claim that every arrangement of 12 u's and 3 s's gives a solution. To find the value of x, we locate the first s and count the number of u's to its left. If the arrangement begins with an s, $x = 0$ because no u's are to its left. To find the value of y, we count the number of u's between the first and second s. If the first and second s are adjacent, then $y = 0$. Similarly, the value of z

is the number of u's between the second and third s, and the value of w is the number of u's to the right of the third s.

Conversely, if we start with any solution, such as $x = 0$, $y = 1$, $z = 2$, $w = 9$ we can write 12 u's and 3 s's in a row

$$s\,u\,s\,u\,u\,s\,u\,u\,u\,u\,u\,u\,u\,u$$

corresponding to this solution. The solution $x = 9$, $y = 0$, $z = 1$, $w = 2$ corresponds to the arrangement

$$u\,u\,u\,u\,u\,u\,u\,u\,u\,s\,s\,u\,s\,u\,u\,.$$

Thus the number of solutions of $x + y + z + w = 12$ in non-negative integers is the same as the number of ways of writing 12 u's and 3 s's in a row. This number is $C(15, 3)$ by the theory in Section 3.2.

We generalize this result to the equation

$$(4.9) \qquad x_1 + x_2 + x_3 + \cdots + x_k = m\,,$$

in k variables whose sum must always be m, by an argument similar to that given in the special case. The number of solutions of equation (4.9) in non-negative integers is the same as the number of arrangements in a row of m u's and $k - 1$ s's, and there are

$$C(m + k - 1, k - 1)$$

such arrangements.

Let m and k be fixed positive integers. The number of solutions of equation (4.9) in non-negative integers is

$$(4.10) \quad C(m + k - 1, k - 1) \qquad \text{or} \qquad C(m + k - 1, m)$$

The second part of (4.10) follows from the first by virtue of the basic property $C(n, r) = C(n, n - r)$.

Problem Set 15†

1. How many solutions are there of $x + y + z + w = 50$ (a) in positive integers?   (b) in non-negative integers?

2. Prove that the number of solutions of $x_1 + x_2 + x_3 + x_4 = 9$ in positive integers is the same as the number of solutions of

$$x_1 + x_2 + x_3 + x_4 + x_5 + x_6 = 9$$

in positive integers.

3. Check that the two forms given in (4.10) are equal.

4. Prove that the number of solutions of equation (4.6) in positive integers equals the number of solutions in positive integers of the equation in $m - k + 1$ variables

$$x_1 + x_2 + x_3 + \cdots + x_{m-k+1} = m.$$

5. Prove that the number of solutions in non-negative integers is the same for the two equations

$$x_1 + x_2 + \cdots + x_6 = 8 \quad \text{and} \quad x_1 + x_2 + \cdots + x_9 = 5.$$

6. How many integers between 1 and 1,000,000 inclusive have sum of digits   (a) equal to 6;   (b) less than 6?

7. How many terms are there in the expansion of

$$\text{(a) } (\alpha_1 + \alpha_2 + \alpha_3 + \alpha_4 + \alpha_5)^{17};$$

$$\text{(b) } (\alpha_1 + \alpha_2 + \cdots + \alpha_k)^t,$$

where k and t are positive integers?

---

†Answers to these and subsequent problems may be given in the $C(n, r)$ notation. For example, an answer such as $C(37, 5) - C(26, 4)$ is acceptable as it stands without further elaboration or simplification.

4.3 Combinations with Repetitions

The symbol $C(n, r)$ denotes the number of combinations of n *different* things, taken r at a time. Suppose now that there are several identical copies of each of the n things, as for example identical copies of the books in a bookstore. Thus we can ask the question: Given n distinct categories of things, each category containing an unlimited supply, how many different combinations of r things are there? (A combination may include several indistinguishable objects from the same category.) This question amounts to asking for the number of solutions of

$$x_1 + x_2 + x_3 + \cdots + x_n = r$$

in non-negative integers, because we can take x_1 of the first thing, x_2 of the second thing, $\cdots$, x_n of the n-th thing. Thus we can use formula (4.10) with k and m replaced by n and r to get the following conclusion.

The number of combinations, r at a time, of n different things each of which is available in unlimited supply is

(4.11) $$C(n + r - 1, r).$$

For example, let us ask how many different sets of three coins can be formed, each coin being a cent, a nickel, a dime or a quarter. Here we have $r = 3$ and $n = 4$, and so the answer, by (4.11), is $C(6, 3)$ or 20. Going back to the analysis that led to (4.11) we note that the question amounts to asking for the number of solutions in non-negative integers of $x_1 + x_2 + x_3 + x_4 = 3$, where we interpret x_1 as the number of cents, x_2 as the number of nickels, x_3 as the number of dimes, and x_4 as the number of quarters used in forming a set of 3 coins.

As another example, consider Problem 1.4 of Chapter 1. Briefly, the problem is this: Consider twenty different books each of which is available in unlimited supply. How many selections of ten books can be made, (a) if repetitions are allowed, (b) if repetitions are not allowed, so that the ten books must all be different? Part (b) is just a matter of choosing ten things out of twenty, so the answer is $C(20, 10)$. Part (a) is a question of the number of combinations, ten at a time, of twenty different things each of which is available in multiple copies. So the answer to part (a) is given by formula (4.11) with $r = 10$ and $n = 20$, namely

$$C(29, 10) \;=\; \frac{29!}{10!\,19!}\,.$$

Problem Set 16

1. In the explanation of formula (4.11) in the text it is stated that each of the things is "available in unlimited supply". Actually the supply need not be unlimited. How many copies of each of the n things must there be?

2. How many different collections of six coins can be formed, if each coin may be a cent, a nickel, a dime, a quarter, a half dollar, or a silver dollar?

3. Poker chips come in three colors, red, white, and blue. How many different combinations of ten poker chips are there?

4. A toy store has marbles in five colors, all uniform in size. They are priced at 10 cents a dozen. How many different color combinations are available for ten cents?

5. Consider the integers with seven digits, namely the integers from 1,000,000 to 9,999,999 inclusive. Separate these into subsets as follows: put numbers into the same subset if and only if their digits as a collection are the same. For example, 8,122,333 and 3,213,283 are in the same subset. How many subsets are there?

4.4 Equations with Restricted Solutions

In Section 4.2 we considered the question of the number of solutions of such an equation as $x + y + z + w = 12$; first the solutions were restricted to the set of positive integers, then to the set of non-negative integers. To say that x is a positive integer is the same as saying that x is an integer satisfying $x > 0$, or that x is an integer satisfying $x \geqslant 1$. To say that x is a non-negative integer is the same as saying that x is an integer satisfying $x \geqslant 0$.

Now we raise the question: How many solutions in integers greater than 5 are there of the equation

$$(4.12) \qquad\qquad x + y + z + w = 48 \, ?$$

For example, $x = 6$, $y = 10$, $z = 12$, $w = 20$ is a solution, and we want to count the number of such solutions. Since each variable must be greater than 5, the subtraction of 5 from each gives a new set of four positive numbers

$$(4.13) \quad r = x - 5, \quad s = y - 5, \quad t = z - 5, \quad u = w - 5$$

whose sum is 28:

$$r + s + t + u = x - 5 + y - 5 + z - 5 + w - 5$$
$$= x + y + z + w - 20 = 28,$$

$$(4.14) \qquad\qquad r + s + t + u = 28 \, .$$

Thus équations (4.14) and (4.12) are related by the substitutions, or transformation, (4.13). For example, the solution $x = 6$, $y = 10$, $z = 12$, $w = 20$ of equation (4.12) corresponds to the solution $r = 1$, $s = 5$, $t = 7$, $u = 15$ of equation (4.14). Here are other examples:

$$
\begin{array}{ccc}
x = 10 & & r = 5 \\
y = 11 & & s = 6 \\
 & \text{corresponds to} & \\
z = 13 & & t = 8 \\
w = 14 & & u = 9 \, ; \\
\end{array}
$$

$$
\begin{array}{ccc}
x = 25 & & r = 20 \\
y = 9 & & s = 4 \\
 & \text{corresponds to} & \\
z = 8 & & t = 3 \\
w = 6 & & u = 1 \, . \\
\end{array}
$$

Now since each of x, y, z, w must be greater than 5, each of r, s, t, u must be greater than 0, that is to say, each of r, s, t, u must be a positive integer. Thus corresponding to each solution of equation (4.12) in integers greater than 5 there is a solution of equation (4.14) in positive integers, and to each solution of equation (4.14) in positive integers there corresponds a solution of equation (4.12) in integers greater than 5. For example, if we start with the solution

$$r = 15, \quad s = 1, \quad t = 8, \quad u = 4$$

of equation (4.14), we use the transformation (4.13) to get the solution

$$x = 20, \quad y = 6, \quad z = 13, \quad w = 9$$

of equation (4.12). This establishes a one-to-one correspondence between the solutions of equation (4.12) in integers exceeding 5, and the solutions of equation (4.14) in positive integers.

Hence we see that the number of solutions of equation (4.12) in integers greater than 5 is the same as the number of solutions of equation (4.14) in positive integers. Applying formula (4.7) of page 55 to equation (4.14), we see that this number is

$$C(28 - 1, 4 - 1) \quad \text{or} \quad C(27, 3).$$

The idea used here works just as well if each variable is subjected to a different condition. For example, let us consider the question: *How many solutions are there of the equation $x + y + z + w = 48$ in integers satisfying*

(4.15) $\dot{x} > 5, \quad y > 6, \quad z > 7, \quad w > 8$?

In this case we would subtract 5 from x, 6 from y, 7 from z, and 8 from w in any solution of the equation to get a new set of numbers (call them $r, s, t,$ and u) each of which is a positive integer. Thus the transformation, this time, is

$$r = x - 5, \quad s = y - 6, \quad t = z - 7, \quad u = w - 8,$$

or

$$x = r + 5, \quad y = s + 6, \quad z = t + 7, \quad w = u + 8.$$

If we substitute these expressions in the equation $x + y + z + w = 48$ we obtain the equation

$$r + 5 + s + 6 + t + 7 + u + 8 \ = \ 48,$$

or

(4.16) $r + s + t + u \ = \ 22 \, .$

Any solution of $x + y + z + w = 48$ in integers subject to the restrictions (4.15) corresponds to a solution in positive integers of the equation (4.16). For example, the solution $x = 6$, $y = 10$, $z = 12$, $w = 20$ corresponds to the solution $r = 1$, $s = 4$, $t = 5$, $u = 12$ of the equation (4.16). There is a one-to-one correspondence between the solutions, so the number of solutions of

$$x + y + z + w \ = \ 48$$

in integers subject to the restrictions (4.15) equals the number of solutions of $r + s + t + u \ = \ 22$ in positive integers. By formula (4.7) of page 55 this number is

$$C(22-1, \ \ 4-1) \quad \text{or} \quad C(21, 3) \, .$$

Let us now formalize these ideas to get some general formulas. Let us replace 48 by m, and so consider the equation

$$x + y + z + w \ = \ m.$$

Furthermore, in place of the conditions (4.15) on x, y, z, and w, suppose we have the restrictions

(4.17) $x > c_1, \ \ y > c_2, \ \ z > c_3, \ \ w > c_4,$

where c_1, c_2, c_3, c_4 are some fixed integers. The transformation is now

$$r = x - c_1, \quad s = y - c_2, \quad t = z - c_3, \quad u = w - c_4,$$

or

$$x = r + c_1, \quad y = s + c_2, \quad z = t + c_3, \quad w = u + c_4.$$

If we substitute these in the equation $x + y + z + w = m$ we get the equation

$$r + c_1 + s + c_2 + t + c_3 + u + c_4 = m,$$

or

(4.18) $$r + s + t + u = m - c_1 - c_2 - c_3 - c_4.$$

Thus the number of solutions of the equation $x + y + z + w = m$ in integers subject to the restrictions (4.17) is the same as the number of solutions of (4.18) in positive integers r, s, t, u. By formula (4.7) of page 55 this number is

(4.19) $$C(m - c_1 - c_2 - c_3 - c_4 - 1, \quad 3).$$

If we replace x, y, z, w, by x_1, x_2, x_3, x_4 respectively, the conclusion can be stated as follows: The number of solutions in integers x_1, x_2, x_3, x_4 of the equation

$$x_1 + x_2 + x_3 + x_4 = m$$

subject to the restrictions

$$x_1 > c_1, \quad x_2 > c_2, \quad x_3 > c_3, \quad x_4 > c_4$$

is given by the formula (4.19).

Suppose now that there are k variables $x_1, x_2, x_3, \cdots, x_k$ and k fixed integers $c_1, c_2, c_3, \cdots, c_k$. Then an immediate extension of the above theory gives the result:

The number of solutions of the equation

(4.20) $$x_1 + x_2 + x_3 + \cdots + x_k = m$$

in integers satisfying the conditions

(4.21) $$x_1 > c_1, \quad x_2 > c_2, \quad x_3 > c_3, \quad \cdots, \quad x_k > c_k$$

is

(4.22) $$C(m - c_1 - c_2 - c_3 - \cdots - c_k - 1, \quad k - 1).$$

Note: Although in the examples leading up to this general result the integers c_1, c_2, etc. were taken to be *positive*, this proposition holds for any integers c_1, c_2, c_3, $\cdots$, c_k, positive, negative, or zero.

Problem Set 17

1. Write out in detail a one-to-one correspondence between the solutions of $x + y + z + w = 27$ in integers greater than 5, and the solutions of $r + s + t + u = 7$ in positive integers.

2. How many solutions are there of $x + y + z + w = 100$ in integers greater than 7?

3. Find the number of solutions of $x_1 + x_2 + x_3 + x_4 + x_5 = 50$ in positive integers (a) with $x_5 > 12$; (b) with $x_5 > 12$ and $x_4 > 7$.

4. Find the number of solutions of $x + y + z + w = 1$ in integers greater than -4, i.e., in integers selected from $-3, -2, -1, 0, 1, 2, 3, 4, 5, \cdots$.

5. Find the number of solutions of $x + y + z + w = 20$ in positive integers (a) with $x > 6$; (b) with $x > 6$ and $y > 6$; (c) with $x > 6$, $y > 6$, and $z > 6$.

6. Find the number of solutions of $x + y + z + w = 20$ in non-negative integers (a) with $x \geqslant 6$; (b) with $x \geqslant 6$ and $y \geqslant 6$.

7. Find a formula for the number of solutions of $x + y + z + w = m$ in non-negative integers satisfying (a) $x \geqslant c_1$; (b) $x \geqslant c_1$ and $y \geqslant c_2$.

8. How many integers between 1 and 1,000,000 inclusive have sum of digits 13?

4.5 Summary

The Fibonacci numbers $1, 2, 3, 5, 8, 13, 21, \cdots$, have the property that each member of the sequence (except the first two) is the sum of the preceding two numbers. This property is stated in the recursion formula

$$F(n) \;=\; F(n-1) + F(n-2).$$

Although in many books the Fibonacci numbers are defined in this way, we approached them by defining $F(n)$ as the number of ways oɪ writing n signs, each plus or minus, so that no two minus signs are adjacent; thus $F(1) = 2$, $F(2) = 3$, $F(3) = 5$, $F(5) = 8$, etc. It was established that, defining $F(0)$ to be 1, we get the entire sequence of Fibonacci numbers from the formula

$$F(n) \;=\; C(n+1, 0)+C(n, 1)+C(n-1, 2)+C(n-2, 3)+\cdots ,$$

where the sum on the right terminates when zero terms (terms of the form $C(u, v)$ with $u < v$) begin to appear.

Let m and k be fixed positive integers. The number of solutions of

$$x_1 + x_2 + x_3 + \cdots + x_k \;=\; m$$

in positive integers is $C(m-1, k-1)$; in non-negative integers is $C(m+k-1, m)$. Furthermore, if $c_1, c_2, c_3, \cdots, c_k$ are fixed integers, then the number of solutions in integers satisfying the conditions

$$x_1 > c_1, \quad x_2 > c_2, \quad x_3 > c_3, \quad \cdots, \quad x_k > c_k$$

is

$$C(m - c_1 - c_2 - c_3 - \cdots - c_k - 1, \quad k - 1).$$

Two solutions are said to be the same if and only if the values of x_1 are identical, and the values of x_2 are identical, and the values of x_3 are identical, and so on. (Questions about the number of solutions of the given equation subject to even more restrictions on the solutions, such as for example solutions in integers from 1 to 7, are treated in the next chapter.)

The number of combinations, r at a time, of n different things each of which (like coins, books, or stamps) is available in an unlimited supply is $C(n + r - 1, r)$. Here n and r denote positive integers, but n may be greater than, equal to, or less than r.

CHAPTER FIVE

The Inclusion-Exclusion Principle; Probability

In this chapter we prove a theorem of a very broad kind and then apply it to particular problems. The idea of *probability* is introduced towards the end of the chapter.

5.1 A General Result

It will be convenient to lead up to the inclusion-exclusion principle by a sequence of three problems listed in increasing order of difficulty. The first problem is not very difficult at all.

PROBLEM 5.1 How many integers between 1 and 6300 inclusive are not divisible by 5? Since precisely every fifth number is divisible by 5, we see that of the 6300 numbers under consideration, exactly 6300/5 or 1260 are divisible by 5. Hence the answer to the question is

$$6300 - 1260 = 5040.$$

PROBLEM 5.2 How many integers between 1 and 6300 inclusive are divisible by neither 5 nor 3? To answer this we could begin by paralleling the argument in Problem 5.1 and say that the number of integers under consideration that are divisible by 5 is 1260, and the number divisible by 3 is 6300/3 or 2100. But

$$6300 - 2100 - 1260$$

is not the correct answer to the problem, because too many integers have been subtracted from the 6300. Numbers like 15, 30, 45, $\cdots$ which are divisible by both 3 and 5 have been removed twice from the 6300 integers under consideration. So we see that we must add back the number of integers divisible by both 3 and 5, that is, divisible† by 15. There are 6300/15 or 420 of those. Thus we get the answer

$$6300 - 2100 - 1260 + 420 = 3360.$$

PROBLEM 5.3 How many integers between 1 and 6300 inclusive are divisible by none of 3, 5, 7? To solve this we can begin with an analogy to the previous argument and first remove from the 6300 integers those divisible by 3, in number 2100, those divisible by 5, in number 1260, and those divisible by 7, in number 900. Thus

$$6300 - 2100 - 1260 - 900$$

is a start toward the answer. However, numbers divisible by both 3 and 5 have been removed twice; likewise numbers divisible by both 3 and 7; likewise numbers divisible by both 5 and 7. Hence we add back the number of integers divisible by both 3 and 5, namely 6300/15 or 420, also the number divisible by both 3 and 7, namely 6300/21 or 300, and also the number divisible by both 5 and 7, namely 6300/35 or 180. We now have

$$6300 - 2100 - 1260 - 900 + 420 + 300 + 180$$

and are closer to the answer. But one final adjustment must be made because of integers divisible by 3, by 5, and by 7, e.g., 105, 210, 315

† A fuller discussion of such divisibility properties is given in Chapter 1 of I. Niven's *Numbers: Rational and Irrational* in this series.

and so on. Such integers are counted in the original 6300, are counted out in the 2100, 1260 and 900, and then counted back in the 420, 300, and 180. The net effect is that each such integer has been counted in once, out three times, and then back in three times. Hence the final adjustment is to count them out again, and so we subtract 6300/105 or 60. Thus the answer to Problem 5.3 is

$$(5.1) \quad 6300 - 2100 - 1260 - 900 + 420 + 300 + 180 - 60 = 2880.$$

There are 2880 integers between 1 and 6300 inclusive that are divisible by none of 3, 5, 7.

The three problems just discussed can be answered by appeal to a general principle. Suppose that we have N objects. Suppose that some of these objects have property α, and some do not. Let $N(\alpha)$ denote the number having property α. Similarly, suppose that some of the objects have property β, and some do not. Let $N(\beta)$ denote the number having property β. If there are other properties γ, δ, $\cdots$, let $N(\gamma)$, $N(\delta)$, $\cdots$ denote the number of objects having property γ, the number having property δ, $\cdots$.

In the problems above the objects are the integers from 1 to 6300 inclusive, and so $N = 6300$. The properties α, β, $\cdots$ are the divisibility properties; for example, an integer has the property γ if it is divisible by 7.

Continuing the general analysis, let $N(\alpha, \beta)$ denote the number of objects having both properties α and β. Let $N(\alpha, \beta, \gamma)$ denote the number having the three properties α, β and γ. In the same way $N(\alpha, \beta, \gamma, \delta)$ denotes the number of objects having the four properties α, β, γ and δ.

Now suppose we ask the question: How many of the N objects do not have property α? The answer, $N - N(\alpha)$, is obtained by a simple subtraction. This is analogous to Problem 5.1.

How many objects have neither the property α nor β? The answer is

$$N - N(\alpha) - N(\beta) + N(\alpha, \beta).$$

This is analogous to Problem 5.2.

How many of the objects have none of the three properties α, β, γ?

The answer is

(5.2)
$$N - N(\alpha) - N(\beta) - N(\gamma)$$
$$+ N(\alpha, \beta) + N(\alpha, \gamma) + N(\beta, \gamma) - N(\alpha, \beta, \gamma).$$

Let us check this result, which is analogous to the answer in Problem 5.3.

First consider an object having none of the properties α, β, γ. Such an object is counted by the term N but by none of the other terms in (5.2). Hence such an object is counted in once.

Next consider an object that has exactly one of the three properties; say it has the property β. Such an object is counted by two terms in (5.2), namely N and $N(\beta)$; but since $N(\beta)$ is prefaced by a minus sign, such an object is not counted by (5.2).

Next consider an object that has exactly two of the properties, say β and γ. Such an object is counted by the terms N, $N(\beta)$, $N(\gamma)$ and $N(\beta, \gamma)$ in (5.2), and by no other terms. Hence, in effect, such an object is not counted at all by (5.2), because of the arrangement of plus and minus signs in that formula.

Finally consider an object that has all three properties α, β and γ. It is counted by every one of the eight terms in (5.2), but again this means that in effect it is not counted at all because of the arrangement of signs.

Summing up the argument, we see that formula (5.2) in effect counts those objects, and only those objects, having none of the properties α, β, γ.

Formula (5.2) can be extended to any number of properties. *The number of objects having none of the properties* α, β, γ, $\cdots$ *is*

(5.3)
$$N$$
$$-N(\alpha) - N(\beta) - N(\gamma) - \cdots$$
$$+N(\alpha, \beta) + N(\alpha, \gamma) + N(\beta, \gamma) + \cdots$$
$$-N(\alpha, \beta, \gamma) - \cdots$$
$$\cdot \ \cdot \ \cdot \ \cdot \ \cdot \ \cdot \ \cdot \ \cdot$$

This is the inclusion-exclusion principle which gives the title to this chapter. To prove it, we shall show that an object having one or more of the properties α, β, γ, $\cdots$ is, in effect, not counted by (5.3). This argument will establish that the expression (5.3) counts precisely those objects having none of the properties, because such objects are counted by the term N but by no other term in (5.3).

Consider an object, say T, that has exactly j of the properties, where j is some positive integer. In formula (5.3), T is counted by the term N. In the second line,

$$-N(\alpha) - N(\beta) - N(\gamma) - \cdots ,$$

the object T is counted j times, or what is the same thing, $C(j, 1)$ times. In the third line

$$+N(\alpha, \beta) + N(\alpha, \gamma) + N(\beta, \gamma) + \cdots ,$$

the object T is counted $C(j, 2)$ times, because this is the number of terms with two of the j properties of T. Similarly the fourth line counts T exactly $C(j, 3)$ times, and so on. Because of the arrangement of plus and minus signs in (5.3), we see that T is counted in effect

$$1 - C(j, 1) + C(j, 2) - C(j, 3) + C(j, 4) - \cdots$$

times. The value of this expression is zero, by property (3.7) of Section 3.6. Thus we have established the general theorem.

Problem Set 18

1. Write out formula (5.3) in full for the case of four properties α, β, γ and δ.

2. How many terms are there in formula (5.3), presuming that there are r properties α, β, γ, $\cdots$?

3. How many integers from 1 to 33,000 inclusive are divisible by none of 3, 5, 11?

4. How many integers from 1 to 1,000,000 inclusive are neither perfect squares, perfect cubes, nor perfect fourth powers?

5. Using the same notation as in formula (5.3), with exactly five properties $\alpha, \beta, \gamma, \delta, \epsilon$ under consideration, write a formula for the number of objects having all three properties α, β and γ, but having neither of the properties δ, ϵ.

6. Presuming a set of objects, and four properties $\alpha, \beta, \gamma, \delta$ under consideration, write a formula for the number of objects having property β but none of the properties α, γ, δ.

5.2   Applications to Equations and to Combinations with Repetitions

PROBLEM 5.4   How many solutions are there of the equation

$$(5.4) \qquad\qquad x_1 + x_2 + x_3 + x_4 = 20$$

in positive integers with $x_1 \leqslant 6$, $x_2 \leqslant 7$, $x_3 \leqslant 8$, and $x_4 \leqslant 9$? In terms of the notation of the preceding section, let the "objects" be the solutions in positive integers of equation (5.4). For example, the set

$$(5.5) \qquad x_1 = 2, \qquad x_2 = 8, \qquad x_3 = 9, \qquad x_4 = 1,$$

is one "object". Say that a solution has property α in case $x_1 > 6$, property β in case $x_2 > 7$, property γ in case $x_3 > 8$, property δ in case $x_4 > 9$. We want to find the number of solutions having none of the properties $\alpha, \beta, \gamma, \delta$, so we can use formula (5.3) of the preceding section.

From Chapter 4 (Section 4.5) we know that the number of solutions of (5.4) in positive integers is $C(19, 3)$. Since this is the total number N of "objects" under consideration, we set $N = C(19, 3)$. Next we want to find the value of $N(\alpha)$, the number of solutions of (5.4) in positive integers with $x_1 > 6$. Again by the results derived in Chapter 4, we see that

$$N(\alpha) \;=\; C(20-6-1,\; 4-1) \;=\; C(13, 3).$$

By a similar argument we conclude that

$$N(\beta) = C(12, 3), \qquad N(\gamma) = C(11, 3), \qquad N(\delta) = C(10, 3).$$

Next, $N(\alpha, \beta)$ denotes the number of solutions of (5.4) in positive integers satisfying both $x_1 > 6$ and $x_2 > 7$, so

$$N(\alpha, \beta) = C(20-6-7-1, \quad 4-1) = C(6, 3).$$

Parallel arguments show that

$$N(\alpha, \gamma) = C(5, 3), \qquad N(\alpha, \delta) = C(4, 3), \qquad N(\beta, \gamma) = C(4, 3),$$
$$N(\beta, \delta) = C(3, 3), \qquad N(\gamma, \delta) = C(2, 3) = 0.$$

All further terms in formula (5.3) are zero. For example, consider $N(\alpha, \beta, \gamma)$. This denotes the number of solutions of equation (5.4) in positive integers satisfying the conditions $x_1 > 6$, $x_2 > 7$, and $x_3 > 8$. There are no such solutions since $6 + 7 + 8 = 21$. Hence the solution of Problem 5.4 can be written

$$C(19, 3) - C(13, 3) - C(12, 3) - C(11, 3) - C(10, 3)$$
$$+ C(6, 3) + C(5, 3) + C(4, 3) + C(4, 3) + C(3, 3)$$
$$= 969 - 286 - 220 - 165 - 120 + 20 + 10 + 4 + 4 + 1 = 217.$$

In many applications of the inclusion-exclusion principle (5.3) there is a symmetry about the properties $\alpha, \beta, \gamma, \cdots$ such that the following conditions hold:

$$N(\alpha) = N(\beta) = N(\gamma) = \cdots ,$$
$$N(\alpha, \beta) = N(\alpha, \gamma) = N(\beta, \gamma) = \cdots ,$$
$$N(\alpha, \beta, \gamma) = \cdots ,$$
$$\bullet \quad \bullet \quad \bullet \quad \bullet \quad .$$

In words, say that the properties $\alpha, \beta, \gamma, \cdots$ are symmetric if the number of objects having any one property equals the number of objects having any other single property, if the number of objects having two of the properties is the same no matter which two are considered, and likewise for three properties, four properties, and so on. Thus the properties are symmetric if the number of objects having a certain j properties (j being fixed) equals the number of objects having any other collection of j properties; furthermore, this must be true for $j = 1$, $j = 2$, $j = 3$ and so on as far as it makes sense to go.

Let the total number of properties $\alpha, \beta, \gamma, \cdots$ be r. If these are symmetric properties, then the formula (5.3) for the number of objects having none of the properties is

$$(5.6) \quad N - C(r, 1)N(\alpha) + C(r, 2)N(\alpha, \beta) - C(r, 3)N(\alpha, \beta, \gamma) + \cdots .$$

The reason for this is that the terms of (5.3) can be collected into batches with equal members, there being $C(r, 1)$ of the sort $N(\alpha)$, $C(r, 2)$ of the sort $N(\alpha, \beta)$, etc.

To illustrate a set of symmetric properties, consider the following question.

PROBLEM 5.5   How many solutions are there of the equation

$$(5.7) \qquad\qquad x_1 + x_2 + x_3 + x_4 = 26$$

in integers between 1 and 9 inclusive?

Again we can use the theory of the preceding section. The "objects" under consideration are all solutions in positive integers of the equation (5.7), so that $N = C(25, 3)$. A solution of the equation has property α in case $x_1 > 9$, property β in case $x_2 > 9$, property γ in case $x_3 > 9$, and property δ in case $x_4 > 9$. These four properties are completely symmetric in the sense that led from formula (5.3) to formula (5.6). Hence we need only compute

$$N(\alpha), \quad N(\alpha, \beta), \quad N(\alpha, \beta, \gamma) \quad \text{and} \quad N(\alpha, \beta, \gamma, \delta).$$

We find that

$$N(\alpha) = C(26 - 9 - 1, 4 - 1) = C(16, 3);$$
$$N(\alpha, \beta) = C(26 - 9 - 9 - 1, 4 - 1) = C(7, 3);$$
$$N(\alpha, \beta, \gamma) = C(26 - 9 - 9 - 9 - 1, 3) = C(-2, 3) = 0;$$
$$N(\alpha, \beta, \gamma, \delta) = 0.$$

Therefore, by formula (5.6), the answer is

$$C(25, 3) - C(4, 1)C(16, 3) + C(4, 2)C(7, 3)$$
$$= 2300 - 2240 + 210 = 270.$$

Let us now generalize from Problem 5.5 to this question: How many solutions does the equation

$$(5.8) \qquad x_1 + x_2 + x_3 + \cdots + x_k = m$$

have in integers from 1 to c inclusive, where c is some fixed positive integer? Again we apply the theory of the preceding section, where the "objects" under study are now all solutions of (5.8) in positive integers. We say that a solution has property α if $x_1 > c$, property β if $x_2 > c$, property γ if $x_3 > c$, and so on. These properties are symmetric, and so we can use formula (5.6). By the theory of page 64, we see that

$$N = C(m - 1, k - 1)$$
$$N(\alpha) = C(m - c - 1, k - 1)$$
$$N(\alpha, \beta) = C(m - 2c - 1, k - 1)$$
$$N(\alpha, \beta, \gamma) = C(m - 3c - 1, k - 1),$$

etc.

Then formula (5.6) gives us the following result. *Let c be any fixed positive integer. The number of solutions of equation* (5.8) *in positive integers not exceeding c is*

$$C(m - 1, k - 1) - C(k, 1)C(m - c - 1, k - 1)$$
$$(5.9) \qquad + C(k, 2)C(m - 2c - 1, k - 1)$$
$$- C(k, 3)C(m - 3c - 1, k - 1)$$
$$+ C(k, 4)C(m - 4c - 1, k - 1) - \cdots$$

where the series continues until zero terms arise.

The special case $m > kc$ is of some interest; for, in this case, equation (5.8) can have no solutions in integers not exceeding c.

For example, if $m = 25$, $k = 4$ and $c = 6$, then (5.8) becomes $x_1 + x_2 + x_3 + x_4 = 25$ and this has no solutions in integers from 1 to 6 because the maximum value of the sum $x_1 + x_2 + x_3 + x_4$, under our restriction, is 24. In this case, the value of expression (5.9) is zero, and we obtain the identity

$$C(24, 3) - C(4, 1)C(18, 3) + C(4, 2)C(12, 3) - C(4, 3)C(6, 3) = 0.$$

As another example of the inclusion-exclusion principle consider the following question which may be thought of as a problem in combinations with repetitions:

A bag of coins contains eight cents, seven nickels, four dimes, and three quarters. Assuming that the coins of any one denomination are identical (for example the eight cents are identical), in how many ways can a collection of six coins be made up from the whole bagful?

In making up a collection of coins, let x be the number of cents, y the number of nickels, z the number of dimes, and w the number of quarters. Then the problem amounts to asking for the number of solutions of the equation

$$x + y + z + w = 6$$

in non-negative integers satisfying the conditions

$$x \leqslant 8, \qquad y \leqslant 7, \qquad z \leqslant 4, \qquad w \leqslant 3.$$

Let N be the count of all solutions in non-negative integers; its value (see page 57) is

$$N = C(6 + 4 - 1, 4 - 1) = C(9, 3).$$

If we say that a solution has property α in case $x \geqslant 9$, property β in case $y \geqslant 8$, property γ in case $z \geqslant 5$, and property δ in case $w \geqslant 4$, then most of the terms in formula (5.3) on page 70 are zero. For example $N(\alpha) = 0$ because there are no solutions of $x + y + z + w = 6$ in non-negative integers with $x \geqslant 9$. In fact the only non-zero terms in this formula are N, $N(\gamma)$, and $N(\delta)$. Furthermore we can calculate that

$$N(\gamma) = C(6 + 4 - 5 - 1, 4 - 1) = C(4, 3);$$
$$N(\delta) = C(6 + 4 - 4 - 1, 4 - 1) = C(5, 3);$$
$$N - N(\gamma) - N(\delta) = C(9, 3) - C(4, 3) - C(5, 3) = 70.$$

Problem Set 19

1. Find the number of solutions of $x_1 + x_2 + x_3 + x_4 = 14$ in integers from 1 to 6 inclusive.

2. Find the number of solutions of $x_1 + x_2 + x_3 + x_4 + x_5 + x_6 = 34$ in positive even integers not exceeding 10.

3. Find the number of solutions of $x_1 + x_2 + x_3 + x_4 = 20$ in integers satisfying $1 \leqslant x_1 \leqslant 6$, $1 \leqslant x_2 \leqslant 7$, $3 \leqslant x_3 \leqslant 9$, $4 \leqslant x_4 \leqslant 11$.

4. Find the number of solutions of $x_1 + x_2 + x_3 + x_4 = 1$ in integers between -3 and 3 inclusive.

5. A bag of coins contains eight cents, seven nickles, four dimes, and three quarters. Assuming that coins of any one denomination are identical, in how many ways can a collection of ten coins be made up from the bagful?

6. In the preceding problem, how many of the collections contain no quarters?

7. The equation $x_1 + x_2 + x_3 + x_4 = 12$ has exactly one solution in positive integers not exceeding 3, as a moment's reflection will show. Apply formula (5.9) to get an identity in the $C(n, r)$ symbols.

8. Find the number of solutions of the equation $y_1 + y_2 + y_3 + y_4 = 14$ in integers between 1 and 9 inclusive.

9. The numerical answer to the preceding problem is the same as in Problem 5.5. (The problems look somewhat similar, the difference being that the constants in the equations are 26 in one instance, 14 in the other.) Show that the equation in the preceding question can be obtained from that in Problem 5.5 by use of the substitution

$$x_1 = 10 - y_1, \quad x_2 = 10 - y_2, \quad x_3 = 10 - y_3, \quad x_4 = 10 - y_4.$$

10. Using the principle sketched in the preceding problem find a specific integer value for c, other than $c = 12$, so that the number of solutions of the two equations

$$x_1 + x_2 + x_3 + x_4 + x_5 = 12 \quad \text{and} \quad y_1 + y_2 + y_3 + y_4 + y_5 = c,$$

in positive integers from 1 to 6, is the same. Then use (5.9) to get an identity between two expressions in $C(n, r)$.

11. Let k, m, c_1, c_2 and c_3 be positive integers. Write a formula for the number of solutions in positive integers of

$$x_1 + x_2 + x_3 + x_4 + \cdots + x_k = m$$

subject to the restrictions $x_1 \leqslant c_1, \quad x_2 \leqslant c_2, \quad x_3 \leqslant c_3.$

12. Find the number of seven-digit positive integers such that the sum of the digits is 19.

5.3   Derangements

As another application of the general theorem of Section 5.1 we turn to quite a different question. Consider the permutations of the numbers $1, 2, 3, \cdots, n$, taken all at a time. Among these permutations there are some, called *derangements*, in which none of the n integers appears in its natural place, that is, 1 is not in its natural place (the first place), 2 is not in its natural place, $\cdots$, and n is not in its natural place. The number of derangements of n things will be denoted by $D(n)$.

As illustrations we note: $D(1) = 0$; $D(2) = 1$ because there is one derangement, 2, 1; $D(3) = 2$ because the derangements are 2, 3, 1 and 3, 1, 2; $D(4) = 9$ because the derangements are

2, 1, 4, 3	3, 1, 4, 2	4, 1, 2, 3
2, 3, 4, 1	3, 4, 1, 2	4, 3, 1, 2
2, 4, 1, 3	3, 4, 2, 1	4, 3, 2, 1.

We want to derive a formula for $D(n)$, valid for any positive integer n. This can be achieved with very little difficulty by use of the inclusion–exclusion principle. To make the idea concrete, let us begin by computing $D(7)$. Let N denote the number of permutations of 1, 2, 3, 4, 5, 6, 7 taken all at a time, so that $N = 7!$. Say that a permutation has property α if 1 is in its natural place, β if 2 is in its proper place, γ if 3 is in its proper place, δ if 4 is in its proper place, ϵ if 5 is in its proper place, ζ if 6 is in its proper place, η if 7 is in its proper place. For example, the permutation

$$7, 2, 6, 1, 5, 3, 4$$

has properties β and ϵ, but no others. A derangement is a permutation having none of the properties α, β, γ, δ, ϵ, ζ, η.

We compute $N(\alpha)$, the number of permutations of 1, 2, 3, 4, 5, 6, 7 such that 1 is in the first place (regardless of whether the others are in their natural positions or not) by putting 1 in first place and permuting the others. The result is $N(\alpha) = 6!$. Similarly, if 2 is held in the second place and the others permuted, we obtain $N(\beta) = 6!$. In fact, it does not matter which of the seven numbers we keep fixed in its natural position; the remaining six can be arranged in 6! ways. Therefore $N(\alpha) = N(\beta) = \cdots = N(\eta) = 6!$.

Next, we compute $N(\alpha, \beta)$ by holding 1 and 2 in the first and second places while the remaining five numbers are permuted. This leads to 5! different arrangements. Again, if any two of the numbers are held in their natural positions while the remaining five are permuted, we get 5! permutations so that

$$N(\alpha, \beta) = N(\alpha, \gamma) = \cdots = N(\beta, \gamma) = \cdots = N(\zeta, \eta) = 5!.$$

Similarly, holding three of the numbers fixed leads to

$$N(\alpha, \beta, \gamma) = \cdots = N(\epsilon, \zeta, \eta) = 4!,$$

holding four fixed leads to $N(\alpha, \beta, \gamma, \delta) = \cdots = 3!$, holding five fixed leads to $N(\alpha, \beta, \gamma, \delta, \epsilon) = \cdots = 2!$, holding six fixed leads to $N(\alpha, \beta, \gamma, \delta, \epsilon, \zeta) = 1!$, and holding all seven fixed leads to $N(\alpha, \beta, \gamma, \delta, \epsilon, \zeta, \eta) = 0! = 1$. Clearly, these are the symmetry conditions described in Section 5.2, and so we may use formula (5.6) to compute

$$D(7) = 7! - C(7, 1) \cdot 6! + C(7, 2) \cdot 5! - C(7, 3) \cdot 4!$$
$$+ C(7, 4) \cdot 3! - C(7, 5) \cdot 2! + C(7, 6) \cdot 1! - C(7, 7) \cdot 0!.$$

We simplify this by expressing each $C(n, r)$ in terms of factorials; for example,

$$C(7, 4) \cdot 3! = \frac{7!}{4! 3!} \cdot 3! = \frac{7!}{4!}.$$

The result can be written

$$(5.10) \quad D(7) = 7! - \frac{7!}{1!} + \frac{7!}{2!} - \frac{7!}{3!} + \frac{7!}{4!} - \frac{7!}{5!} + \frac{7!}{6!} - \frac{7!}{7!}$$

$$= 7!\left[1 - \frac{1}{1!} + \frac{1}{2!} - \frac{1}{3!} + \frac{1}{4!} - \frac{1}{5!} + \frac{1}{6!} - \frac{1}{7!}\right].$$

This entire argument generalizes directly to $D(n)$, the number of derangements of n things, and yields the following equations:

$$D(n) = n! - C(n, 1)(n-1)! + C(n, 2)(n-2)!$$
$$- \cdots + (-1)^n C(n, n)0!$$

$$= n! - \frac{n!}{1!(n-1)!}(n-1)! + \frac{n!}{2!(n-2)!}(n-2)!$$
$$- \cdots + (-1)^n \frac{n!}{n!0!}0!$$

$$= n! - \frac{n!}{1!} + \frac{n!}{2!} - \cdots + (-1)^n \frac{n!}{n!}.$$

Thus

$$(5.11) \quad D(n) = n!\left[1 - \frac{1}{1!} + \frac{1}{2!} - \frac{1}{3!} + \cdots + (-1)^n \frac{1}{n!}\right].$$

There is another interpretation of $D(n)$, which we now explain in terms of the special case $D(7)$. Consider a fixed permutation of the integers from 1 to 7, for example

$$P_0: \quad 7, 2, 6, 1, 5, 3, 4.$$

Say that a permutation of the integers from 1 to 7 is *incompatible with* P_0 if it does not have 7 in the first place, nor 2 in the second place, nor 6 in the third place, nor 1 in the fourth place, nor 5 in the fifth place, nor 3 in the sixth place, nor 4 in the seventh place. For example, 1, 3, 5, 7, 2, 4, 6 is incompatible with P_0, whereas 1, 3, 5, 7, 2, 6, 4 is not. The question is: How many permutations are there that are incompatible with P_0?

If we think about the definition of compatibility for a moment and compare it with the definition of derangement, we notice that a derangement is just a permutation incompatible with the "natural" order 1, 2, 3, 4, 5, 6, 7. Since the number of permutations incompatible with some fixed ordering clearly does not depend on which fixed ordering ("natural" or otherwise) is given, we conclude that the number of permutations incompatible with P_0 is $D(7)$, the number of derangements.

We can also show this directly by applying the argument at the beginning of this section; we merely interpret

α as the property that a permutation has 7 in first position,

β as the property that a permutation has 2 in second position,

γ as the property that a permutation has 6 in third position,

. . . .

η as the property that a permutation has 4 in seventh position,

and rederive formula (5.10).

There is nothing special about the one permutation P_0 under discussion. In general, we can say that *if we take any fixed permutation of the integers from 1 to 7, the number of permutations incompatible with it is* $D(7)$. The derangements are simply all the permutations that are incompatible with the natural arrangement 1, 2, 3, 4, 5, 6, 7.

More generally, the following statements can be made. Say that two permutations $a_1, a_2, \cdots, a_n$ and $b_1, b_2, \cdots, b_n$ of the integers 1, 2, $\cdots$, n are *incompatible* if $a_1 \neq b_1$, $a_2 \neq b_2$, $\cdots$, and $a_n \neq b_n$. The number of permutations of the integers from 1 to n that are incompatible with any fixed permutation is $D(n)$, the number of derangements. Furthermore, derangements are simply permutations of the integers from 1 to n that are incompatible with the natural ordering 1, 2, 3, $\cdots$, n.

Problem Set 20

1. Evaluate $D(5)$ and $D(6)$.

2. List all the permutations of 1, 2, 3, 4 that are incompatible with the particular permutation 4, 3, 2, 1.

3. Find the number of derangements of the integers from 1 to 10 inclusive, satisfying the condition that the set of elements in the first five places is   (a) 1, 2, 3, 4, 5, in some order;   (b) 6, 7, 8, 9, 10, in some order.

4. Find the number of permutations of 1, 2, 3, 4, 5, 6, 7 that do not have 1 in the first place, nor 4 in the fourth place, nor 7 in the seventh place.

5. How many permutations of the integers from 1 to 9 inclusive have exactly three of the numbers in their natural positions, and the other six not?

6. A simple code is made by permuting the letters of the alphabet, with every letter replaced by a different one. How many codes can be made in this way?

7. Prove that $D(n) - nD(n - 1) = (-1)^n$ for $n \geqslant 2$.

5.4   Combinatorial Probability

Probability, an important branch of mathematics with an extensive literature, will be treated here in a very limited fashion. We shall restrict attention to a few questions closely related to the main subject of this book. Because of this restriction it will suffice to give a simple definition of probability which, although inadequate for a more sophisticated study of the subject, encompasses all the problems brought into our discussion.

To be specific, we shall confine attention to situations where we can presume what are called *equally likely cases*. For example, if a coin is tossed, we shall take it for granted that the two outcomes, heads and tails, are equally likely. If a die (plural "dice") is cast, we shall assume that the six outcomes, namely 1, 2, 3, 4, 5, or 6 coming up, are equally likely to occur. Or if a card is drawn at random from an ordinary deck, we shall assume that all 52 cards have an equal chance of being drawn, that it is just as likely that the three of hearts (say) will turn up as any other card.

The probability assigned to the three of hearts turning up is 1/52. In general, probability is defined as the ratio of the number of "favorable" cases to the total number of equally likely cases:

$$\frac{\text{Number of favorable cases}}{\text{Total number of equally likely cases}}.$$

Thus the probability of getting heads when a coin is tossed is 1/2; of a 4 coming up when a die is cast is 1/6; of an even number turning up when a die is cast is 3/6 or 1/2; of getting an ace in a single random draw from a deck of cards is 4/52 or 1/13.

An important condition imposed on this definition is that the cases entering into the calculation be equally likely cases. For example, consider the question: What is the probability of getting a total of 12 when two dice are thrown? We could argue *incorrectly* that the sum of the two numbers turning up on a pair of dice may be 2, or 3, or 4, $\cdots$, or 12, so the total number of cases is 11, and so the probability of throwing a 12 is 1/11. This answer is incorrect because these 11 cases are not equally likely. The chances of throwing a 12 are clearly not as great as those of throwing (say) 8, because for a 12, there must be a 6 turned up on each die, whereas for an 8 there may be a 4 on each die, or a 3 and a 5, or a 2 and a 6.

When two dice are thrown the proper number of equally likely outcomes can be found by thinking of the dice as two distinct independent objects, say one white die and one blue die. There are 6 possibilities for the white die and 6 for the blue die, and so by the multiplication principle of Chapter 2 there are 36 equally likely cases:

1, 1	1, 2	1, 3	1, 4	1, 5	1, 6
2, 1	2, 2	2, 3	2, 4	2, 5	2, 6
3, 1	3, 2	3, 3	3, 4	3, 5	3, 6
4, 1	4, 2	4, 3	4, 4	4, 5	4, 6
5, 1	5, 2	5, 3	5, 4	5, 5	5, 6
6, 1	6, 2	6, 3	6, 4	6, 5	6, 6.

Of these 36 cases there is only one, namely 6, 6, that gives a total of 12. Hence the probability of getting a total of 12 is 1/36.

Consider the question: What is the probability of a sum of 8 when two dice are thrown? From the above table of 36 cases we see that a sum of 8 arises in the 5 cases   2, 6   3, 5   4, 4   5, 3   6, 2. Hence the answer is 5/36.

Consider the question: What is the probability of getting one head and two tails when three coins are tossed? To get the total number of equally likely cases we conceive of the three coins as distinct, then use the multiplication principle of Chapter 2, and find that there are $2 \cdot 2 \cdot 2$ or eight cases, namely

$$HHH \quad HTH \quad THH \quad TTH$$
$$HHT \quad HTT \quad THT \quad TTT$$

where H stands for heads and T for tails. Thus the answer to the question is $3/8$ since the favorable cases are HTT, THT and TTH.

PROBLEM 5.6   If ten coins fall to the floor, what is the probability that there are five heads and five tails?

SOLUTION: We conceive of the coins as distinct, a first coin, a second coin, and so on. There are 2^{10} outcomes because each coin can land in two possible ways, heads or tails. An outcome can be designated by a string of ten letters, each either an H (for heads) or a T (for tails); for example

(5.12) $T T H H T H H H T T$

means that the first coin is tails, the second tails, the third heads, etc. The number of favorable cases, therefore, is the number of ways that five H's and five T's can be written in a row, and by the work of Chapter 3, this number is $C(10, 5)$. Hence the answer to the question is

$$\frac{C(10, 5)}{2^{10}} = \frac{63}{256}.$$

PROBLEM 5.7   What is the probability that six cards drawn at random from a standard deck of 52 cards will be red cards?

SOLUTION. The total number of cases is the number of ways of selecting six out of 52, and this is $C(52, 6)$. There being 26 red cards in a deck, the number of favorable cases is $C(26, 6)$, the number of ways of choosing six out of 26. Hence the answer is

$$\frac{C(26, 6)}{C(52, 6)}.$$

PROBLEM 5.8 What is the probability of getting a total of 13 when four dice are thrown?

SOLUTION. Since each die can come up in six ways the total number of cases is 6^4. Consider the dice as identifiable in some way, such as by color, so that we can refer to the first die, the second die, etc. If the number turning up on the first die is x_1, on the second die x_2, on the third die x_3, and on the fourth die x_4, then the number of favorable cases is the number of solutions of

$$x_1 + x_2 + x_3 + x_4 = 13$$

in positive integers from 1 to 6. By (5.9) this number of solutions is

$$C(12, 3) - C(4, 1)C(6, 3) = 220 - 80 = 140.$$

Hence the answer is $140/6^4$ or $35/324$.

PROBLEM 5.9 If a permutation of the integers $1, 2, 3, \cdots, n$ is taken at random, what is the probability that it is a derangement?

SOLUTION. The total number of permutations is $n!$ and the number of favorable cases is $D(n)$ as given in (5.11). Hence the probability is

$$(5.13) \qquad \frac{D(n)}{n!} = 1 - \frac{1}{1!} + \frac{1}{2!} - \frac{1}{3!} + \frac{1}{4!} - \cdots + (-1)^n \frac{1}{n!}.$$

This probability has some interesting aspects, some of which will be mentioned here. (Others will be elicited in the next problem set.) For $n = 1, 2, 3, 4, 5, 6, 7, 8$, the values of $D(n)/n!$ are

$$(5.14) \qquad 0, .5000, .3333, .3750, .3667, .3681, .3679, .3679,$$

to four decimal places of accuracy. Note that the four place approximation to the value of $D(n)/n!$ does not change from $n = 7$ to $n = 8$. It is interesting that this does not change beyond $n = 8$, so that .3679 is accurate for $D(n)/n!$ to four decimal places for all n from 7 onwards, $n = 7$, $n = 8$, $n = 9$, and so on. In other words, no matter how large n is, $D(n)/n!$ remains within .00005 of .3679.

As n increases without bound, the right side of (5.13) has more and more terms, and $D(n)/n!$ tends to the limiting value $1/e$ where e is a basic mathematical constant.

In computing the probability of the occurrence of an event it is sometimes more convenient to begin by computing the "complementary probability", namely the probability that the event will not occur. The probability of an event is defined as

$$p = \frac{\text{Number of favorable cases}}{\text{Total number of equally likely cases}},$$

so the complementary probability is defined as

$$q = \frac{\text{Number of unfavorable cases}}{\text{Total number of equally likely cases}}.$$

Since the number of favorable cases added to the number of unfavorable cases is the total number of cases, we see that

$$p + q = 1 \quad \text{or} \quad p = 1 - q.$$

Problem Set 21

1. Check the calculations giving the values in (5.14).

2. Find the probability of getting two tails if two coins are tossed.

3. What is the probability of getting a total of 7 when two dice are thrown?

4. Two dice, one red and one white, are tossed. What is the probability that the white die turns up a larger number than the red die?

5. If four dice are thrown, what is the probability that the four numbers turning up will be all different?

6. If seven dice are thrown, what is the probability that exactly three 6's will turn up?

7. Show that the terms of the binomial expansion of $(\frac{1}{6} + \frac{5}{6})^7$ are the probabilities that when seven dice are cast the number of 6's turning up will be respectively 0, 1, 2, 3, 4, 5, 6, 7.

8. What is the probability of getting a total of 15 when five dice are thrown?

9. When eight coins are tossed what is the probability of (a) exactly five heads; (b) at least five heads?

10. What is the probability that four cards dealt at random from an ordinary deck of 52 cards will contain one from each suit, that is to say, one heart, one spade, one club and one diamond?

11. Find the probability that when 13 cards are dealt from an ordinary deck of 52 cards (a) at least two are face cards; (b) exactly one ace is present; (c) at least one ace is present.

12. The letters of the alphabet are written in random order. What is the probability that x and y are adjacent?

13. If a five-digit integer is chosen at random, what is the probability that (a) the sum of the digits is 20; (b) the product of the digits is 20?

14. A teacher is going to separate ten boys into two teams of five each to play basketball by drawing five names out of a hat containing all ten names. As the drawing is about to start, one boy says to a good friend, "I hope we get on the same team." His friend replies, "Well, we have a fifty-fifty chance." Is he right, in the sense that the probability that the two boys will be on the same team is $\frac{1}{2}$?

15. A man took the eight spark plugs out of his auto to clean them. He intended to put each one back into the same cylinder it came from, but he got mixed up. Assuming that the plugs were put back in random fashion, what is the probability that at least one went back into the cylinder it came from? at least two?

16. A solitaire type of card game is played as follows: The player has two shuffled decks, each with the usual 52 cards. With the decks face down the player turns up a pair of cards, one from each deck.

If they are matching cards (for example, if both are the seven of spades) he has lost the game. If they are not matching cards he continues and turns up another pair of cards, one from each deck. Again he has lost if they are a matching pair. The player wins if he can turn up all 52 pairs, none matching. What is the probability of a win?

17. In the preceding problem suppose the game is played with two "decks" of 13 cards each, for example the spades from two decks of cards. What is the probability of a win in this case?

18. In Problem 16 suppose that a win is defined differently: The player wins if there is exactly one matching pair in the entire 52 pairs. What is the probability of a win?

5.5 Summary

Consider a collection of N different objects, some of which have property α, some property β, some property γ, and so on. Let $N(\alpha)$ be the number of objects having property α, $N(\beta)$ the number having property β, $\cdots$, $N(\alpha, \beta)$ the number having both properties α and β, $N(\alpha, \beta, \gamma)$ the number having all three properties α, β, and γ, and so on. Then the number of objects having none of the properties is

$$N$$
$$-N(\alpha) - N(\beta) - N(\gamma) - \cdots$$
$$+N(\alpha, \beta) + N(\alpha, \gamma) + N(\beta, \gamma) + \cdots$$
$$-N(\alpha, \beta, \gamma) - \cdots$$

$$\cdot \ \cdot \ \cdot \ \cdot \ \cdot \ \cdot \ \cdot$$

Suppose that there are r properties under consideration. Also suppose that the number of objects having any one property is the same as the number of objects having any other single property, that the number of objects having two properties is the same no matter which two are considered, and likewise for three properties, four properties, and so on. Then the number of objects having none of the properties can be written in the simpler form

$$N - C(r, 1)N(\alpha) + C(r, 2)N(\alpha, \beta) - C(r, 3)N(\alpha, \beta, \gamma) + \cdots .$$

With the use of this inclusion-exclusion principle, as it is called, the discussion of the equation

$$(5.15) \qquad x_1 + x_2 + x_3 + \cdots + x_k = m$$

is continued from the preceding chapter. We are now able to find the number of solutions of an equation of type (5.15) under the conditions that each variable is restricted to a specific set of consecutive integral values. Whereas detailed formulas were not developed in general, the following case was treated: Let c be any fixed positive integer; the number of solutions of equation (5.15) in positive integers from 1 to c inclusive is

$$
\begin{aligned}
C(m - 1, k - 1) &- C(k, 1)C(m - c - 1, k - 1) \\
&+ C(k, 2)C(m - 2c - 1, k - 1) \\
&- C(k, 3)C(m - 3c - 1, k - 1) \\
&+ C(k, 4)C(m - 4c - 1, k - 1) - \cdots ,
\end{aligned}
$$

where the series continues until zero terms arise.

The discussion of combinations with repetitions is continued from the preceding chapter to a wider variety of cases, again by use of the inclusion-exclusion principle.

Define $D(n)$ as the number of derangements of 1, 2, 3, $\cdots$, n, that is, the number of permutations with 1 not in the first place, 2 not in the second place, $\cdots$, and n not in the n-th place. It was established that

$$D(n) = n!\left[1 - \frac{1}{1!} + \frac{1}{2!} - \frac{1}{3!} + \frac{1}{4!} - \frac{1}{5!} + \cdots + (-1)^n \frac{1}{n!}\right].$$

Say that two permutations of n objects are *incompatible* if in the two arrangements, all pairs of objects in corresponding positions consist of two distinct objects. If P is a fixed permutation of the integers from 1 to n, the number of permutations incompatible with P is $D(n)$. Derangements are permutations incompatible with the natural ordering 1, 2, 3, $\cdots$, n.

Probability was defined in simple combinatorial situations as the ratio of the number of favorable cases to the total number of equally likely cases. The meaning of "equally likely cases" was taken as intuitively clear in certain basic situations, and then extended to more complex ones by use of the multiplication principle of Chapter 3.

CHAPTER SIX

Partitions of an Integer

In this chapter we discuss partitions of an integer, or what is the same thing, partitions of a collection of identical objects. In case the objects are not identical, the problem comes under the heading "partitions of a set" and is discussed in Section 8.2.

The partitions of a positive integer are the ways of writing that integer as a sum of positive integers. The partitions of 5, for example, are

$$5 \quad 4+1 \quad 3+1+1 \quad 2+1+1+1$$
$$3+2 \quad 2+2+1 \quad 1+1+1+1+1$$

Since there are seven partitions of 5, we write $p(5) = 7$; in general, we let $p(n)$ denote the number of partitions of the positive integer n. In such a partition as $3+2$ above, the numbers 3 and 2 are called the summands. Thus 5 has one partition with one summand, two partitions with two summands, two partitions with three summands, one with four summands, and one with five summands.

Whereas 5 has two partitions with three summands, the equation $x_1 + x_2 + x_3 = 5$ has six solutions in positive integers; they are

$$(3, 1, 1), \quad (1, 3, 1), \quad (1, 1, 3), \quad (2, 2, 1), \quad (2, 1, 2), \quad (1, 2, 2).$$

In counting the number of solutions of an equation, order is taken into account; but in counting the number of partitions, the order of the summands is irrelevant.

6.1 Graphs of Partitions

Let us look at the partitions of 6:

(6.1)

$1 + 1 + 1 + 1 + 1 + 1$	$4 + 1 + 1$	$5 + 1$
$2 + 1 + 1 + 1 + 1$	$3 + 2 + 1$	$4 + 2$
$3 + 1 + 1 + 1$	$2 + 2 + 2$	$3 + 3$
$2 + 2 + 1 + 1$		6

There are eleven, so we write $p(6) = 11$. Also we see that the number of partitions of 6

(6.2)

into 6 summands is 1,

into 5 summands is 1,

into 4 summands is 2,

into 3 summands is 3,

into 2 summands is 3,

into 1 summand is 1.

The notation $q_k(n)$ will denote the number of partitions of n with k or fewer summands. For $n = 6$, the listing (6.2) above shows that

(6.3)

$$q_1(6) = 1 \qquad q_3(6) = 7 \qquad q_5(6) = 10$$
$$q_2(6) = 4 \qquad q_4(6) = 9 \qquad q_6(6) = 11.$$

Since the number 6 cannot be partitioned into more than six summands, we would expect that $q_6(6)$ would be the same as $p(6)$. Similarly $q_n(n)$ means the number of partitions of n having n or fewer summands, and so

(6.4)
$$q_n(n) = p(n) .$$

Partitions can also be classified according to the size of the summands. The listing (6.1) shows that the number of partitions of 6

(6.5)

with 6 as the largest summand is 1,

with 5 as the largest summand is 1,

with 4 as the largest summand is 2,

with 3 as the largest summand is 3,

with 2 as the largest summand is 3,

with 1 as the largest summand is 1.

Note the resemblance of this list to the list (6.2). This is no coincidence, as we shall see. Furthermore, if we define $p_k(n)$ as the number of partitions of n with summands no larger than k, we find that

(6.6)
$$p_1(6) = 1 \qquad p_3(6) = 7 \qquad p_5(6) = 10$$
$$p_2(6) = 4 \qquad p_4(6) = 9 \qquad p_6(6) = 11 .$$

This list resembles (6.3). In general it is true that $p_k(n) = q_k(n)$. Let us look at some special cases to see why this is so.

The partitions of 6 into three summands are

(6.7) $4 + 1 + 1, \quad 3 + 2 + 1, \quad 2 + 2 + 2.$

The partitions of 6 with 3 as the largest summand are

(6.8) $3 + 1 + 1 + 1, \quad 3 + 2 + 1, \quad 3 + 3.$

To see why it is no accident that there are the same number (three) of partitions listed in (6.7) and (6.8), we use the so-called *graphs of partitions*. The graph of the partition $4 + 1 + 1$ is

. . . .

.

.

Similarly, the graphs of $3 + 2 + 1$ and $2 + 2 + 2$ are

. . .   . .

. .   . .

.   . .

Thus the graph of a partition of n with k summands simply consists of k rows of dots, one row for each summand; the row representing the largest summand appears at the top, that representing the next largest summand appears under it, and so on. There are as many rows as there are summands, and the number of dots in each row corresponds to the size of each summand. The total number of dots in the graph of a partition of n is n.

The *reverse* of a graph is obtained by interchanging the horizontal and vertical rows of dots; for example,

GRAPH   REVERSE OF THE GRAPH

· · · ·   · · ·
·   ·
·   ·
                     ·

$4 + 1 + 1$ $3 + 1 + 1 + 1$

· · ·   · · ·
· ·   · ·
·   ·

$3 + 2 + 1$ $3 + 2 + 1$

· ·
· ·   · · ·
· ·   · · ·

$2 + 2 + 2$ $3 + 3$

· · · · · ·   · · · ·
· · · ·   · ·
·   · ·
·   · ·
                        ·

$6 + 4 + 1 + 1$ $4 + 2 + 2 + 2 + 1 + 1$

The reverse of a graph of a partition of n is again a graph of a partition of n. If the original graph represents a partition with k summands (i.e. has k rows), then the reverse graph has k dots in its first (longest) row and hence represents a partition with maximum summand k. For example, the partition of 12 into 4 summands $6 + 4 + 1 + 1$ has the graph

```
. . . . . .
. . . .
.
.
```

The reverse graph

```
. . . .
. .
. .
. .
.
.
```

represents the partition $4 + 2 + 2 + 2 + 1 + 1$ of 12, where 4 is the maximum summand. Thus the one-to-one correspondence between graphs and reverse graphs can be interpreted as a one-to-one correspondence between partitions of n with k summands and partitions of n with greatest summand k. It follows that the number of partitions of n into k summands is the same as the number of partitions of n with maximum summand k.

Moreover, since the number of partitions of n into 1, or 2, or 3, $\cdots$, or k summands is the same as the number of partitions of n with maximum summand 1, or 2, or 3, $\cdots$, or k, we may say:

The number of partitions of n into k or fewer summands equals the number of partitions of n having summands no larger than k; in symbols,

(6.9) $$q_k(n) = p_k(n).$$

This result is illustrated for the special case $n = 6$ in the lists of equations (6.3) and (6.6).

Problem Set 22

1. Evaluate $p(1)$, $p(2)$, $p(3)$, $p(4)$ and $p(5)$.

2. Evaluate $p_1(n)$ and $q_1(n)$.

3. Evaluate $q_2(8)$, $q_2(9)$ and, in general, $q_2(n)$.

4. Find the value of $p_{99}(99) - p_{98}(99)$.

5. Evaluate $p_{67}(67) - p_{65}(67)$.

6. Prove that $p_n(n) = p_{n+1}(n)$ and, in general, that $p_k(n) = p_n(n)$ if $k > n$.

7. Prove that $p_n(n) = p_{n-1}(n) + 1$.

6.2   The Number of Partitions

The number of partitions of n has been denoted by $p(n)$, the number of partitions of n with k or fewer summands by $q_k(n)$, and the number of partitions of n with summands no larger than k by $p_k(n)$. The relations obtained so far are

$$(6.10) \qquad p_k(n) = q_k(n) \qquad \text{and} \qquad p(n) = q_n(n) = p_n(n) .$$

In order to calculate the numerical values of these partitions we establish one more result:

$$(6.11) \qquad p_k(n) = p_{k-1}(n) + p_k(n - k).$$

To prove this for integers n and k satisfying $1 < k < n$, we separate the $p_k(n)$ partitions of n with summands no larger than k into two types:

         (a) those having k as a summand;

         (b) those not having k as a summand.

We observe first that the partitions of type (b) are precisely the $p_{k-1}(n)$ partitions of n having summands no larger than $k - 1$. Next we note that, since the summand k occurs at least once in each partition of type (a), we can remove a summand k from each of these partitions. If we do so, the resulting partitions are precisely the partitions of $n - k$ into summands no larger than k, in number $p_k(n - k)$. Thus (6.11) is established for integers n and k such that $1 < k < n$.

As an illustration of this argument we take the case $n = 6$, $k = 4$, so that (6.11) becomes $p_4(6) = p_3(6) + p_4(2)$. All the partitions of the number 6 are listed in (6.1) of the preceding section. There are nine partitions of 6 having summands no larger than 4, so that $p_4(6) = 9$. These nine partitions are separated into type (a), those having 4 as a summand, and type (b), those not having 4 as a summand:

Type (a)	Type (b)
$4 + 1 + 1$	$1 + 1 + 1 + 1 + 1 + 1$
$4 + 2$	$2 + 1 + 1 + 1 + 1$
	$3 + 1 + 1 + 1$
	$2 + 2 + 1 + 1$
	$3 + 2 + 1$
	$2 + 2 + 2$
	$3 + 3$

The partitions of type (b) are all partitions of 6 having summands no larger than 3; the number of these is $p_3(6)$. When we remove a summand 4 from each partition of type (a) we get the partitions $1 + 1$ and 2. The number of these is $p_4(2)$ because

$$p_4(2) = p_2(2) = p(2) = 2.$$

Formula (6.11) is valid for positive integers k and n satisfying $1 < k < n$. To make a table of values for $p_k(n)$ we need a few additional observations. First, for $k = 1$ we note that

(6.12) $p_1(n) = 1$ for all $n \geqslant 1$,

because there is only one partition of n with summands no larger than 1. Next, there is no partition of n with a summand exceeding n, and so

(6.13) $p_k(n) = p_n(n)$ if $k \geqslant n$.

In case $n = 1$ this gives

$$1 = p_1(1) = p_2(1) = p_3(1) = \cdots .$$

Also, there is exactly one partition of n having n as a summand, and hence

(6.14) $p_n(n) = 1 + p_{n-1}(n)$.

With these results it is a simple matter to make a table of values of $p_k(n)$. To begin, we can write 1's in the first horizontal row and the first vertical column because of formulas (6.12) and (6.13). Then the best way to proceed, perhaps, is to fill in the values of $p_2(n)$ for $n = 2, 3, 4, \cdots$, then $p_3(n)$ for $n = 2, 3, 4, \cdots$, then $p_4(n)$ for $n = 2, 3, 4, \cdots$, and so on, using formulas (6.11), (6.13) and (6.14).

TABLE OF VALUES OF $p_k(n)$

	$k = 1$	$k = 2$	$k = 3$	$k = 4$	$k = 5$	$k = 6$	$k = 7$
$n = 1$	1	1	1	1	1	1	1
$n = 2$	1	2	2	2	2	2	2
$n = 3$	1	2	3	3	3	3	3
$n = 4$	1	3	4	5	5	5	5
$n = 5$	1	3	5	6	7	7	7
$n = 6$	1	4	7	9	10	11	11
$n = 7$	1	4	8	11	13	14	15

Problem Set 23

1. Extend the table of values of $p_k(n)$ as far as $n = 12$ and $k = 12$.

2. Evaluate $q_7(5)$, $q_7(7)$ and $q_7(9)$.

3. Evaluate $p(7)$, $p(8)$, $p(9)$ and $p(10)$.

6.3 Summary

The number of partitions of a positive integer n, denoted by $p(n)$, is the number of ways of writing n as a sum of positive integers. In such a partition as $7 = 4 + 2 + 1$ there are three summands, 4, 2 and 1. The order of the summands does not matter, so that $7 = 2 + 1 + 4$ is the same partition. By $q_k(n)$ is meant the number of partitions of n having k or fewer summands; by $p_k(n)$ is meant the number of partitions of n with no summand greater than k. The following results were established:

$$p_k(n) = q_k(n),$$
$$p(n) = p_n(n) = p_{n+1}(n) = p_{n+2}(n) = p_{n+3}(n) = \cdots,$$
$$p_k(n) = p_{k-1}(n) + p_k(n - k) \quad \text{for } 1 < k < n.$$

A short table of partitions was developed by use of these results together with the following simple observations:

$$p_1(n) = 1 \quad \text{and} \quad p_n(n) = 1 + p_{n-1}(n).$$

CHAPTER SEVEN

Generating Polynomials

In this chapter we shall use polynomials to "generate" the solutions of a class of problems. For example, we shall solve Problem 1.5 of Chapter 1: In how many ways is it possible to make change for a dollar bill? The method introduced in this chapter is, in its level of sophistication, just one step above the enumeration of cases.

In order to find the number of ways of changing a dollar bill, we first examine the well-known technique of multiplying polynomials. We shall be concerned, in particular, with multiplying polynomials whose coefficients are 1. For example,

$$(1 + x + x^2 + x^4 + x^8)(1 + x^3 + x^6 + x^9)$$
$$= 1 + x + x^2 + x^3 + 2x^4 + x^5 + x^6 + 2x^7$$
$$+ 2x^8 + x^9 + 2x^{10} + 2x^{11} + x^{13} + x^{14} + x^{17}.$$

Now suppose we are interested in the terms of the product only up to x^9. Then we would neglect terms involving higher powers of x and we would write

$$(1 + x + x^2 + x^4 + x^8)(1 + x^3 + x^6 + x^9)$$
$$= 1 + x + x^2 + x^3 + 2x^4 + x^5 + x^6 + 2x^7 + 2x^8 + x^9 + \cdots.$$

There would be no need to calculate powers of x beyond x^9 in the process of multiplication. To illustrate this point, let us find the expansion, up to x^7, of the product

$$(1 + x)(1 + x^2)(1 + x^3)(1 + x^4)(1 + x^5)(1 + x^6)(1 + x^7).$$

Working from the right-hand end we could write the multiplication process as follows:

$$(1 + x)(1 + x^2)(1 + x^3)(1 + x^4)(1 + x^5)(1 + x^6)(1 + x^7)$$

$$= (1 + x)(1 + x^2)(1 + x^3)(1 + x^4)(1 + x^5)$$
$$\cdot (1 + x^6 + x^7 + \cdots)$$

$$= (1 + x)(1 + x^2)(1 + x^3)(1 + x^4)$$
(7.1) $$\cdot (1 + x^5 + x^6 + x^7 + \cdots)$$

$$= (1 + x)(1 + x^2)(1 + x^3)(1 + x^4 + x^5 + x^6 + x^7 + \cdots)$$

$$= (1 + x)(1 + x^2)(1 + x^3 + x^4 + x^5 + x^6 + 2x^7 + \cdots)$$

$$= (1 + x)(1 + x^2 + x^3 + x^4 + 2x^5 + 2x^6 + 3x^7 + \cdots)$$

$$= 1 + x + x^2 + 2x^3 + 2x^4 + 3x^5 + 4x^6 + 5x^7 + \cdots.$$

A considerable amount of work is saved since the full expansion includes terms up to x^{28}. This saving in labor can be achieved, of course, only if we are not concerned with terms beyond x^7. As we shall see, such a limitation will be acceptable in the problems of this chapter.

Problem Set 24

1. Expand the product $(1 + x)(1 + x^2)(1 + x^4)(1 + x^8)(1 + x^{16})$ including terms up to x^{16}.

2. Expand the product

$$(1 + x)(1 + x^2)(1 + x^3)(1 + x^4)(1 + x^5)(1 + x^6)(1 + x^7)(1 + x^8)$$

including terms up to x^8.

3. Multiply out the product

$$(1 + x + x^2 + x^3 + x^4 + x^5 + x^6 + x^7)(1 + x^2 + x^4 + x^6)(1 + x^3 + x^6)$$
$$\cdot (1 + x^4)(1 + x^5)(1 + x^6)(1 + x^7)$$

including terms up to x^7.

7.1   Partitions and Products of Polynomials

Let us look at the term $5x^7$ in the expansion of the product (7.1) of binomials of the form $(1 + x^n)$, $n = 1, 2, \cdots, 7$. The coefficient 5 tells us, in effect, that x^7 turns up five times in the multiplication process. Tracking down these five cases we see that x^7 arises from the products

$$x^7, \quad x^6x, \quad x^5x^2, \quad x^4x^3, \quad x^4x^2x,$$

where the factors 1 have been omitted for simplicity. The exponents in these five cases correspond to the equations

$$7 = 7, \quad 7 = 6 + 1, \quad 7 = 5 + 2, \quad 7 = 4 + 3, \quad 7 = 4 + 2 + 1.$$

We observe that these five equations are precisely the partitions of the number 7 with *distinct* summands.

As a second example, consider all partitions of 6 with distinct summands,

$$6 = 6, \quad 6 = 5 + 1, \quad 6 = 4 + 2, \quad 6 = 3 + 2 + 1.$$

Here we have four equations, or four partitions, and this corresponds to the coefficient 4 in the term $4x^6$ of the expansion (7.1).

If we wanted to use polynomial products to find the number of partitions of 8 with distinct summands, the expansion (7.1) would be inadequate since it stops with $(1 + x^7)$. We would look at the coefficient of x^8 in the expansion of

(7.2) $(1 + x)(1 + x^2)(1 + x^3)(1 + x^4)(1 + x^5)(1 + x^6)$

$$\cdot (1 + x^7)(1 + x^8).$$

(See Problem 2 of Problem Set 24.)

Another point can be made. The coefficients of x, x^2, x^3, x^4, x^5, x^6, x^7 in the expansion (7.1) are respectively the numbers of partitions of 1, 2, 3, 4, 5, 6, 7 with distinct summands. Similarly, the coefficients of x, x^2, x^3, x^4, x^5, x^6, x^7, x^8 in the expansion of the product (7.2) are respectively the number of partitions of 1, 2, 3, 4, 5, 6, 7, 8 with distinct summands. It follows that the expansions of (7.1) and (7.2) are identical up to the term involving x^7, that is, up to $5x^7$.

Can we use polynomial multiplication to get at the ordinary partitions of a number, without the "distinct summands" restriction? We can, provided we choose the correct polynomials for multiplication. Consider the product

$$(1 + x + x^2 + x^3 + x^4 + x^5 + x^6 + x^7)$$

(7.3) $\cdot (1 + x^2 + x^4 + x^6)(1 + x^3 + x^6)$

$$\cdot (1 + x^4)(1 + x^5)(1 + x^6)(1 + x^7).$$

Let us look at the third, second and first factors in the forms

$$1 + x^3 + x^6 = 1 + x^3 + x^{3+3},$$

$$1 + x^2 + x^4 + x^6 = 1 + x^2 + x^{2+2} + x^{2+2+2},$$

$$1 + x + x^2 + x^3 + x^4 + x^5 + x^6 + x^7 = 1 + x^1 + x^{1+1} + x^{1+1+1}$$

$$+ x^{1+1+1+1} + x^{1+1+1+1+1} + x^{1+1+1+1+1+1} + x^{1+1+1+1+1+1+1}.$$

Viewing these factors in this way (and not altering the factors $1 + x^4$, $1 + x^5$, $1 + x^6$, $1 + x^7$) we see that the coefficient of x^7 in the entire product expansion can be thought of as the number of ways of writing 7 as a sum of numbers selected from one or more of the following batches, where at most one member may be taken from any one batch.

First batch   1,   1 + 1,   1 + 1 + 1,   1 + 1 + 1 + 1,

        1 + 1 + 1 + 1 + 1,   1 + 1 + 1 + 1 + 1 + 1,

        1 + 1 + 1 + 1 + 1 + 1 + 1;

Second batch: 2,   2 + 2,   2 + 2 + 2;

Third batch: 3,   3 + 3;

Fourth batch: 4;

Fifth batch: 5;

Sixth batch: 6;

Seventh batch: 7.

But this is just an elaborate description of *the number of partitions of 7*.

Thus we see that the coefficients of x, x^2, x^3, x^4, x^5, x^6, x^7 in the expansion of the product (7.3) are simply the numbers of partitions of 1, 2, 3, 4, 5, 6, 7 respectively. In the notation of the preceding chapter, these coefficients are the numerical values of $p(1)$, $p(2)$, $p(3)$, $p(4)$, $p(5)$, $p(6)$, $p(7)$.

As another example, consider the product

$$(7.4) \quad \begin{aligned} & (1 + x + x^2 + x^3 + x^4 + x^5 + x^6 + x^7 + x^8 + x^9) \\ & \cdot (1 + x^3 + x^6 + x^9)(1 + x^5)(1 + x^7)(1 + x^9). \end{aligned}$$

An argument similar to that used with the product (7.3) shows that the coefficients of x, x^2, x^3, x^4, x^5, x^6, x^7, x^8, x^9 are the numbers of partitions of 1, 2, 3, 4, 5, 6, 7, 8, 9, with odd summands only.

These examples suggest the following general principle. *Let a, b, c, d, e be unequal positive integers. Then the coefficient of x^n in the expansion of*

$$(7.5) \quad \begin{aligned} & (1 + x^a + x^{2a} + x^{3a} + \cdots)(1 + x^b + x^{2b} + x^{3b} + \cdots) \\ & \cdot (1 + x^c + x^{2c} + x^{3c} + \cdots)(1 + x^d + x^{2d} + x^{3d} + \cdots) \\ & \cdot (1 + x^e + x^{2e} + x^{3e} + \cdots) \end{aligned}$$

equals the number of partitions of n with summands restricted to a, b, c, d, e. Each factor in (7.5) must include all exponents not exceeding n.

To illustrate this last remark, consider the case $n = 34$ and $a = 6$; the first factor in (7.5) would be

$$1 + x^6 + x^{12} + x^{18} + x^{24} + x^{30}.$$

No harm would be done by the presence of higher powers such as x^{36}, x^{42}, and so on, but these are not necessary in case $n = 34$.

There is, of course, no reason to restrict the summands to five items a, b, c, d, e. The extension of formula (7.5) to more summands merely involves additional appropriate factors, and the contraction to fewer summands merely involves the removal of appropriate factors.

Question: What product can be used to give the number of partitions of 20 with summands 3, 4, 5, 6? *Answer:* The number of such partitions is the coefficient of x^{20} in the expansion of the product

$$(1 + x^3 + x^6 + x^9 + x^{12} + x^{15} + x^{18})$$

(7.6)
$$\cdot (1 + x^4 + x^8 + x^{12} + x^{16} + x^{20})$$

$$\cdot (1 + x^5 + x^{10} + x^{15} + x^{20})(1 + x^6 + x^{12} + x^{18}).$$

Finally, we note that there is another interpretation of the coefficient of x^{20} in this expansion. It is the number of solutions, in nonnegative integers, of

$$3y + 4z + 5u + 6v = 20;$$

for, each such solution corresponds to a partition of 20 with summands 3, 4, 5, 6. For example, the solution $y = 1$, $z = 3$, $u = 1$, $v = 0$ corresponds to the partition $20 = 3 + 4 + 4 + 4 + 5$.

Problem Set 25

1. Give an interpretation of each of the following in terms of partitions:

(a) the coefficient of x^{12} in the expansion of

$$(1 + x^2 + x^4 + x^6 + x^8 + x^{10} + x^{12})(1 + x^4 + x^8 + x^{12})(1 + x^6 + x^{12})$$
$$\cdot (1 + x^8)(1 + x^{10})(1 + x^{12});$$

(b) the coefficient of x^9 in the expansion of

$$(1 + x + x^2 + x^3 + x^4 + x^5 + x^6 + x^7 + x^8 + x^9)$$
$$\cdot (1 + x^2 + x^4 + x^6 + x^8)(1 + x^3 + x^6 + x^9);$$

(c) the coefficient of x^6 in the expansion of

$$(1 + x)(1 + x^2)(1 + x^3)(1 + x^4)(1 + x^5)(1 + x^6).$$

2. Calculate the indicated coefficients in the preceding question.

3. Write a polynomial product whose expansion can be used to find

(a) the number of partitions of 38 with summands restricted to 6, 7, 12, 20;

(b) the number of partitions of 15 with summands greater than 2;

(c) the number of partitions of 9 with distinct (i.e. unequal) summands.

Calculate the number of partitions in each case.

4. How many solutions are there in non-negative integers of the equation

$$2y + 3z + 5w + 7t = 18?$$

5. How many solutions in positive integers are there of the equation

$$3u + 5v + 7w + 9t = 40?$$

7.2 Change for a Dollar Bill

In the light of the general principle formulated in the preceding section, it is not difficult now to determine in how many ways it is possible to break a dollar bill into change. Since coins come in the denominations 1, 5, 10, 25 and 50 cents, our task is to find the number of partitions of 100 with summands restricted to 1, 5, 10, 25, 50. Thus we can apply the formulation (7.5) with

$$a = 1, \quad b = 5, \quad c = 10, \quad d = 25, \quad e = 50;$$

the answer to the question is the coefficient of x^{100} in the expansion of the product $P_1P_2P_3P_4P_5$, where the P's are the polynomials

$$P_1 = 1 + x + x^2 + x^3 + x^4 + \cdots + x^{99} + x^{100},$$

$$P_2 = 1 + x^5 + x^{10} + x^{15} + x^{20} + \cdots + x^{95} + x^{100},$$

$$P_3 = 1 + x^{10} + x^{20} + x^{30} + x^{40} + \cdots + x^{90} + x^{100},$$

$$P_4 = 1 + x^{25} + x^{50} + x^{75} + x^{100},$$

$$P_5 = 1 + x^{50} + x^{100}.$$

All calculations will be made up to x^{100}. We compute

$$P_4P_5 = 1 + x^{25} + 2x^{50} + 2x^{75} + 3x^{100} + \cdots,$$

$$P_3P_4P_5 = 1 + x^{10} + x^{20} + x^{25} + x^{30} + x^{35} + x^{40} + x^{45} + 3x^{50}$$
$$+ x^{55} + 3x^{60} + x^{65} + 3x^{70} + 3x^{75}$$
$$+ 3x^{80} + 3x^{85} + 3x^{90} + 3x^{95} + 6x^{100} + \cdots,$$

$$P_2P_3P_4P_5 = 1 + x^5 + 2x^{10} + 2x^{15} + 3x^{20} + 4x^{25} + 5x^{30} + 6x^{35}$$
$$+ 7x^{40} + 8x^{45} + 11x^{50} + 12x^{55} + 15x^{60} + 16x^{65} + 19x^{70}$$
$$+ 22x^{75} + 25x^{80} + 28x^{85} + 31x^{90} + 34x^{95} + 40x^{100} + \cdots.$$

The final multiplication need not be done in detail, since we are concerned only with the coefficient of x^{100}. We notice that each term in the polynomial product $P_2P_3P_4P_5$ enters exactly once in contributing to the coefficient of x^{100} in the product of P_1 and $P_2P_3P_4P_5$. It follows that this coefficient can be calculated simply by adding all the coefficients in $P_2P_3P_4P_5$ (including the constant term 1):

$$1 + 1 + 2 + 2 + 3 + 4 + 5 + 6 + 7 + 8 + 11 + 12$$
$$+ 15 + 16 + 19 + 22 + 25 + 28 + 31 + 34 + 40.$$

This sum is 292, and so there are 292 ways of changing a dollar bill.

Problem Set 26

1. Find the number of ways of changing a hundred dollar bill into bills of smaller denominations, namely 1, 5, 10, 20, 50 dollar bills.

2. In how many ways can the sum of 53 cents be made up in coins of denominations 1, 5, 10, 25 cents?

3. Find the number of solutions in non-negative integers of the equation

$$5y + 10z + 25w + 50t = 95.$$

4. Find the number of solutions in positive integers of the equation

$$5y + 10z + 25w + 50t = 155.$$

7.3   Summary

The incomplete multiplication of polynomials with unit coefficients —incomplete in the sense that the result is obtained only up to a certain power of the variable x —is used to determine the number of certain partitions and solutions of equations.

For five summands, the procedure is illustrated by the following general principle. Let a, b, c, d, e be unequal positive integers. Then the coefficient of x^n in the expansion of

$$(1 + x^a + x^{2a} + x^{3a} + \cdots)(1 + x^b + x^{2b} + x^{3b} + \cdots)$$

$$\cdot(1 + x^c + x^{2c} + x^{3c} + \cdots)(1 + x^d + x^{2d} + x^{3d} + \cdots)$$

$$\cdot(1 + x^e + x^{2e} + x^{3e} + \cdots)$$

equals the number of partitions of n with summands restricted to a, b, c, d, e. (Each of the five factors in parentheses in the product must include all exponents not exceeding n.) This coefficient is also the number of solutions in non-negative integers y, z, w, u, v of the equation

$$ay + bz + cw + du + ev = n.$$

This theory is used to determine, for example, the number of ways of making change for a dollar bill.

CHAPTER EIGHT

Distribution of Objects
Not All Alike

Many problems of combinatorial analysis can be stated in terms of the number of ways of distributing *objects* in *boxes*. Some of these distribution problems were considered in earlier chapters. We now make a brief classification of the various types of questions.

First, the objects may be considered to be alike, and the boxes also indistinguishable from one another. These are partition problems. For example, the number of ways of distributing nine objects in four boxes is the same as the number of partitions of 9 into at most four summands. Problems of this sort were discussed in Chapters 6 and 7.

Next, the objects may be alike, but the boxes may be thought of as different. Under these conditions, the number of ways of distributing nine objects in four boxes equals the number of solutions of

$$x_1 + x_2 + x_3 + x_4 = 9$$

in non-negative integers. If no box is to be empty, solutions in positive integers are to be counted. Similarly, other restrictions on the number of elements in the boxes correspond to restrictions on the solutions of the equations. Questions of this sort were studied in Chapters 4 and 5.

In the present chapter we study the distribution of objects that are not all alike. The words "not all alike" admit two interpretations: (1) objects all different in the sense of no two alike; (2) a mixed collection of objects, some alike and some different, such as coins, for example. In the first section we discuss the case of objects all different, with boxes also different; in the second section, the case of objects all different with boxes alike; in the third section, objects some alike and some different, with boxes different.

8.1 Objects Different, Boxes Different

If m objects, no two alike, are to be distributed in k boxes, no two alike, the number of ways this can be done is k^m since there are k alternatives for the disposal of the first object, k alternatives for the disposal of the second, and so on.

But now suppose the additional requirement that there be no empty box is imposed; that is, we are to count only those distributions in which each box receives at least one object. Of course we must now have at least as many objects as boxes, $m > k$; otherwise no such distribution can be made. Let $f(m, k)$ denote the number of ways of putting m different objects into k different boxes, with no box empty. For example, $f(3, 2) = 6$. For convenience we define $f(m, k) = 0$ if $m < k$.

We derive a formula for $f(m, k)$ by using the inclusion-exclusion principle of Chapter 5. The method is illustrated by the computation of $f(m, 7)$. Consider the total number of arrangements, 7^m, of m different objects in seven different boxes. Say that such an arrangement has property α in case the first box is empty, property β in case the second box is empty, and similarly properties γ, δ, ϵ, ζ, η for the other five boxes respectively. To find the number of distributions with no box empty, we simply count the number of distributions having none of the properties α, β, γ, etc. We can apply formula (5.6) of page 74 because of the symmetry of the seven properties. Here $N = 7^m$ is the total number of distributions. By $N(\alpha)$ we mean the number of distributions with the first box empty, and so $N(\alpha) = 6^m$. Similarly, $N(\alpha, \beta)$ is the number of distributions with the first two boxes empty. But this is the same as the number of distributions into five boxes, and hence $N(\alpha, \beta) = 5^m$. Thus we can write

$$N = 7^m, \quad N(\alpha) = 6^m, \quad N(\alpha, \beta) = 5^m, \quad N(\alpha, \beta, \gamma) = 4^m,$$

$$N(\alpha, \beta, \gamma, \delta) = 3^m, \quad N(\alpha, \beta, \gamma, \delta, \epsilon) = 2^m$$

$$N(\alpha, \beta, \gamma, \delta, \epsilon, \zeta) = 1^m, \quad N(\alpha, \beta, \gamma, \delta, \epsilon, \zeta, \eta) = 0.$$

Applying formula (5.6) of page 74 with $r = 7$ we get

$$f(m, 7) = 7^m - C(7, 1)6^m + C(7, 2)5^m - C(7, 3)4^m$$
$$+ C(7, 4)3^m - C(7, 5)2^m + C(7, 6)1^m.$$

By a direct generalization of this with k in place of 7, we see that

(8.1)
$$f(m, k) = k^m - C(k, 1)(k - 1)^m + C(k, 2)(k - 2)^m$$
$$- C(k, 3)(k - 3)^m + \cdots + (-1)^{k-1}C(k, k - 1)1^m.$$

If $m < k$ then $f(m, k) = 0$. In such cases formula (8.1) can be used to give identities about $C(n, r)$. For example, if $m = 6$ and $k = 7$, then (8.1) tells us that

$$7^6 - C(7, 1)6^6 + C(7, 2)5^6 - C(7, 3)4^6 + C(7, 4)3^6$$
$$- C(7, 5)2^6 + C(7, 6)1^6 = 0.$$

Problem Set 27

1. Find the number of distributions of five different objects in three different boxes, with no box empty.

2. Find the value of $f(5, 2)$.

3. It is stated in the text that $f(3, 2) = 6$. Verify this both by an actual count of the cases, and by use of formula (8.1).

4. In how many ways is it possible to distribute k distinct objects in k distinct boxes with no box empty? Answer this question in two ways, namely by direct consideration and by use of formula (8.1), and derive an identity.

5. Prove that if m is any positive integer less than 8,

$$8^m - C(8, 1)7^m + C(8, 2)6^m - C(8, 3)5^m + C(8, 4)4^m$$
$$- C(8, 5)3^m + C(8, 6)2^m - C(8, 7) = 0.$$

8.2   Objects Different, Boxes Alike (Partitions of a Set)

If a set contains m elements, it is always presumed as part of the meaning of the word "set" that the elements are different from one another. Thus the number of ways that m different objects can be put into k like boxes is the same as the number of partitions of a set of m elements into k subsets. Note that nothing is said about the number of elements in the k subsets. However, in some problems it will be specified that the subsets are non-empty.

Let $G(m, k)$ denote the number of distributions of m different things into k like boxes, i.e., boxes that are not ordered, and cannot be distinguished in any way. To say it another way, $G(m, k)$ is the number of separations of m different objects into k or fewer batches; we include the words "or fewer" because one or more of the batches may be empty. For example, consider $G(3, 2)$. Denoting the three objects by $A, B,$ and $C,$ we see that there are four cases:

(8.2)

$A, B,$ and C in one box, nothing in the other;

A in one box, B and C in the other;

B in one box, A and C in the other;

C in one box, A and B in the other.

Thus $G(3, 2) = 4$.

Now let $g(m, k)$ denote the number of distributions of m different objects in k like boxes, *with no box empty*. Thus $g(m, k)$ is the number of ways of separating m different objects into k non-empty batches, or the number of ways of separating a set of m things into k non-empty subsets. Looking at the cases listed as (8.2) we see that

$$g(3, 1) = 1 \quad \text{and} \quad g(3, 2) = 3.$$

In general, we can separate the $G(m, k)$ distributions into those where no box is empty, those where exactly one box is empty, those where exactly two boxes are empty, and so on, to get

(8.3)
$$G(m, k) = g(m, k) + g(m, k - 1) + g(m, k - 2)$$
$$+ g(m, k - 3) + \cdots + g(m, 1).$$

Next we derive a formula for $g(m, k)$. There is a simple relationship between $g(m, k)$ and $f(m, k)$; it parallels the relationship between combinations and permutations in the elementary theory. To see this, consider any distribution counted by $g(m, k)$; since there are $k!$ ways of numbering the k boxes to change them from like to unlike boxes, each distribution gives rise to $k!$ distributions of the $f(m, k)$ type. It follows that

$$f(m, k) = g(m, k) \cdot k! \qquad \text{or} \qquad g(m, k) = f(m, k)/k!$$

In view of equation (8.1) of the preceding section, this last equation can be rewritten in the form

(8.4)
$$g(m, k) = \frac{1}{k!} [k^m - C(k, 1)(k - 1)^m + C(k, 2)(k - 2)^m$$
$$- \cdots + (-1)^{k-1} C(k, k - 1)1^m].$$

It is an easy matter to determine the value of $g(m, k)$ by (8.4), and then to determine $G(m, k)$ by (8.3). Also, since formula (8.4) gives the number of partitions of a set of m elements into k nonempty subsets, the total number of partitions of a set of m elements can be obtained by adding the values of $g(m, k)$ for all the appropriate values of k, namely $k = 1$, $k = 2$, $\cdots$, $k = m$. Thus the total number of partitions of a set of m elements is

$$g(m, 1) + g(m, 2) + g(m, 3) + \cdots + g(m, m),$$

where each term of this sum can be evaluated by use of (8.4).

Problem Set 28

1. In how many ways is it possible to separate the nine letters $a, b, c, d, e,$ f, g, h, i into three non-empty batches?

2. If we separate four distinct objects into four non-empty batches, it is clear that there is just one way to do it. Check that formula (8.4) gives this result.

3. In how many ways is it possible to separate m distinct objects into two non-empty batches?

4. In how many ways is it possible to factor the number 30,030 into three positive integer factors (a) if 1 is allowed as a factor, (b) if each factor must be greater than 1? (Order does not count: $30 \cdot 77 \cdot 13$ is the same factoring as $13 \cdot 30 \cdot 77$.)

5. Find the total number of ways of partitioning a set of five (distinct) elements.

6. Without using the formulas of the text, establish from the meaning of the symbolism that $g(m, m) = 1$. Hence prove the identity

$$m! = m^m - C(m, 1)(m - 1)^m + C(m, 2)(m - 2)^m$$
$$- C(m, 3)(m - 3)^m + \cdots + (-1)^{m-1}C(m, m-1)(1)^m.$$

7. Without using the formulas of the text, establish that

$$g(m, m - 1) = C(m, 2).$$

Then use a similar kind of analysis to evaluate $g(m, m - 2)$.

8.3   Objects Mixed, Boxes Different

Consider several different objects, each of which may be in more than one copy; for example, a collection of stamps, or of books. Let there be a copies of the first object, b copies of the second, c of the third, and so on. Let the total number of objects be n, so that

(8.5) $a + b + c + \cdots = n.$

These objects are to be distributed into several unlike boxes as follows: α objects into the first box, β into the second box, γ into the third box, and so on. Each distribution into the boxes will use up all the objects, so that the sum of α, β, γ and so on is n:

$$(8.6) \qquad \alpha + \beta + \gamma + \cdots = n.$$

We shall use the symbolism†

$$(8.7) \qquad [a, \ b, \ c, \ \cdots \ \| \ \alpha, \beta, \gamma, \ \cdots]$$

to denote the number of distributions of the objects in the boxes, as specified. As an example, we consider the notation $[1, \ 2, \ 2 \ \| \ 2, \ 3]$, where $n = 5$. One way to visualize the five objects is to think of colored balls, say one red ball, two blue balls, and two white balls. The two blue balls are identical; the two white balls are identical. The problem is to find the number of ways of putting two of the balls into the first box, and three into the second box. It is not difficult to verify that there are five ways of doing this, that is,

$$[1, \ 2, \ 2 \ \| \ 2, \ 3] \ = \ 5.$$

We shall not derive any general formula for the number of distributions denoted by (8.7). The problem of this distribution number is rather difficult, and so we shall analyze some special cases only. First we examine two basic properties of the distribution number (8.7). One property is that the order of the terms on either side of the vertical separator is immaterial. For example,

$$[1, \ 2, \ 2 \ \| \ 2, \ 3] \ = \ [2, \ 1, \ 2 \ \| \ 2, \ 3] \ = \ [2, \ 2, \ 1 \ \| \ 3, \ 2].$$

The second, less obvious, property is that the two sides can be interchanged, as in the examples

$$[1, \ 2, \ 2 \ \| \ 2, \ 3] \ = \ [2, \ 3 \ \| \ 1, \ 2, \ 2],$$
$$(8.8) \qquad [4, \ 5, \ 6 \ \| \ 2, \ 2, \ 3, \ 8] \ = \ [2, \ 2, \ 3, \ 8 \ \| \ 4, \ 5, \ 6].$$

† Adapted from H. Rademacher and O. Toeplitz, *The Enjoyment of Mathematics*, Princeton, 1957, with permission.

We now establish the validity of the second statement, i.e., of equation (8.8). The notation [4, 5, 6 ⫴ 2, 2, 3, 8] means the number of ways of putting 4 red balls, 5 blue balls, and 6 white balls into 4 boxes, with 2 balls in the first box, 2 in the second box, 3 in the third box, and 8 in the fourth box. The balls are distinguishable only by color. In any distribution we shall denote by x_1 the number of red balls put into the first box, and similarly by x_2, x_3, x_4 the numbers of red balls put into the second, third, and fourth boxes respectively. In the same way, let y_1, y_2, y_3, y_4 denote the numbers of blue balls put into the boxes, and z_1, z_2, z_3, z_4 the number of white balls. Then the notation [4, 5, 6 ⫴ 2, 2, 3, 8] can be interpreted as the number of solutions in non-negative integers of the system of equations

$$(8.9) \quad \begin{aligned} x_1 + x_2 + x_3 + x_4 &= 4 & x_1 + y_1 + z_1 &= 2 \\ y_1 + y_2 + y_3 + y_4 &= 5 & x_2 + y_2 + z_2 &= 2 \\ z_1 + z_2 + z_3 + z_4 &= 6 & x_3 + y_3 + z_3 &= 3 \\ & & x_4 + y_4 + z_4 &= 8 \end{aligned}$$

Now let us consider the right hand side of equation (8.8). The symbolism [2, 2, 3, 8 ⫴ 4, 5, 6] denotes the number of ways of putting 2 green balls, 2 orange balls, 3 yellow balls, and 8 black balls into 3 boxes with 4 balls in the first box, 5 balls in the second box, and 6 balls in the third box. Let t_1, t_2, t_3 denote the numbers of green balls put in the first, second and third boxes respectively, in any distribution. Similarly, let u_1, u_2, u_3 denote the numbers of orange balls, v_1, v_2, v_3 the numbers of yellow balls, and w_1, w_2, w_3 the numbers of black balls, put in the first, second and third boxes respectively. Then the notation [2, 2, 3, 8 ⫴ 4, 5, 6] can be interpreted to mean the number of solutions in non-negative integers of the system of equations

$$(8.10) \quad \begin{aligned} t_1 + t_2 + t_3 &= 2 & t_1 + u_1 + v_1 + w_1 &= 4 \\ u_1 + u_2 + u_3 &= 2 & t_2 + u_2 + v_2 + w_2 &= 5 \\ v_1 + v_2 + v_3 &= 3 & t_3 + u_3 + v_3 + w_3 &= 6 \\ w_1 + w_2 + w_3 &= 8 & & \end{aligned}$$

To see that the system of equations (8.10) is the same as the system of equations (8.9), let

$$t_1 = x_1 \qquad u_1 = x_2, \qquad v_1 = x_3, \qquad w_1 = x_4,$$

$$t_2 = y_1, \qquad u_2 = y_2, \qquad v_2 = y_3, \qquad w_2 = y_4,$$

$$t_3 = z_1, \qquad u_3 = z_2, \qquad v_3 = z_3, \qquad w_3 = z_4.$$

This shows that (8.8) holds. A similar argument with more elaborate systems of equations can be used to prove that

(8.11) $\quad [a, b, c, \cdots \| \alpha, \beta, \gamma, \cdots] = [\alpha, \beta, \gamma, \cdots \| a, b, c, \cdots]$

for any integers satisfying $a + b + c + \cdots = \alpha + \beta + \gamma + \cdots = n$. A result of this type in mathematics is called a *duality* principle.

As a special case of (8.11), consider the situation where $\alpha = 1$, $\beta = 1$, $\gamma = 1$ and so on:

(8.12) $\quad [a, b, c, \cdots \| 1, 1, 1, \cdots, 1] = [1, 1, 1, \cdots, 1 \| a, b, c, \cdots];$

here each block of 1's has n terms, and $a + b + c + \cdots = n$. The notation on the left of (8.12) can be interpreted to mean the number of permutations of n things taken all at a time, where a of the things are alike, another b alike, another c alike, and so on. The number of such permutations, as given in the summary of Chapter 3, is

(8.13) $$\frac{n!}{a!b!c! \cdots}.$$

Now we can assert that the right member of (8.12) also has the value (8.13). Thus (8.13) is the number of ways of distributing n distinct things in boxes with a in the first box, b in the second box, c in the third box, and so on.

Problem Set 29

1. Find the numerical values of the following:

(a) $[1, 1, 1, 1 \| 1, 1, 1, 1]$

   (b) $[1, 1, 1, 1, 1, 1, 1, 1, 1 \, \| \, 4, 5]$

   (c) $[1, 1, 1, 1, 1, 1, 1, 1, 1, 1 \, \| \, 1, 1, 1, 1, 1, 1, 4]$

   (d) $[30, 10 \, \| \, 10, 10, 10, 10]$

   (e) $[2, 1, 1 \, \| \, 2, 1, 1]$

   (f) $[2, 2, 2 \, \| \, 2, 2, 2]$

   (g) $[4, 4, 4 \, \| \, 6, 6]$

2. Express each of the following in the notation of previous chapters:

   (a) $[1, 1, 1, \cdots, 1 \, \| \, 1, 1, 1, \cdots, 1]$, with n ones on each side of the separator;

   (b) $[1, 1, 1, \cdots, 1 \, \| \, 1, 1, 1, \cdots, 1, n - r \,]$, with n ones to the left of the separator, and r ones to the right;

   (c) $[1, 1, 1, \cdots, 1 \, \| \, r, n - r \,]$, with n ones to the left of the separator;

   (d) $[a_1, a_2, a_3, \cdots, a_k \, \| \, r, n - r \,]$, where

$$a_1 + a_2 + a_3 + \cdots + a_k = n$$

and each of the a's is not less than r.

3. Evaluate $[2, 1, 1, 1, \cdots, 1 \, \| \, 2, 1, 1, 1, \cdots, 1 \,]$, with k ones on each side of the separator.

8.4 Summary

The number of distributions of m different objects in k different boxes is k^m. If no box is to be empty, the notation $f(m, k)$ is used for the number of distributions, with $f(m, k) = 0$ in case $m < k$. It was shown that

$$f(m, k) = k^m - C(k, 1)(k - 1)^m + C(k, 2)(k - 2)^m$$

$$- C(k, 3)(k - 3)^m + \cdots + (-1)^{k-1}C(k, k - 1)1^m.$$

If we have m different objects and k boxes that are indistinguishable from each other, the notation $G(m, k)$ is used for the total number of distributions of the objects in the boxes, and $g(m, k)$ for the number of distributions with no box empty. It is proved that

$$g(m, k) = f(m, k)/k!$$

and

$$G(m, k) = g(m, k) + g(m, k - 1) + g(m, k - 2) + \cdots + g(m, 1).$$

Another interpretation of $G(m, k)$ is the number of partitions of a set of m (distinct) elements into k (unordered) subsets; note that there is no restriction on the number of elements in the subsets. However, if the k subsets are required to be non-empty, the number of partitions of the set is $g(m, k)$. The total number of ways of partitioning a set of m (distinct) elements is $G(m, m)$. To evaluate this for any specific value of m, we use the result

$$G(m, m) = g(m, m) + g(m, m-1) + g(m, m-2) + \cdots + g(m, 1),$$

together with $g(m, k) = f(m, k)/k!$ and the formula above for $f(m, k)$.

Let $a, b, c, \cdots$ and $\alpha, \beta, \gamma, \cdots$ be two sets of positive integers having the same sum n:

$$a + b + c + \cdots = n, \qquad \alpha + \beta + \gamma + \cdots = n.$$

Let there be n objects of which a are alike, another b are alike, another c are alike, and so on. The number of distributions of these objects into boxes, with α objects in the first box, β objects in the second box, γ objects in the third box, etc., is denoted by $[a, b, c, \cdots \| \alpha, \beta, \gamma, \cdots]$. It was shown that

$$[a, b, c, \cdots \| \alpha, \beta, \gamma, \cdots] = [\alpha, \beta, \gamma, \cdots \| a, b, c, \cdots].$$

CHAPTER NINE

Configuration Problems

The questions discussed in this chapter are related to geometric patterns or configurations of one kind or another. We begin with a concept which is widely used throughout mathematics—the pigeonhole principle.

9.1 The Pigeonhole Principle

If eight pigeons fly into seven pigeonholes, at least one of the pigeon holes will contain two or more pigeons. More generally, if $n + 1$ pigeons are in n pigeon holes, at least one of the holes contains two or more pigeons.

This simple form of the pigeonhole principle can be generalized as follows: If $2n + 1$ pigeons are in n pigeonholes at least one of the holes contains three or more pigeons. Here is an even stronger statement that includes all the preceding assertions as special cases: If $kn + 1$ pigeons are in n pigeonholes, at least one of the holes contains $k + 1$ or more pigeons.

It is not difficult to prove this; for, if it were not so, then every hole would contain k or fewer pigeons. Thus there would be n holes with k or fewer pigeons in each hole, and so a total of at most nk pigeons could be accommodated. But this is a contradiction because there are $kn + 1$ pigeons in all. Hence we have established the result by an indirect proof.

Problem Set 30

1. Given the information that no human being has more than 300,000 hairs on his head, and that New York City, by a recent census, has a population of 7,781,984, observe that there are at least two persons in New York with the same number of hairs on their heads. What is the largest integer that can be used for n in the following assertion? There are n persons in New York with the same number of hairs on their heads.

2. Assume the information that at least one of a_1 and b_1 has a certain property P, and at least one of a_2 and b_2 has property P, and at least one of a_3 and b_3 has property P. Prove that at least two of a_1, a_2, a_3 or at least two of b_1, b_2, b_3 have property P.

3. Assume the same information as in the preceding question, and also that at least one of a_4 and b_4 has property P, and at least one of a_5 and b_5 has property P. Prove that at least three of a_1, a_2, a_3, a_4, a_5 or at least three of b_1, b_2, b_3, b_4, b_5 have property P.

4. Assume that at least one of a_1, b_1, c_1 has property Q, and likewise for a_2, b_2, c_2, and likewise for $a_3, b_3, c_3, \cdots$, and likewise for a_{10}, b_{10}, c_{10}. What is the largest integer that can be used for k to make the following assertion correct? At least k of $a_1, a_2, a_3, \cdots, a_{10}$, or at least k of $b_1, b_2, b_3, \cdots, b_{10}$, or at least k of $c_1, c_2, c_3, \cdots, c_{10}$, have property Q.

5. Assume that at least two of a_1, b_1, c_1 have property T, and likewise for $a_2, b_2, c_2, \cdots$, and likewise for a_5, b_5, c_5. What is the largest integer that can be used for r to make the following assertion correct? At least r of a_1, a_2, a_3, a_4, a_5, or at least r of b_1, b_2, b_3, b_4, b_5, or at least r of c_1, c_2, c_3, c_4, c_5 have property T.

9.2 Chromatic Triangles

Consider six points in a plane, no three of which are collinear (on a straight line). There are $C(6, 2)$ or fifteen line segments connecting the points. Let these fifteen segments be colored in any way by the use of two colors, say red and white; all the segments may be red, all may be white, or some may be red and the rest white. Say that any triangle connecting three of the points is *chromatic* if its sides have the same color.

We shall prove that no matter how the fifteen line segments are colored, it is always possible to find a chromatic triangle. It is a property of the number 6 that 6 is the smallest number of points in the plane (no three collinear) such that, no matter how each of the segments joining pairs of points is colored in one of two colors, it is always possible to find a chromatic triangle.

Proof that it is always possible to find a chromatic triangle: Take any one of the six points, say A, and consider the five segments AB, AC, AD, AE, AF emanating from A. (See Figure 9.1.) By the pigeonhole principle, at least three of these five segments must have the same color. There is no loss of generality in presuming that the three segments having the same color are AB, AC, and AD. (In Figure 9.1, where one color is indicated by dashed lines, the other by solid lines, it is actually AB, AC, and AE that have the same color. But since we can interchange the letters on the points B, C, D, E, and F —in the case illustrated we would interchange the labels on the points D and E —we can always fix it so that the segments AB, AC, and AD have the same color.)

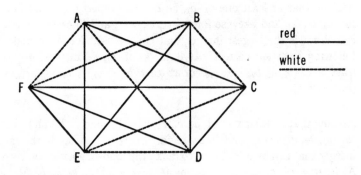

Figure 9.1

Next, there is no loss of generality in presuming that the three segments AB, AC, and AD are red. For if they were white, we would simply reverse the color of every one of the fifteen line segments with no effect on the existence of a chromatic triangle: any red chromatic triangle would become a white chromatic triangle, and vice versa; furthermore, no new chromatic triangles would be created in the process.

We now take the three red segments, AB, AC, and AD emanating from A and consider the triangle BCD formed by their endpoints. There are two possibilities: either all three sides of BCD are white, or it has at least one red side. If all three sides of BCD are white, then BCD is a chromatic triangle. On the other hand, if at least one side of triangle BCD is red, then this red side together with the appropriate two of the three red segments AB, AC, and AD, forms a red chromatic triangle. In full detail, if BC is red, then ABC is a chromatic triangle; if BD is red, then ABD is a chromatic triangle; if CD is red, then ACD is a chromatic triangle. This completes the proof.

We note two other ways of stating the same principle. Among any six persons, it is possible to find three who are mutually acquainted, or it is possible to find three no two of whom are acquainted. Among any six persons, it is possible to find three each of whom has shaken hands with the other two, or it is possible to find three no two of whom have shaken hands.

Problem Set 31

1. Prove that 6 is the smallest number of points having the chromatic triangle property; that is, exhibit 5 points in the plane, no 3 collinear, with each of the 10 line segments joining pairs of points colored in one of two colors, either red or white, in such a way that the configuration has no chromatic triangle. (Note that if 5 such points are exhibited, this implies that 6 is the smallest number.)

2. Consider 17 points in the plane, no 3 collinear, with each of the segments joining the points colored red, white, or blue. Prove that there is a chromatic triangle no matter what color pattern is present. (The reader might wish to solve the analogous problem for an integer

larger than 17. The number 17 is the smallest that can be used in this problem, in the sense that the proposition is not true for 16 or fewer points. However the proof that 17 is the smallest, given by R. E. Greenwood and A. M. Gleason in 1955, is beyond the scope of this book.)

Additional problems on chromatic triangles are included in the Miscellaneous Problems following Chapter 11.

9.3   Separations of the Plane

Consider n straight lines in a plane satisfying the following conditions: (1) each line is infinite in extent in both directions; (2) no two lines are parallel; (3) no three lines are concurrent, i.e. no three lines meet in a point. Into how many regions is the plane separated by the n lines? Let $f(n)$ denote the number of regions into which n such lines separate the plane; we find, by simple observation, that $f(1)=2$, $f(2)=4$, $f(3)=7$ (see Figure 9.2). The problem is to evaluate $f(n)$ in the general case.

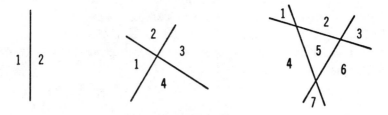

Figure 9.2

To solve this problem we employ a technique which has already been used in Section 3.8. It consists in finding expressions for the differences $f(k) - f(k-1)$ for $k = 2, 3, \cdots, n$ and adding them. Their sum is just $f(n) - f(1)$ since each intermediate term is subtracted and then added. Such a sum is often called a "telescoping" sum. To find the appropriate expressions in this case, consider $n-1$ straight lines in the plane that separate it into $f(n-1)$ regions. Now introduce the n-th line. Far out on the line—farther out than any intersection point—this n-th line is dividing a region in two. Then, if we move along the line, we observe that whenever this n-th line crosses one of the other lines, it splits another region in two. For example, let $n = 4$; if we move along the fourth line in Figure 9.3 from left to right, we see that it splits region "4", and then successively regions "5", "6", and "3" as it crosses the three other lines. Thus the fourth line creates four new regions. By the same reasoning we conclude that the n-th line creates n new regions, and we express this fact by the equation $f(n) = n + f(n - 1)$, or

(9.1) $$f(n) - f(n - 1) = n.$$

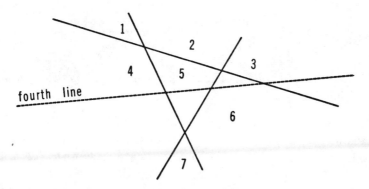

Figure 9.3

Now we apply the method of the "telescoping" sum; that is, we write equation (9.1) followed by its counterparts with n replaced successively by $n - 1$, $n - 2$, $\cdots$, 3, 2:

$$f(n) - f(n - 1) = n,$$
$$f(n - 1) - f(n - 2) = n - 1,$$
$$f(n - 2) - f(n - 3) = n - 2,$$
$$\cdots \cdots$$
$$f(3) - f(2) = 3,$$
$$f(2) - f(1) = 2.$$

When these equations are added, the sum of all the left members is simply $f(n) - f(1)$. Thus we have

$$f(n) - f(1) = 2 + 3 + \cdots + (n - 2) + (n - 1) + n.$$

The right side of this equation is the sum of the natural numbers from 2 to n. Now by Section 3.8 the sum of the natural numbers from 1 to n is $n(n + 1)/2$, and so

$$f(n) - f(1) = \frac{n(n + 1)}{2} - 1.$$

Next we replace $f(1)$ by its known value, 2, and add 2 to both sides of our equation to obtain the final solution,

(9.2) $$f(n) = \frac{n(n + 1)}{2} + 1 = \frac{n^2 + n + 2}{2}.$$

As another illustration of the "telescoping sum" method, consider the following

PROBLEM: Let there be $n + k$ lines in the plane satisfying these conditions: (1) k of the lines are parallel to each other; (2) there are no other cases of parallel lines; (3) no three of the $n + k$ lines are concurrent. Into how many regions is the plane separated by the $n + k$ lines?

SOLUTION: Let $G(n, k)$ denote the number of regions of separation. For example, $G(1, 2) = 6$ and $G(2, 2) = 10$. The argument leading to equation (9.1) can be modified to get a similar kind of equation in this case; that is, we study the effect of introducing the k-th parallel line, thus changing the number of regions of separation from $G(n, k - 1)$ to $G(n, k)$. The k-th parallel line crosses n lines, and so creates $n + 1$ new regions. Thus

$$G(n, k) = n + 1 + G(n, k - 1),$$

or

(9.3) $$G(n, k) - G(n, k - 1) = n + 1.$$

Again we write this equation followed by its counterparts with k replaced successively by $k - 1$, $k - 2$, $\cdots$, 2, 1:

$$G(n, k) - G(n, k - 1) = n + 1,$$

$$G(n, k - 1) - G(n, k - 2) = n + 1,$$

$$G(n, k - 2) - G(n, k - 3) = n + 1,$$

$$\cdots \cdots \cdots \cdots$$

$$G(n, 3) - G(n, 2) = n + 1,$$

$$G(n, 2) - G(n, 1) = n + 1,$$

$$G(n, 1) - G(n, 0) = n + 1.$$

Here we have k equations, each having the right member $n + 1$. When we add these equations, the sum of the right members is $k(n + 1)$, and the sum of the left members is $G(n, k) - G(n, 0)$, so

$$G(n, k) - G(n, 0) = k(n + 1).$$

The symbol $G(n, 0)$ denotes the number of regions created by n lines none of which are parallel and no three of which are concurrent; this number is the same as $f(n)$ in the preceding problem, and hence we can use equation (9.2) to get

$$G(n, k) - \frac{n^2 + n + 2}{2} = k(n + 1),$$

or

$$G(n, k) = \frac{n^2 + 2nk + n + 2k + 2}{2}.$$

Problem Set 32

1. Consider n straight lines in the plane, no two of which are parallel. However, three of the lines, and only three, are concurrent. Into how many regions is the plane separated?

2. A set of k parallel lines in the plane is intersected by another set of m parallel lines. Into how many regions is the plane separated?

3. In the preceding question, introduce another line, parallel to no previous line, and passing through none of the mk previous intersection points. Into how many regions is the plane separated?

4. Let there be $q + t$ straight lines in the plane satisfying the following conditions: no two lines are parallel; q of the lines pass through a certain point A; t of the lines pass through another point B; no line passes through both A and B. Into how many regions is the plane separated?

5. Let there be $k + q$ straight lines in the plane satisfying the following conditions: k of the lines are parallel to each other; there are no other cases of parallel lines; q of the lines, but none of the k parallel lines, pass through a certain point A. Into how many regions is the plane separated?

6. In addition to the $k + q$ lines in the preceding question, let there be introduced n more straight lines in the plane, such that there are no other cases of parallelism beyond the k parallel lines, and no further cases of concurrency beyond the q lines intersecting at the point A. Into how many regions is the plane separated?

9.4 Summary

The pigeonhole principle, in its simplest form, states that if $n + 1$ pigeons are in n holes, then at least one of the holes contains two or more pigeons. More generally, if $kn + 1$ pigeons are in n holes, then at least one of the holes contains $k + 1$ or more pigeons.

This principle is applied to prove that, given six points in the plane, no three collinear, if each of the 15 line segments joining pairs of points is colored with one of two colors, then there is a chromatic triangle present for every possible color pattern. By "chromatic triangle" is meant one whose three sides are of the same color.

The "telescoping sum" method is used to prove that a plane is separated into $\frac{1}{2}(n^2 + n + 2)$ regions by n straight lines satisfying the conditions (a) no two lines are parallel, and (b) no three lines are concurrent. A somewhat more general situation is handled by the same method and further generalizations are indicated in the problems.

CHAPTER TEN

Mathematical Induction

Consider the sums of the odd integers:

(10.1)

$$1 = 1$$
$$1 + 3 = 4$$
$$1 + 3 + 5 = 9$$
$$1 + 3 + 5 + 7 = 16$$
$$1 + 3 + 5 + 7 + 9 = 25$$
$$1 + 3 + 5 + 7 + 9 + 11 = 36$$

A clear pattern emerges in the sums 1, 4, 9, 16, 25, 36; they are the squares of the natural numbers 1, 2, 3, 4, 5, 6. These equations suggest the general proposition that the sum of the first n odd positive integers is equal to n^2, or, stated in symbols,

(10.2) $$1 + 3 + 5 + 7 + \cdots + (2n - 1) = n^2.$$

Of course the verification of the first few cases in equations (10.1) does not in any way guarantee that the general formula (10.2) is correct for every positive integer n. Perhaps the easiest way to prove formula (10.2), which is valid for every positive integer n, is to use mathematical induction.

10.1   The Principle of Mathematical Induction

Let us use the symbol P_n to denote equation (10.2). To every positive integer n there corresponds an equation of the form (10.2); for example, the equations listed in (10.1) are of this form, and we designate them by P_1, P_2, P_3, P_4, P_5, P_6. Moreover, we can tell by actual calculation that all six statements of equality are true. The assertion "P_n is true for every positive integer n" actually comprises the infinitely many assertions "P_1 is true, P_2 is true, P_3 is true, $\cdots$". So far, we have seen only that P_1, P_2, $\cdots$, P_6 are true and we want to establish the truth of all (infinitely many) of these propositions. *The principle of mathematical induction states that we can establish the truth of any such infinite sequence of propositions if we can prove two results:*

  (i) *that P_1 is true;*

  (ii) *that P_{k+1} follows from P_k for every positive integer k.*

Other ways of stating (ii) are that "P_k implies P_{k+1}" and "P_{k+1} is implied by P_k".

The idea is that if we can prove (ii), that P_k implies P_{k+1}, then we can conclude

$$P_1 \text{ implies } P_2,$$
$$P_2 \text{ implies } P_3,$$
$$P_3 \text{ implies } P_4,$$
$$P_4 \text{ implies } P_5,$$

and so on. So if we prove (i) we will have a start on this chain, and the truth of P_2, P_3, P_4, P_5, and so on, will follow by (ii) from the truth of P_1.

Let us return to the special case where the proposition P_n is the equation (10.2). There is no difficulty with (i), since P_1 is simply $1 = 1$. To prove (ii), we must show that

$$P_k: \quad 1 + 3 + 5 + 7 + \cdots + (2k - 1) \; = \; k^2$$

implies:

$$P_{k+1}: \quad 1 + 3 + 5 + 7 + \cdots + (2k - 1) + (2k + 1) \; = \; (k + 1)^2;$$

that is, we are to assume P_k and prove that P_{k+1} follows as a consequence. Assuming the proposition P_k, let us add $2k + 1$ to both sides of the equation:

$$1 + 3 + 5 + 7 + \cdots + (2k - 1) + (2k + 1) = k^2 + (2k + 1)$$
$$= k^2 + 2k + 1$$
$$= (k + 1)^2.$$

Thus P_{k+1} follows from P_k, and we have proved the validity of equation (10.2) for all positive integers n.

As a second illustration, consider the sums of the cubes of the natural numbers:

(10.3)
$$1^3 = 1,$$
$$1^3 + 2^3 = 9,$$
$$1^3 + 2^3 + 3^3 = 36,$$
$$1^3 + 2^3 + 3^3 + 4^3 = 100,$$
$$1^3 + 2^3 + 3^3 + 4^3 + 5^3 = 225,$$
$$1^3 + 2^3 + 3^3 + 4^3 + 5^3 + 6^3 = 441.$$

The numbers 1, 9, 36, 100, 225, 441 on the right sides of these equations are all squares, namely the squares of 1, 3, 6, 10, 15, 21. If we look at Pascal's triangle on page 41 we note that these numbers are in the third vertical column, and so can be written, in terms of combination symbols, as

$$C(2, 2), \quad C(3, 2), \quad C(4, 2), \quad C(5, 2), \quad C(6, 2), \quad C(7, 2).$$

Might it be that $C(n + 1, 2)$ is the appropriate number whose square is the sum of the cubes of the natural numbers from 1 to n? Since

$$C(n + 1, 2) = \tfrac{1}{2}n(n + 1),$$

this conjecture may be expressed by

(10.4)
$$1^3 + 2^3 + 3^3 + 4^3 + \cdots + n^3 = [C(n + 1, 2)]^2$$
$$= \tfrac{1}{4}n^2(n + 1)^2.$$

Let us now regard (10.4) as the proposition P_n, or rather as the infinite collection of propositions, one for $n = 1$, a second for $n = 2$, a third for $n = 3$, and so on; then equations (10.3) are the propositions P_1, P_2, P_3, P_4, P_5, P_6. To prove P_n by mathematical induction, we must establish (i) that P_1 is true, and (ii) that P_k implies P_{k+1} for every positive integer k. Now P_1, the first of equations (10.3), simply states that $1^3 = 1$, and this is clearly true.

Before proving (ii), let us write out P_k and P_{k+1} in full, by replacing n by k, and then n by $k + 1$ in (10.4),

$$P_k: \quad 1^3 + 2^3 + 3^3 + 4^3 + \cdots + k^3 = \tfrac{1}{4}k^2(k + 1)^2;$$

$$P_{k+1}: \quad 1^3 + 2^3 + 3^3 + 4^3 + \cdots + k^3 + (k + 1)^3$$
$$= \tfrac{1}{4}(k + 1)^2(k + 2)^2.$$

We are to assume P_k and establish P_{k+1}. Adding $(k + 1)^3$ to both sides of the equation P_k, we obtain

$$1^3 + 2^3 + 3^3 + 4^3 + \cdots + k^3 + (k + 1)^3 = \tfrac{1}{4}k^2(k + 1)^2 + (k + 1)^3.$$

The question is whether this is the same as P_{k+1}. Using basic algebra we shall see that it is. P_{k+1}.

$$\tfrac{1}{4}k^2(k + 1)^2 + (k + 1)^3 = (k + 1)^2[\tfrac{1}{4}k^2 + (k + 1)]$$
$$= (k + 1)^2\left[\frac{k^2 + 4k + 4}{4}\right]$$
$$= \tfrac{1}{4}(k + 1)^2(k + 2)^2,$$

and so the proof of (10.4) is complete.

Problem Set 33

1. Prove that $1 + 2 + 3 + 4 + \cdots + n = \tfrac{1}{2}n(n + 1)$ by mathematical induction.

2. Prove that $1^2 + 2^2 + 3^2 + 4^2 + \cdots + n^2 = n(n + 1)(2n + 1)/6$ by mathematical induction.

3. Let $K(n)$ denote the number of unordered pairs of integers selected from $1, 2, 3, \cdots, n$, subject to the restriction that no pair is consecutive. For example, $K(5)$ is the count of the pairs

$$1, 3 \quad 1, 4 \quad 1, 5 \quad 2, 4 \quad 2, 5 \quad 3, 5$$

and so $K(5) = 6$. By such counting it can be determined that

$$K(3) = 1 \quad K(4) = 3 \quad K(5) = 6$$
$$K(6) = 10 \quad K(7) = 15 \quad K(8) = 21.$$

Make a conjecture about $K(n)$ from this information, and, if possible, prove your conjecture by mathematical induction.

4. Some of the following equations hold for all positive integers n. Try to establish each by mathematical induction.

(a) $1 + 4 + 7 + 10 + \cdots + (3n - 2) = n^2 + n - 1$;

(b) $1 \cdot 2 + 2 \cdot 3 + 3 \cdot 4 + \cdots + n(n + 1) = (n^3 + 3n^2 + 2n)/3$;

(c) $1^2 + 3^2 + 5^2 + \cdots + (2n - 1)^2 = (4n^3 - n)/3$;

(d) $1 \cdot 3 + 3 \cdot 5 + 5 \cdot 7 + \cdots + (2n - 1)(2n + 1)$
$$= (5n^3 + 10n - 6)/3;$$

(e) $1 \cdot 2 + 3 \cdot 3 + 5 \cdot 4 + 7 \cdot 5 + \cdots + (2n - 1)(n + 1)$
$$= (n^3 + 5n^2 - 4n + 2)/2;$$

(f) $1 \cdot 1 \cdot 2 + 2 \cdot 2 \cdot 3 + 3 \cdot 3 \cdot 4 + \cdots + n \cdot n \cdot (n + 1)$
$$= n(3n^3 + 10n^2 + 9n + 2)/12.$$

10.2   Notation for Sums and Products

In writing such an equation as

$$1 + 2 + 3 + \cdots + n = \tfrac{1}{2}n(n + 1)$$

there is some difficulty with the notation. Whereas with $n = 10$ there is no doubt as to what is meant by $1 + 2 + 3 + \cdots + n$, in the case $n = 2$ one must interpret $1 + 2 + 3 + \cdots + n$ as simply

$1 + 2$. There is a notation that avoids this confusion and at the same time has the virtue of greater compactness, namely

$$\sum_{j=1}^{n} j \quad \text{in place of} \quad 1 + 2 + 3 + \cdots + n.$$

This is read "sigma j, $j = 1$ to n", and means "sum the element j for all integer values from $j = 1$ to $j = n$". Here are some other illustrations:

$$\sum_{j=1}^{n} j^2 \quad \text{means} \quad 1^2 + 2^2 + 3^2 + \cdots + n^2;$$

$$\sum_{j=1}^{100} j(j + 3) \quad \text{means} \quad 1 \cdot 4 + 2 \cdot 5 + 3 \cdot 6 + 4 \cdot 7 + \cdots + 100 \cdot 103;$$

$$\sum_{j=1}^{n} (j^3 + 1) \quad \text{means} \quad (1^3 + 1) + (2^3 + 1) + (3^3 + 1)$$
$$+ \cdots + (n^3 + 1);$$

$$\sum_{j=4}^{n-1} (j^3 + 1) \quad \text{means} \quad (4^3 + 1) + (5^3 + 1) + (6^3 + 1)$$
$$+ \cdots + ((n - 1)^3 + 1).$$

We note that constant factors can be moved to the left of the sigma:

(10.6) $$\sum_{j=1}^{n} 4j^2 = 4 \sum_{j=1}^{n} j^2, \quad \sum_{j=1}^{n} 5(j^3 + 1) = 5 \sum_{j=1}^{n} (j^3 + 1);$$

the reason is that the constant factor multiplies each term in the sum and may therefore be written as a factor in front of the entire sum. Also we note that expressions consisting of several terms may be summed termwise; for example,

$$\sum_{j=1}^{n} (j^2 + 3j) = \sum_{j=1}^{n} j^2 + \sum_{j=1}^{n} 3j,$$

(10.7)

$$\sum_{j=1}^{n} (j^3 + 3j^2 - j) = \sum_{j=1}^{n} j^3 + \sum_{j=1}^{n} 3j^2 - \sum_{j=1}^{n} j.$$

This is a consequence of a mere re-grouping of terms.

The sum of the natural numbers from 1 to n and the sum of their squares were evaluated in Chapter 3, page 47. The sum (10.4) of the cubes of the natural numbers from 1 to n was found by mathematical induction in the preceding section. With the sigma notation, these sums can be written as follows:

$$\sum_{j=1}^{n} j = \tfrac{1}{2}n(n+1),$$

(10.8)
$$\sum_{j=1}^{n} j^2 = \tfrac{1}{6}n(n+1)(2n+1),$$

$$\sum_{j=1}^{n} j^3 = \tfrac{1}{4}n^2(n+1)^2.$$

Note that the symbol j is a "dummy"; we could just as well write

$$\sum_{k=1}^{n} k = \tfrac{1}{2}n(n+1), \quad \text{and} \quad \sum_{r=1}^{n} r^2 = \tfrac{1}{6}n(n+1)(2n+1)$$

instead of the first two formulas in (10.8). Let us use sigma notation to evaluate the sum

$$1\cdot1\cdot2 + 2\cdot2\cdot3 + 3\cdot3\cdot4 + \cdots + n\cdot n\cdot(n+1).$$

We write it in the form

$$\sum_{j=1}^{n} j^2(j+1) \quad \text{or} \quad \sum_{j=1}^{n} (j^3 + j^2).$$

Using the property illustrated in (10.7) and formulas (10.8) we get

$$\sum_{j=1}^{n} (j^3 + j^2) = \sum_{j=1}^{n} j^3 + \sum_{j=1}^{n} j^2$$

$$= \tfrac{1}{4}n^2(n+1)^2 + \tfrac{1}{6}n(n+1)(2n+1)$$

$$= n(n+1)(n+2)(3n+1)/12,$$

where we have omitted the simple algebra involved in arriving at the last formulation.

As another example, consider the sum

$$1 + 4 + 7 + 10 + \cdots + (3n - 2)$$

which, in sigma notation, can be written

$$\sum_{j=1}^{n} (3j - 2).$$

Again using (10.8) along with basic properties described above, we have

$$\sum_{j=1}^{n} (3j - 2) = \sum_{j=1}^{n} 3j - \sum_{j=1}^{n} 2 = 3 \sum_{j=1}^{n} j - \sum_{j=1}^{n} 2$$

$$= \frac{3n(n + 1)}{2} - 2n = \frac{n(3n - 1)}{2}.$$

Sums whose terms are preceded by alternating plus and minus signs are written in sigma notation with the help of $(-1)^j$; for example,

$$\sum_{j=1}^{8} (-1)^j j^2 = -1^2 + 2^2 - 3^2 + 4^2 - 5^2 + 6^2 - 7^2 + 8^2,$$

$$\sum_{j=0}^{7} (-1)^j C(7, j) = C(7, 0) - C(7, 1) + C(7, 2) - C(7, 3)$$

$$+ C(7, 4) - C(7, 5) + C(7, 6) - C(7, 7).$$

As another illustration, consider the formula from Chapter 8 for the number of distributions of m distinct objects into k distinct boxes with no box empty:

$$f(m, k) = k^m - C(k, 1)(k - 1)^m + C(k, 2)(k - 2)^m$$

$$- C(k, 3)(k - 3)^m + \cdots + (-1)^{k-1} C(k, k - 1)(1)^m.$$

This can be written in compact form as

$$f(m, k) = \sum_{j=0}^{k-1} (-1)^j C(k, j) (k - j)^m.$$

Also in Chapter 8 the number of partitions of a set of m (distinct) elements into k (non-distinct) subsets with no subset empty was denoted by $g(m, k)$, with the relation

$$g(m, k) = f(m, k)/k!.$$

Thus a compact formula for $g(m, k)$ would be

$$g(m, k) = \sum_{j=0}^{k-1} (-1)^j C(k, j) (k - j)^m/k!.$$

If in this formula we replace $C(k, j)$ by its factorial form, there is a cancellation of $k!$ and the result becomes

$$g(m, k) = \sum_{j=0}^{k-1} \frac{(-1)^j (k - j)^m}{j!(k - j)!}.$$

There is also a convenient shorthand notation for products; it uses the upper case Greek letter pi, $\prod$, in place of the upper case sigma. For example, $n!$ can be written

$$n! = \prod_{j=1}^{n} j.$$

Here are some other examples:

$$\prod_{j=1}^{n} (j^2 + 1) \quad \text{means} \quad (1^2 + 1)(2^2 + 1)(3^2 + 1) \cdots (n^2 + 1);$$

$$\prod_{j=1}^{n} (3j - 1) \quad \text{means} \quad 2 \cdot 5 \cdot 8 \cdot 11 \cdots (3n - 1);$$

$$\prod_{j=1}^{7} (1 + x^j) \quad \text{means} \quad (1 + x)(1 + x^2)(1 + x^3)(1 + x^4)$$
$$\cdot (1 + x^5)(1 + x^6)(1 + x^7).$$

Problem Set 34

1. Express the following sums without the sigma notation:

$$\text{(a)} \ \sum_{j=1}^{5} j^2; \qquad \text{(b)} \ \sum_{j=1}^{4} (2j^2 - 1); \qquad \text{(c)} \ \sum_{k=3}^{6} (k^2 + 2).$$

2. Evaluate the following sums by use of the sigma notation and formulas (10.8):

    (a) $3 + 6 + 9 + 12 + \cdots + 3n;$

    (b) $2 + 5 + 8 + 11 + \cdots + (3n - 1);$

    (c) $1 \cdot 3 + 3 \cdot 5 + 5 \cdot 7 + 7 \cdot 9 + \cdots + (2n - 1)(2n + 1);$

    (d) $1 \cdot 2 + 3 \cdot 3 + 5 \cdot 4 + 7 \cdot 5 + \cdots + (2n - 1)(n + 1);$

    (e) $5 + 9 + 13 + 17 + 21 + \cdots + (4n + 1).$

3. Write formulas similar to formulas (10.8) for the sums

$$\text{(a)} \quad 1 + 2 + 3 + \cdots + (n - 1);$$

$$\text{(b)} \quad 1 + 2 + 3 + \cdots + (n + 1);$$

$$\text{(c)} \quad 1^2 + 2^2 + 3^2 + \cdots + (n + 1)^2.$$

4. Find the numerical value of

$$\sum_{j=1}^{100} (-1)^j \cdot j.$$

5. Write the equation

$$C(n, 0) + C(n, 1) + C(n, 2) + C(n, 3) + \cdots + C(n, n) = 2^n$$

in sigma notation.

6. Identify

$$\sum_{j=0}^{n} (-1)^j C(n,j)$$

as a sum discussed earlier in this book, and so evaluate it.

7. Prove

$$\sum_{j=0}^{n} 2^j = 2^{n+1} - 1$$

by mathematical induction. Hence prove that, in Pascal's triangle (page 41), the sum of the elements in any row equals the sum of all elements in all preceding rows, with 1 added.

8. Evaluate the product $\prod_{j=2}^{6} (j + 1)$.

9. Express the product $\prod_{j=1}^{n} (2j)$ in factorial notation.

10. Verify that

$$\prod_{j=1}^{n} (2j - 1) = \frac{(2n)!}{2^n \cdot n!}.$$

11. Let $f(n)$ be defined by

$$f(n) = \sum_{j=1}^{n} j \cdot j!.$$

Verify that $f(1) = 1$, $f(2) = 5$, $f(3) = 23$, and find the numerical values of $f(4)$, $f(5)$, and $f(6)$. Then compare these with the numerical values of $2!$, $3!$, $4!$, $5!$, $6!$, and $7!$, conjecture a formula for $f(n)$, and try to prove it by mathematical induction.

10.3 Summary

The proof technique known as mathematical induction can be used to establish an infinite sequence of propositions $P_1, P_2, P_3, \cdots$, provided one can show

(i) that P_1 is true,

(ii) that P_{k+1} follows from P_k for every positive integer k.

The sigma notation for sums and the pi notation for products are explained.

CHAPTER ELEVEN

Interpretations of a Non-Associative Product

Consider the mathematical expression

$$2^{3^4}.$$

There appear to be two ways of interpreting this—one by starting with 2^3 and so interpreting the expression as 8^4; another by starting with 3^4 and so interpreting the expression as 2^{81}. These ways lead to different results because 8^4 is 4096 whereas 2^{81} is much larger. We can indicate these two interpretations by using parentheses; thus

$$(11.1) \qquad (2^3)^4 = 8^4, \quad 2^{(3^4)} = 2^{81}, \quad \text{and} \quad (2^3)^4 \neq 2^{(3^4)}.$$

Now in actual fact there is a convention or agreement in mathematics as to precisely how 2^{3^4} is to be interpreted, namely as the second form in (11.1),

$$2^{3^4} = 2^{(3^4)} = 2^{81}.$$

For the purposes of this chapter we disregard this convention. We look upon (11.1) as a demonstration that exponentiation is not associative, in contrast, for example, to addition and multiplication;

$$(2 + 3) + 4 = 2 + (3 + 4), \qquad (2 \cdot 3) \cdot 4 = 2 \cdot (3 \cdot 4).$$

Ignoring the conventional meaning for such expressions as

$$(11.2) \qquad\qquad 2^{3^{4^5}} \quad \text{or} \quad a^{b^{c^d}},$$

we ask how many interpretations there are when four numbers are stacked up this way in exponential fashion. More generally, how many interpretations are there when n numbers are stacked up in exponential fashion?

11.1 A Recursion Relation

To simplify the typography we shall write the second expression in (11.2) as though it were a "product" $abcd$. We presume that such "products" are non-associative, so that the 3-products $a(bc)$ and $(ab)c$ are different. All possible interpretations of a 4-product can be readily enumerated:

$$(11.3) \quad a((bc)d), \quad a(b(cd)), \quad (ab)(cd), \quad (a(bc))d, \quad ((ab)c)d.$$

Let us define $F(n)$ as the number of interpretations of a non-associative n-product; then the enumeration (11.3) shows that $F(4) = 5$. Also, we know that $F(3) = 2$, because of the two cases $a(bc)$ and $(ab)c$. There is only one interpretation of a 2-product ab, and likewise only one interpretation for a 1-product a, and hence we can write $F(2) = 1$, $F(1) = 1$.

The general problem of this chapter is the evaluation of $F(n)$, the number of interpretations of an n-product

$$(11.4) \qquad\qquad x_1 x_2 x_3 \cdots x_n$$

with no associative property. $F(n)$ can be thought of as the number of ways of putting parentheses on (11.4) to make it non-ambiguous.

To illustrate what we are about to do, let us take the special case $n = 6$. In putting parentheses on a 6-product, one possible first step is to split the product into two parts. This can be done in any of the following five ways:

$$\text{(a)} \qquad x_1(x_2x_3x_4x_5x_6),$$

$$\text{(b)} \qquad (x_1x_2)(x_3x_4x_5x_6),$$

$$(11.5) \qquad \text{(c)} \qquad (x_1x_2x_3)(x_4x_5x_6),$$

$$\text{(d)} \qquad (x_1x_2x_3x_4)(x_5x_6),$$

$$\text{(e)} \qquad (x_1x_2x_3x_4x_5)x_6.$$

In how many ways can additional parentheses be installed? In expression (a), there are $F(5)$ interpretations of $x_2x_3x_4x_5x_6$. In expression (b), there are $F(4)$ interpretations of $x_3x_4x_5x_6$. In expression (c), there are $F(3)$ interpretations for each of $x_1x_2x_3$ and $x_4x_5x_6$, and so $F(3) \cdot F(3)$ interpretations in all for (c). Expressions (d) and (e) are similar to (b) and (a) respectively. Putting all this information together we see that

$$F(6) \;=\; F(5) + F(4) + F(3)F(3) + F(4) + F(5).$$

Since $F(1) = 1$ and $F(2) = 1$, this can be written in the more symmetric form

$$F(6) \;=\; F(1)F(5)+F(2)F(4)+F(3)F(3)+F(4)F(2)+F(5)F(1).$$

By a similar argument we can conclude that

$$F(7) \;=\; F(1)F(6) + F(2)F(5) + F(3)F(4) + F(4)F(3)$$
$$+ F(5)F(2) + F(6)F(1),$$

and, in general, that

$$(11.6) \qquad \begin{aligned} F(n) \;=\;& F(1)F(n-1) + F(2)F(n-2) \\ &+ F(3)F(n-3) + \cdots + F(n-1)F(1). \end{aligned}$$

With the sigma notation for sums the recursion relation (11.6) can be written in the form

$$F(n) \;=\; \sum_{j=1}^{n-1} F(j)F(n-j)$$

and used to calculate successive values of $F(n)$ as n increases through the natural numbers. For example, if we take $F(1) = 1$ and $F(2) = 1$ as our starting values, we can find

$$F(3) = F(1)F(2) + F(2)F(1) = 1 + 1 = 2,$$

$$F(4) = F(1)F(3) + F(2)F(2) + F(3)F(1) = 2 + 1 + 2 = 5,$$

$$F(5) = F(1)F(4) + F(2)F(3) + F(3)F(2) + F(4)F(1)$$

$$= 5 + 2 + 2 + 5 = 14,$$

and so on.

Problem Set 35

1. Find the number of interpretations of (i) a 6-product, (ii) a 7-product, (iii) an 8-product, in a non-associative system.

2. What is the conventional non-ambiguous meaning of $5^{4^{3^2}}$?

3. Enumerate the fourteen interpretations of a 5-product, analogous to the formulation (11.3) in the text.

11.2   The Development of an Explicit Formula

Consider any non-associative product such as

$$(11.7) \qquad (((x_1x_2)(x_3x_4))x_5)(((x_6x_7)x_8)x_9).$$

The parentheses, which serve to indicate the arrangement of association of the elements, occur in pairs, with a left and a right parenthesis in each pair. To any product such as (11.7) we attach two numbers, denoted by n and k; n is the number of elements in the product [$n = 9$ in the example (11.7)], and k denotes the number of elements preceding the rightmost of the left parentheses. (In the example (11.7) the rightmost of the left parentheses is the one immediately preceding x_6, and hence $k = 5$.) As another example consider

$$(11.8) \qquad x_1(x_2(((x_3(x_4x_5))x_6)x_7)),$$

where $n = 7$ and $k = 3$. In any such product the rightmost of the left parentheses is followed by two elements and the corresponding right parenthesis;† in (11.7) this pattern is $(x_6 x_7)$, and in (11.8) it is $(x_4 x_5)$.

Next we define a transformation which takes any product and transforms it into a product having one element less. The transformation removes the rightmost of the left parentheses, the element following it, and the corresponding right parenthesis. Thus (11.7) is transformed into

$$(11.9) \qquad (((x_1 x_2)(x_3 x_4))x_5)((x_7 x_8)x_9),$$

and (11.8) into

$$(11.10) \qquad x_1(x_2(((x_3 x_5)x_6)x_7)).$$

In (11.9) we see that $n = 8$ and $k = 5$, and in (11.10) $n = 6$ and $k = 2$.

In general, an n-product with k elements preceding the rightmost of the left parentheses is transformed into an $(n - 1)$-product because one element is removed. The transformed expression either has k elements preceding the rightmost of the left parentheses (this is the case whenever that parenthesis is adjacent to another left parenthesis), or the transformed product has fewer than k elements preceding it.

Let us denote by $F(n, k)$ the number of non-associative n-products with exactly k elements preceding the rightmost of the left parentheses. It turns out that the following relation holds:

$$(11.11) \qquad \begin{aligned} F(n, k) \;=\; & F(n - 1, k) + F(n - 1, k - 1) \\ & + F(n - 1, k - 2) + \cdots + F(n - 1, 0). \end{aligned}$$

We illustrate this in the case $n = 5$ and $k = 3$. There are five products corresponding to these specific values of n and k; that is to say, $F(5, 3) = 5$. We list these five products in the left column and the corresponding transformed products in the right column:

† By "such a product", we mean one which has been made unambiguous by the insertion of sufficiently many parentheses.

Product	Transformed product	n	k
$(x_1x_2)(x_3(x_4x_5))$	$(x_1x_2)(x_3x_5)$	4	2
$x_1(x_2(x_3(x_4x_5)))$	$x_1(x_2(x_3x_5))$	4	2
$x_1((x_2x_3)(x_4x_5))$	$x_1((x_2x_3)x_5)$	4	1
$(x_1(x_2x_3))(x_4x_5)$	$(x_1(x_2x_3))x_5$	4	1
$((x_1x_2)x_3)(x_4x_5)$	$((x_1x_2)x_3)x_5$	4	0

The first two transformed products are of the $F(4, 2)$ type, the next two of the $F(4, 1)$ type, and the last one of the $F(4, 0)$ type. In fact, these collections of types are complete, so that $F(4, 2) = 2$, $F(4, 1) = 2$, $F(4, 0) = 1$. Furthermore, there is no product of the $F(4, 3)$ type, and so $F(4, 3) = 0$. Thus by actual count we have verified the special case

$$F(5, 3) = F(4, 3) + F(4, 2) + F(4, 1) + F(4, 0)$$

of (11.11).

A proof of (11.11) is suggested by this example. First, if any product of the $F(n, k)$ type is transformed by the procedure described above, there results a product of one of the types listed on the right side of (11.11). Secondly, the transformation is reversible as follows: take any product of a type listed on the right side of (11.11); replace the $(k + 1)$-st element, say y, by two elements in parentheses, say (yz); this procedure gives a product of the type $F(n, k)$. So we have a one-to-one correspondence between the types of products listed on the two sides of equation (11.11), and the result is thereby established.

Now if, in formula (11.11), we replace k by $k - 1$ the result is

$$F(n, k - 1) = F(n - 1, k - 1) + F(n - 1, k - 2)$$
$$+ F(n - 1, k - 3) + \cdots + F(n - 1, 0).$$

Subtracting this from (11.11), we get

$$F(n, k) - F(n, k - 1) = F(n - 1, k)$$

or

(11.12) $F(n, k) = F(n, k - 1) + F(n - 1, k).$

This formula somewhat resembles the result

$$C(n, r) = C(n - 1, r) + C(n - 1, r - 1).$$

There is a connection between the functions $F(n, k)$ and $C(n, r)$ which we now reveal by comparing brief numerical tables.

To develop a table of values of $F(n, k)$ we use (11.12) along with certain basic results. Because parentheses are not needed in the simple cases $n = 1$ and $n = 2$, let us confine attention to values of $n \geqslant 3$. For any value of n, the corresponding values of k are $0, 1, 2, \cdots, n - 1$. (It turns out to be convenient in the formulas to ignore the case $k = n$, for which there are no products.) The values of $F(n, 0)$ and $F(n, n - 1)$ can easily be determined from the definition of $F(n, k)$. First, $F(n, 0)$ means the number of n-products having no element preceding the rightmost of the left parentheses. There is one such product illustrated, in the case $n = 8$, by

$$(((((((x_1 x_2) x_3) x_4) x_5) x_6) x_7) x_8,$$

and so $F(n, 0) = 1$. Now the rightmost of the left parentheses is followed by at least two elements (since we do not enclose a single element in parentheses), and so there is no product of type $F(n, n - 1)$. Thus we have

(11.13) $F(n, 0) = 1, \quad F(n, n - 1) = 0 \quad$ for all $n \geqslant 3$.

With this information and the easily established result $F(3, 1) = 1$, it is now possible to use (11.12) to develop a table of values.

TABLE OF VALUES OF $F(n, k)$

k n	0	1	2	3	4	5	6	7	8	9
3	1	1	0							
4	1	2	2	0						
5	1	3	5	5	0					
6	1	4	9	14	14	0				
7	1	5	14	28	42	42	0			
8	1	6	20	48	90	132	132	0		
9	1	7	27	75	165	297	429	429	0	
10	1	8	35	110	275	572	1001	1430	1430	0
11	1	9	44	154	429	etc.				
12	1	10	54	208	637					
13	1	11	65	273	910					
14	1	12	77	350	1260					

This is to be compared with a table of values of $C(n, r)$, that is, with Pascal's triangle. In every row of Pascal's triangle, we list the differences of adjacent pairs of values, the left one subtracted from the right one, by writing these in parentheses between each pair; but we do not list negative differences (see the table on p. 148).

A comparison of these tables shows that the entries in the $F(n, k)$ table turn up as differences in the $C(n, r)$ table; for example,

$$F(7, 3) = C(8, 3) - C(8, 2),$$

$$F(8, 4) = C(10, 4) - C(10, 3),$$

$$F(9, 6) = C(13, 6) - C(13, 5),$$

$$F(12, 3) = C(13, 3) - C(13, 2).$$

These results suggest the general proposition

(11.14) $F(n, k) = C(n+k-2, k) - C(n+k-2, k-1).$

This conjecture is correct, but of course it cannot be proved by an examination of a few special cases in the tables.

TABLE OF VALUES OF $C(n, r)$; DIFFERENCES IN PARENTHESES

r / n	0	1	2	3	4	5	6	7
1	1(0)	1	0	0	0	0	0	0
2	1(1)	2	1	0	0	0	0	0
3	1(2)	3(0)	3	1	0	0	0	0
4	1(3)	4(2)	6	4	1	0	0	0
5	1(4)	5(5)	10(0)	10	5	1	0	0
6	1(5)	6(9)	15(5)	20	15	6	1	0
7	1(6)	7(14)	21(14)	35(0)	35	21	7	1
8	1(7)	8(20)	28(28)	56(14)	70	56	28	8
9	1(8)	9(27)	36(48)	84(42)	126(0)	126	84	36
10	1(9)	10(35)	45(75)	120(90)	210(42)	252	210	120
11	1(10)	11(44)	55(110)	165(165)	330(132)	462(0)	462	330
12	1(11)	12(54)	66(154)	220(275)	495(297)	792(132)	924	792
13	1(12)	13(65)	78(208)	286(429)	715(572)	1287(429)	1716(0)	1716

11.3 Proof of the Conjecture

Before proving the conjecture (11.14) we write it in a different form by making an algebraic calculation:

$C(n+k-2, k) - C(n+k-2, k-1)$

$$= \frac{(n + k - 2)!}{k!(n - 2)!} - \frac{(n + k - 2)!}{(k - 1)!(n - 1)!}$$

$$= \frac{(n + k - 2)!}{k!(n - 1)!} [(n - 1) - k] .$$

Thus (11.14) can be written as

$$(11.15) \qquad F(n, k) = \frac{(n + k - 2)!}{k!(n - 1)!} (n - k - 1) .$$

We note that this is true for $k = 0$, because

$$F(n, 0) = \frac{(n - 2)!}{0!(n - 1)!} (n - 1) = 1$$

agrees with the value calculated before. Also we note that (11.15) gives the correct results $F(3, 1) = 1$ and $F(3, 2) = 0$.

We are now in a position to prove (11.15) by mathematical induction. It is necessary to argue in a slightly more sophisticated way than in the proofs by induction of the preceding chapter, because there are now two variables, n and k. However, we can reduce this problem to one in a single variable by the following device. Let P_m denote all cases of (11.15) with $n + k = m$. Since $n \geqslant 3$ we start with $m = 3$:

P_3 is equation (11.15) in the one case $n = 3$, $k = 0$;

P_4 is (11.15) in the cases $n = 4$, $k = 0$ and $n = 3$, $k = 1$;

P_5 is (11.15) in the cases $n = 5$, $k = 0$; $n = 4$, $k = 1$;

$$n = 3, \ k = 2.$$

Similarly P_6 would consist of 4 cases, P_7 of 5 cases, and so on. Our inductive proof of (11.15) will consist in proving (i) that P_3 is true, and (ii) that P_m implies P_{m+1}.

We have already checked that P_3 holds, so we turn to (ii). Assuming that P_m holds, we are to prove P_{m+1}, that is, equation (11.15), for any pair of integers n and k whose sum is $m + 1$. So in what follows we regard n and k as integers for which $n + k = m + 1$. Of course, in proving that P_m implies P_{m+1} we make use of P_m, and so we use (11.15) for $F(n, k - 1)$ and $F(n - 1, k)$ because

$$n + k = m + 1 \text{ implies } n + (k - 1) = m \text{ and } (n - 1) + k = m.$$

Thus P_m includes the two statements

$$F(n, k - 1) = \frac{(n + k - 3)!}{(k - 1)!(n - 1)!} (n - k)$$

and

$$F(n - 1, k) = \frac{(n + k - 3)!}{k!(n - 2)!} (n - k - 2).$$

Making use of (11.12), we get

$$F(n, k) = F(n, k - 1) + F(n - 1, k)$$

$$= \frac{(n+k-3)!}{(k-1)!(n-1)!} (n-k) + \frac{(n+k-3)!}{k!(n - 2)!} (n - k - 2)$$

$$= \frac{(n + k - 3)!}{k!(n - 1)!} [k(n - k) + (n - 1)(n - k - 2)]$$

$$= \frac{(n + k - 3)!}{k!(n - 1)!} (n + k - 2)(n - k - 1)$$

$$= \frac{(n + k - 2)!}{k!(n - 1)!} (n - k - 1),$$

and so (11.15) is established.

11.4   A Formula for $F(n)$

Our aim now is to answer the question posed in the introduction to this chapter: What is the number $F(n)$ of n-products in a non-associative system? By using the results of the intervening sections, we now derive a simple formula for $F(n)$.

First we observe that the total number of n-products consists of those with no element preceding the rightmost of the left parentheses, plus those with one element preceding it, plus those with two elements preceding it, $\cdots$, plus those with all but one preceding it, plus those with all preceding it. In symbols,

(11.16)
$$F(n) = F(n, 0) + F(n, 1) + \cdots + F(n, n - 2)$$
$$+ F(n, n - 1) + F(n, n).$$

In view of formula (11.13) and the fact that $F(n, n) = 0$, we may write (11.16) in the form

(11.16')
$$F(n) = \sum_{j=0}^{n-2} F(n, j).$$

Next, we write formula (11.11), derived in Section 11.2, with n replaced by $n + 1$ and k replaced by $n - 1$. This yields

(11.17)
$$F(n + 1, n - 1) = F(n, n - 1) + F(n, n - 2)$$
$$+ \cdots + F(n, 0).$$

But $F(n, n - 1)$ is zero, so we may write (11.17) as

$$F(n + 1, n - 1) = \sum_{j=0}^{n-2} F(n, j),$$

and, comparing it with (11.16'), we see that

(11.18)
$$F(n) = F(n + 1, n - 1).$$

Finally, we apply formula (11.15), derived in Section 11.3, to the right member of (11.18); in other words, we replace n by $n + 1$ and k by $n - 1$ in (11.15) and obtain

$$F(n+1, n-1) = \frac{[(n+1) + (n-1) - 2]!}{(n - 1)!n!} [n+1 - (n-1) - 1]$$

$$= \frac{(2n - 2)!}{n!(n - 1)!}.$$

Substituting this into (11.18) gives the desired result

$$F(n) = \frac{(2n-2)!}{n!(n-1)!}$$

for the number of ways of meaningfully inserting parentheses into an expression of the form $x_1 x_2 x_3 \cdots x_n$.

11.5 Summary

A mathematical "product" is non-associative if $a(bc) = (ab)c$ does not hold in all cases. The word "product" is in quotation marks because for the purposes of this chapter ab can represent the result of any binary operation on elements a and b yielding a non-associative system. One illustration of this arises from interpreting ab as the exponential form a^b.

In a non-associative system there are two interpretations of the 3-product abc, namely $a(bc)$ and $(ab)c$. The topic of this chapter is the number of interpretations, denoted by $F(n)$, of a non-associative n-product $x_1 x_2 x_3 \cdots x_n$. First a recursion relation

$$F(n) = \sum_{j=1}^{n-1} F(j)F(n-j)$$

is established; then the explicit formula

$$F(n) = \frac{(2n-2)!}{n!(n-1)!}$$

is derived. We proved this result by separating $F(n)$ into parts, with $F(n, k)$ denoting the number of n-products having exactly k elements preceding the rightmost of the left parentheses. Properties of $F(n, k)$ developed in formulas (11.11) and (11.12) resulted in a table of values for this function. On comparing these values with differences in Pascal's triangle, it was easy to guess how $F(n, k)$ is related to the $C(m, j)$. This guess, conjecture (11.14), was proved by mathematical induction, and thus $F(n)$ was evaluated.

Miscellaneous Problems

1. A class is given a true-false test consisting of 12 questions. One of the students, rather unprepared, decides on the following strategy. He answers 3 of the questions about which he feels absolutely certain, and then handles the other 9 by tossing a coin to make his decision in each case. Assuming that the student answered those 3 correctly, establish that his probability of getting at least half the answers right is greater than 9/10.

2. How many terms of the sequence of natural numbers 1, 2, 3, 4, $\cdots$ must be added to give a sum exceeding one million?

3. Consider the sequence 2, 22, 84, 212, $\cdots$, whose terms are obtained by taking $j = 1$, $j = 2$, $j = 3$, $\cdots$ in the expression $4j^3 - 3j^2 + j$. Find a formula for the sum of the first n terms.

4. If 12 boys are separated at random into 3 teams of 4 each, what is the probability that 2 particular boys will be on different teams?

5. In the preceding question, what is the probability that 3 particular boys will be completely separated, one on each team?

6. Given a set of N objects of which $N(\alpha)$ have a certain property α, and $N(\alpha, \beta)$ have both properties α and β, etc., prove that

$$3N + N(\alpha, \beta) + N(\alpha, \gamma) + N(\beta, \gamma) \geqslant 2N(\alpha) + 2N(\beta) + 2N(\gamma).$$

7. Write a polynomial product so that the coefficient of x^{100} denotes the number of partitions of 100 into unequal positive odd integers.

8. In a certain mythical country, postage stamps come in the following denominations: 3 kinds of 1 cent stamps (the regular kind and two commemoratives), 3 kinds of 2 cent stamps, 2 kinds of 3 cent stamps, and one kind each of 4 cent, 5 cent, 10 cent and 20 cent stamps. Write a polynomial product so that the coefficient of x^{20} denotes the number of ways of getting 20 cents worth of stamps.

9. Prove that the Fibonacci numbers $F(0) = 1$, $F(1) = 2$, $F(2) = 3$, $F(3) = 5$, $F(5) = 8$, etc. have the property

$$F(n) = 2 + \sum_{j=0}^{n-2} F(j) \qquad \text{if } n > 2.$$

10. For any given positive integer n, prove that

$$\sum_{j+k=n+1} C(j, k) = 1 + \sum_{j+k<n} C(j, k),$$

where the sum on the left includes all terms $C(j, k)$ with non-negative integers j, k satisfying $j + k = n + 1$, and the sum on the right all such terms with $j + k < n$. (Suggestion: Use the result of the preceding problem.)

11. Of the 30! permutations of the integers $1, 2, 3, \cdots, 30$, how many have the property that multiples of 3 are not in adjacent places, that is, no two of the integers 3, 6, 9, 12, 15, 18, 21, 24, 27, 30 are adjacent?

12. Find the number of permutations of the 8 letters a, b, c, d, e, f, g, h, taken all at a time, subject to the condition that b does not immediately follow a, c does not immediately follow b, $\cdots$, and h does not immediately follow g.

13. A collection of 100 coins, 20 of which are cents, 20 nickels, 20 dimes, 20 quarters, and 20 fifty cent pieces, are to be put into 5 distinct boxes. In how many ways can this be done if no box is to be empty? (Presume that the 20 coins of each single denomination are indistinguishable.)

14. Find the number of permutations of the 8 letters $AABBCCDD$, taken all at a time, such that no two adjacent letters are alike.

15. How many permutations are there of the 9 letters $D, D, D, E, E, E,$ $F, F, F,$ taken all at a time, subject to the restriction that no two D's are adjacent?

16. What would be the answer to the preceding question if the additional restriction were imposed that no two E's are adjacent?

17. What would be the answer to the preceding question if yet another restriction were imposed, namely that no two F's are adjacent?

18. Find the number of quintuples (x, y, z, u, v) of positive integers satisfying both equations

$$x + y + z + u = 30 \quad \text{and} \quad x + y + z + v = 27.$$

19. Of the solutions in positive integers of $x + y + z + w = 26$, how many have $x > y$?

20. Evaluate $[n, n, n, n, [\![2n, 2n]$, that is, the number of ways of dividing $4n$ objects, which are alike in batches of n, equally between two persons.

21. In how many ways is it possible to separate nj different objects into n batches with j objects in each batch?

22. Which would you expect to be larger, the number of partitions of 1000 into 3 positive even integers, or the number of partitions of 1000 into 3 positive odd integers? Give a proof of your conjecture.

23. Which would you expect to be larger, the number of partitions of 1000 into 4 positive even integers, or the number of partitions of 1000 into four positive odd integers? Give a proof of your conjecture.

24. Which would you expect to be larger, the number of partitions of 1000 into positive even integers, or the number of partitions of 1000 into positive odd integers? Give a proof of your conjecture. (This question differs from the preceding two questions in that the number of summands is now unrestricted.)

25. How many integers between 1 and 1,000,000 inclusive have the property that at least two consecutive digits are equal? (For example, 1007 has the property but 1017 does not.)

26. Find the number of permutations of the letters of the alphabet, taken all at a time, such that (i) no letter is in its natural place, and (ii) the letters A and B are adjacent.

27. Find the number of permutations of the 6 letters a, b, c, d, e, f, taken all at a time, subject to the condition that letters which are consecutive in the alphabet are not adjacent. (For example, a and b are not adjacent, b and c are not adjacent, etc.)

28. Prove that the number of people through all of history who have shaken hands (with other people) an odd number of times is even.

29. In any group of people, prove that there are two persons having the same number of acquaintances within the group. (Presume, of course, that if A is acquainted with B, then B is acquainted with A.)

30. Given n points in the plane, no 3 collinear, let each of the line segments joining pairs of points be colored one of two colors, say red and white. Then from each point there emanate $n - 1$ line segments, some red and some white. Prove that no matter what configuration of colors is used, there are two points out of which there emanate the same number of red segments, and hence also the same number of white segments.

31. Let there be $m + 1$ equally spaced parallel lines, intersected at right angles by $k + 1$ equally spaced parallel lines. Presuming $m \leqslant k$, what is the total number of squares in the network?

32. *The Tower of Hanoi Puzzle.* There are 8 circular discs placed over one of three vertical pegs. The discs are of 8 unequal radii, with the largest disc at the bottom of the pile on one peg, covered by successively smaller discs so that the smallest one is on top. The problem is to transfer the tower of discs from the peg on which they rest initially to one of the other two pegs. The rules are that the discs may be moved freely, one at a time, from peg to peg, except that no disc can ever be placed on top of a smaller disc. The question is whether it is possible under these rules to move the tower of discs from one peg to another, and if so, how many moves are needed to effect the transfer.

33. Given 6 points in the plane, no 3 collinear, let each of the line segments joining the points be colored one of two colors, say red or white. Prove that no matter what configuration of colors is used,

there are always at least *two* chromatic triangles present, that is, two triangles whose three sides have the same color. (The two triangles need not be of the same color; one may be a red chromatic triangle, and the other white.)

34. In the preceding problem prove that there need not be 3 chromatic triangles. That is, exhibit a configuration of colored segments with only 2 chromatic triangles.

35. Given 7 points in the plane, no 3 collinear, let each of the line segments joining the points be colored one of two colors, say red or white. Prove that no matter what configuration of colors is used, there are always at least three chromatic triangles present.

36. Consider 66 points in the plane, no 3 collinear, with each of the line segments joining these points colored one of 4 colors. Prove that for any arrangement of colors whatsoever there is always a chromatic triangle present, i.e. a triangle whose 3 sides have the same color. (The information that with 17 points and 3 colors there is a chromatic triangle might be useful.)

37. Consider 17 points in a plane, no three collinear, with each of the segments joining two points colored red, white or blue. Prove that there are at least two chromatic triangles in the configuration.

38. Consider 24 points in the plane, no 3 collinear, with each of the segments joining the points colored one of two colors, say red or white. Prove that no matter what distribution of colors is made, it is always possible to find 4 points such that the 6 line segments joining them are of the same color. (The reader might wish to solve this problem with a larger integer substituted for 24. The smallest number that can be used to replace 24 is 18, in the sense that the proposition is not true for 17 or fewer points. However the proof that 18 is the smallest, given by R. E. Greenwood and A. M. Gleason in 1955, is beyond the scope of this book.)

39. Given n points on the circumference of a circle, there are $C(n, 2)$ or $n(n - 1)/2$ line segments joining pairs of points. Suppose the n points are spaced so that no 3 line segments have a common intersection point inside the circle. What is the total number $I(n)$ of intersection points inside (not on the circumference of) the circle? For example, $I(4) = 1$, $I(5) = 5$, $I(6) = 15$.

40. In the preceding problem, into how many regions is the interior of the circle divided by the line segments joining the n points? Let $R(n)$ be the number of regions; for example, $R(2) = 2$, $R(3) = 4$, $R(4) = 8$, $R(5) = 16$.

41. Given n equally spaced points on the circumference of a circle (the vertices of a regular n-gon); consider the

$$C(n, 3) = \tfrac{1}{6}n(n-1)(n-2)$$

triangles that can be formed by straight line segments linking the points. How many of these triangles are isosceles?

42. If n identical dice are thrown, how many possible outcomes are there? (Say that two outcomes are the same if they contain the same number of ones, the same number of twos, $\cdots$, and the same number of sixes.)

43. Consider n planes in 3-dimensional space satisfying the following conditions: no two are parallel; no two lines of intersection are parallel; no four intersect in a point. Into how many regions is space separated by the planes?

44. What is the probability that a randomly selected permutation of $1, 2, 3, \cdots, n$ has the "2" somewhere between the "1" and the "3"?

45. Find the number of permutations of $2n$ things which are alike in pairs (for example $AABBCCDDEE\cdots$) taken all at a time, such that no two adjacent things are alike.

46. Find the probability that a randomly selected permutation of $1, 2, 3, \cdots, n$ taken all at a time has exactly j of the numbers out of their natural positions.

47. How many permutations are there of the $n + k$ letters

$$AAA\cdots ABBB\cdots B,$$

of which n are A's and k are B's, subject to the condition that no three A's are adjacent?

48. Find the number of permutations of 1, 2, 3, $\cdots$, $2n$ taken all at a time, such that no odd number is in its natural position.

49. Suppose that the prime factorization of an integer n has exactly m factors, all distinct. How many factorings are there of n into k factors, where k is some integer $\leqslant m$, (i) if each factor must be greater than 1, (ii) if 1 is allowed as a factor? (Factorings that differ only in the order of the factors are not counted separately.)

50. Consider the integers 1, 2, 3, $\cdots$, n. Let $K(n,j)$ denote the number of subsets of these n integers satisfying the conditions (i) each subset contains j integers, (ii) no subset contains a consecutive pair of integers. For example, $K(5, 3) = 1$ because the only subset of 1, 2, 3, 4, 5, satisfying the conditions is 1, 3, 5. By separating the subsets counted by $K(n, j)$ into two types, those that contain n and those that do not, obtain a recursion relation for $K(n, j)$. Then use this relation to construct a short table of values of $K(n, j)$, say up to $n = 100$ and $j = 10$. This table, when contrasted with Pascal's triangle, should suggest a conjecture about the value of $K(n, j)$. Find the proper conjecture and then prove it by mathematical induction.

51. Three persons, strangers to one another, enter a room in which there are 3 mutual acquaintances. Prove that among the 6 people there are at least 3 other triples each of which consists of 3 strangers or 3 mutual acquaintances. A more definite statement of the problem follows: Say that a set of 3 persons has property α in case they are pairwise strangers, property β in case they are pairwise acquainted. Consider six persons A, B, C, D, E, F, such that A, B, C have property α, and D, E, F have property β. Prove that the sum of the number of triples with property α and the number of triples with property β is at least 5.

52. A flight of stairs has 14 steps. A boy can go up the stairs one at a time, two at a time, or any combination of ones and twos. In how many ways can the boy go up the stairs?

53. How many integers between 1 and 1,000,000 inclusive have the property that no digit is smaller than a digit to its left? (For example 1468 has the property stated, but 1648 does not.)

Answers and Solutions

Answers are given for almost all problems. Solutions are given for many, although for the most part the "solution" is a mere sketch, in some instances nothing more than a suggestion or two. If the reader's answer to a problem is not the same as the one given here, he should allow for the possibility that the difference is merely one of form. For it should be kept in mind that most problems admit more than one method of solution and that two answers may be equal without looking the same.

Problem 1.1, page 1.   1, 2 or 3

We give here an analysis of years having 365 days; the analysis for 366 day years is similar. First, let us call Sunday a type 0 day, Monday a type 1 day, Tuesday type 2, $\cdots$, Saturday type 6. If January 13 is a type 0 day, then February 13 is a type 3 day since it is 31 or $3 + 28$ days later, March 13 is type 3, April 13 is type 6, May 13 is type 1, $\cdots$, December 13 is type 5. The entire list of types from January 13 to December 13 is

$$0, 3, 3, 6, 1, 4, 6, 2, 5, 0, 3, 5.$$

There are two Friday the thirteenths, since Friday is of type 5. The analysis thus far has been on the assumption that January 13 is a Sunday. The easiest way to proceed is to vary what is meant by type 0. For example, if we redefine type 0 to be Monday, then Friday is of type 4, and the list above shows that in such a year there is only one Friday the thirteenth. Thus the list reveals the answer to the problem by consideration of all seven interpretations of what is meant by type 0. For a 366 day year, the corresponding list is 0, 3, 4, 0, 2, 5, 0, 3, 6, 1, 4, 6.

Problem 1.2, page 2.   10

There is 1 kind of block with six blue faces; 1 kind with five blue faces; 2 kinds with four blue faces, because the two red faces may be opposite or adjacent to each other; 2 kinds with three blue faces, because there may be, or may not be, two blue faces opposite one another. The number of different kinds of blocks with two blue faces is the same as the number with four blue faces; with one blue face, the same as with five blue faces; with no blue face, the same as six blue faces.

Problem 1.3, page 3, is solved on page 27.

Problem 1.4, page 4, is solved on page 59.

Problem 1.5, page 4, is solved on page 106.

Problem Set 1, page 5

1. 55   **2.** 138   **3.** 185   **4.** $n + r - 1$ **5.** $k - r + 1$ **6.** $h + 1$

7. 80 integers from $x = 145$ to $x = 224$.

8. (a) 49   (b) 44   (c) 35

Argument for part (c). Subtract 11 from each integer: 6, 12, 18, 24, $\cdots$, 210. Divide each by 6: 1, 2, 3, 4, $\cdots$, 35. These operations have not changed the number of elements.

9. (a) 181: the integers 11, 22, 33, $\cdots$, 1991;
   (b) 121: delete from the integers in (a) the following: 33, 66, 99, $\cdots$, 1980; these are 60 in number; hence $181 - 60$;
   (c) 167: delete from 6, 12, 18, 24, $\cdots$, 1998 the integers 12, 24, 36, $\cdots$, 1992; thus $333 - 166$.

10.   9: 4 cents, 2 nickels, 1 dime, 1 quarter, 1 fifty-cent piece (alternatively, replace 2 nickels, 1 dime by 1 nickel, 2 dimes).

11.   39

Let a, b, c denote a cents, b nickels, c dimes. Then with no 25 cent piece the solutions in triples a, b, c are

47, 0, 0	42, 1, 0	37, 2, 0	37, 0, 1	32, 3, 0
32, 1, 1	27, 4, 0	27, 2, 1	27, 0, 2	22, 5, 0
22, 3, 1	22, 1, 2	17, 6, 0	17, 4, 1	17, 2, 2
17, 0, 3	12, 7, 0	12, 5, 1	12, 3, 2	12, 1, 3
7, 8, 0	7, 6, 1	7, 4, 2	7, 2, 3	7, 0, 4
2, 9, 0	2, 7, 1	2, 5, 2	2, 3, 3	2, 1, 4

With one 25 cent piece the solutions are

22, 0, 0	17, 1, 0	12, 2, 0	12, 0, 1	7, 3, 0
7, 1, 1	2, 4, 0	2, 2, 1	2, 0, 2	

12. 7

13. 3

14. 3, 4, 5, 6, 8, 9, 10, 12, 15, 18, 20, 24, 30, 36, 40, 45, 60, 72, 90, 120, 180, 360

A regular polygon with n sides has exterior angle $360/n$ degrees, and so an interior angle has size $360 - (360/n)$ degrees. Hence we choose all positive integers n such that $360/n$ is an integer, except $n = 1$ and $n = 2$.

15. 36

Let the colors be denoted by R, G, B and W, say for red, green, blue and white. There are 4 cases of solids painted one color: all R, all G, all B, all W. Solids painted two colors yield 18 cases: if the colors are R and G there are 3 cases because the number of R-faces may be 1, 2 or 3; similarly there are 3 cases for each of the other color combinations RB, RW, GB, GW, BW. There are 12 different kinds of solids painted three colors: if the colors are R, G, B, there are 3 cases—for example, one case with two R-faces, one G-face and one. B-face. Solids painted four colors can be of 2 kinds: orient the tetrahedron so that the bottom is R and there is a G-face towards you; then the other two faces can be BW or WB.

16. 6

17. 36

Problem Set 2, page 10

1. 676 (or 26·26)

2. 600 (or 25·24)

3. 3380 (or 26·26·5)

4. 3000 (or 5·25·24)

5. 30 (or 6·5)

6. 64 (or 8·2·2·2)

7. 4968 (or 23·12·3·6)

8. 243 (or 3·3·3·3·3); 768 (or 3·4·4·4·4)

Problem Set 3, page 11

1. 6; 120; 40320

2. 132; 2; 30; 5040

3. 120

4. 25

5. 6

6. 2

7. 720

8. 11880; 151200

9. 210

10. (b) and (c) are false.

Problem Set 4, page 17

1. 210, 1680 and 380

3. $P(n, 1) = n$; $P(m, 1) = m$; $P(n + m, 1) = n + m$

4. $P(n, n) = n!$ and $P(n, n - 1) = n(n - 1)(n - 2) \cdots 2 = n!$

5. 12144 (or 24·23·22)

6. 13824 (or 24·24·24); 14400 (by adding 24·24 to 13824)

7. 4536 (or 9·9·8·7); 2240, since there are 5 choices for the units' digit (digit on the right end), 8 choices for the thousands' digit, 8 choices for the hundreds' digit, and 7 choices for the tens' digit.

8. 120 (or 5·4·3·2); 72 (or 4·3·2·3)

9. 720 (or $6 \cdot 6 \cdot 5 \cdot 4$);   420

10. 103920

There are $P(8, 8) = 40320$ integers with 8 digits; $P(8, 7) = 40320$ integers with 7 digits; $P(8, 6) = 20160$ integers with 6 digits. Integers with 5 digits are separated into two types depending on the digit on the left end; if the left end digit is 5, there are $1 \cdot 5 \cdot 6 \cdot 5 \cdot 4 = 600$ possibilities because, taking the digits from left to right, there is one possibility for the first digit, 5 possibilities for the second digit (namely the digits 3, 4, 6, 7, 8 since integers with 0, 1 or 2 in this place would be less than 53000); if the first digit is 6, 7, or 8, there are $3 \cdot 7 \cdot 6 \cdot 5 \cdot 4 = 2520$ possibilities. The answer is obtained by adding these various results.

11. 90360

The solution of the previous problem can be used as a model, but must be modified because of the presence now of the digit 0. This digit cannot be used as the first or left end digit in an integer. The number of possibilities can be obtained by thinking about the number of possibilities for each digit position, from left to right. Thus,

8 digit numbers: $7 \cdot 7 \cdot 6 \cdot 5 \cdot 4 \cdot 3 \cdot 2 \cdot 1 = 35280$;

7 digit numbers: $7 \cdot 7 \cdot 6 \cdot 5 \cdot 4 \cdot 3 \cdot 2 = 35280$;

6 digit numbers: $7 \cdot 7 \cdot 6 \cdot 5 \cdot 4 \cdot 3 = 17640$;

5 digit numbers beginning with the digit 5: $1 \cdot 4 \cdot 6 \cdot 5 \cdot 4 = 480$;

5 digit numbers beginning with the digit 6 or 7: $2 \cdot 7 \cdot 6 \cdot 5 \cdot 4 = 1680$.

Problem Set 5, page 21

1. 15, 35 and 84

3. (a) $C(10, 2) = C(10, 8) = 45$;   (b) 45

4. $C(720, 10)$ or $\dfrac{720!}{10! \, 710!}$

6. $C(20, 2)$ or   190; $C(20, 3)$ or   1140

7. $10! - 2 \cdot 9! = 8 \cdot 9!$

The number of unrestricted arrangements is $10!$. The number of arrangements with two specific persons together is $2 \cdot 9!$ because the two persons can be regarded as a unit, but in two ways.

8. Let n be the largest of the five integers, so that we must prove that $n(n-1)(n-2)(n-3)(n-4)$ is divisible by $5!$. Now we solve the problem by observing that $C(n, 5)$ is an integer given by the formula

$$C(n, 5) = \frac{n(n-1)(n-2)(n-3)(n-4)}{5!}.$$

More generally, the formula for the integer $C(n, r)$ shows that the product of r consecutive integers is divisible by $r!$.

9. (a) 362880 or 9!;   (b) 5760 or 2(5!4!);   (c) 17280 or 6!4!;   (d) 2880 or 5!4!

In part (c) the red books may be treated as a unit, so there are 6 items to be permuted; this gives 6!. But in any one of these arrangements the red books can be permuted in 4! ways. In part (d), the green books can be permuted in their allocated positions in 5! ways, the red books in 4! ways.

10. (a) $2C(30, 3)C(30, 5) + C(30, 4)C(30, 4)$

Add the results of three cases, namely 3 professors, 4 professors, or 5 professors. For example, the 3 professors case implies 5 business men, and so there are $C(30, 3)C(30, 5)$ possibilities.

(b) $C(60, 8) - C(30, 8)$

If none of the eight were a business man, the number of possibilities would be $C(30, 8)$. This is then subtracted from the total number of unrestricted possibilities.

11. 79 (or $4 \cdot 5 \cdot 4 - 1$)

12. 4

There are as many zeros as the number of occurrences of 10 as a factor. Now 5 occurs as a factor four times, namely in 5, 10, 15, 20; and 2 occurs as a factor many more times.

13. 12

The argument is similar to that in the preceding problem, with this difference: the terms 25 and 50 in the product have 5 as a factor twice.

14. 7^5, because there are 7 choices for each flag.

15. (a) $7 \cdot 6^4$;   (b) $P(7, 5) = 7 \cdot 6 \cdot 5 \cdot 4 \cdot 3 = 2520$

16. 2024

The total number of unrestricted subsets is $C(26, 3) = 2600$. From this number we subtract the number of cases with three consecutive letters, such as J, K, L. There are 24 of these. Then we subtract the number of cases with two, but not three consecutive letters; if the letters are A, B there are 23 cases; B, C, 22 cases; $\cdots$; X, Y, 22 cases; Y, Z, 23 cases; so 552 in all. The answer is thus $2600 - 24 - 552$.

17. $k!/(k - n)!$

First choose n of the k boxes to receive one object each; this can be done in $C(k, n)$ ways. For each such choice, the things can be put in the boxes in $n!$ ways. Thus the answer is $C(k, n) \cdot n!$.

Problem Set 6, page 24

1. 5040 or 7!

2. 3600

Start with the solution of the preceding problem and subtract the number of cases where the two persons, say A and B, are in adjacent seats. Taking A and B as a unit we see that there are 6! cases with A to the left of B, and 6! cases the other way about. Thus the answer is $7! - 6! - 6!$.

3. 144

The ladies can be seated in alternate seats in 3! ways. The answer is obtained by multiplying this by 4!, the number of ways the men can be seated for any fixed arrangement of the ladies.

4. 12

Given any of the 3! seating arrangements of the ladies, the men can be seated in exactly two ways.

5. 120

The number of firing orders is simply the number of ways of arranging 1, 2, 3, 4, 5, 6 in a circle.

6. 30

Let one of the colors be white. Then since one face must be white, let it be the bottom of the block. The top can be colored in any of the 5 remaining colors. That done, the vertical faces are to be colored with the 4 remaining colors. This now amounts to a problem in circular permutations, because the cubical block can now be rotated about a vertical axis through the center of the block without altering the colors of the top and bottom. Hence there are 3! ways of coloring the vertical faces, and this is multiplied by 5 to get the answer.

7. 2

Starting with a blank block, number two opposite faces 1 and 6, and place the block with the 6 on top. The four vertical faces are to be numbered 2, 3, 4, 5. Number the front face 2, and the back face 5. There remain two choices for the numbers 3 and 4.

Problem Set 7, page 30

1. (a) 168 or $8!/(5!2!)$ (b) $21!/(2!2!2!2!3!9!)$

2. Choose a out of n, then b out of $n - a$, then c out of $n - a - b$. This gives $C(n, a)C(n - a, b)C(n - a - b, c)$, which can be evaluated further to give the factorial answer.

3. 5035

We subtract from the total number 6435 of unrestricted paths the number that includes the block from 5th to 6th on E. From 1st and A to 5th and E there are $C(8, 4)$ paths. From 6th and E to 9th and H there are $C(6, 3)$ paths. Hence from 6435 we subtract

$$C(8, 4) \cdot C(6, 3).$$

4. $15!/(4!5!6!)$

Denoting by R, B, U the motions of distance one unit to the right, back, and up, we see that the problem is the same as finding the number of permutations, all at a time, of the fifteen letters

$$R\ R\ R\ R\ B\ B\ B\ B\ B\ U\ U\ U\ U\ U$$

5. $17!/(4!5!6!2!)$

Problem Set 8, page 33

1. 15, 10, 5   **2.** $C(10, 4)$ **3.** $C(49, 10)$

4. (a) $C(n - 1, r) = C(n - 2, r) + C(n - 2, r - 1)$;

(b) $C(n - 1, r - 1) = C(n - 2, r - 1) + C(n - 2, r - 2)$

5. (a) $C(n - 1, r) = \dfrac{(n - 1)!}{r!(n - r - 1)!}$

(b) $C(n - 1, r - 1) = \dfrac{(n - 1)!}{(r - 1)!(n - r)!}$

6. Adding the results of the preceding problem, we get

$$C(n - 1, r) + C(n - 1, r - 1)$$

$$= \frac{(n - 1)!}{r!(n - r - 1)!} + \frac{(n - 1)!}{(r - 1)!(n - r)!}$$

$$= \frac{(n - 1)!(n - r) + (n - 1)!r}{r!(n - r)!} = \frac{(n - 1)!n}{r!(n - r)!}$$

$$= \frac{n!}{r!(n - r)!} = C(n, r).$$

7. $C(n, r) = C(n - 2, r - 2) + 2C(n - 2, r - 1) + C(n - 2, r)$

8. $n = r = 0$

Problem Set 9, page 37

1. 6; $n + 1$

2. $(x + y)^6 = C(6, 0)x^6 + C(6, 1)x^5y + C(6, 2)x^4y^2 + C(6, 3)x^3y^3 + C(6, 4)x^2y^4 + C(6, 5)xy^5 + C(6, 6)y^6$;

with $x = y = 1$, this sum equals 2^6 or 64.

3. $(1 - 1)^6 = 0$

4. $C(10, 7) = 120$

5. $u^7 + 7u^6v + 21u^5v^2 + 35u^4v^3 + 35u^3v^4 + 21u^2v^5 + 7uv^6 + v^7$

8. 180 terms; *bdsw* and *bfpu* are actual terms.

Problem Set 10, page 40

1. $x^4 + y^4 + z^4 + 4x^3y + 4xy^3 + 4x^3z + 4xz^3 + 4y^3z + 4yz^3 + 6x^2y^2$
$$+ 6x^2z^2 + 6y^2z^2 + 12x^2yz + 12xy^2z + 12xyz^2$$

2. $10!/(2!2!2!2!2!)$ **3.** $6!$ **4.** 3^8; 4^{17}

5. 3^{12} because the numbers are precisely the coefficients in the expansion of $(x + y + z)^{12}$.

Problem Set 11, page 42

1. 1, 9, 36, 84, 126, 126, 84, 36, 9, 1
1, 10, 45, 120, 210, 252, 210, 120, 45, 10, 1
1, 11, 55, 165, 330, 462, 462, 330, 165, 55, 11, 1
1, 12, 66, 220, 495, 792, 924, 792, 495, 220, 66, 12, 1
1, 13, 78, 286, 715, 1287, 1716, 1716, 1287, 715, 286, 78, 13, 1

2. By formula (3.6) the sum of the elements of the ninth row is 2^8. Similarly the sums of the elements of preceding rows are 2^7, 2^6, etc. So it must be verified that

$$2^8 = 2^7 + 2^6 + 2^5 + 2^4 + 2^3 + 2^2 + 2^1 + 2^0 + 1.$$

By virtue of the identity

$$a^n - 1 = (a - 1)(a^{n-1} + a^{n-2} + \cdots + a + a^0),$$

we have $2^8 - 1 = (2 - 1)(2^7 + 2^6 + \cdots + 2^0)$ or

$$2^8 - 1 = 2^7 + 2^6 + \cdots + 2^0$$

which is equivalent to the equation we wanted to verify.

3. This can be deduced from equation (3.7) by transposing terms with minus signs.

Problem Set 12, page 43

1. 63 or $2^6 - 1$

2. 6560 or $3^8 - 1$, because on each issue a member has three choices: yes, no, or abstention.

3. 1023 or $2^{10} - 1$

4. 254, because there are 2^7 types for a family of 7 children, 2^6 for 6 children, and so on.

Problem Set 13, page 47

1. 5050 or $\frac{1}{2}(100)(101)$

2. Denoting the sum by s we have $2s = 101 + 101 + \cdots + 101$ with 100 summands. Hence $2s = 10100$ and $s = 5050$.

3. Denoting the sum by S we have

$$S = 1 + 2 + 3 + \cdots + (n-2) + (n-1) + n$$
$$S = n + (n-1) + (n-2) + \cdots + 3 + 2 + 1$$
$$2S = (n+1) + (n+1) + \cdots + (n+1) = n(n+1),$$
$$S = \tfrac{1}{2}n(n+1)$$

4. 338350 or $\frac{1}{6}(100)(101)(201)$

5. (a) 99   (b) 101   **6.** (a) $n-1$ (b) $n+1$.

7. 4851; 5151

With $x = 1$ the equation becomes $y + z = 99$ with 98 solutions in positive integers; with $x = 2$ we have $y + z = 98$ with 97 solutions in positive integers; $\cdots$; with $x = 98$ we have $y + z = 2$ with 1 solution. The total number of solutions in positive integers is

$$98 + 97 + \cdots + 2 + 1 = \tfrac{1}{2}(98)(99).$$

8. $\frac{1}{2}(n-2)(n-1)$; $\frac{1}{2}(n+1)(n+2)$

9. 10; 15; $\frac{1}{2}(n+1)(n+2)$

The number of terms in the expansion of $(x + y + z)^4$ is the number of solutions of $a + b + c = 4$ in non-negative integers.

10. Write equation (3.8) with $r = 4$ and n replaced by $m + 3$, $m + 2$, $m + 1$, $\cdots$, 6, 5, to get

$$C(m + 2, 3) \ = \ C(m + 3, 4) - C(m + 2, 4)$$

$$C(m + 1, 3) \ = \ C(m + 2, 4) - C(m + 1, 4)$$

$$C(m, 3) \ = \ C(m + 1, 4) - C(m, 4)$$

$$\cdots \cdots \cdots \cdots \cdots$$

$$C(5, 3) \ = \ C(6, 4) - C(5, 4)$$

$$C(4, 3) \ = \ C(5, 4) - C(4, 4)$$

Adding these we get

$$C(4, 3) + C(5, 3) + \cdots + C(m, 3) + C(m + 1, 3) + C(m + 2, 3)$$
$$= C(m + 3, 4) - C(4, 4).$$
$$\tfrac{1}{6}(4)(3)(2) + \tfrac{1}{6}(5)(4)(3) + \cdots + \tfrac{1}{6}(m + 2)(m + 1)(m)$$
$$= \tfrac{1}{24}(m + 3)(m + 2)(m + 1)(m) - 1.$$

Transpose the term -1 and multiply by 6 to get

$$(3)(2)(1) + (4)(3)(2) + (5)(4)(3) + \cdots + (m + 2)(m + 1)(m)$$
$$= \tfrac{1}{4}(m + 3)(m + 2)(m + 1)(m).$$

The term $(m + 2)(m + 1)m$, for example, can be written as $m^3 + 3m^2 + 2m$, so the whole left side can be separated into three sums

$$(1^3 + 2^3 + 3^3 + \cdots + m^3) + 3(1^2 + 2^2 + 3^2 + \cdots + m^2)$$
$$+ 2(1 + 2 + 3 + \cdots + m).$$

Writing S for the sum of the cubes from 1^3 to m^3, and substituting the known formulas for the other sums, we get

$$S + \tfrac{1}{2}m(m + 1)(2m + 1) + m(m + 1)$$
$$= \tfrac{1}{4}(m + 3)(m + 2)(m + 1)m.$$

This reduces to $S = \tfrac{1}{4}m^2(m + 1)^2$ and so the answer is

$$1^3 + 2^3 + 3^3 + \cdots + m^3 = \tfrac{1}{4}m^2(m + 1)^2.$$

Problem Set 14, page 54

1. $F(11) = 233.$

2. $F(n)$ is even if $n = 1, 4, 7, 10, 13, 16, \cdots$. In general $F(n)$ is even if n is of the form $3k + 1$, and $F(n)$ is odd in all other cases. This is an immediate consequence of Formula (4.4) and the fact that the sum of two integers is odd only if one of them is odd and the other even.

3. $F(n + 1) = F(n) + F(n - 1)$

4. Add the result of the preceding question to formula (4.4).

5. $C(11, 6)$

6. $C(15, 5)C(16, 6)$
Ignoring the B's momentarily we observe that the A's and C's can be arranged in order in any one of $C(15, 5)$ ways. Then there are 16 places between the A's and C's and at the ends where the B's may be inserted. Thus for each arrangement of A's and C's, there are $C(16, 6)$ ways of inserting the B's.

7. 7350
Ignoring the i's momentarily we note that the other letters can be arranged in order in $7!/(4!2!) = 105$ ways. Then there are 8 places between and at the ends of these letters where the i's may be inserted. Hence there are $C(8, 4)$ or 70 ways of inserting the i's. The answer is $70 \cdot 105$.

Problem Set 15, page 58

1. $C(49, 3)$; $C(53, 3)$

2. We note that $C(8, 3) = C(8, 5)$

4. It suffices to establish that $C(m - 1, k - 1) = C(m - 1, m - k)$, and this follows from formula (2.4).

5. Use formula (4.10).

6. (a) $C(11, 6)$

Ignoring the integer 1,000,000 the sum of whose digits is not 6, we interpret the integers from 1 to 999,999 as having six digits by allowing zero as a digit. For example the integer 8365 can be written 008365. If we write $x_1, \cdots, x_6$ for the six digits, we can interpret the problem as the number of solutions of $x_1 + x_2 + \cdots + x_6 = 6$ in non-negative integers.

(b) $C(10, 5) + C(9, 4) + C(8, 3) + C(7, 2) + C(6, 1) + 1$

7. (a) $C(21, 17)$

Each term of the expansion is of the form $\alpha_1^{z_1} \alpha_2^{z_2} \alpha_3^{z_3} \alpha_4^{z_4} \alpha_5^{z_5}$ (with an appropriate coefficient), where the sum of the exponents is 17; thus $x_1 + x_2 + x_3 + x_4 + x_5 = 17$. Hence the answer is the number of solutions of this equation in non-negative integers.

(b) $C(t + k - 1, t)$

Problem Set 16, page 60

1. r **2.** $C(11, 6)$ **3.** $C(12, 10)$ **4.** $C(16, 12)$.

5. $C(16, 7) - 1$

The question amounts to asking for the number of combinations, seven at a time, of the ten digits 0, 1, 2, $\cdots$, 9, each of which may be repeated in the combination. The "-1" in the answer accounts for the case of seven zeros, to which there corresponds no integer.

Problem Set 17, page 65

1. One of the twenty parts of the answer is: 6, 8, 7, 6 corresponds to 1, 3, 2, 1.

2. $C(71, 3)$

3. (a) $C(37, 4)$ (b) $C(30, 4)$

4. $C(16, 3)$

5. (a) $C(13, 3)$ (b) $C(7, 3)$ (c) None

6. (a) $C(17, 3)$ (b) $C(11, 3)$

7. (a) $C(m - c_1 + 3, 3)$ (b) $C(m - c_1 - c_2 + 3, 3)$

8. $C(18, 5) - 6C(8, 5)$

Set aside the integer 1,000,000 the sum of whose digits is not 13. We interpret the integers from 1 to 999,999 as having six digits by allowing zero as a digit. If we write $x_1, \cdots, x_6$ for the six digits we can interpret the problem as the number of solutions of $x_1 + x_2 + \cdots + x_6 = 13$ in non-negative integers not exceeding nine. Ignoring the "not exceeding nine" limitation momentarily, we note that the equation has $C(18, 5)$ solutions in non-negative integers. Next, the number of solutions in non-negative integers with $x_1 > 9$ is seen to be $C(8, 5)$. This is subtracted from $C(18, 5)$, and analogous subtractions are made for the cases $x_2 > 9$, $x_3 > 9$, etc.

Problem Set 18, page 71

1. $N - N(\alpha) - N(\beta) - N(\gamma) - N(\delta) + N(\alpha, \beta) + N(\alpha, \gamma) + N(\alpha, \delta)$
$$+ N(\beta, \gamma) + N(\beta, \delta) + N(\gamma, \delta) - N(\alpha, \beta, \gamma) - N(\alpha, \beta, \delta)$$
$$- N(\alpha, \gamma, \delta) - N(\beta, \gamma, \delta) + N(\alpha, \beta, \gamma, \delta)$$

2. 2^r, the total number of subsets of a set of r objects.

3. 16000

Let divisibility by 3, 5, 11 be denoted by α, β, γ, respectively. Then formula (5.3) gives

$$33000 - 11000 - 6600 - 3000 + 2200 + 1000 + 600 - 200.$$

4. 998910

The fourth powers are included among the squares, so they can be left out of the consideration. Say that an integer has property α if it is a perfect square, property β if a perfect cube. An integer has both properties α and β if it is a perfect sixth power. Thus we make the computation

$$N - N(\alpha) - N(\beta) + N(\alpha, \beta) = 1,000,000 - 1000 - 100 + 10.$$

5. $N(\alpha, \beta, \gamma) - N(\alpha, \beta, \gamma, \delta) - N(\alpha, \beta, \gamma, \epsilon) + N(\alpha, \beta, \gamma, \delta, \epsilon)$

6. $N(\beta) - N(\beta, \alpha) - N(\beta, \gamma) - N(\beta, \delta) + N(\beta, \alpha, \gamma) + N(\beta, \alpha, \delta)$
$$+ N(\beta, \gamma, \delta) - N(\beta, \alpha, \gamma, \delta)$$

Problem Set 19, page 77

1. $C(13, 3) - 4C(7, 3)$

2. $C(16, 5) - 6C(11, 5) + 15C(6, 5)$
The question amounts to asking for the number of solutions of $y_1 + y_2 + \cdots + y_6 = 17$ in positive integers not exceeding 5, because any even integer x_1 can be written as $2y_1$, where y_1 is again an integer.

3. $C(14, 3) - C(8, 3) - 2C(7, 3) - C(6, 3)$
Let N denote the number of solutions of the equation which satisfy the conditions $x_1 > 0$, $x_2 > 0$, $x_3 > 2$, > 3. x_4 Thus $N = C(14, 3)$ by the formula (4.22). If one of these solutions has $x_1 > 6$, say it has property α. Likewise let $x_2 > 7$, $x_3 > 9$ and $x_4 > 11$ correspond to properties β, γ and δ. Thus we want to find how many of the $C(14, 3)$ solutions have none of the properties $\alpha, \beta, \gamma, \delta$. By use of formula (4.22) we compute

$$N(\alpha) = C(8, 3), \quad N(\beta) = C(7, 3), \quad N(\gamma) = C(7, 3), \quad N(\delta) = C(6, 3).$$

All further terms in formula (5.3) are zero.

4. $C(16, 3) - 4C(9, 3)$

5. $C(13, 3) - C(4, 3) - C(5, 3) - C(8, 3) - C(9, 3) + C(4, 3)$
This amounts to finding the number of solutions of

$$x_1 + x_2 + x_3 + x_4 = 10$$

in non-negative integers subject to the restrictions $x_1 \leqslant 8$, $x_2 \leqslant 7$, $x_3 \leqslant 4$, $x_4 \leqslant 3$.

6. $C(12, 2) - C(3, 2) - C(4, 2) - C(7, 2)$
This amounts to finding the number of solutions of $x_1 + x_2 + x_3 = 10$ in integers satisfying the inequalities $0 \leqslant x_1 \leqslant 8$, $0 \leqslant x_2 \leqslant 7$, $0 \leqslant x_3 \leqslant 4$.

7. $C(11, 3) - 4C(8, 3) + 6C(5, 3) = 1$

8. $C(13, 3) - 4C(4, 3)$

10. $c = 23$; $C(11, 4) - 5C(5, 4) = C(22, 4) - 5C(16, 4)$
$$+ 10C(10, 4) - 10C(4, 4)$$
The substitution or transformation $x_j = 7 - y_j$ for $j = 1, 2, 3, 4, 5$ will solve the problem.

11. $C(m-1, k-1) - C(m-1-c_1, k-1) - C(m-1-c_2, k-1)$

$\qquad - C(m-1-c_3, k-1) + C(m-1-c_1-c_2, k-1)$

$\qquad + C(m-1-c_1-c_3, k-1) + C(m-1-c_2-c_3, k-1)$

$\qquad\qquad - C(m-1-c_1-c_2-c_3, \ k-1)$

12. $C(24, 6) - C(15, 6) - 6C(14, 6)$

Denote the digits from left to right by $x_1, \cdots, x_7$. Then the answer is the number of solutions of $x_1 + \cdots + x_7 = 19$ in non-negative integers not exceeding 9, but with the additional restriction that x_1 is positive.

Problem Set 20, page 81

1. $D(5) = 44$; $D(6) = 265$

2. 1234   2134   3142   1243   2143   3214   1432   2413   3412

3. (a) 1936

The integers 1, 2, 3, 4, 5 can be put into the first five places in $D(5)$ ways, because there are $D(5)$ derangements of five things; the remaining integers from 6 to 10 can be put into the last five places in $D(5)$ ways, so the answer is $D(5) \cdot D(5)$.

  (b) $(5!)^2 = 14400$

Any arrangement of 6, 7, 8, 9, 10 in the first five places is a derangement, so there are $5!$ possibilities; the same is true for the integers 1, 2, 3, 4, 5 in the last five places.

4. 3216

We use the inclusion-exclusion principle with three properties of the permutations: 1 in the first place; 4 in the fourth place; 7 in the seventh place. Thus the answer is $7! - 6! - 6! - 6! + 5! + 5! + 5! - 4!$.

5. 22260

There are $C(9, 3) = 84$ ways of choosing the three numbers which are to be in their natural positions; for each such choice, there are $D(6) = 265$ derangements of the other six numbers. The product of 84 and 265 is the answer.

6. $D(26)$ or $26! \left[1 - \dfrac{1}{1!} + \dfrac{1}{2!} - \dfrac{1}{3!} + \cdots + \dfrac{1}{26!} \right]$

7. $D(n) - nD(n-1) = n!\left[1 - \dfrac{1}{1!} + \cdots + \dfrac{(-1)^n}{n!}\right]$

$$- n!\left[1 - \dfrac{1}{1!} + \cdots + \dfrac{(-1)^{n-1}}{(n-1)!}\right]$$

After the subtraction is performed, the only remaining term is

$$n!\left[\dfrac{(-1)^n}{n!}\right].$$

Problem Set 21, page 86

2. $\frac{1}{4}$ **3.** $\frac{1}{6}$.

4. 5/12

There are 36 equally likely cases. Of these, 15 have a larger number on the white die.

5. 5/18

There are 6^4 equally likely cases. For convenience we suppose that the dice are of different colors, say white, red, blue and green. When the dice are thrown we can argue that any outcome on the white die will be satisfactory, so 6 possibilities; but whatever the outcome on the white die, we want a different outcome on the red die, so 5 possibilities; similarly there are 4 possibilities on the blue die, and 3 on the green die. So the number of favorable cases is $6 \cdot 5 \cdot 4 \cdot 3$. (Another way of calculating the number of favorable cases is to count the number of four-digit integers made up entirely with the digits 1, 2, 3, 4, 5, 6, and having distinct digits. Any such integer, say 3516, can be interpreted as meaning that the white die comes up "3", the red die "5", the blue die "1", and the green die "6".)

6. $7 \cdot 5^5/6^7$

There are 6^7 equally likely cases. To calculate the number of favorable cases, we count the number of seven digit numbers (one digit for each die) made up entirely of the digits 1, 2, 3, 4, 5, 6, and having exactly three sixes present. This is seen to be $1 \cdot 1 \cdot 1 \cdot 5 \cdot 5 \cdot 5 \cdot C(7, 3)$.

8. $651/6^5$ or $[C(14, 4) - 5C(8, 4)]/6^5$

There are 6^5 equally likely cases. The number of favorable cases is the same as the number of solutions of $x_1 + x_2 + x_3 + x_4 + x_5 = 15$ in integers from 1 to 6.

9. (a) 7/32

There are 2^8 equally likely cases. Of these the number of favorable cases is $C(8, 5)$, because it amounts to the number of ways of choosing five out of eight coins.

(b) 93/256   or $[C(8, 5) + C(8, 6) + C(8, 7) + C(8, 8)]/2^8$.

10. $13^4/C(52, 4)$

The number of selections of four cards from a deck is $C(52, 4)$. The number of selections of four cards, one from each suit, is $[C(13, 1)]^4$, or 13^4.

11. (a) $1 - [C(40, 13) + 12C(40, 12)]/C(52, 13)$

Compute the complementary probability. The total number of equally likely cases is $C(52, 13)$. The number of selections of 13 cards with no face cards present is $C(40, 13)$; with exactly one face card present is $C(12, 1)C(40, 12)$.

(b) $C(4, 1)C(48, 12)/C(52, 13)$

(c) $1 - C(48, 13)/C(52, 13)$

This answer is arrived at by computing the complementary probability. (The answer by a direct method looks different.) The number of selections of 13 cards with no aces present is $C(48, 13)$.

12. 1/13

There are 26! orders in all. Of these, x and y are adjacent in $2 \cdot 25!$ cases.

13. (a) $[C(23, 4) - C(14, 4) - 4C(13, 4) + 4C(4, 4)]/90000$

There are 90000 five digit integers. The number of favorable cases is the number of solutions of $x_1 + x_2 + x_3 + x_4 + x_5 = 20$ in non-negative integers not exceeding 9, but with the additional restriction that x_1 must be positive. The inclusion-exclusion principle along with formula (4.22) can then be used.

(b) 1/1800

There are 50 five-digit integers satisfying the conditions of the problem. Twenty of them have digits 5, 4, 1, 1, 1, and thirty of them have digits 5, 2, 2, 1, 1.

14. No, the probability is 4/9

There are $C(10, 5)/2$ equally likely cases, because this is the number of ways that 10 boys can be separated into two teams of 5. To compute the number of favorable cases, we set aside the two friends and choose three out of eight to accompany them on "favorable" teams; this gives $C(8, 3)$ favorable cases.

15. $1 - D(8)/8!$; $1 - [D(8) + 8D(7)]/8!$

The answers given arise from the complementary probability in each part. The number of equally likely cases is 8!. The number of ways in which no spark plug can go back into its original cylinder is $D(8)$, the number of derangements of 8 things. Furthermore, the number of arrangements with exactly one plug in its original cylinder is $8D(7)$.

16. The probability of a win is the same as the probability that the arrangement of cards in one deck is compatible with that in the other. Since there are 52! possible arrangements and $D(52)$ derangements, the ratio of the number of favorable cases to the total number of equally likely cases is

$$\frac{D(52)}{52!} = 1 - \frac{1}{1!} + \frac{1}{2!} - \frac{1}{3!} + \cdots + \frac{1}{52!} \qquad \text{(approximately .3679)}.$$

17. $1 - \dfrac{1}{1!} + \dfrac{1}{2!} - \dfrac{1}{3!} + \cdots - \dfrac{1}{13!}$

(To four decimal places, this answer is the same as that to Problem 16.)

18. The probability of a win is the probability that a shuffled deck will produce a total derangement except for one card. There are 52 ways of holding one card fixed and $D(51)$ derangements of the remaining 51 cards. Hence, the answer is

$$52\frac{D(51)}{52!} = \frac{D(51)}{51!} = 1 - \frac{1}{1!} + \frac{1}{2!} - \frac{1}{3!} + \cdots - \frac{1}{51!}.$$

(This differs from the answer to Problem 16 by 1/52! which is an extremely small number.)

Problem Set 22, page 96

1. 1, 2, 3, 5, 7   **2.** $p_1(n) = 1,$ $q_1(n) = 1$

3. $q_2(8) = 5,$ $q_2(9) = 5,$ $q_2(n) = 1 + \frac{1}{2}n$ if n is even,

$\qquad\qquad\qquad q_2(n) = \frac{1}{2}(n+1)$ if n is odd.

4. 1   **5.** 2

6. The largest summand occurring among all the partitions of n is n itself, and hence there are no partitions counted by $p_{n+1}(n)$ not already counted by $p_n(n)$; similarly for $p_k(n)$ with $k > n$.

7. There is only one partition, namely n itself, that is counted by $p_n(n)$ but not by $p_{n-1}(n)$.

Problem Set 23, page 99

1. Partial solution:

k $\diagdown$ n	1	2	3	4	5	6	7	8	9	10	11	12
8	1	5	10	15	18	20	21	22	22	22	22	22
9	1	5	12	18	23	26	28	29	30	30	30	30
10	1	6	14	23	30	35	38	40	41	42	42	42
11	1	6	16	27	37	44	49	52	54	55	56	56
12	1	7	19	34	47	58	65	70	73	75	76	77

2. 7, 15, 28   **3.** 15, 22, 30, 42

Problem Set 24, page 101

1. $1 + x + x^2 + x^3 + x^4 + x^5 + x^6 + x^7 + x^8 + x^9 + x^{10} + x^{11} + x^{12}$

$\qquad\qquad\qquad + x^{13} + x^{14} + x^{15} + x^{16} + \cdots$

2. $1 + x + x^2 + 2x^3 + 2x^4 + 3x^5 + 4x^6 + 5x^7 + 6x^8 + \cdots$

3. $1 + x + 2x^2 + 3x^3 + 5x^4 + 7x^5 + 11x^6 + 15x^7 + \cdots$

Problem Set 25, page 105

1. (a) the number of partitions of 12 with even summands;
   (b) the number of partitions of 9 with summands not exceeding 3;
   (c) the number of partitions of 6 with distinct summands.

2. (a) 11   (b) 12   (c) 4

3. (a) $(1 + x^6 + x^{12} + x^{18} + x^{24} + x^{30} + x^{36})$
   $\cdot (1 + x^7 + x^{14} + x^{21} + x^{28} + x^{35})(1 + x^{12} + x^{24} + x^{36})(1 + x^{20})$;

   (b) $(1 + x^3 + x^6 + x^9 + x^{12} + x^{15})(1 + x^4 + x^8 + x^{12})$
   $\cdot (1 + x^5 + x^{10} + x^{15})(1 + x^6 + x^{12})(1 + x^7 + x^{14})(1 + x^8)$
   $\cdot (1 + x^9) \cdots (1 + x^{15})$;

   (c) $(1 + x)(1 + x^2)(1 + x^3)(1 + x^4)(1 + x^5)(1 + x^6)(1 + x^7)$
   $\cdot (1 + x^8)(1 + x^9)$; 5, 17, 8 partitions respectively.

4. 14
Compute the coefficient of x^{18} in the expansion of

$$(1 + x^2 + x^4 + x^6 + \cdots + x^{18})(1 + x^3 + x^6 + \cdots + x^{18})$$
$$\cdot (1 + x^5 + x^{10} + x^{15})(1 + x^7 + x^{14}).$$

5. 3
The answer is the number of solutions of

$$3U + 5V + 7W + 9T = 16$$

in non-negative integers, as can be seen by use of the transformation $u = 1 + U, \quad v = 1 + V, \quad w = 1 + W, \quad t = 1 + T.$ This is the coefficient of x^{16} in the expansion of

$$(1 + x^3 + x^6 + x^9 + x^{12} + x^{15})(1 + x^5 + x^{10} + x^{15})$$
$$\cdot (1 + x^7 + x^{14})(1 + x^9).$$

Problem Set 26, page 108

(In these solutions P_1, P_2, P_3, P_4, P_5 denote the polynomials given in the text on page 107.)

1. 343

Compute the coefficient of x^{100} in the expansion of $P_1P_2P_3QP_5$, where $Q = 1 + x^{20} + x^{40} + x^{60} + x^{80} + x^{100}$.

2. 49

Compute the coefficient of x^{58} in the expansion of $P_1P_2P_3P_4$. Each polynomial can be abbreviated to exclude powers higher than x^{58}.

3. 34

This is the coefficient of x^{95} in the expansion of $P_2P_3P_4P_5$.

4. 16

Apply the transformation $y = 1 + Y$, $z = 1 + Z$, $w = 1 + W$, $t = 1 + T$ to get the equation $5Y + 10Z + 25W + 50T = 65$ and then find the number of solutions of this equation in non-negative integers. This is the coefficient of x^{65} in the expansion of $P_2P_3P_4P_5$.

Problem Set 27, page 111

1. 150 or $3^5 - 3 \cdot 2^5 + 3$ **2.** $f(5, 2) = 2^5 - 2 = 30$

4. $k! = k^k - C(k, 1)(k - 1)^k + C(k, 2)(k - 2)^k - C(k, 3)(k - 3)^k$
$$+ \cdots + (-1)^{k-1}C(k, k - 1)$$

5. The expression in the problem comes from formula (8.1) with $k = 8$; since there are no ways of distributing fewer than 8 objects into 8 boxes with no box empty, $f(m, 8) = 0$ for $m < 8$.

Problem Set 28, page 114

1. 3025 or $\dfrac{3^9 - 3 \cdot 2^9 + 3}{3!}$ **2.** $\dfrac{4^4 - 4 \cdot 3^4 + 6 \cdot 2^4 - 4}{4!} = 1$

3. $2^{m-1} - 1$

4. (a) 122   (b) 90

The number 30,030 has six distinct prime factors, and we want to separate these into three sets. The notation for part (a) is $G(6, 3)$, for part (b) is $g(6, 3)$.

5. 52   **7.** $g(m, m - 2) = C(m, 3) + 3C(m, 4)$

Problem Set 29, page 117

1. (a) 24   (b) 126 or $C(9, 4)$ (c) 151200 or $P(10, 6)$
    (d) 286   (e) 7   (f) 21   (g) 19

Solution of (d). This is $C(13, 3)$, the number of solutions of $x + y + z + w = 10$ in non-negative integers.

Solution of (g). This is $C(8, 2) - 3C(3, 2)$, the number of solutions of $x + y + z = 6$ in non-negative integers not exceeding 4.

2. (a) $n!$ (b) $P(n, r)$ (c) $C(n, r)$ (d) $C(r + k - 1, r)$

Solution of (d). This is the number of solutions of

$$x_1 + x_2 + \cdots + x_k = r$$

in non-negative integers.

3. $\frac{1}{4}(k^2 + 3k + 4) \cdot k!$

Denote the two like objects by A, A. The first box is to contain two objects. The number of distributions with at least one A in the first box is $(k + 1)!$. The number of distributions with the A's in boxes other than the first is $C(k, 2)C(k, 2) \cdot (k - 2)!$, because there are $C(k, 2)$ ways of choosing the two objects to go in the first box, $C(k, 2)$ ways of choosing the two boxes for the A's, and $(k - 2)!$ ways of distributing the other $k - 2$ objects.

Problem Set 30, page 121

4. $k = 4$

Suppose that at most three of $a_1, a_2, \cdots, a_{10}$, and at most three of $b_1, b_2, \cdots, b_{10}$, and at most three of $c_1, c_2, \cdots, c_{10}$ have property Q. Then by simple addition at most nine of the entire thirty items have property Q. This contradicts the given information.

5. $r = 4$

Problem Set 31, page 123

1. One way to handle this is to color AB, BC, CD, DE, EA blue, and all other line segments red.

2. Denote one of the seventeen points by A and denote the others by B_1, B_2, $\cdots$, B_{16}. Consider the sixteen line segments emanating from A, namely AB_1, AB_2, $\cdots$, AB_{16}. By the pigeonhole principle at least six of these segments are of one color, say blue. We may as well take these six blue segments to be AB_1, AB_2, $\cdots$, AB_6. Now if there is at least one blue segment among the fifteen segments linking B_1, B_2, B_3, B_4, B_5, B_6, then we have a blue chromatic triangle. (For example if the segment B_3B_5 is blue, then AB_3B_5 is a blue triangle.) On the other hand if there is no blue segment in this batch of fifteen, this means that all segments linking the points B_1, B_2, B_3, B_4, B_5, B_6 are red or white. In this case we apply the basic result proved in Section 9.2.

Problem Set 32, page 127

1. $\frac{1}{2}(n^2 + n)$

This result can be obtained from the answer $\frac{1}{2}(n^2 + n + 2)$ in the text for the number of regions created by n lines, no two parallel, no three concurrent. For if in that case we slide one of the lines across the plane in such a way that it becomes concurrent with two other lines, then one region is lost.

2. $(m + 1)(k + 1)$

3. $(m + 1)(k + 1) + m + k + 1$
The new line creates $m + k + 1$ new regions.

4. $qt + 2q + 2t - 1$

Denote the number of regions by $F(q, t)$. If we remove one of the q lines we see that $2 + t$ regions are lost, and so $F(q, t)$ exceeds $F(q - 1, t)$ by $2 + t$. Thus we have

$$F(q, t) - F(q - 1, t) = 2 + t,$$
$$F(q - 1, t) - F(q - 2, t) = 2 + t,$$
$$F(q - 2, t) - F(q - 3, t) = 2 + t,$$
$$\cdots \cdots \cdots$$
$$F(2, t) - F(1, t) = 2 + t,$$
$$F(1, t) - F(0, t) = 1 + t.$$

(Note the slight difference in the last equation.) Adding these we get the answer by use of $F(0, t) = 2t$.

5. $kq + 2q + k$

Denote the number of regions by $H(q, k)$. If one of the k parallel lines is removed, the number of regions is reduced by $q + 1$. Hence we see that $H(q, k) - H(q, k - 1) = q + 1$. Forming a telescoping sum as in the preceding question, and using $H(q, 0) = 2q$, we get the answer.

6. $kq + 2q + k + nk + nq + n(n + 1)/2$

Denote the number of regions by $H(q, k, n)$ so that $H(q, k, 0)$ is the same as $H(q, k)$ of the preceding question. If one of the n lines is withdrawn, there is a decrease of $n + k + q$ regions. Thus,

$$H(q, k, n) - H(q, k, n - 1) = k + q + n,$$

and from this we can proceed as in the two preceding solutions.

Problem Set 33, page 132

3. A comparison with Pascal's triangle suggests the conjecture

$$K(n) = C(n - 1, 2) = \tfrac{1}{2}(n - 1)(n - 2).$$

This turns out to be correct, because $K(n + 1) = K(n) + n - 1$ by the following observation: $K(n + 1)$ counts not only the pairs counted by $K(n)$ but also the pairs

$$1, n + 1 \qquad 2, n + 1 \qquad 3, n + 1 \qquad \cdots \qquad n - 1, n + 1.$$

4. (a) False (b) True (c) True (d) False (e) False (f) True

Problem Set 34, page 138

2. (a) $\displaystyle\sum_{j=1}^{n} 3j = \frac{3n(n + 1)}{2}$

(c) $\displaystyle\sum_{j=1}^{n} (2j-1)(2j+1) = \sum_{j=1}^{n} (4j^2-1) = 4\sum_{j=1}^{n} j^2 - n$

$$= \frac{2n(n+1)(2n+1)}{3} - n$$

$$= \frac{n(4n^2+6n-1)}{3}$$

3. (a) $\dfrac{n(n-1)}{2}$ **(c)** $\dfrac{(n+1)(n+2)(2n+3)}{6}$

4. 50   **6.** 0   **8.** 2520   **9.** $2^n n!$ **11.** $f(n) = (n+1)! - 1$

Problem Set 35, page 143

1. (i) 42   **(ii)** 132   **(iii)** 429

2. 5^{262144}

Solutions of Miscellaneous Problems

1. Consider the complementary probability, namely the chances of getting fewer than half the answers correct. The number of equally likely possibilities is 2^9. The student fails to get at least three right out of nine in $C(9, 0) + C(9, 1) + C(9, 2)$ cases, the terms of this sum corresponding to none, one or two right. Noting that this sum is $1 + 9 + 36 = 46$, we see that the complementary probability is $46/512$, which is less than $1/10$.

2. 1414

The answer to the question is the smallest positive integer n such that $\frac{1}{2}(n^2 + n) > 1,000,000$. The corresponding equation

$$\tfrac{1}{2}(n^2 + n) = 1,000,000$$

has a positive root between 1413 and 1414.

3. $n^3(n + 1)$

The problem is to evaluate

$$\sum_{j=1}^{n} (4j^3 - 3j^2 + j) \quad \text{or} \quad 4\sum_{j=1}^{n} j^3 - 3\sum_{j=1}^{n} j^2 + \sum_{j=1}^{n} j.$$

Formulas for these sums can be found in the Summary of Chapter 3 and the answer to Problem 10 of Set 13. Thus we get

$$n^2(n + 1)^2 - \tfrac{1}{2}n(n + 1)(2n + 1) + \tfrac{1}{2}n(n + 1),$$

which reduces to the answer given.

4. 8/11

It makes no difference whether or not the teams are "identified", that is, given specific labels such as the red team, the blue team and the green team. Here is a solution using identified teams. The total number of ways of forming the teams is $C(12, 4)C(8, 4)$, by first choosing four boys for the red team and then four for the blue. Label the particular boys A and B; the number of ways of forming the teams with A on the red and B on the blue is $C(10, 3)C(7, 3)$. Consequently the answer is $6C(10, 3)C(7, 3)/[C(12, 4)C(8, 4)]$.

5. 16/55

Using the background of the preceding solution, with the boys labeled A, B, C, we note that there are $C(9, 3)C(6, 3)$ ways of forming the teams with A on the red, B on the blue and C on the green. Hence the answer is $6C(9, 3)C(6, 3)/[C(12, 4)C(8, 4)]$.

6. The number of objects having neither of the properties α, β is $N - N(\alpha) - N(\beta) + N(\alpha, \beta)$. This is not negative and so

$$N - N(\alpha) - N(\beta) + N(\alpha, \beta) \geqslant 0$$

or

$$N + N(\alpha, \beta) \geqslant N(\alpha) + N(\beta).$$

Similarly we have

$$N + N(\alpha, \gamma) \geqslant N(\alpha) + N(\gamma) \quad \text{and} \quad N + N(\beta, \gamma) \geqslant N(\beta) + N(\gamma),$$

and the result follows by addition of these inequalities.

7. $(1 + x)(1 + x^3)(1 + x^5)\cdots(1 + x^{99})$ or $\displaystyle\prod_{j=1}^{50}(1 + x^{2j-1})$

8. $\displaystyle\left\{\sum_{j=0}^{20} x^j\right\}^3\left\{\sum_{j=0}^{10} x^{2j}\right\}^3\left\{\sum_{j=0}^{6} x^{3j}\right\}^2\cdot\sum_{j=0}^{5} x^{4j}\cdot\sum_{j=0}^{4} x^{5j}\cdot\sum_{j=0}^{2} x^{10j}\cdot\sum_{j=0}^{1} x^{20j}.$

9. Add the equations $F(n) - F(n - 1) = F(n - 2),$
$$F(n - 1) - F(n - 2) = F(n - 3),$$
$$F(n - 2) - F(n - 3) = F(n - 4),$$
$$\cdot\ \cdot\ \cdot\ \cdot\ \cdot\ \cdot\ \cdot$$
$$F(2) - F(1) = F(0).$$

10. The relation $F(n) = C(n + 1, 0) + C(n, 1) + C(n - 1, 2) + \cdots$
from the Summary of Chapter 4 can be written as

$$F(n) = \sum_{j+k=n+1} C(j, k).$$

Similarly we see that

$$F(n - 2) = \sum_{j+k=n-1} C(j, k), \qquad F(n - 3) = \sum_{j+k=n-2} C(j, k),$$
$$\cdots, \qquad F(0) = \sum_{j+k=1} C(j,k).$$

Adding these to $1 = C(0, 0)$ we get

$$F(n - 2) + F(n - 1) + \cdots + F(0) + 1 = \sum_{j+k<n} C(j, k).$$

The conclusion then follows by use of the preceding problem.

11. $(20!)(21!)/11!$

Set aside the multiples of 3 momentarily; the other twenty integers can be permuted in 20! ways. Given any one of these permutations, there are 21 spaces between and at the ends of the integers. Choose 10 of these spaces to insert the multiples of 3; thus $C(21, 10)$ choices. But then the multiples of 3 can be inserted in 10! ways. So the answer is

$$(20!)\cdot C(21, 10)\cdot(10!).$$

12. 16687.

Say that a permutation has property α_1 in case a is followed immediately by b; property α_2 in case b is followed immediately by c; $\cdots$; property α_7 in case g is immediately followed by h. The problem is to find the number of permutations having none of these properties, and this can be done by use of the inclusion-exclusion principle. It can be seen that $N(\alpha_1) = N(\alpha_2) = \cdots = N(\alpha_7) = 7!$, $N(\alpha_1, \alpha_2) = 6!$, $N(\alpha_1, \alpha_2, \alpha_3) = 5!$, etc. Thus the answer is

$$8! - C(7, 1)\cdot 7! + C(7, 2)\cdot 6! - C(7, 3)\cdot 5! + C(7, 4)\cdot 4!$$
$$- C(7, 5)\cdot 3! + C(7, 6)\cdot 2! - C(7, 7)\cdot 1!$$

13. $\{C(24, 4)\}^5 - 5\{C(23, 3)\}^5 + 10\{C(22, 2)\}^5 - 10\{C(21, 1)\}^5$
$$+ 5\{C(20, 0)\}^5$$

Ignore momentarily the condition that no box is to be empty. Label the boxes A, B, C, D, E. Then the number of distributions of the cents is $C(24, 4)$, the number of solutions of $x_1 + x_2 + x_3 + x_4 + x_5 = 20$ in non-negative integers, where x_1 is interpreted as the number of cents in box A, etc. Hence the number of distributions of all the coins is $\{C(24, 4)\}^5$. Now introduce the condition that no box be empty and use the inclusion-exclusion principle. Say that a distribution has property α in case box A is empty, property β in case box B is empty, etc. Thus we see that

$$N = \{C(24, 4)\}^5, \quad N(\alpha) = \{C(23, 3)\}^5, \quad N(\alpha, \beta) = \{C(22, 2)\}^5,$$

and so on, which give the answer.

14. 864

First disregard the restriction that no two adjacent letters be alike. The total number of permutations is then

$$N = \frac{8!}{2!2!2!2!} = 2520.$$

Now apply the inclusion-exclusion principle, where a permutation has property α in case the A's are adjacent, property β in case the B's are adjacent, etc. It can be calculated that

$$N(\alpha) = \frac{7!}{2!2!2!} = 630, \quad N(\alpha, \beta) = \frac{6!}{2!2!} = 180,$$

$$N(\alpha, \beta, \gamma) = 60, \quad N(\alpha, \beta, \gamma, \delta) = 24.$$

Hence the answer is

$$N - 4N(\alpha) + 6N(\alpha, \beta) - 4N(\alpha, \beta, \gamma) + N(\alpha, \beta, \gamma, \delta) \;=\; 864.$$

15. 700

First permute the E's and F's to get $(6!)/(3!3!)$ or 20 permutations. Then in each of these 20 permutations insert the D's in any 3 of the 7 spaces between letters or at the ends. Thus the answer is $20C(7, 3)$.

16. 340

In the solution to the preceding problem separate the 20 permutations of the E's and F's into three types: 4 permutations having no E's adjacent; 12 permutations having exactly two E's adjacent; 4 permutations with all three E's adjacent. The D's can be inserted in $C(7, 3)$, $C(6, 2)$, and $C(5, 1)$ ways respectively for these three types. Hence the answer is $4C(7, 3) + 12C(6, 2) + 4C(5, 1)$.

17. 174

First consider all arrangements with DE on the left end, followed by the other seven letters. With the F's omitted these arrangements are six in number, namely

  (1) *DEDDEE* (2) *DEDEDE* (3) *DEDEED*

  (4) *DEEEDD* (5) *DEEDED* (6) *DEEDDE*

The F's can be inserted in the following number of ways in these six arrangements: $C(3, 1)$, $C(5, 3)$, $C(4, 2)$, $C(3, 3)$, $C(4, 2)$, $C(3, 1)$ This totals 29, and the answer is obtained by multiplying by 6 to allow for other pairs of letters on the left end, besides DE.

18. 2600

To any solution of $x + y + z + v = 27$ in positive integers, there corresponds a unique solution of the other equation since

$$u \;=\; 30 - x - y - z.$$

Hence the question amounts to asking for the number of solutions of

$$x + y + z + v \;=\; 27$$

in positive integers. The answer is $C(26, 3)$.

19. 1078

By symmetry the number of solutions with $x > y$ equals the number with $x < y$. The total number of solutions is $C(25, 3)$ or 2300. The number of solutions with $x = y$ is

$$\sum_{x=1}^{12} C(25 - 2x,\ 1) \ = \ \sum_{x=1}^{12} (25 - 2x) \ = \ 144,$$

because for a fixed value of x the equation $2x + z + w = 26$ or $z + w = 26 - 2x$ has $C(25 - 2x, 1)$ solutions in positive integers. Hence the answer is $(2300 - 144)/2$.

20. $(n + 1)(2n^2 + 4n + 3)/3$

The question amounts to asking for the number of selections of $2n$ objects from $4n$ objects, given that the $4n$ objects are identical in sets of n. (Thus there are just 4 different kinds of objects.) This is the same as asking for the number of solutions of $x_1 + x_2 + x_3 + x_4 = 2n$ in non-negative integers not exceeding n. By the work of Chapter 5 this is $C(2n + 3, 3) - 4C(n + 2, 3)$.

21. $(nj)!/\{(j!)^n n!\}$

A first batch of j objects can be chosen in $C(nj, j)$ ways, a second batch in $C(nj - j, j)$ ways, and so on. Since the order of the batches does not matter, the answer is

$$C(nj,\ j)\,C(nj - j,\ j)\,C(nj - 2j,\ j) \cdots C(3j,\ j)\,C(2j, j)/n!\ .$$

22. Partitions into positive even integers.

There are no partitions of 1000 into three positive odd integers.

23. Partitions into four positive odd integers.

Let $a + b + c + d$ be a partition of 1000 into four positive even integers, with $a \leqslant b \leqslant c \leqslant d$. Then

$$(a - 1) + (b - 1) + (c - 1) + (d + 3)$$

is a partition of 1000 into four positive odd integers. Moreover this gives a one-to-one correspondence between *all* the partitions into four even integers and *some* of the partitions into four odd integers. The correspondence gives only "some" of the partitions into odd integers because $d + 3$ exceeds $c - 1$ by at least 4, and so such a partition as $249 + 249 + 251 + 251$ is not present.

24. Partitions into positive odd integers.

Any partition into even summands can be transformed into one having odd summands by separating each even summand $2j$ into two parts, 1 and $2j - 1$. For example $200 + 300 + 500$ is transformed into $1 + 1 + 1 + 199 + 299 + 499$. Thus each partition with even summands is transformed into a unique partition with odd summands, but this procedure does not give *all* partitions with odd summands.

25. 402130

Count the integers *not* having the property. For example, there are 9^6 integers with 6 digits such that no two adjacent integers are equal. Thus the answer is $1,000,000 - (9^6 + 9^5 + 9^4 + 9^3 + 9^2 + 9)$.

26. $-24 + \sum\limits_{j=0}^{22} (-1)^j \{C(24, j) + C(23, j) + 46C(22, j)\}(24 - j)!$.

First consider those permutations with B in first place and A in second place. Of these there are

$$D(24) \qquad \text{or} \qquad \sum\limits_{j=0}^{24} (-1)^j C(24, j)(24 - j)!,$$

because these permutations are derangements. Next consider those with A in second place and B in third place. Of these there are, by an argument using the inclusion-exclusion principle as in the theory for derangements,

$$\sum\limits_{j=0}^{23} (-1)^j C(23, j)(24 - j)!.$$

Finally with A and B in any other specified adjacent positions, there are

$$\sum\limits_{j=0}^{22} (-1)^j C(22, j)(24 - j)!$$

possibilities.

27. 90

Apply the inclusion-exclusion principle to the 6! unrestricted partitions, taking α as the property that a and b are adjacent, β the property that b and c are adjacent, and so on.

28. Each time two people shake hands, the number of people who have shaken hands an odd number of times changes by 2, 0, or -2.

29. The possible number of acquaintances of each person in a group of n people is one of the n integers 0, 1, 2, $\cdots$, $n-1$. If no two people have the same number of acquaintances, then all n integers are represented. But 0 and $n-1$ cannot occur simultaneously because it would mean one person is acquainted with everybody, another with nobody.

30. This is simply the preceding question in a different form.

31. $m(3mk - m^2 + 3k + 1)/6$

We count the number $s_1(k, m)$ of squares of side 1, then the number $s_2(k, m)$ of squares of side 2, etc. Then the total number of squares in the grid is

$$S(k, m) = \sum_{i=1}^{m} s_i(k, m).$$

Now $s_1(k, 1) = k$, $s_1(k, m) = ms_1(k, 1) = mk$; similarly,

$$s_2(k, m) = (m - 1)s_2(k, 2) = (m - 1)(k - 1),$$

and so on. We evaluate

$$S(k, m) = mk + (m - 1)(k - 1) + (m - 2)(k - 2) + \cdots + 1(k - m + 1).$$

Reversing the order of the terms in this sum, we write

$$\begin{aligned} S(k, m) &= k - m + 1 + 2(k - m + 2) + 3(k - m + 3) \\ &\qquad + \cdots + m(k - m + m) \\ &= (k - m)(1 + 2 + 3 + \cdots + m) \\ &\qquad + (1^2 + 2^2 + 3^2 + \cdots + m^2) \\ &= (k - m)\frac{m(m + 1)}{2} + \frac{m(m + 1)(2m + 1)}{6}, \end{aligned}$$

and this is the number given above

32. It is possible in 255 moves.

The problem can be stated for n discs, requiring say, $f(n)$ moves. A simple analysis reveals that $f(n) = 2f(n - 1) + 1$.

33. Let the points be A, B, C, D, E, F. By the work of Section 9.2 we may presume that ABC (say) is a red chromatic triangle. If DEF is not chromatic it has a white side, say DE. If ADE is not chromatic then at least one of AD and AE is red. Likewise if BDE and CDE are not chromatic, at least one of BD and BE, and at least one of CD and CE, are red. So at least two of AD, BD, CD are red, or at least two of AE, BE, CE are red. In the first case consider the triangles ABD, ACD, BCD, and in the second case ABE, ACE, BCE.

34. Here is one pattern. Let the sides of ABC be red, and the sides of DEF red, and let all other segments be white.

35. By the solution to Problem 33, we can take any six of the points and get two chromatic triangles. Let A be one of the vertices of one of these triangles. Then apply the solution to Problem 33 to the six points other than A.

36. From any one of the points, say A, there are 65 emanating segments. Of these, at least 17 are of one color; say that $AB_1, AB_2, \cdots, AB_{17}$ are red. If any line segment joining two of $B_1, B_2, \cdots, B_{17}$ is red, there is a red chromatic triangle. Otherwise we can apply the 17 points, 3 colors result in Problem 2 of Set 31.

37. This problem can be solved by a slight sharpening of the argument given in the solution of Problem 2 of Set 31. Take A *not as any one* of the points, but as a point which is not the vertex of a chromatic triangle, and use the result of Problem 33 of this set.

38. From any one of the points there are 23 emanating segments of which at least 12 are of one color. Say that $AB_1, AB_2, \cdots, AB_{12}$ are red segments. If among the 12 points B_1 to B_{12} there is a red chromatic triangle, then such a triangle together with the point A gives a solution. Otherwise consider the 11 segments $B_1B_2, B_1B_3, \cdots, B_1B_{12}$; at least 6 of these, say $B_1B_2, B_1B_3, \cdots, B_1B_7$, are of one color. If the color is red, the points B_2, B_3, B_4, B_5 give a solution. If the color is white, then consider the six points $B_2, B_3, \cdots, B_7$. There is a chromatic triangle, necessarily white, among these six points. This triangle, together with B_1, gives a solution.

39. $n(n-1)(n-2)(n-3)/24$

Any four of the points on the circle determine a unique intersection point, so $C(n, 4)$ is the answer.

40. $C(n, 4) + 1 + \frac{1}{2}n(n-1)$

Adding one point at a time, consider the increase $R(j) - R(j-1)$ in the number of regions as we pass from $j-1$ to j points. Let P be the j-th point, and Q any of the $j-1$ points. If the line PQ has k intersection points inside the circle, then the line PQ creates $k+1$ new regions. But all the lines PQ (with P fixed and Q any one of the $j-1$ points) create $C(j, 4) - C(j-1, 4)$ intersection points by the result of the preceding problem. Thus we have

$$R(j) - R(j-1) = j - 1 + C(j, 4) - C(j-1, 4),$$

and the problem can be solved by summing this from $j = 2$ to $j = n$.

41. $(n^2 - n)/2$ if n is odd and not a multiple of 3; $(n^2 - 2n)/2$ if n is even and not a multiple of 3; subtract $2n/3$ in case n is a multiple of 3.

42. $C(n+5, 5)$

This is the number of solutions of $x_1 + x_2 + \cdots + x_6 = n$ in non-negative integers, where x_1 is the number of the dice showing ones, x_2 the number showing twos, and so on.

43. $(n^3 + 5n + 6)/6$

We make use of the number of regions into which a plane is separated by n lines of which no two are parallel and no three concurrent. This was denoted by $f(n)$ in Section 9.2, and it was established that

$$f(n) = \frac{1}{2}(n^2 + n + 2).$$

Now in the present problem if we introduce one plane at a time, and if the j-th plane thereby causes an increase of $g(j) - g(j-1)$ in the number of regions of space, then it can be argued that

$$g(j) - g(j-1) = f(j-1).$$

The answer is obtained by summing this equation from $j = 2$ to $j = n$.

44. 1/3

Consider any arrangement of the n integers; 1, 2, 3 occur somewhere, say in the i-th, the j-th and the k-th positions, respectively. Now hold all other integers fixed in their positions, but permute 1, 2, 3. There are 6 ways of placing 1, 2, 3 into the i-th, j-th and k-th positions; two of these ways are favorable, in the sense that 2 occurs between 1 and 3. Since this reasoning may be applied to every selection of positions i, j, k, we see that the probability is $\frac{2}{6}$ or $\frac{1}{3}$.

45. $\displaystyle\sum_{j=0}^{n} \frac{(-1)^j C(n, j) \cdot (2n - j)!}{2^{n-j}}$

Apply the inclusion-exclusion principle to the unrestricted permutations, taking the property α_1 to be A's adjacent, property α_2 to be B's adjacent, etc.

46. $C(n, j) D(j)/n!$

Choose $n - j$ integers to be in their natural positions, and then the others can be arranged in $D(j)$ ways, where $D(j)$ denotes derangements.

47. $\displaystyle\sum_{j=0}^{n} C(k + 1, j) C(k + 1 - j, n - 2j)$

First line up the B's, with $k + 1$ spaces between them and at the ends. Then consider the number of permutations having j pairs of A's in j of the spaces, and $n - 2j$ single A's in another $n - 2j$ spaces.

48. $\displaystyle\sum_{j=0}^{n} (-1)^j C(n, j)(2n - j)!$

Use the inclusion-exclusion principle applied to the total number $(2n)!$ of permutations. Say that a permutation has property α_1 in case 1 is in its natural position, α_2 in case 3 is in its natural position, and so on.

49. (i) $g(n, k)$ of Chapter 8;
(ii) $G(n, k)$ of Chapter 8.

50. The recursion relation is $K(n, j) = K(n - 2, j - 1) + K(n - 1, j)$. The proper conjecture is $K(n, j) = C(n - j + 1, j)$.

51. Consider the table:

	Column 1	Column 2	Column 3
Row 1:	AD	BD	CD
Row 2:	AE	BE	CE
Row 3:	AF	BF	CF

If a row contains two pairs of strangers, we get another triple with property α. If a row contains three pairs of strangers, we get three triples with property α. Two similar observations can be made about a column containing two pairs, or three pairs, of acquaintances. Next, if the table contains seven or more pairs of strangers, there must be one row with three pairs of strangers, and the problem is solved. A similar argument applies if the table contains seven or more pairs of acquaintances. If the table contains six pairs of strangers and three pairs of acquaintances, then either some row has three pairs of strangers or every row has two pairs of strangers. In either case the problem is solved. The rest of the argument is left to the reader.

52. 610

Say that the boy can go up n steps in $f(n)$ ways, so we are to determine $f(14)$. Now $f(n) = f(n - 1) + f(n - 2)$ because the boy can move to the n-th step directly from either of the two preceding steps. This recursion relation is the same as that for the Fibonacci numbers $F(n)$ of Section 4.1, but the beginning values here are $f(1) = 1$ and $f(2) = 2$; so $f(n) = F(n - 1)$, and so $f(14) = F(13)$.

53.   4995   or $\displaystyle\sum_{j=1}^{9} (10 - j)C(j + 4, 4)$

Disregarding the integer 1,000,000 we note that all the others can be thought of as six-digit integers, with digits $x_1, x_2, \cdots, x_6$ from left to right, where zeros are allowed as digits. Define the differences $d_1, d_2, \cdots, d_5$ between adjacent digits by $d_1 = x_2 - x_1$, $d_2 = x_3 - x_2$, $\cdots$, $d_5 = x_6 - x_5$; the integers with the desired property have non-negative values for the differences d_1 to d_5. Furthermore, their digits are uniquely determined from each set of values $x_1, d_1, d_2, d_3, d_4, d_5$, and each such set satisfies the equation $d_1 + d_2 + d_3 + d_4 + d_5 = x_6 - x_1$. The number of solutions of this equation in non-negative integers is $C(x_6 - x_1 + 4, 4)$. Writing j for $x_6 - x_1$ we can assemble the answer given keeping in mind that $0 \leqslant x_1 \leqslant x_6 \leqslant 9$.

Bibliography

[1] H. Hadwiger, H. Debrunner and V. Klee, *Combinatorial Geometry in the Plane*, Holt, Rinehart and Winston, New York, 1964.

[2] John Riordan, *An Introduction to Combinatorial Analysis*, John Wiley, New York, 1958.

[3] H. J. Ryser, *Combinatorial Mathematics*, Carus Monograph No. 14, John Wiley, New York, 1963.

[4] W. A. Whitworth, *Choice and Chance*, Hafner, New York, 1959.

General combinatorial problems are treated in [2], [3] and [4] whereas [1] deals with questions akin to Chapter 9 of this book. References [1], [2], [3] are advanced books; reference [4] is a reprinting of an older book, easy to read, but not very up-to-date.

Index

Symbols